Crisis in the European Monetary Union

After decades of economic integration and EU enlargement, the economic geography of Europe has shifted, with new peripheries emerging and the core showing signs of fragmentation. This book examines the paths of the core and peripheral countries, with a focus on their diverse productive capabilities and their interdependence.

Crisis in the European Monetary Union: A Core-Periphery Perspective provides a new framework for analysing the economic crisis that has shaken the Eurozone countries. Its analysis goes beyond the short-term, to study the medium and long-term relations between 'core' countries (particularly Germany) and Southern European 'peripheral' countries. The authors argue that long-term sustainability means assigning the state a key role in guiding investment, which in turn implies industrial policies geared towards diversifying, innovating and strengthening the economic structures of peripheral countries to help them thrive.

Offering a fresh angle on the European crisis, this volume will appeal to students, academics and policymakers interested in the past, present and future construction of Europe.

Giuseppe Celi is Associate Professor of Economics at the University of Foggia, Italy. He has been the coordinator of the university's Economic Theory PhD programme.

Andrea Ginzburg was Professor of Economic Policy at the University of Modena and Reggio Emilia, Italy.

Dario Guarascio is a researcher in applied economics at the National Institute of Public Policy Analysis (INAPP), Italy. He is in charge of the research unit 'Skills and labour market transitions'.

Annamaria Simonazzi is Professor of Economics at La Sapienza University of Rome, Italy. She is co-editor of *Economia & Lavoro* and on the editorial board of *inGenere*.

Routledge Studies in the European Economy

Crisis in the European Monetary Union

A Core-Periphery Perspective

Giuseppe Celi, Andrea Ginzburg,
Dario Guarascio and
Annamaria Simonazzi

Routledge
Taylor & Francis Group

LONDON AND NEW YORK

First published 2018
by Routledge

2 Park Square, Milton Park, Abingdon, Oxfordshire OX14 4RN
52 Vanderbilt Avenue, New York, NY 10017

Routledge is an imprint of the Taylor & Francis Group, an informa business

First issued in paperback 2019

British Library Cataloguing in Publication Data
A catalog record for this book is available from the British Library

Library of Congress Cataloging in Publication Data
A catalog record for this book has been requested

ISBN: 978-1-138-68583-3 (hbk)
ISBN: 978-0-367-87862-7 (pbk)

Typeset in Times New Roman
by Wearset Ltd, Boldon, Tyne and Wear

Contents

Figures

Tables

Acknowledgements

The authors wish to thank all friends and colleagues who have discussed various drafts of this work throughout its elaboration or provided insights around the issues this book deals with. In particular, the authors wish to thank Adalgiso Amendola, Aldo Barba, Federico Bassi, Antonella Bellino, Riccardo Bellofiore, Mario Biagioli, Francesco Bogliacino, Sergio Cesaratto, Valeria Cirillo, Giovanni Dosi, Giorgio Fodor, Michael Landesmann, Cristina Marcuzzo, Mario Pianta, Annalisa Rosselli, Roberto Schiattarella, Antonella Stirati and Attilio Trezzini. Moreover, the authors are grateful to Gianluca Orefice for kindly making available CEPII data and to Corrado Polli for providing his precious support for the empirical analysis carried out in Chapter 6. Giuseppe Celi thanks Mariella, for her patience and support. Dario Guarascio has a loving and thankful thought for Eva, Albertina, Noè, Giorgio, Nicoletta, Massimo, Bardo, Lina and Pietro.

Introduction

On 25 March 2017, the European Union heads of state met in Rome to celebrate the 60th anniversary of the Treaty of Rome. Four days later, with a letter to the president of the European Council, the UK officially notified its intention to withdraw from the EU. Behind the celebrations, the crisis of the Southern periphery – and indeed of the whole Eurozone (EZ) – still awaits a sustainable solution.

The European project was designed (and expected) to promote convergence and harmonization between and within countries. After several decades of economic integration and enlargement, almost two decades of tighter monetary integration, and a long economic and financial crisis, the reality looks very different. Divergence has been increasing in many domains, with weaker member states and regions falling behind their stronger companions. Moreover, economic and social inequality is on the rise within each of the member states. The flow of capital from the centre to the South came to a sudden stop, replaced by flows of young and high-skilled labour heading North. Wage and price flexibility in the Southern countries has not yet produced new job opportunities, which continue to be concentrated elsewhere. European enlargement and the centripetal forces of European construction have changed the economic geography of the Union: new peripheries now gravitate around a changing core, the barycentre of the EU moving from North–South to North–East.

This book starts from the conviction that in order to understand where we are heading it is important to understand how we got where we are now. In trying to provide an answer to the current crisis we must look beyond the short run, analysing the different trajectories of the peripheral and core countries in terms of the interdependence between economies with different productive capabilities. Our analysis starts from three methodological premises.

History and path dependence

The current crisis is the culmination of a process of integration that has profoundly changed the structure of each member state, their interrelations and their power relations. One of the side effects of the economic crisis that began in 2008 was the rediscovery of the terms 'centre' and 'periphery' to analyse the economic situations of the European countries. Study of the evolution of the centre-periphery relations may help towards an understanding of the dynamics of the European integration processes of the second half of the twentieth century, based on both their chronology and the processes of geographical redistribution of international production. As the Italian philosopher Giambattista Vico observed (Vico, [1725–1728] 2011: 61), chronology and geography are the 'two eyes of history'. As far as chronology is concerned, it should be recalled that all the countries of the Southern European periphery can be defined as latecomers, though Italy embarked on a path of industrialization and integration into European trade earlier than any of the other peripheral countries. As for geography, the changing geographies of production are contingent outcomes of the co-evolution of the asymmetric power relationships between individual and collective actors and institutions.

Globalization and Europeanization

We need to bear in mind the background against which this co-evolution occurred, namely European integration of the peripheral countries and globalization. As from the beginning of the 1970s, the countries of Europe were caught up between two different levels of deregulation, global and European. Analysis should consider the interweaving between globalization and Europeanization, or in other words the particular way the globalization process, which originated in the US, was translated into Europe through the formation of the European Union and the Monetary Union. At the global level, the growing importance of the financial sector affected the rate and quality of growth of the capitalist economies, which moved from the two engines represented by investment and exports to the single engine of exports, occasionally complemented by consumption booms. Europeanization can be interpreted as EU-wide application of a policy of deregulation of goods and capital similar to the Anglo-Saxon model. Deregulation of labour markets and financialization affected the timing, shape and direction of the European integration process. However, the neoliberal agenda proved difficult to reconcile with preservation of key elements of the European social model and the presence of a solid welfare state.

Embeddedness

When joining the euro, the member states relinquished their national management tools. The single currency was formed without creating any supra-national governance to take their place. Moreover, the entire institutional architecture of the Monetary Union was based on the assumption that the countries that met the Maastricht criteria for accession were all on a level playing field. Convergence was interpreted with reference to financial rather than real indicators, and it was believed that any problem encountered could and would be addressed in time (neo-functionalism). Thus, construction of the European institutions was disembedded from the specific social and political institutions that provide a solid and durable foundation for any monetary union, and with no consideration for the different levels of development of its members. Insufficient political cohesion and misguided economic theory played a role in shaping what was pre-eminently a political project. The crisis made it evident that this institutional structure was not sustainable.

Old and new peripheries (and core countries)

The interaction between these various factors reshaped economic and geopolitical relations between the European economies. German reunification and collapse of the Soviet Union opened the way to Eastern enlargement, and to a geographical reorganization of production at the European level. Germany's economic weight in Europe increased correspondingly. New peripheries came to the fore, while the core showed signs of internal fragmentation.

The outbreak of the crisis and its unequal consequences must be interpreted against this background. Mistakenly interpreted as a standard fiscal/balance of payments problem, the crisis was the final effect of the interaction between the international financial crisis and the incomplete nature of the European institutions. A change of strategy is even more important today, since the crisis marks another major structural break in world trade, similar to the breaks that occurred in the 1970s and the first decade of the new millennium. In the first decade of the new millennium, Germany once again succeeded in reorganizing its economy and exploiting the benefits of wage restraint, industrial outsourcing to Eastern European countries, and the 'exorbitant privilege' of belonging to the Monetary Union enjoying a dominant position within it. The crisis has shown not only an inability to replicate the German export-led model across Europe, but also the limitations of this model for Germany itself. In fact, the conditions that ensured the success of German exports in the years between 2005 and 2007 no longer hold.

There is still very little hope of a radical change in policies along new lines, which would mean changing the EZ rules. The will to advance towards budgetary and political union is non-existent in Europe today. This not only means that the Eurozone is bound to remain a fragile institution, but it actually justifies Orphanides' disconsolate conclusion that 'In its current form, the euro poses a threat to the European project' (2015: 19).

The book is divided into two parts. Part I focuses on the medium term. After the first introductory chapter, it offers an overview of the evolution of the European Monetary Union (EMU) from its inception, and goes on to discuss the crisis that befell it. Part II takes a longer view, opening out a structural scenario within which to interpret the medium/short-run developments.

The formation of the EMU, from the Werner Report (1970) to the Delors Report (European Council, 1989) and beyond, followed a rugged path in which the balance of power between countries, momentous changes in international economic relations and paradigm shifts in economic theory led to a flawed institutional construction which was very different from the initial goals and expectations. If the Werner Report was still embedded in an economic culture that saw economic policy instruments jointly concurring in stabilizing the economy – the initial design envisaged a single monetary policy coupled with a 'Centre of Decision for Economic Policy' to avoid regional and structural disequilibria – the Delors Report and the EMU enshrined the separation between an independent European Central Bank (ECB) and fiscal and political powers, which remained under the control of the nation state. Chapter 1 tells the story of how the European Union moved on from Werner to Maastricht. As discussed in the chapter, the 'metallistic' notion of money lay behind this separation: according to this view, money is just a means for simplifying transactions, not a social institution that depends on the central authority of the state. This notion of money is key to interpret the evolution of the economic policy that emerged in response to the events of the 1970s and 1980s. It served to safeguard the financial interests that were rapidly growing in national and international weight (financialization). The difficulties faced by traditional Keynesian demand management policies in the stagflation period following the first oil shock offered the excuse for the establishment of a new (old) theoretical paradigm, advocating the self-regulation of markets and the principle of non-interference of monetary and fiscal policies with the market mechanism.

This neoliberal policy consensus, which replaced the Bretton Woods consensus, was transposed into the European context (*Europeanization*, as we call it) through the adoption of two complementary role models: the German model and the US model. The former – whose influence was based on Germany's successful adjustment to the new inflationary environment following the collapse of Bretton Woods – advocated price stability as the only strategy for growth. The new theoretical paradigm, via a vertical Phillips curve, had it that disinflation could be obtained without costs in terms of unemployment. The latter role model – legitimized by the outstanding performance of the US economy in the first half of the 1980s – promoted the liberalization of labour, product and capital markets as the recipe for growth. The interaction of these two models paved the way to the European road to global finance and monetary integration. As a result, the institutions of the EMU left the currency disembedded from the fiscal, social and political institutions required to make a currency union viable. It is this institutional incompleteness that lies behind the European leaders' (political) inability to prevent the international financial crisis from developing into full-blown sovereign and economic crisis. The political choices underlying the economic design are also at the heart of the growing divide between core and periphery countries in Europe.

Chapter 2 specifically explores the European core-periphery divergences in the period preceding the crisis (1999–2008). The German current account surplus has dominated the debate on the root causes of the crisis. Our analysis rejects the monothematic explanation of the German surplus in terms of wage moderation, in favour of a multidimensional approach that includes, besides cost competitiveness, other factors, such as the German linkages with the high-growth markets of the emerging countries and offshoring towards Central and Eastern European countries. We suggest that the Hartz reforms mostly affected the 'non-corporatist' part of the labour market, increasing the segmentation of the German labour market. The growing share of low-paid workers and working poor in total German employment contributed to keeping the cost of services low, thus indirectly supporting the competitiveness of the export industry and, by reducing the purchasing power of a large part of the population, bringing about a reduction in the quality of imported consumption goods. Finally, the de-synchronization of the German real estate cycle from the global cycle of the period 1997–2012 resulted in falling house prices in Germany and waning residential investments, a decline in household consumption and a consequent improvement in the current account.

All these factors contributed to the reorganization of the German industrial fabric and reshuffle of German markets, thus playing a major role in the expansion of its surpluses and the emergence of two peripheries: the Southern periphery (SP, hereafter) and the Eastern periphery (EP, hereafter). As from the introduction of the euro, the SP experienced a weakening of its industrial base and an increasing dependence on foreign financial flows. Conversely, the EP became part of a 'Central European Manufacturing Core' headquartered in Germany, dramatically enlarging and strengthening its manufacturing base, while partly crowding out suppliers located in the SP.

Just as not all the peripheries are alike, nor do the core countries share the same destiny: Germany's successful economic performance in the last decade contrasts with France's economic and political decline. Chapter 3 briefly outlines the evolution of the French economy since the formation of Monetary Union. A great country that aimed to provide guidance in the process of European integration, France ended up sharing many traits in common with the countries of the Southern periphery: declining rate of accumulation and high unemployment, public deficits coupled with increasing current account imbalances, internal inequalities. After Mitterrand's failure to embark on an isolated expansionary policy in 1983, France discarded its dirigist post-war economic strategy to adopt a vast programme of liberalization. To 'anaesthetize' (Levy, 2008) the social and economic effects of these measures, and particularly the flexibilization of the labour market, social spending was substantially increased. With the fiscal constraints imposed by entry into the Monetary Union, the increase in social spending contributed to crowding out resources from public investments and industrial policy. Attempts to rehabilitate the instruments of public intervention came up against the problem that the dismantlement of most of the tools of statist industrial policy in the 1980s and 1990s had stripped the state of critical institutional and fiscal capacities. After decades of neoliberalism, the French authorities lacked the vision, policy instruments and financial means to forge an effective, statist response to the 2008 crisis.

The development of the French trade balance is one significant indicator of the increasing difficulties of the French economy. We demonstrate that the reversal in the French trade balance was essentially imputable to the automotive sector, whose progressive deterioration since 2004 went hand in hand with the international relocation of production undertaken by the French companies

(Renault, PSA). The French firms' internationalization strategies differed greatly from those pursued by the German companies. While the latter outsourced parts and components, maintaining final assembly at home (especially in the medium- to high-quality segments), the French automotive industry relocated the entire process (with the bulk of the medium- to high-quality segments produced abroad). These different approaches to internationalization produced a positive impact on the trade balance in Germany, but had a negative impact in France. We conclude that the interpretation of trade deficits as purely macroeconomic phenomena, disregarding their microeconomic origin, is at the root of misguided therapies that risk exacerbating the problem. The initial cost in terms of loss of industrial jobs and erosion of the domestic productive structure, due for instance, to the strategies of international de-localization of national firms, is aggravated by further decline in employment and productive capacity as a result of defla- tionary macroeconomic policies.

The deflationary measures adopted in Europe in response to the 2008 eco- nomic crisis are extensively discussed in Chapter 4. Unlike the US, in many European countries (especially in the EZ) the crisis evolved as a devastating double-dip recession. The first slump, in 2008–2009, was driven by a fall in European exports in a context of rapid, sharp and synchronized collapse of world trade, due to the direct and indirect effects associated with the fall in US GDP. While the US government, in synergy with the Federal Reserve, set robust expansionary measures in motion in 2009, the EZ failed to adopt adequate countercyclical policies. Instead, public resources were lavished to bail out the banking system. In 2010 the second EZ recession set in as a result of the auster- ity measures implemented by European governments to neutralize the sovereign default risk. In this chapter, we present an interpretation of the crisis that differs from the 'consensus narrative' (CEPR, 2015), which saw the crisis as a standard balance of payment crisis along the lines of the models applied to the developing countries. In addition, we provide an overview of the austerity policies imple- mented in the SP as from the outset of the crisis, highlighting the dramatic con- sequences on the industrial fabric of their economies.

We argue that the consensus narrative – which stresses the profligacy of the deficit countries, overlooking the complementary huge and persistent surpluses by the core countries, ignores the circumstances leading to the 'sudden stop' in cross- border lending, disregards the part played by house prices in the financial crisis and downplays the role of the flawed institutional architecture of the EMU – prac- tically amounts to a justification of the austerity measures implemented over the period 2010–2014. The agenda covered a range of contractionary measures: cuts in public expenditure and increase in taxation to reduce the public debt and deficit; privatizations of public assets; and structural reforms to render the labour and product markets more flexible in order to enhance price competitiveness and promote exports. Instead of aligning the 'spendthrift' countries with the most vir- tuous countries of the EZ, austerity policies contributed to widening the divides – between core and periphery, and between peripheries. While Germany and the EP – closely integrated with German production networks – soon started to recover, the SP plunged into deep and prolonged recession, with devastating effects on their productive capacity, which shrank by 25 per cent in Italy and Spain, and by 30 per cent in Greece, while even increasing in the core. The socio-economic consequences of this productive collapse in the SP were dramatic: unemployment (especially among the young) surged, large-scale South–North migrations resumed and poverty reached alarming levels.

Polarization and divergence also occurred within the core, as indeed within the countries of the periphery, characterized by historical regional divides. Chapter 5 focuses on the internal divides within two countries, Germany and Italy, representative, respectively, of the core and the periphery. The increasing segmentation of the German labour market is the other side of the coin of Germany's economic success: on the one hand, high-skilled manufacturing workers employed in the export sector benefiting from protection and high wages on the other, low-paid workers, working poor and precarious labourers, employed prevalently in the services sector. Labour market segmentation and increasing income inequality in Germany shed new light on the origins of the German trade surplus. The increase in the share of low-wage employment in Germany coincides with a marked rise in the incidence of low-quality consumption goods in German imports. This evidence holds two important implications. First, it highlights the relevance of 'income effects', besides internal devaluation, in generating the German trade surplus. Second, it underlies the transformation under way in Germany's trade network, i.e. the diversion of German imports from the 'luxury' goods of the SP to the low-quality, cheaper consumption goods of China, the growing interconnections with China and the EP, and the declining linkages with the SP.

A core-periphery pattern is also to be seen within the peripheral countries. Focussing on the North–South divide in Italy, we show how the asymmetric involvement of Italian regions in the internationalization processes – further intensified over the last two decades – abandonment of the industrial policy, preferring a market-oriented agenda, and the differential impact of the 2008 crisis contributed to widening the socio-economic distance between the Italian Mezzogiorno and the rest of the country. Since 2008, the fall in Southern GDP has been twice that of the Centre-North, with more marked decline in investment, employment and productive capacity in the South. The structural polarization between the Southern regions and the rest of Italy has been exacerbated by a significant revival in internal migration from the South to the Centre-North. Unlike in the past, recent migration flows from the Mezzogiorno are made up of highly educated young people, a circumstance that penalizes even further the future development of the Mezzogiorno.

Chapter 6 concludes the first part by presenting a picture of the evolution of core-periphery trade relations since the introduction of the euro. The years following establishment of the EMU have seen Germany occupying the position of trade leader in Europe. The reorganization of its industrial platform, including its extensions abroad (mainly in the EP), is reflected in the evolution of its trade network: the changes in the geographical composition of trade flows signal modifications in the relative importance of the various areas and countries directly and indirectly linked to the German economy. We focus on two distinct trade networks. The first network (N1) traces all the bilateral trade relations between six countries: the two main core countries – Germany and France – and the countries of the SP – Greece, Italy, Spain and Portugal. The second network (N2) extends the coverage to include, besides Germany and France, China and three clusters of countries belonging respectively to the SP, the EP, the Euro-9 (the remaining EZ countries). We observe how the structure of the two networks evolved before and after introduction of the euro, and before and after the crisis: that is, in the years 1999, 2008 and 2014. In 1999, Germany was running surpluses with all its partners (France and SP countries) in N1, and a deficit with the Euro-9 (N2). The SP had strong links with all the other EU countries and ran deficits with all of them, with the exception of the EP, which in turn had limited links with the whole network except Germany.

China was still a minor player in terms of trade volumes. The picture changed dramatically in 2008. Germany's surplus towards the whole network (N2) skyrocketed (113.5 billion dollars), driven by a huge surplus with the SP and France. The sharp increase in trade volumes with the EP evidences the creation of production connections with the Eastern European countries. The value of the EP's exports to Germany exceeded the value of the SP's exports, indicating the gradual displacement of SP producers within the German manufacturing platform. Finally, the spectacular growth of Chinese exports (ten times higher than in 1999) reminds us that the processes of productive reorganization occurring in Europe are interwoven with global trends. The trade network in 2014 reveals how deeply the 2008 crisis has reshaped the structure of trade, which is now dominated by the German–EP–China triangle: Germany runs a surplus with China and a deficit with the EP, which in turn runs a deficit with China. Underlying the formation of this triangle is: (i) the need for Germany to compensate for the sharp fall in the SP's imports, and its success in reorienting its exports to China; (ii) the increased economic importance of the EP, which is reflected in its capacity to run a surplus with Germany.

Resuming the discussion on the importance of the automotive sector in accounting for the economic decline of France and the success of Germany that we developed in Chapter 3, we present the trends of the automotive industry in Europe, showing their relevance in explaining the overall trends.

In the second part of the book, we shift the analysis of European core-periphery relationships from the short/medium run to the long run, providing a structural framework that, opening up an historical and global perspective, helps to interpret the evolution of the SP in the process of Europeanization and in the crisis.

The three decades following the Second World War saw sustained growth in the industrial world, favoured by a stable international economic environment. The first three decades of the 'Pax Americana' rested on two fundamental pillars: the Bretton Woods agreement and US hegemony. Fixed (but adjustable) exchange rates and controls on capital movements provided a stable international monetary framework; the deficit of the US balance of payments guaranteed the necessary liquidity for international transactions. Two engines sustained the growth process, following the sequence investment–income–imports. High domestic demand in the US (and in the other industrialized countries) resulted in high world demand, stimulating world export growth which was transmitted to the capital goods sector. The high import content reinforced the expansion of the world market through the foreign trade multiplier. The two engines of investment and exports represented a powerful combination fuelling post-war growth. This mechanism broke down in the early 1970s, leaving only exports as the main driver of (a more modest) growth, occasionally supported by private consumption. Given the stagnation of wages since the 1980s, consumption sprees were financed by debt, and therefore unsustainable in the long run.

Chapter 7 focuses on the factors that interrupted the golden age of post-war capitalist development in the late 1960s and early 1970s, and argues that the great inflation of the 1970s, associated with political and social tensions, opened the way to three fundamental, intertwined discontinuities in the modus operandi of western capitalist countries. The first discontinuity was associated with the transition from 'politicized' management of economic policy based on discretionality, to 'de-politicized' management based on the automatism of rules (Burnham, 2001; Krippner, 2011). De-politicization should not be understood as the removal of politics, but rather as redefinition of the boundary between the political and the economic so as to allow policymakers to govern the economy 'at one remove' (Burnham, 2001). The second discontinuity was the transition from the inflation phase of the 1970s to the next phase, that of 'financialization', defined as a process in which financial activities play an increasingly leading role in the formation of the profits of the economy. The third discontinuity was the slowdown in capital accumulation and its de-linking from exports, the latter remaining the main driving force of domestic growth.

The final part of the chapter considers how these global changes, and specifically the process of financialization, have been transferred to the countries of the European periphery. Since the beginning of the 1970s, the countries of Europe had been in the throes of two different forms of deregulation, global and European. We look at the interweaving between globalization and Europeanization, or in other words the specific way the globalization process, which originated in the US, was translated into Europe through the formation of the European Union and the Monetary Union. We argue that the US neoliberal model, intermediated by European construction, institutions and norms designed in conformity with the German model, has modelled the structure and affected the functioning of the peripheral economies, substantially weakening their resilience.

Chapter 8 focuses in detail on the weakening of the investment engine for the countries of the Southern European periphery since the mid-1970s. An analysis of the main phases of the development of the European countries since the second post-war period provides evidence of considerable differences in the productive structures of the countries of the centre and the SP of Europe at the start of the Europeanization process. These differences entailed the asymmetric capacity of countries at differing levels of development to adjust to external shocks.

Distancing ourselves from the thesis of 'premature tertiarization', we provide an interpretative framework in which the crisis of the mid-1970s, raising the bar in the standards required to compete in international markets, represented a crucial turning point in the relations between the core and the periphery in Europe. While Germany succeeded in restructuring its economy through processes of creative destruction and reconstruction, undertaken with the support of industrial policies, the peripheral countries, adopting policies of premature liberalization, fell behind, suffering erosion of their productive structures. The aggregate demand gap resulting from the crisis was filled with a kind of bank-led 'privatized Keynesianism' (which in some countries took the form of a construction and consumption bubble) that concealed – until the outbreak of the global crisis – the existence of a demand-and-supply constraint on development in the European peripheral countries. This longer-term perspective helps us better to assess the limitations of the solely macroeconomic alternatives that have been proposed to steer the EZ economy out of its present quagmire. While internal devaluation (wage flexibility) in the deficit (Southern European) countries has shown its destructive potential, expansion of internal demand in the 'core' countries (Germany) or unqualified EZ-wide reflationary measures, though indispensable, do not get to the root of the development and debt sustainability problems of Southern European countries, which continue to lack a sufficiently broad and differentiated productive structure. The problems associated with the structural rigidity of peripheral economies depend on their limited ability to operate in a regime where innovation and product-led innovation prevail, and not on scant labour flexibility.

Chapter 9 discusses the policy implications of the analysis developed in the previous chapters, with particular focus on industrial policies. Given the differences in the levels of development of the various EU countries and their varying capacities to cope with change, fiscal policy should be assigned two complementary targets: the role of actively promoting – through investment – the removal of development bottlenecks and renewal of the productive base, and a redistributive and compensative function. This new strategy entails attributing strategic importance to investment guidance by the state through industrial policies geared to diversifying, innovating and strengthening the economic structures of peripheral countries. In order to restore more sustainable growth, the EU must implement a multilevel policy aiming at rebalancing the core-periphery divide in Europe. The severity of the crisis and its dramatic consequences have led to the return of the concept of 'industrial policy' in the economic strategies of the EU. Though positive, the first examples of this reorientation of strategy – the Investment Plan for Europe (Junker plan) and Industry 4.0 – have so far failed to show the capacity to support a process of structural convergence and, in the case of Industry 4.0, given the structural heterogeneity existing in Europe, the new technologies risk remaining concentrated in the more advanced area. We conclude that a change of strategy is even more urgent today, since the crisis marks another major structural break in world trade, similar to those of the 1970s and the first decade of the new millennium, while the innovation drive risks further widening the divide within Europe.

References

Burnham, P. (2001). New Labour and the politics of depoliticisation. *The British Journal of Politics & International Relations*, 3(2), 127–149.

CEPR (2015). *Rebooting the Eurozone: Step 1 – Agreeing a Crisis Narrative*. Centre for Economic Policy Research. http://voxeu.org/epubs/cepr-reports/rebooting-eurozone-step-1-agreeing-crisis-narrative [accessed 13 September 2017].

European Council (1989). Committee for the Study of Economic & Monetary Union. *Report on Economic and Monetary Union in the European Community*. Unipub.

Krippner, G. R. (2011). *Capitalizing on Crisis*. Cambridge, MA: Harvard University Press.

Levy, J. D. (2008). From the dirigiste state to the social anaesthesia state: French economic policy in the longue durée. *Modern & Contemporary France*, 16(4), 417–435.

Orphanides, A. (2015). The euro area crisis five years after the original sin. *MIT Sloan School Working Paper No. 5147-15*.

Vico, G. [1725–1728] (2011). *Princìpi di scienza nuova*. Milano: Mondadori.

Werner, P. (1970). *Report to the Council and the Commission on the Realisation by Stages of Economic and Monetary Union in the Community – 'Werner Report'* – (definitive text) [8 October 1970]. Bulletin of the European Communities, Supplement 11/1970. [EU Council of the EU Document] http://aei.pitt.edu/1002/ [accessed 13 September 2017].

Part I
A medium-term perspective

1 The Euro crisis

A faulty institutional construction

1 Introduction

'The problems we are seeing in Europe today', Sen (2012) has argued,

> are mainly the result of policy mistakes: punishments for bad sequencing
> (currency unity first, political unity later); for bad economic reasoning
> (including ignoring Keynesian economic lessons as well as neglecting the
> importance of public services to European people); for authoritarian
> decision-making; and for persistent intellectual confusion between reform
> and austerity. Nothing in Europe is as important today as a clear-headed
> recognition of what has gone so badly wrong in implementing the grand
> vision of a united Europe.

The current euro problems are the result of three forgotten unions: financial,
fiscal and political (Matthijs and Blyth, 2015). The unresolved conflict between
national and supra-national sovereignty left the union without an institution
responsible for a common fiscal governance, at the same time when the scope of
national policy was increasingly constrained by automatic rules. Financial liberalization and capital market integration were not supported by the construction
of common institutions to ensure financial stability. Banking regulation was left
to national institutions, which proved clearly unable to cope with the globalization of capital markets and 'too big to fail' financial organizations. Finally, the
missing political union left the European community with a democratic deficit
and a deep crisis of legitimacy that stemmed from the EU's faulty institutions
and the subsequent crisis resolution policies (Schmidt, 2015).

Many of the issues challenging the survival of the monetary union today were
long debated, but not solved, prior to the inception of the euro (Mourlon-Druol,
2014). This ill-designed institutional construct is the consequence of unresolved
political issues as much as of economic theory's illusion of the possibility to
eschew polity from money. Forgetting Polanyi's lesson that 'markets need political authority to stabilise them' (McNamara, 2015: 29), the link between political sovereignty and fiscal authority, on the one hand, and money creation and
the central bank, on the other, has been weakened to a degree rarely, if ever,

known before (Goodhart, 1998: 409). The divorce between money creation and the establishment and maintenance of a stable sovereign power is at the roots of the current troubles of the EMU.

The asymmetrical construction of the EMU, where monetary union exists without economic union, differs from the model of integrated monetary and economic governance conceived by prominent early thinkers of the EMU (Verdun, 2007). The period that separates the Werner Report (1970), when the idea of a common currency was first broached, and the Delors Report (European Council, 1989), when it was brought back to life, was one of intense economic turbulence. The tension between national policy autonomy and economic interdependence, global transformation in production and the surge of finance, the U-turn in economic theory and policy that has shaped policymakers' views on macroeconomic responses to global transformations: these elements have all played a critical role in the evolution of the institutional foundations of the European Union. Despite the Delors Report's claim to have moved in continuity with the Werner Report, the two reports are worlds apart. The institutional construction of the EMU reflects the interests and beliefs of its two main actors – Germany's reliance on rules to buttress its deep concern for moral hazard by other member states and France's vacillating commitments to Keynesianism and austerity (Matthijs and Blyth, 2015: 12) – as well as their evolving unequal relationship, and France's increasing weakness (Vail, 2015; Brunnermeier *et al.*, 2016).

In this chapter, we analyse the steps that led to the institutional construction of the EMU. Its uneven path reflects the changing global economic environment and the European countries' response to it.

Three aspects will be considered.

1   The failure of demand management policies in the stagflation period of the 1970s and the surge of a new theoretical paradigm. The idea that it was possible to successfully steer the economy was punctured by the bad decade of the 1970s and the theoretical explanations that were offered for the inherent failings of the 1960-type macro-models (Goodhart, 2007: 27). After the dollar devaluation, the Bretton Woods consensus, based on fixed (but adjustable) exchange rates, capital controls and monetary (and more generally, economic) policy independence, was replaced by a neoliberal policy consensus that set price stability as the primary objective, eliminated the controls on capital movement and relinquished the independence of monetary and fiscal policy.

2   The Europeanization process. The European Union's political and economic dynamics became part of the organizational logic of national politics and policy-making through the adoption of two role models: Germany and the US. Germany was the nation that had adjusted most successfully following the demise of the Bretton Woods system. Germany's view that stable prices are essential to achieve growth and higher employment contributed to creating a consensus on a scheme that asserted the primacy of disinflation and price stability – an objective that the new economic theory maintained could

be pursued at no cost in terms of unemployment. The US's astonishing growth performance in the first part of the 1980s, mistakenly ascribed to the liberalization of labour, products and capital markets, boosted the process of financial and labour deregulation in Europe.

3   Global finance and monetary union. The internationalization of capital movements thwarted any attempt to safeguard the independence of monetary policy in a regime of fixed exchange rates. The two experiences of exchange rate cooperation – the Snake between 1973 and 1978, and the European Monetary System (EMS) between 1979 and 1992/1995 – demonstrated the fragility of any exchange rate agreement aimed at creating an area of monetary stability in a period of strong dollar fluctuations. The Snake utterly failed to reduce the variability of the nominal exchange rate vis-à-vis the Deutsche mark (DM). The EMS was more successful, but entailed several realignments and almost collapsed in the 1992 exchange rate crisis. The exchange rate agreements were made even more fragile by the decision to abolish the controls on capital movements, which left the monetary union as the only alternative to a return to free floating (Padoa-Schioppa, 1987).

The final section of the chapter deals with the euro crisis. While it was acknowledged from the outset that the euro area was far from meeting the conditions for an Optimum Currency Area (OCA), it was believed that these conditions would be met in the making, if only the institutional features of the various countries could be made to conform to the ideal theoretical model. The institutional structure of the EMU as well as the structural reforms required of debtor countries as a condition for financial assistance respond to that conviction. In line with the OCA approach, mainstream interpretations of the crisis have stressed the sub-optimality of the euro area. We agree with McNamara (2015) that this is the wrong diagnosis: the euro crisis is not due to economic sub-optimality, but to ill-designed economic and political institutions. As we shall argue in the following chapters, the successful association of countries at different levels of development cannot be achieved simply by coercing the weakest members to behave in conformity with the theory by adopting the institutions of the 'model' country. This means that partial reforms tinkering with single aspects of the crisis will not get to the root of the euro crisis; even worse, the current policy mix is condemning the Southern European countries to indefinite stagnation. If, as Hopkin (2015: 183) argues, the fate of the euro hangs on the outcome of the crisis in the Southern European democracies, 'the collapse of political authority that could result from prolonging the squeeze [on their economies] threatens the euro project itself'.

2   The Werner Report and the idea of Europe

The Werner Report was the first concrete attempt to build a European identity after the signing of the Treaty of Rome in 1957. The international context of the time helps to understand why the EMU came onto the agenda.

During the 1960s, progress in European integration, with completion of the customs union and the establishment of the Common Agricultural Policy (CAP), marked progress in integration and supported the aspiration of a common action to contrast the US hegemony. The French stance against the asymmetric functioning of the International Monetary System and what de Gaulle termed 'le privilège exorbitant de l'Amérique' on the one hand pushed for reform of the system, and on the other, advocated a 'European Europe' independent of the United States and with a strong influence in the world. However, what de Gaulle wanted was a 'Europe of states' in which each country would retain its sovereignty, and he was determined to curb any move towards supra-nationality.[1]

The early signs of the breakdown of the Bretton Woods system – turbulence in the international currency markets, the dollar crisis (and the so-called 'Triffin Dilemma'[2]) – heralded the increasing fragility of the international system of fixed exchange rates. While the growth of the Eurodollar market limited the scope for running a monetary policy independent from that of the US, the devaluation of the French franc and the revaluation of the DM in 1969[3] highlighted the lack of coordination on monetary questions among the Six (the six member states of the EC in 1969: France, Germany, Italy, the Netherlands, Belgium and Luxembourg) raising the fear that exchange rate instability, fuelled by increased capital mobility, would disrupt the CAP and any project of further integration.

These factors signalled the need for greater European integration. The European Council of December 1969 in the Hague declared its wish to move forward to Economic Monetary Union. The initiative came from the German Chancellor Willy Brandt, who suggested that, in a first phase, the European Commission (EC) member states should jointly formulate medium-term objectives and aim at harmonization of short-term policies. In a second phase, 'a monetary union of permanently fixed exchange rates could then be achieved' and Germany was prepared to transfer part of its reserves to a common European institution (Gros and Thygesen, 1992: 12). For its part, France stressed the need for the early creation of a system of BP (balance of payments) assistance and a common exchange policy towards third currencies. The study commissioned to detail how the EMU could be achieved resulted in the Werner Report.

The deep differences between the two main actors' economic philosophies were reflected in the difference of opinions regarding the mechanisms that should lead to a successful EMU, and they would persist throughout the subsequent history of increasing integration. They were so ingrained in national thinking that mutual incomprehension often ensued. Thus, despite the common recognition of the importance of harmonizing economic policies and attaining convergence of economic performances to achieve monetary integration, what this meant differed significantly. As Brunnermeier *et al.* (2016: 3) observe, 'economic governance' for Germany meant convergence around a common stability culture, while for France it meant common initiatives to direct economic development. Consequently, the sensitive issue of exchange rates stability was seen by Germany as a problem of consistent domestic economic policies, by France as the achievement of internal and external equilibrium that might require financial assistance and, eventually, international solidarity (Keynes' stance at Bretton Woods and Meade's analysis of the balance of payments were still vivid memories).

The confrontation within the group of high-ranking national and EC officials who worked on the Werner Report would resurface whenever important decisions regarding the institutional set-up of the Union were at stake, notably the establishment of the EMS, the Delors Report and the setting up of the EMU. It came to be referred to as the 'economists' versus 'monetarists' debate (Tsoukalis, 1977; Kruse, 1980; Verdun, 2000a, 2000b, 2002; Maes and Verdun, 2005). But this is a misnomer. Indeed, it can be more properly framed within the discussion on the role of money in terms of cartalist versus metallist positions (see Section 4). According to the cartalist view (in this debate improperly labelled 'monetarist'), money can and does affect the real variables; an influence denied by the metallist position (labelled 'economist'), according to which money can only affect the level of prices. This labelling was retained on subsequent occasions of institutional decision-making to denote the two positions (Wyplosz, 2006). However, by then both contenders would share the same metallistic faith in the irrelevance of monetary policy. While the Germans would adhere to their metallist view (wrongly dubbed 'economist', but monetarist in its correct economic meaning), the French (together with the whole southern front) would argue from an 'ultra-monetarist' position, denying any real effect of money even in the short run.

Thus, the weak-currency countries, France, Belgium and Luxembourg, 'underlined the potential driving role of monetary integration' (Gros and Thygesen, 1992: 14), arguing that 'the economy is led by deliberate monetary decisions'. For them, therefore, common monetary institutional arrangements meant the narrowing of exchange rate margins, the pooling of reserves, and mutual financial support systems. The obligation on surplus countries to share the burden of defending the parities made the functioning of the exchange rate system more symmetrical and favoured the harmonization of economic policies. Thus, a common monetary policy, to be adopted in the early stages, could produce economic policy convergence (Verdun, 2007: 198–199).[4] By contrast, according to the strong-currency countries, Germany and the Netherlands, far-reaching economic policy coordination (fiscal policy and perhaps even incomes policy) should precede the introduction of a common monetary policy (Rosenthal, 1975: 107–108). At the European Council meeting in Luxembourg in April 1976, Schmidt's remark '[I am stunned] that some may believe that one can correct budgetary mechanisms or wage mistakes by monetary mechanisms' nicely rendered the unyielding German view (quoted in Mourlon-Druol, 2014: 1282).

Germany opposed policies aimed at narrowing margins and the early institution of the exchange stabilization fund, on the ground that 'the convergence of economic policies will in itself curb exchange rate variations between the European currencies' (Ungerer, 1997). A single currency would come only at the end of the process, as the 'finishing touch' to a harmonization that would have already been carried out. Italy's position evolved over time, possibly reflecting the evolution of its labour market, which suggested a more favourable consideration of exchange rate 'flexibility'. According to Verdun (2007), in the end, Italy favoured the view that monetary union should come after economic union. Conversely, according to Ungerer (1997), Italy sided with France.

Another point of divergence concerned the transfer of responsibility on economic (fiscal) policy from the national to the community level. Much emphasis was put on avoiding the risk of longer-run divergence in economic performance. To counter this risk, a 'Centre of Decision for Economic Policy' should be given authority over budgetary policies to exercise a decisive influence on economic policy, including national budgetary policies and public financial transfers, needed to avoid regional and structural disequilibria.[5] Equally worth noting is the awareness of the need for regional, employment and industrial policies to tackle structural divergences.[6] Germany and the Netherlands argued for a central economic policy institution with political responsibility (such as a Council for short-term economic policy, or a Commission provided with political responsibility) and an autonomous European central bank. The French opposed this scheme, 'that smacked of political integration' (Eichengreen, 2007: 193). Less attention was paid to achieving convergence in inflation. According to Gros and Thygesen (1992: 13), this difference in objectives, compared with the Delors Report, was only partly due to past experience of relatively small divergences in inflation rates, reflecting the 'rather different view of how economies work and interact which prevailed twenty years ago'. Fully in line with the economic theory of the 1990s, they concluded: 'the rejection of the "center of decision for economic policy" was not surprising since, at least from today's point of view … EMU does not require the degree of centralization of fiscal policy foreseen by the Werner Report' (ibid.: 14).

The Interim Report, officially presented on 8 October 1970, marked a precarious compromise. Envisaging progressive actions in parallel on the economic convergence and monetary cooperation fronts, it provided for the establishment of an economic and monetary union in three stages over a ten-year period (1971–1980). In the second stage, 'the definition and general thrust of economic policy should be made progressively more binding and there should be a proper harmonisation of monetary and budgetary policies'. The harmonization of the financial structures should make it possible to arrive at a true common capital market, and community measures should take care of regional and employment policies. Monetary union meant 'the total and irreversible convertibility of currencies, the elimination of margins of fluctuation in exchange rates, the irrevocable fixing of parity rates and the complete liberalization of movements of capital' which 'may be accompanied by the maintenance of national monetary symbols or the establishment of a sole Community currency' (Werner, 1970: 10). It was supposed to come as the culmination of the process in 1980, with transfer of power from the national to the Community level through the creation of a 'centre of decision for economic policy' that would be 'politically responsible to a European Parliament' (elected by universal suffrage), and a 'Community system for the central banks'.

The Werner Plan envisaged a degree of political integration much higher than the various countries, let alone France, were willing to accept. The weakness of the dollar, putting pressure on the DM and threatening the sustainability of the common market, the vagueness of the commitments in the first stages and the provision of opting-out clauses may have played a role. Treading in de Gaulle's footsteps, President Pompidou deemed only economic and financial cooperation as part of the first stage to be realistic, while plans for transferring vital powers over monetary matters to the Community institutions – as envisaged for the second stage – were considered either unrealistic or undesirable. 'In obvious deference to the French reluctance to discuss institutional arrangements for the final stage and the transfer of responsibility to the EC level, the Commission hardly referred to these issues' (Ungerer, 1997: 114).[7] Speaking in the Bundestag in 1970, Chancellor Brandt described the plan for economic and monetary union by stages as 'the European Community's new Magna Carta'. A more sober view was expressed by Helmut Schmidt, his Minister of Defence, who argued in favour of

> expectations more closely geared to realities: wider and deeper cooperation, without necessarily institutional perfection.... The political unification of Western Europe continues to be a principal goal of our foreign policy ... [but it] is jeopardized if its architects aim for the unattainable. Pragmatism and gradualism offer better chances.
>
> (Schmidt, 1970: 44, 40)

Primarily concerned with safeguarding monetary stability, the Bundesbank reiterated two demands. The margins for fluctuation should not be reduced until there had been genuine harmonization of economic and financial policies; and the future council of the chairmen of the central banks in charge of laying down monetary policy guidelines should, from the outset, be independent of the Council of Ministers, though they should take the Council's guidelines for economic policy into account.

At the Council meetings of 23 November and 14 December 1970, the French delegation was extremely reluctant to agree to successive transfers of powers to the Community institutions and rejected the idea that there should be automatic transition from the first to the second stage. Germany, for its part, expressed reservations about the financing clauses without any tangible achievements to show in relation to policy coordination. In the official ratification of the plan for economic and monetary union by the Council of Ministers of the Community on 22 March 1971, member states' differences led to a messy compromise that postponed sensitive issues to the future. Only stage one, planned to run from 1 January 1971 to 31 December 1973, was clearly defined. Among the measures planned for this stage was the gradual adoption of common standpoints in monetary relations with non-Community countries and international organizations, particularly the United States and the International Monetary Fund, and the gradual narrowing of the margins of fluctuation between European currencies.[8] The central banks were asked to take action, on an experimental and unofficial basis, to reduce the margins of exchange rate fluctuations as from June 1971.

The member states' political resolution committing them to establishing economic and monetary union was only a few months prior to the US decision, on 15 August 1971, to devalue the dollar. This event thwarted achievement of the goal set out in the Werner Plan, already weakened by the absence of any real political will, but made the question of a coordinated floating of the European currencies more compelling.

3 The Snake and the EMS

'La ligne droite' of Franco-German relations

The US dollar depreciation inaugurated a period of wide European currency fluctuations. The Smithsonian Agreement (announced in December 1971) broadened the fluctuations of each currency against the dollar to 2.25 per cent. Thus, each pair of European currencies could fluctuate by as much as 9 per cent against each other. The member states' response to the turmoil of the 1970s was to seek to reproduce stable exchange rates within the context of the EC. The first attempt was a failure. The Community mechanism for the progressive tightening of the margins of fluctuation among the member states' currencies, known as the 'Snake in the tunnel', entered into force in April 1972. With the Snake, short-term and very short-term financial facilities were established to extend financial support to weak-currency countries, although on German insistence their extent was strictly limited (Eichengreen, 2007: 248). Moreover, the question of the European Monetary Cooperation Fund, which should have supported the exchange rate system, was left unresolved. The diverse impacts of the dollar and oil crises on the European economies and the diverse national responses to unemployment and inflation increased the divergence among the European currencies.

While most of Europe was struggling with stagflation, West Germany stood out as a model of price stability. Yet the unscrupulous devaluation of the dollar ('benign neglect') put pressure on the DM, which appreciated against the other European currencies, shattering the Snake. Besides straining the common market, the DM appreciation threatened to make the process of restructuring the German economy far more costly (see Chapter 8). Though capital controls were used by Germany to stem the inflows in order to contain the DM appreciation without losing control of the money supply, the German government (but not the Bundesbank) had to reconsider the opportuneness of a more reliable system of fixed exchange rates.

The turbulence in the Snake had demonstrated that no regional monetary arrangement could work without Franco-German agreement. The 'straight line' (*la ligne droite*) which came into being in 1974 when Valéry Giscard d'Estaing was elected French President and Helmut Schmidt German Chancellor, favoured the EMS initiative. However, the traditional preoccupations – asymmetry versus stability – counterposed France and Germany. At the European Council meeting in Copenhagen in April 1978,

> France's insistence on symmetry would be satisfied by creating a 'trigger mechanism' based on an agreed set of indicators that would force strong-currency countries to relax monetary conditions and weak-currency countries to tighten them when stability was at risk. This would be supplemented by binding intervention obligations and, after a two-year transitional period, by the pooling of foreign-exchange reserves.
>
> (Eichengreen, 2007: 285)

Although Chancellor Schmidt might by now have favoured deeper monetary integration, he had to overcome the opposition of the Bundesbank. Its head, Ottmar Emminger, attempted to veto provisions that could put the German foreign reserves at risk, and obtained elimination of the trigger mechanism and the pooling of reserves and, more importantly, the Chancellor's assurance that the Bundesbank's commitment to unlimited intervention would always be subordinate to its mandate to price stability: '*ultra posse nemo obligatur*. And where the *ultra posse* lies one decides for oneself', avowed Schmidt in a private meeting at the Bundesbank (Bundesbank Archive, 1978).

Doubts and opposition to the EMS in the periphery: Italy's last 'Keynesian' debate

In Italy, several economists declared their opposition to participation in the EMS, doing so in parliament, at the Bank of Italy,[9] in government and in the press (Baffigi, 2016: 9). Judging the EMS premature, they believed it would impose too many sacrifices on a country with huge territorial disparities and that lagged behind the rest of the area. They were concerned that the fixed exchange rate target would conflict with the objective of full employment; a concern made more real by the increasing globalization of finance. Given the differences among countries' initial economic conditions, the expected fragility of the EMS would have created an opportunity for speculative attacks. The high interest rates required to defend the exchange against 'hot money' would conflict with the investment required to overcome the structural crisis caused by under-investment (Caffè, 1979). By preventing full control of monetary policy, the EMS would have deprived Italy of a key tool for the management of economic crises. Finally, convergence required a fiscal policy targeted on reduction of the geographical divide. Such a policy, which was explicitly envisaged by both the Werner and the MacDougall Report (1977), was no longer adequately considered in the EMS project.

The lack of any commitment on special funds for less developed regions would have increased divergence. In the Italian Parliament, Luigi Spaventa took a position strongly opposed to the EMS, which he feared would become an area of deflation. In his view, the EMS agreement lacked three fundamental features to make it sustainable: guarantees on its symmetric functioning; adequate mutual financial assistance; and measures to support less prosperous member countries. Italy's low per capita income, high unemployment, fragile industrial structure, wide regional differences and high cost and price differentials – which persisted despite the efforts made and the progress achieved – suggested that convergence to the EC average could only be gradual.

> It would be impossible, for us, as for the other EC member countries, to adapt to Germany's pace of inflation, which represents a factor of imbalance no smaller than our rate of inflation. Membership would guarantee the exchange rate stability, but it would be achieved at the cost of a lower level of development, employment and income.
>
> (Spaventa, 1978, our translation)

Spaventa concluded that the conditions attached to the use of community funds, which mandated that they must not alter competition, ran counter to their very function, which should be to upgrade the less-developed member states to the competitiveness level of the most advanced ones. The rigid exchange rate constraint would unnecessarily maximize the social and economic costs of the recovery. The trade unions and the main party of the left (PCI) were initially opposed to the EMS on similar grounds. From a monetarist perspective, also Monti (1978) argued against entering a fixed exchange rate agreement before the (monetary) causes of inflation had been tackled.

Those supporting participation had mostly political reasons to do so: the curbing of anti-Atlantic sentiments, and avoiding Italy's economic isolation. Especial influence was exerted by the Federalist movement. Adopting a functionalist approach, it supported the EMS as an unsatisfactory, but expedient, first step towards a political union. Starting from the conviction that it was impossible to create a monetary union without an adequate constitutional framework (that is, a political union), the Federalists believed that the EMS would have created such contradictions as to make resolution of the question of the political and institutional structure unavoidable (Mosconi, 1980, quoted in Masini, 2004: 132–133). With the creation of the EMS, the European economies would be on a razor's edge, poised between a speedy progression towards monetary and political union or relapse into disorderly fluctuating exchange rates.

The economic reasons advanced in favour of Italy's participation in the EMS foreshadowed the view that assigns to European integration the function of correcting otherwise uncontainable old national vices and bringing deviant countries into line. The exchange constraint offered the opportunity to create the conditions to 'normalize' the economy, forcing the social partners to find a solution to the price-wage spiral and to engage in the process of restructuring and modernizing the economy (Andreatta, 1978; Modigliani, 1978).[10] This debate preluded a shift in economic thinking on the relation between democracy and economics which is still at the basis of the current discussion on the 'democratic deficit' of the EMU. In an indirect reply to a blunt private letter from Padoa-Schioppa, prompted by his criticism of the Pandolfi Plan,[11] Federico Caffè – a highly esteemed Italian eco-nomist – explained his doubts about joining the EMS on the basis of 'issues such as the conditions of workers in Europe, the situations of social exclusion and the "strangulation" that could be expected from membership of a monetary system under German hegemony' (quoted in Baffigi, 2016: 10). He stressed the need not to impoverish the range of tools that can be used for economic policy, including public expenditure or the adoption of controls, against the new approach, which 'assumes one can separate the policies regarding production, considered of purely technical nature, from social choices to be submitted to political judgment within democratic procedures' (ibid.). Caffè argued that it should be society that sets social objectives, giving economists (technocrats) the task of finding the best way to achieve them; rather than being the technicians who set the goals – what is pos-sible or desirable – and society having to adapt.

The change in paradigm

The Italian debate on the EMS reflected a more general process 'of policy failure, policy paradigm innovation, and policy emulation' which unfolded among the states of the European Union in the years between the Snake and the EMS and that eventually produced 'a new, neoliberal view of monetary policy' (McNamara, 1998: 5). 'The Bretton Woods system', wrote McNamara (1998: 9),

> was based on the idea that a liberal, open, multilateral system did not have to preclude an extensive role for the state in the domestic economy – that market liberalism would be 'embedded' within a larger context of social goals, like full employment and the welfare state's 'safety net'.

This premise was based on capital controls, autonomy of monetary and fiscal policy and fixed (but adjustable) exchange rates (Vianello, [2009] 2013). The crisis of the 1970s called into question the power of national monetary policies designed to protect the domestic polity against the changing global economy.[12] The *unreformed* old policies of demand management could no longer offer a solution to the stagflation caused by structural changes in demand, production and finance (see Chapter 8). Rising capital mobility made the principles under-lying Bretton Woods no longer viable. Without the support of capital controls, exchange rates stability required monetary policy to cease targeting any other objective, such as employment and other societal aims. With politically accept-able levels of employment and growth no longer assured, commitment to stability would be continuously tested by financial markets, making the objective of exchange rate stability more and more costly.

Policy failure in the aftermath of the first oil crisis opened the way for altern-atives to Keynesian policies. Monetarism offered an alternative paradigm. Reversing the Keynesian thesis, it asserted that the private sector was inherently stable and efforts to manipulate the economy (which was assumed to be in full employment) were ineffective and counterproductive. The notion of money and the real effects of monetary policy were reconsidered: from the 1970s onwards, there was growing consensus that, in the long run, monetary policy is unable to affect the level of real activity, but can only affect the level of prices. Denying any effect even in the short run, the rational expectation approach would soon also sweep away the objection that real effects in the short run may affect (via investment) the structure of the economy, thus modifying its long-run path of growth.

While monetarist theories provided a legitimation for neoliberal, anti-inflationary policies, though 'tempered by fixed exchange rates', Germany, the nation that had adjusted most successfully after the demise of Bretton Woods, became the role model. From the mid-1970s, monetary targets were used by the majority of continental European governments to buttress more restrictive policies. At first, this shift reflected a pragmatic policy reaction to the changed global economic circumstances of the 1970s, rather than any strong 'monetarist' convictions (Houben, 2000: 141–142). Central banks were in uncharted territory. The dollar devaluation had left the system without a nominal anchor; the high inflation made the nominal interest rate no longer a reliable indicator of the tightness of the monetary policy stance; finally, the inflationary effects of the oil crisis – occurring within a context of high liquidity brought about by massive exchange interventions and further increased in 1974–1975 to counter the effects of the oil crisis – contributed to 'wide acceptance that rapid growth in the money stock and in prices go hand in hand' (ibid.).

Spearheaded by Germany, all European countries adopted monetary and credit targets to tackle price and wage increases. Emulation of Germany's (pragmatic) monetarism produced a convergence of policies, which, in turn, made the (relative) stability of exchange rates in the EMS possible, within an international context of increasing capital mobility and variable exchange rates. The by-product was 'eurosclerosis', a term coined by Herbert Giersch in the 1970s to describe the conditions of high unemployment and slow job creation characterizing the European countries in the 1970s and 1980s. The Mitterrand experiment had demonstrated that, in the new European setting, there was no longer room for any unilateral expansionary policy at the nation-state level (see Barba and Pivetti, 2016 for a critical view). With the EC unable or unwilling to orchestrate a coordinated action, this meant the abandonment of any strategy of fiscal stimulus in the EC. By contrast, in the same period, fuelled by a huge fiscal expansion, the United States was achieving phenomenal economic growth. The economic stagnation in Europe was blamed on labour market rigidities, government over-regulation and overly generous social benefits (Simonazzi, 2003). Increasingly, the European Social Model came to be viewed as a stumbling block on the road towards the American way of growth. The Reagan–Thatcher presidencies thus provided a complementary role model based on labour market flexibility, financial deregulation, privatization and state retrenchment.

The developments of economic theory in the 1980s provided justification for the drastic change in objectives and paradigms. Price stability became the overarching goal, to be achieved within a paradigm assuming full employment and self-regulating financial markets. An important fallout of the monetarist approach was the demise of the basic tool of Keynesian policy: the Phillips curve. If the unemployment rate is at the full employment equilibrium level (the natural rate of unemployment), it cannot be changed through monetary or fiscal policy. Expansionary policy was no longer viewed as a boost to the economy, but rather as a harbinger of higher inflation (McNamara, 1998: 146). The independence of the natural rate of unemployment from inflation explained stagflation and provided the blue-print for policy. By acting on expectations, credible commitments to curbing inflation could reduce inflation at almost no cost in terms of output and employment. Whence derived the suggestion to refrain from any policy intervention, but rather to pursue price stability through automatic rules. For a weakly credible institution, it could pay to borrow credibility from a government with a long-proven anti-inflationary stance. This could be done by committing to fixed exchange rates, an experiment which characterized the last period of the EMS, before its 1992 crisis. Thus, although in the monetarist approach money supply was the only appropriate target for monetary policy, commitment to fixed exchange rates could strengthen the credibility of the pledge to reduce inflation, thereby reducing the real cost of disinflation.

While the 1970s debate on Italy's participation in the EMS took place within the (neo)Keynesian field, by the end of the 1980s the discussion on Italy's participation in the EMU was conducted entirely in terms of the new macroeconomic theory. Rules and constraints were now deemed necessary to separate and shield the economy from the political sphere. The new approach conquered the economic profession and the political arena 'as completely as the Holy Inquisition conquered Spain', to borrow Keynes' expression (Keynes, 1936: 32). Also some of those who had previously advanced doubts on the opportuneness of Italy's joining the EMS on Keynesian grounds were conquered by the new paradigm. 'The economic debate that accompanied the launching of the EMS initiative', wrote Spaventa (1991: 8), 'was heated, but fairly simple in its terms: with the new classical macroeconomics still in its infancy, a number of themes which later became relevant in the literature were then absent'.

> As a corollary of these theoretical developments, the asymmetry issue was turned on its head. While the early debate considered the lack of symmetry as a major shortcoming of the system, in the new literature this is instead regarded as a virtue, as long as the n-th country, the one free to set monetary policy independently, pursues price stability as its major objective.
>
> (Ibid.: 9)

Moreover, 'these models have … provided Germany with a powerful justification for rejecting recurrent demands for greater coordination on the part of other members of the system' (ibid.). So much for French and Italian complaints about the lack of symmetry and coordination in the EMS.

For a while, reliance on rules (in turn: the fixed exchange rates in the new EMS, the Bundesbank's monetary stance, the central bank's independence, the financial markets) seemed able to deliver the discipline required to keep the polity from interfering. But, then, Polanyi's lesson on the impossibility of separating market and polity was relearned the hard way when this approach inevitably failed.

Why did political leaders and economists of progressive persuasion, who did not consider themselves monetarists, endorse restrictive monetary and fiscal policies strongly oriented by the monetarist doctrine? The view that European integration would have the function of correcting old national vices, considered otherwise incorrigible, played a role. The external constraint, conceived 'as a whip' on the production system (the exchange rate appreciation) or 'as a bridle' on excessive debt expansion (capital flights as a threat or a punishment for profligate behaviours), would have opened the way to a linear progress of growth. Moreover, monetarism seemed to provide an answer to two important issues that progressive policymakers tended to underestimate: inflation and the (lack of) effectiveness of unreformed Keynesian policies. The changes of the global context required an overhaul of the Keynesian policies and of the social contract upon which they were founded in ways compatible with preservation of the welfare state. To deal with the problem of inflation and with the exhaustion of the capacity of Keynesian policies to address change, recourse to monetarism was certainly not the only option (see Chapter 7).

The embedded liberalism of the Bretton Woods era failed to cope with the changing economic and financial context. A new norm of competitive liberalism, rooted in the view that harsh measures must be taken to adjust to changing international economic conditions, then prevailed. The complete victory of this approach, epitomized by the TINA acronym – There Is No Alternative – would wipe out even the memory of different courses of action. 'The conservative orthodoxy shared by socialists and conservatives alike in Europe, at first a "second best" alternative, soon evolved to become a first best, one that could be sold to societal groups as the appropriate remedy to relieve the traumas of stagflation and Eurosclerosis' (McNamara, 1998: 10).

4 The bumpy road to the EMU

Remarking on the oscillating Europeanism of the German government, De Cecco (1992: 13) pointed out that Germany tended to move closer to Europe in times of economic and political weakness, only to distance itself again in times of economic strength. Yet, the plans devised when Germany felt weak came to be implemented when the German cycle was over and they were no longer needed. This had been the fate of the Werner Plan. Again, the agreement on the EMS came on the eve of another shift of American policy. Paul Volcker's succession to Arthur Burns in 1979 marked the change of US priorities in monetary policy: foremost among them became 'taking on inflation'. Following the monetary squeeze, US short-term interest rates skyrocketed, ushering in a period of dollar appreciation, disinflation and third-world debt crisis. In its first years, the EMS enjoyed a period of relative tranquillity. The turn in the US monetary policy, controls on capital movements and several realignments required to compensate the differentials with German inflation contributed to its survival.

The second part of the 1980s saw accelerated progress towards economic and monetary unification. The process of economic integration had resulted in extensive interdependence of the European economies, but growth had been disappointing, especially when compared to the USA's economic success. This divergence in performance was interpreted as due to the gains generated by the US's ever-freer markets of goods, labour and finance. The Single European Act, signed in February 1986, set the European Community the objective of establishing a single market for goods and services by 31 December 1992. An EC directive (1988) mandated the removal of capital controls by 1 June 1990. Though member states with shaky finances were authorized to proceed more slowly, most of them accomplished the objective before the deadline.

The fragility of the EMS, continuously threatened by the enormous build-up of international financial capital, prompted the leap towards removal of capital controls. According to Padoa-Schioppa (1994: 142), concern for the survival of the single market,[13] threatened by complete freedom of capital, was the technical reason inducing to see no alternative to monetary union. However, there was nothing to be feared from the abolition of controls, argued the new monetarist theory, which solved Wallich's irreconcilable triad (Wallich, 1973) between fixed exchange rates, independence of monetary policy and freedom of capital movements by sacrificing, at no cost, the national monetary policy. 'Since the only consequence of a restrictive monetary policy ... would be a lowering of the inflation rate, without any lasting loss of employment, free capital movements would represent a healthy factor of monetary discipline, without any substantial contraindications' (Simonazzi and Vianello, 2001: 266). Padoa-Schioppa (1994: 223) noted that it would have been much more difficult for this argument to be accepted in the intellectual climate of the 1970s, when monetary policy was given the task of finding an equilibrium between employment and inflation. Contrary to the widespread fear that the EMS with fixed exchange rates and free capital mobility might be unstable, the new orthodoxy argued that abiding by the rules can strengthen credibility. Removal of capital controls signalled that a country was committed and able to withstand the assaults of the market, before acceding to the monetary union. Writing in 1990, Giavazzi and Spaventa contended that 'financial liberalization seems to have strengthened, rather than weakened the EMS' (p. 447) (see Pivetti, 1992 and 1998 for a criticism of this position).

The Maastricht Treaty and the European Monetary Union

It is well known how economic and political events engendered the speedy establishment of the European Monetary Union. Deeper monetary integration suited France, weary of the asymmetric working of the system, which meant that France (and the weaker-currency countries) unfairly bore a disproportionate share of the adjustment burden.[14] It suited also Germany for economic reasons, since it insulated the DM (and the European currencies) from the vagaries of the dollar. There were also more specific political reasons. Chancellor Kohl saw monetary integration as a way to further the cause of a politically integrated Europe,[15] as did Genscher, his foreign minister, who 'insisted that economic and monetary union (EMU) negotiations be linked to negotiations on deeper political integration and foreign policy coordination'. At its meeting in June 1988, recalling that '[i]n adopting the Single Act, the Member States of the Community confirmed the objective of progressive realization of economic and monetary union' the European Council entrusted to a 'Committee, chaired by Mr Jacques Delors, President of the European Commission, the task of studying and proposing concrete stages leading towards this union' (European Council, 1989: 3 Foreword).

The Delors Report went to great lengths to present the monetary union as a natural, indeed unavoidable, consequence of the Single Act while, at the same time, claiming continuity with the Werner Report.[16]

> We agreed on three stages taken over from the Werner Report: stage one, devoted to enhancing coordination, from 1 July 1990; stage two, a transition stage on the way to the final stage, preparing the ground for what were ultimately to be the institutions for Economic and Monetary Union; and the last stage, at which the exchange rates between the currencies themselves and between them and the single currency would be laid down irrevocably.[17]

Yet, small details and important omissions produced a very different design: there were no longer capital controls to defend the exchange in the transition to the common currency, no central budget for the EU to accompany the EMU, no union-wide system of fiscal federalism, nor any transfer of fiscal prerogatives to the community level. The original view that removal of capital controls and centralization of monetary policy should come at the end of a more advanced process of political integration was replaced with a concept of monetary integration as a 'catalyst' or 'stepping stone' to political integration (Pivetti, 1998). Addressing German concerns, the report envisaged binding rules for national fiscal policies and suggested that sound fiscal policy should be a precondition to joining the monetary union.

The Delors Report had just been published (April 1989) and the decision to move to the treaty stage just taken (in the European Council of December 1989), when international circumstances changed again with the fall of the Berlin Wall and the question of German reunification. The prospect of a reunited Germany worried its partners.[18] Now the French switched to the view of the monetary union as a stepping-stone to political union, to embed a united Germany in a larger Europe, trusting in their veto power to bend the rules in their favour. Italy too was convinced that political union was still on the agenda.

The debates leading to the Maastricht Treaty only superficially resembled the two positions that had confronted each other since the Werner Report. This time the discussion took place within the same monetarist field, reflecting different shades of monetarism. In the 'economists' camp, Germany, concerned about monetary and price stability, wanted a long convergence process, no set date for launching the process and a small initial group of countries. A common monetary policy (with a common interest rate) and different inflation rates would lead to perverse real interest rates – what came to be known as the Walters critique. Thus, the common currency should be the final step of a long process of gradual alignment of national policies and nominal variables, with the resulting ever-closer integration of the national economies. 'The introduction of a common currency would then form the inevitable keystone, amounting, as it were, to a kind of "coronation"' (Issing, 2008: 302).

The 'monetarists' camp, associated with France and Italy, argued, on the basis of the new classical macroeconomic theory, that once a new currency had been established, past expectations would become irrelevant. With the establishment of strong institutions, the irreversible fixing of exchange rates would 'force' the necessary economic adjustment. The argument was that pre-entry disinflation would be slow and costly, but it would be almost immediate and essentially costless if achieved after entry into the monetary union. Thus, the discussion saw 'moderate monetarists' arguing in favour of gradualism and 'ultra-monetarists' in favour of a 'big-bang'. Unconvinced by the ultra-monetarists' arguments,[19] Germany pressed for its own ideas on monetary union. The ECB should follow the Bundesbank's architecture and be totally independent of the polity. Countries' policies should be subjected to the judgment of financial markets. The proposed directive for capital liberalization should be 'irrevocable, without safeguard clauses and prior harmonization of capital taxation and financial regulation as requested by Italy', declared Stoltenberg's memorandum (15 March 1988) (Gros and Thygesen, 1992: 315).

By the time the intergovernmental conference to set down the rules convened in December 1990, German unification was a *fait accompli*. The German position hardened: a politically independent ECB, with price stability as its primary objective and structured federally – that is, on the Bundesbank's blue-print[20] – together with the notorious fiscal conditionality, sanctioned the separation of monetary and fiscal policy. The parallel political agenda scored only modest results and by the 1990s, the link between monetary and political integration had been dropped from the agenda.

The 1992 crisis and beyond

Since 1987, the 'convergence game' played by financial markets, taking advantage of the weaker countries' higher interest rates needed to defend the parity, had favoured the stability of the system. The respite granted by markets in spite of the accumulation of disequilibria made it possible to transform vague plans for a monetary union into a Treaty. The Maastricht Treaty, signed in February 1992, set down the convergence criteria and defined the path to the creation of the Economic and Monetary Union. The rejection of the Treaty by the Danish voters in the June referendum was entirely unexpected by the political class (though not by speculators, Simonazzi and Vianello, 1996). Faced with the problems of financing the Eastern reconstruction and its looming inflationary consequences, the Bundesbank drew its opt-out clause, shattering the EMS and with it France's long, painful road to disinflation.

'La ligne droite' of Franco-German relations – which had been reshaped after the break-up of the Soviet Union with the French consent to German unification in exchange for German consent to monetary union – suffered a new setback after the EMS 1992 crisis, but was again redressed in the course of the decade. The sharp depreciation of the Lira (50 per cent against the DM between 1992 and 1995) signalled the risks of freely fluctuating exchange rates within the common market. However, Germany was concerned that member states with a weaker historical performance could join the EMU with no clear checks and balances to deal with poor performance after exchange rates had been locked (i.e. post-stage three). The Treaty focused on the risk of free-riding by any country that, on the brink of default on its debt, could force the other Euro area members and the Eurosystem to provide support (Wyplosz, 2006). It contained three provisions to deal with this risk: ECB's independence, no monetary financing of public deficits, and no bail-out by other member states. The first two provisions aimed at separating the ECB from the state. The central bank was strictly forbidden to finance budget deficits, i.e. it was not allowed to operate on the primary debt market. To ensure that it would abide by these legal requirements, it was made strongly independent from governments. A no bail-out clause (Art. 103) shielded governments and all official institutions (including the Eurosystem and the Commission) from the obligation to support any country in financial difficulties. The 1997 Stability and Growth Pact (SGP) extended the convergence criteria laid down in the Maastricht Treaty as permanent requirements, committed the member states to an Official Medium Term Objective of balanced budgets, and set up a formal procedure for its enforcement.

In 1998, the European Central Bank and its European System of Central Banks were created with the mandate, by statute, of guaranteeing price stability (as well as securing the other objectives of the EU, without prejudice to price stability). The ECB was prohibited from purchasing sovereign bonds at issue. The TARGET2 payment system was designed to take care of capital mobility and symmetric access to the financial markets. The SGP was deemed to strengthen the inflation-targeting strategies of the central bank. The institutional structures of the euro were widely believed to prevent a country in difficulties from being bailed out by other euro members or having its sovereign debt purchased by the ECB.[21] Despite all the restrictions, in pre-EMU debates there was relatively little discussion of sovereign default (Whelan, 2013) or how to deal with financial instability. The entire construct was based on the idea that deregulated private capital markets together with fiscal rules would by themselves discipline the countries' imbalances and guarantee convergence. Financial markets priced-in almost no default risk in the pre-crisis years. The stage was set for the Monetary Union to start.

5 The EMU's institutional flaws

Money 'instrumentum regni'

We argued in Section 1 that the current economic problems are the result of the mistaken idea that the EMU could be disembedded from the social and political institutions at the basis of any monetary union. Politics was considered as a sort of 'noise', and rules were needed to constrain politicians to conform with the theoretical model. Thus, the institutional structure of the Eurozone was built on the separation between the ECB, responsible for the Eurozone's monetary policy and constitutionally independent of governments, and political and fiscal powers left with the nation states but constrained through pacts and treaties, with markets as guardians and no political authority to stabilize them.

This construction runs counter to the historical evidence, which indicates that monetary sovereignty has been part of the prerogatives of the state, of the *instrumenta regni*, at least since Roman times (Keynes, [1923] 1971, quoted in De Cecco, 2001). Why, therefore, did European countries voluntarily surrender national sovereignty on money without creating a parallel political entity? The reasons may reside partly in the difficulty of renouncing political sovereignty that led to acceptance of the neo-functionalist idea of a gradual progression towards a more complete union. The economic theory that came to dominate by the end of the 1980s, and the interpretation of the nature of money that the latter implied may have also played a role. Assuming that the relationship between the state's fiscal power and money creation is a crucial mechanism of inflation, it asserts the need to sever this relationship by separating the Treasury from the Central Bank.

This view has a long tradition: it rests on the 'metallistic' notion of money, according to which, far from being a social institution, money is substantially a means to facilitate exchanges, a product of the market that derives its value from the purchasing power of the commodity upon which it is based (Goodhart, 1998). De Cecco (2001: 95) recalls that the obsession to exorcise the fiscal power of money played a role in the inter-war German hyperinflation. Unlike Britain, which, being the financial centre of the time, could sell its bonds on the international market, Germany had to rely for the financing of its war deficit on the internal placement of its bonds, underwritten largely by the Central Bank. The League of Nations, responsible for the financial administration of the Weimar Republic and under the influence of the British Treasury and the Bank of England, banned the monetary financing of public deficits. However, it did not restrain the ability to borrow on the international capital market. The preoccupation with the fiscal power of money led to disregard of the creation of funds by large investment banks. It was even less concerned about the accumulation of foreign debt by German local authorities, of short-term debt by German enterprises, and by the huge short-term liabilities accumulated by large German banks with the banks of the creditor countries. On the contrary,

It seemed, indeed, to many of them [the regulators], that the newfound stability ... which coincided with equally stable exchange rates, attracted foreign capital inflows which were extremely beneficial to the economy of these countries and for the world economy as a whole.... As long as the budgets of the state and of the central bank were kept separate, it seemed to them to be ensuring lasting international monetary stability.

(Ibid.: 98, our translation)

Recent examples of the negative consequences of assuming that monetary and fiscal policy can be kept separate and their interactions neglected abound. Commenting, ten years later, on the 1981 'divorce' between the Treasury and the Bank of Italy, the then treasury ministry Andreatta (1991) observed that the EMS implied the divorce, and these two policies together contributed to bringing about the disinflation in Italy. He did not mention the upsurge in the public debt due to the historically high real interest rates. Major examples of the dangerous dynamics of financial stability in the context of monetary union are provided by Spain and Ireland – two fundamentally fiscally sound countries thrown into crisis by their own banking systems.

The Maastricht Treaty was inspired by the same myopia: the same focus on the state/central bank nexus as the only cause of inflation; the same disregard of financial and banking aspects of monetary policy and of their international repercussions. Banks and financial markets were treated as markets like any other, with which to interfere as little as possible. Money was regarded as a commodity like any other – 'having developed from a private sector cost minimization process to facilitate trading' (Goodhart, 1998: 407) – that could, indeed should, be separated from the state authority. The

thrust of the M[etallist] team's theoretical analysis is that this divorce is all to the good; indeed, it is largely the purpose of the exercise. The blame for recent inflation has been placed on political myopia, via the time inconsistency analysis, and the ability of the political (fiscal) authorities to bend and misuse monetary powers for their own short-term objectives.

(Ibid.)

Optimum Currency Area

The same monetarist approach underlies the Optimum Currency Areas (OCA) theory, which was rediscovered as a tool to assess the costs and benefits of the monetary union. The post-war studies on economic integration considered two distinct problems. The first (Meade, 1957; Scitovsky, 1957) was concerned with the question of whether a monetary union facilitates the successful formation of an economic union. The second (Mundell, 1961; McKinnon, 1963; Kenen, 1969) attempted to identify the economic conditions of an area within which it may be optimal to have fixed exchange rates (Optica, 1976). Because the former approach starts from the given situation of a custom or economic union, which may be empirically far from optimal, it was the one that shaped the debate in the first round of discussions on the road to monetary union (the Werner Report). It was the latter question, however, that shaped much of the academic debate on EMU sustainability, investigating whether the Eurozone satisfied the criteria for an OCA. While it was quite clear that the Eurozone was far from satisfying these criteria, there was no reason why it should. Indeed, argues Goodhart (1998), history is full of instances of viable monetary unions between radically diverse regions. The US and the USSR before its political dissolution are only the most outstanding examples; the North and South of Italy, or post-unification East and West Germany provide other examples. The key determinant, concludes McNamara (2015), is the existence of political borders.

According to the Cartalist theory of money, a monetary union relies, for its viability, on the central authority of the state. The OCA approach, based on the Metallist form theory, cannot predict (or explain) the formation of a monetary union; it can only be 'a normative theory, of what should be'. Thus, having successfully excluded money and its link with the functions and role of government from the picture, the OCA approach can proceed to set down the supply conditions that must be met for an OCA – wage and price flexibility, factor mobility, specialization or diversity of production, nature of the shocks – and to investigate the antidotes for specific market imperfections. In this approach, demand enters only as an asymmetric 'shock': the problem is then to assess if and how quickly supply conditions adjust to bring the economy back to equilibrium. The analysis is based on a production function where differences in products, when considered, play no relevant role in the dynamic macroeconomic adjustment. There is no consideration for differences in the productive structures and stages of development of the various countries which played such a prominent role in the debates on the Werner Report and on participation in the EMS. On the contrary, it is argued that, since trade between EU countries consists mostly of intra-industry trade, the implication is that all countries are on the same level playing field. The focus is then on mitigating short-term cyclical downturns occurring in parts of the EMU, rather than on the ways to compensate for structural differences among the EMU economies. The OCA works as a closed system: although it admits of different impacts of an external shock on the members, the adjustment occurs within the OCA. Finally yet importantly, because the OCA approach focuses on the individual countries' characteristics, it misses the systemic perspective: by ignoring the interdependence among countries, it can neglect the effects of each country's policies on the rest of the area. Thus, it is possible to ignore the deflationary effects deriving from the abolition of policy instruments at the national level, not compensated at the supra-national level. Then, one can compare the benefits, in terms of reduction of transaction costs, against the costs in terms of adjustment difficulties.[22] However, concludes Goodhart (1988: 424), the political economy reasons for the formation of a monetary union (that is, the political relationship between control over money and sovereign power) are so overwhelming 'that the balance of purely economic benefits and costs entailed by OCA must presumably be of second order importance'.

The reasons for the consensus

To the (mostly US) economists who argued against the viability of the EMU on the basis that it did not meet the criteria for an OCA, the Euro-enthusiasts countered that these conditions would be met in the making. The institutional structure could be designed in such a way as to let the economy be guided by automatic rules, thus creating a straitjacket to which in the end the economy and the society would have to adjust. The EC's approach is indicative. It defended the EMU on three grounds: first, questioning the importance of differences between countries and maintaining that the monetary union would reduce them, leading to convergence; second, denying the effectiveness of monetary and exchange rate policies in reducing the differences between countries; and third, arguing that these policies may be not only ineffective but also harmful in the hands of politicians (De Grauwe, 2016). The old concerns that, if countries have different capabilities, no degree of wage flexibility or financial transfer will suffice, were brushed aside. With the market in charge, any discretionary policy could be avoided. 'Once all deficits are brought "close to balance", there will be enough room for the automatic stabilizers to fully operate' (European Commission, 2001: 62). All that was needed was discipline by countries in sticking to the rules.[23] Thus, the lack of concern about potential sovereign debt problems may have rested on the confidence that the fiscal rules, combined with market discipline, would make a default in the euro area unlikely, as argued by Whelan (2013), or that their full implications were not fully recognized when they were adopted, as suggested by Wyplosz (2006: 238). It is also possible that, as suggested by Costantini (2015: 48), austerity reflected shared elite convictions, rather than representing simply an imposition of one country on the others or dictates of technocrats. Smaller countries

> persuaded themselves that maintaining the Commission's powers would provide a long run guarantee of equal and symmetric implementation of the rules across the Union, neglecting the effects that the policies they were implementing and the framework they were validating would have on the real distribution of power within (and on) the EU.[24]

From the EMU to the crisis

The SGP was immediately put to the test. Facing prolonged slow growth after the bursting of the tech bubble in the US, many European countries allowed the stabilizers to operate. Germany and France were the first to violate the pact, with smaller member states following suit. Repeatedly breached, the pact was declared 'stupid' by the then European Commission President, Romano Prodi.

> The Ecofin and the Commission quickly broke ranks, as ministers proved reluctant to follow up on the Commission's recommendations for warnings. Ecofin was also far more amenable than the Commission to winding down

infraction proceedings on the basis of mere promises to do better. The conflict went so far that the Commission, in 2004, brought suit against Ecofin at the European Court of Justice for suspending Pact rules in the cases of Germany and France.

(Costantini, 2015: 45)

Commenting on the episode, Issing (2008: 305) observed ironically 'But can one really expect the Council of Ministers to see its way to imposing sanctions – especially on a big country – in the case of an excessive deficit?'

The pact was suspended in late 2003 – a move partly censured by the European Court of Justice.

> In the end, following consultations with governments, the Commission produced in late 2004 a reform blueprint that aimed at smoothing the SGP's roughest edges without touching its essential components. In March 2005, the ECOFIN Council accepted most of the Commission's recommendations. The 3 per cent budget ceiling was retained as the centrepiece of the pact, but the decision to declare a country in excessive deficit could now rely on a wider set of parameters, including the behaviour of the cyclically adjusted budget, the level of the debt, the duration of a slow-growth period and the possibility that the deficit is associated to productivity-enhancing expenditures [i.e. implementation of structural reforms].
>
> (Wyplosz, 2006: 238)

The 2005 Pact resolved the conflict between 'hawks' (the Commission and several member states, including Netherlands, Austria and Luxembourg) and 'doves' (Schroeder, but not his finance minister, Hans Eichel) by 'formally maintaining the constraints while at the same time substantially eroding them'. The Cyclically Adjusted Budget (CAB) was transformed into a tool for budget surveillance. Its estimation method was revised, without solving any of its basic faults. Output was considered uniquely supply determined, and the effects of demand (i.e. private and public investment) on actual and hence potential output were neglected. Indeed,

> it validates measures that have the opposite effect: downward movements of output due to budget cuts are incorporated into the estimate of potential output, and thus are not recognized as policy failures.... Hence the CAB works as an ex-post justification for further austerity, locking Europe in a vicious spiral.
>
> (Costantini, 2015: 35, 54)[25]

Costantini concludes that

> instead of indicating how fiscal policy can best obtain the economic objective that a community prefers, [the CAB] becomes a tool for constraining

the community's political choices to the demands of a theory on which no consensus exists and which yields sharply different results depending on when and where it is applied.

(Ibid.: 40; see also Palumbo, 2013)[26]

6 In the crisis: bail-outs, politics, reforms

It is well known how the international financial crisis degenerated into a bank-sovereign debt loop, dragging the Eurozone periphery into a deep economic depression. We leave to Chapter 4 a critical review of the mainstream explanations of the crisis. In this section, we briefly discuss the main stages in the evolution of the crisis and its connection with the institutional setting of the EMU. Due to the void at the heart of the institutional architecture of the euro, the 'ECB continues to face the crucial political challenge of being the only notable monetary authority that lacks a fiscal counterpart' (Braun, 2017: 16). The absence of a centralized fiscal authority and the institutional separation of monetary and fiscal policy give rise to a coordination problem – a 'game of chicken' – between the ECB and the European institutions, which has caused destructive delays in tackling the various phases of the economic and financial crisis. Moreover, the ECB's loneliness creates an uneasy balance between independence and accountability.

The banks-sovereign debt loop

The euro crisis has been blamed on the 'sudden stop' of capital flows to the periphery. However, the problem was the start as much as the stop. Haldane (2011) suggested a different metaphor: the 'big fish small pond' problem. The seeds of emerging market crises are sown in the build-up phase, as inflows overwhelm the absorptive capacity of recipient countries' capital markets. At some point, continuation of the 'carry trade' becomes riskier or less profitable as financial instability *in the 'centre'* generates increased risk perceptions, attracting finance back to 'centre' countries (the flight to quality) (Ginzburg and Simonazzi, 2011).

In the first years of the EMU, core countries' financial institutions channelled increasing amounts of capital towards the periphery, funding themselves in international financial markets (O'Connell, 2015).[27] The financial deregulation and the huge liquidity of the international financial market was one factor; the possibility to use government debt as collateral for central banks loans, and their being considered at zero risk by Basle regulations (thus not weighing on the capital requirements) was another (Whelan, 2013). Banks could operate a profitable carry trade in which balance sheets were expanded with low-interest ECB financing and international funding on the liability side and higher-yielding sovereign debt on the asset side, causing nominal interest rates convergence. In the European periphery, external credit flows and domestic credit expansion fuelled an economic expansion, while providing the financing for the induced expansion of imports. Financial fragility, balance of payments disequilibria and distorted sectoral structures all pointed to a crisis foretold. As in past episodes, the bubble and the short-term convergence in economic and financial indicators were mistaken for real sustainable convergence, reinforcing confidence in a self-fulfilling mechanism.

When the Eurozone was established, policymakers paid little mind to the banking sector, even as they abolished capital controls and permitted the free flow of financial services. The 2007–2008 global financial crisis was the occasion for a general reassessment of financial risks. It was soon clear how deeply the European banks were engulfed by the subprime debts and over-exposed to debtors in the periphery (we return to this issue in Section 2 of Chapter 4). Vanishing international liquidity[28] and the huge losses on speculative investment brought many large and small European banks to the brink of insolvency. In the EMU structure, supervision of banks and costs of bank failure were left to individual states. Thus, the true 'doom-loop' should have been that between creditor banks and governments in the 'core' countries. O'Connell (2016: 14) recalls that the exposure to the 'periphery' of banks with their headquarters located in the centre 'reached almost the equivalent of a quarter of their GDP at the end of 2009. But, already by September 2012 with the increase of lending from official sources that exposure had been reduced almost by 40 per cent.'

The way in which the creditor countries solved their bank-state loop was twofold: the ECB's generous provision of liquidity and the 'triangular bail-out' process.

Infringement versus overreaching: the expansion of ECB/ government interactions[29]

The ECB took action in two areas during the long crisis: as a lender of last resort in the banking crisis, in support of the member states' security markets in the fight against deflation. In implementing these 'technical tasks' it inevitably encroached on fiscal and political dimensions. The Maastricht separation between monetary and fiscal policy is, and cannot but be, a legal fiction. Monetary tightness worsens the fiscal balance, via reduced fiscal receipts and higher cost of the debt; in turn, the sovereign market tensions affect the real economy through the bank-lending channel. On the other hand, the increase in taxation required to balance the budget increases prices. Thus, monetary policy affects prices only indirectly through its interaction with fiscal policy. The impossibility of disentangling the effects of monetary and fiscal policy allowed German institutions to criticize the ECB for trespassing.

During 2008–2009, the euro-system intervened to ease the squeeze on banks by generous provision of liquidity, thereby averting a full-scale banking crisis: 'full allotment tenders' were introduced in October 2008 for Medium Refinancing Operations (MRO), and in May 2009 for Long-Term Refinancing Operations (LTRO). Rather than fixing the total quantity of credit, the ECB announced the interest rate and 'solvent banks' could borrow as much as they wanted from their national central banks, against eligible collateral and applicable haircuts. Eligibility criteria for collateral were significantly relaxed.[30] Meanwhile, the ECB also worked towards 'persuading' debtor countries to take responsibility for their banks' excesses and to come to deal with conditionality. In late 2010, the ECB pushed Ireland into a bail-out by threatening to cut off Emergency Liquidity Assistance (ELA).[31] At the end of 2007, Irish monetary and financial institutions had accumulated a gross external debt of around 400 per cent of GDP[32] (Febrero *et al.*, 2016: 10, fn. 5). German banks figured pre-eminently in lending to Ireland: they were owed 139 billion dollars – 4.2 per cent of German GDP – with the Hypo Real Estate, subsequently taken over by the German government, having the highest exposure.[33]

This threat was made at other times. With Cyprus in 2013, when 'the ECB forced a resolution of the Cypriot banking crisis by announcing that it would stop authorising ELA within days unless Cyprus entered a rescue programme to restore solvency to its two big bust banks' (*The Economist*, 2015). ECB officials regularly threatened to cut off credit to the Greek banking system if a default was implemented. Lastly, on 4 February 2015, the Governing Council of the ECB threatened to remove the concession to obtain liquidity on collateral that was formally ineligible, since it consisted of debt issued or guaranteed by the Greek government, which was junk-rated and therefore barred by the ECB's collateral rules. The ECB was prepared to waive that requirement if Greece complied with the terms of its bail-out. 'By pushing Greek banks into greater reliance on ELA', concluded *The Economist* (2015), 'the ECB has moved a step closer to calling time on the Greek government's campaign to secure a more favourable deal from its European creditors'.

The handling of the Greek debt crisis provides the textbook example of the triangular bail-out, a 'revolving door strategy' by which loans are extended to debtor countries on duress to repay surplus countries' creditors (mostly banks), thus freeing governments in the centre from having to openly bail out their financial institutions.[34] Strong political and economic reasons precluded a Greek default[35] that would have severely affected German and French banks, heavily exposed to Greece. The 2009 bail-out of German banks, deeply involved in the international subprime crisis, 'had proved to be politically unpopular and "helping out the Greeks" was perhaps seen as less politically unpopular than "bailout out the banks, again"' (Whelan, 2013: 18). The memory of Lehman Brothers was still burning and fears of contagion could not be easily dismissed. The ECB played a crucial role in both presenting a Greek default as a potential disaster for the euro area[36] and delaying the decision to allow such a default. The loan was eventually granted at almost punitive rates. The rescue of Greece was conditional on the adoption of the policies prescribed by the creditor institutions (see Chapter 4 for a detailed discussion of such policies). Conditionality turned out to be excessive and counterproductive. In spite of repeated efforts to cut the primary budget, the severity of the recession and the burden represented by the service of the debt unleashed a downward spiral between fiscal austerity and falling GDP that dramatically increased the debt/GDP ratio. When the prospect of a Greek default became more concrete, and with most private holders of

Greek sovereign bonds being paid off, no obstacle remained for a (partial) default. By July 2011, the euro area's leaders agreed to the restructuring of Greece's private sovereign debts, which occurred in March 2012. It was termed a 'voluntary' exchange to avoid a 'credit event'.

Instead of containing the crisis, the Greek bail-out made the fragility of the Eurozone construction evident. Within one year, Ireland and Portugal, which had been 'persuaded' by the ECB to bail out their banks, had to undergo similar interventions. Speculation on sovereign debt restructuring and possible exit from the Eurozone caused a sell-off of public bonds and a capital flight: interest rates in the Eurozone 'periphery' rose steeply. When the president of the ECB finally uttered his famous 'whatever it takes', fundamentally changing investors' perception of the sovereign risk, debtor countries' economies had been wrecked by the double-dip recession igniting the last phase of the loop, the debtors' state-banks doom-loop. In fact, the sovereign debt crisis soon backfired on the banks, which had used the liquidity created by the ECB (the big bazooka)[37] to buy the public bonds unloaded by foreign investors. Arguably in defiance of the German monetary authorities, the ECB eventually replaced the SMP Programme with Outright Monetary Transactions (OMT), a commitment to unlimited intervention on the secondary market, to be provided under strict conditionality.

A 'ligne droite' instead of a common polity

In their famous walk at Deauville on 18 October 2010, the German chancellor and the French president, once again bypassing the usual EU deliberation procedures, agreed to affirm the no-bail-out principle.[38] The Private Sector Involvement (PSI) clause sanctioned the partial bail-in of EMU governments' bondholders, and opened the way to the ensuing banking crises.[39] Thus, the debt/bank loop was cut by ensuring that bank creditors (including depositors) lost out when banks failed. Immediately, the yields of Irish and Portuguese bonds shot up, followed by the Spanish and Italian ones.

In dealing with the crisis, after 2008 the primary concern was not employment or growth, nor even inflation, but moral hazard and structural reforms (Braun, 2017: 16). The institutional response to the crisis was thus convergence before solidarity. Assistance was granted subject to a conditionality which went way beyond the fiscal field to encompass the whole spectrum of policies: labour market regulation, pay and industrial relations, privatization, welfare (see Chapter 4). The presumption was that structural reforms within each country (domestic devaluation) would act on the supply side by increasing the market's response to shocks, and on the demand side by improving confidence.

Last-minute interventions and partial reforms of the institutional framework continually followed the deepening of the crisis. In 2010, the European Financial Stabilization Facility (EFSF) was followed by the European Financial Stabilization Mechanism (EFSM) to provide financial assistance to member states of the European Union in economic difficulty. They were replaced in 2012 by a new bail-out fund, the European Stabilization Mechanism (ESM), as a permanent firewall for the Eurozone, with a maximum lending capacity of €500 billion. It required PSI and was subject to conditionality in the form of a macro-economic adjustment programme.

Institutional, procedural and material experimentation was implemented with a high degree of discretion in abiding by or breaching the institutional and functional constraints, but it was often 'too little, too late' in tackling predictable disaster. The ECB's policy was insufficiently accommodative during the first stages of the crisis. It increased the interest rates in 2010, and became largely passive after 2011, contributing, directly and indirectly, to worsening the shift of fiscal policy towards austerity. The management of the crisis, the timing and the conditions of the measures implemented spread a climate of emergency that prepared the ground for a further reform of the SGP that enhanced the power of the Commission against the countries found in default of compliance with the fiscal rules. With common fiscal policy tuned on fiscal consolidation, the independence of the ECB raised a serious issue of democratic deficit. The ability of euro-area countries to service their debt essentially depends on the 'goodwill' of a central bank not subject to any form of democratic accountability or control.

The crisis imposed substantial institutional change on the EMU. Several organizations were created and two pillars of the Maastricht construction – the no-bail-out clause and the prohibition of monetary financing of sovereign debt (arts 124 and 123 of the current treaty) – were circumvented. Yet these reforms neither fixed the 'architectural' flaws of the EMU nor encouraged a domestic change of course by Germany. Governance, in particular, drifted from the community method to the intergovernmental method and to a de facto one-country leadership (Wyplosz, 2017: 116).

The Banking Union (2013), which includes the Single Supervisory Mechanism (SSM) and the Single Resolution Mechanism (SRM), was intended to break the doom-loop between banks and government, on the assumption that this would create more stable banks and thus prevent the imposition of banking failure on the public purse. However, with the Single Resolution Mechanism (SRM) still largely inadequate, and the no-bail-out clause extending to the banking system of an ailing country, the costs of dealing with bank failure would presumably be transferred to shareholders, bondholders and even depositors, before any claims were made on public funds (Lapavitsas *et al.*, 2017). Moreover, with the continuation of the recession, the problems of the banks have changed from holding excessive amounts of public debt to holding large volumes of problematic private debt. Meanwhile, the stalling of the proposal for a common deposit insurance indicates that the sharing of risk is not yet on the agenda.

7 Conclusions

Insufficient political cohesion and misguided economic theory played a role in shaping what was pre-eminently a political project. The single currency was launched without creating the institutions required to enable the different European member states to prosper within a monetary union without exchange rate flexibility and an independent monetary policy and with fiscal autonomy severely constrained. The convergence was interpreted with reference to financial rather than real indicators, and it was believed that any problem encountered could and would be addressed (neo-functionalism). The crisis made evident that this institutional structure was not sustainable.

The management of the crisis exacerbated it. At the meeting of the G20 in London in 2009, participants had agreed on a coordinated expansion. However, the policy responses on the two sides of the Atlantic differed significantly. The US tackled the twin problems of cleaning up the banks and sustaining the economy jointly, using monetary and fiscal policy in combination. Conversely, the EU gave member states responsibility for their banks, targeted fiscal equilibria at the national level, while disregarding the area-wide fiscal stance. There was no supra-national fiscal authority to cushion the effects of a recession. With European countries' fiscal policy U-turn in the spring of 2011, the EU and US economy started to diverge: the 2012–2013 recession was uniquely European. With the Eurozone crisis spiralling, the response was more fiscal austerity. In 2012 a new 'fiscal compact' was agreed as a condition for the ECB's intervention in support of the debtor countries. Adoption of the Six-pack, the Two-pack and the Fiscal Compact (Dodig and Herr, 2015) committed EZ members to 'avoiding moral hazard problems', thus de facto preventing any expansionary fiscal policy to counteract the crisis. The blatantly different performances of the US and the EZ finally prompted reconsideration of some tenets of economic theory, such as the sign and value of the fiscal multipliers, the efficacy of an expansionary monetary policy and the need for fiscal activism. Yet this reassessment did not find adequate response in policy-making, still biased towards fiscal consolidation and structural reforms.

The view of markets as self-equilibrating persists in the policy solutions now being developed and imposed (or self-imposed). Liberalization and integration of financial markets were implemented without adequate policies and institutions for supervision and financial crisis management and resolution (Bibow, 2015). The ECB and the national supervisory bodies failed to appreciate the increasing risks connected with the large European banks' aggressive 'search for yields'. With the Banking Union, financial supervision has been placed at the EU level, and government bail-outs have been replaced with creditor bail-ins (even bank deposits in the case of bank failure). The idea is that of 'a microeconomic problem rather than a systemic macroeconomic problem'. However, 'far from bank vulnerability occurring on an isolated basis, the norm is for bank vulnerability to be systemic, rendering the bail-in solution unsustainable' (Dow, 2016: 7–8). Thus, none of these reforms will avert the need for public bail-outs when the next crisis hits. Meanwhile, a deposit insurance scheme is still waiting.

To restore banks' profitability the economy needs to restart; but highly indebted countries are limited in their ability to pursue proactive fiscal-stimulus policies. 'The adoption of policies under the threat of European sanctions tends to increase "institutional uncertainty" ' (Bastasin and Messori, 2017). By nurturing rather than reducing radical uncertainty, it negatively affects investment, and is thus likely to be counterproductive. To address the problems caused by the flawed institutional construction, the ECB's programme of quantitative easing is greatly inadequate. And the lack of a fiscal counterpart has left the Eurozone with a severe problem of governance and the ECB with a severe problem of democratic accountability.

Notes

1 For de Gaulle, Europe could only ever be a confederation, with power exercised not by an independent body but by the representatives of the member states (ministers or representatives at the highest level), who had a right of veto. Already in 1960, he asked Alain Peyrefitte to draw up 'a note on the practical ways of stifling supranationality' (Palayret 1994: 374–377).

2 The 'Triffin dilemma' refers to the conflicting objectives arising from the use of a national currency, such as the US dollar, as global reserve currency. In fact, the country whose currency is the global reserve currency must be willing to provide international liquidity: that is, it must run a structural trade deficit, which, in the long run, may undermine its status of reserve currency.

3 The 9.3 per cent revaluation of the Deutsche mark on 24 October 1969, which followed the 12.5 per cent devaluation of the French franc on 8 August 1969, was the result of a long negotiation in which Germany finally accepted to compromise its domestic objectives in order to preserve European integration. The revaluation, favoured by the Bundesbank, which was no longer able to fully sterilize the capital inflows, encountered the opposition of German industrialists worried that a major recession would result (see Eichengreen, 2007: 238–241).

4 Elena Danescu (2017: 6–7) writes that Pierre Werner saw the monetary aspect as a priority for European integration, though his position could hardly sit with the cartalist view. In his view, in fact,

> making positive progress towards monetary union would not mean that the national sovereignty of the Community countries would have to be encroached on, since, as 'the history of confederations and federations has amply demonstrated, the last bastion of national sovereignty is not the currency but tax, as the distributor of national income'.

5   To ensure the cohesion of economic and monetary union, transfers of responsibility from the national to the Community plane will be essential. These transfers will be kept within the limits necessary for the effective operation of the Community and will concern essentially the whole body of policies determining the realization of general equilibrium. In addition, it will be necessary for the instruments of economic policy to be harmonized in the various sectors.

(Werner Report, 1970: 10)

> The realization of global economic equilibrium may be dangerously threatened by differences of structure. Cooperation between the partners in the Community in the matter of structural and regional policies will help to surmount these difficulties, just as it will make it possible to eliminate the distortions of competition. The solution of the big problems in this field will be facilitated by financial measures of compensation. In an economic and monetary union, structural and regional policies will not be exclusively a matter for national budgets.

(Ibid.: 11)

6   In the framework of an economic and monetary union it is not enough to pay attention to policies of global economic equilibrium alone. It will also be necessary to envisage measures bearing on structural problems, the essence of which will be profoundly modified by the realization of this process. In this context the Community measures should primarily concern regional policy and employment policy. Their realization would be facilitated by an increase in financial intervention effected at Community level. In addition, it will be necessary to arrive progressively at Community guidance for policies on industry, transport, power, housing, and the environment.

(Werner Report, 1970: 25)

7 The resolution, which had no legal force, made no mention of the concept of an 'economic policy centre', but it did state that economic and monetary union 'means that the main economic policy decisions will be taken at Community level, and therefore that the necessary powers will be transferred from the national to Community level'.

8   To reinforce solidarity within the Community – in the matter of foreign exchange, the central banks are invited, from the beginning of the first stage, to restrict on an experimental basis the fluctuations of rates between Community currencies within narrower bands than those resulting from the application of the margins in force in relation to the dollar. This objective would be achieved by concerted action in relation to the dollar. According to circumstances and to the results achieved in the standardization of economic policies new measures may be taken. These will consist of a transition from a de facto regime to a de jure regime of intervention in Community currencies and the progressive narrowing of the margins of fluctuation between Community currencies.

(Werner Report, 1970: 28)

9 Already in 1973, at the start of the Snake, the Bank of Italy had stressed the need for an adequate amount of credits administered by a regional institution and the pooling of reserves with this institution (Banca d'Italia, 1973: 398).

10 In his biography, Modigliani explains that the article had been written with Padoa-Schioppa, who could not sign it because of the restrictions imposed by the Bank of Italy on its functionaries (quoted in Masini, 2004: 49).

11 Padoa-Schioppa had provided a substantial contribution to the three-year plan of Treasury Minister Pandolfi ('Una proposta per lo sviluppo, una scelta per l'Europa'), published in September 1978 as a road map for Italy to join the EMS. The plan included a series of commitments and targets on wage policy and public finance, in preparation of Italy's participation in the EMS.

12 As Offe (1984) observed, a paradoxical result of the steady expansion of the state's role in managing the economy over the post-war period was that economic events were redefined as the product of state actions rather than the blind operation of the market. Where the government defined price stability as a policy objective, for example, inflation appeared to be the result of a failed state policy rather than an exogenous 'shock' to the economy (quoted in McNamara, 1998).

13 So much so that 'in a report prepared for the EEC Commission in 1986–87, the question was raised as to whether financial liberalisation would not entail the need to adopt flexible exchange rates within the Community, too' (Padoa-Schioppa, 1987: 87).

14 Eichengreen (2007: 349) recalls that Balladur, France's finance minister, wrote a memorandum to the ECOFIN Council in early 1988 where, never explicitly mentioning Germany, he denounced the anomaly of 'a system that exempts any countries whose policies are too restrictive from the necessary adjustment' as demonstrated by 'the fact that some countries have piled up current account surpluses for several years equal to between 2 and 3 percent of their GDP' and advocated a rapid pursuit of the

monetary construction of Europe as the only possible solution. The Italian Treasury ministry, Amato, followed suit (23 February 1988): arguing that Italy had taken risks in pledging to dismantle exchange controls, he required the creation of a fund to recycle capital flows.

15 Brunnermeier *et al.* (2016: 8) argue that for many politicians, especially for former German chancellor Helmut Kohl, economic aspects did not play a major role in the origins of the euro area. Rather, the currency union was a high-minded European political project that went way beyond economic realities. It was needed to stop the recurrence of war between France and Germany.

16 In a recorded interview on how the idea of a single currency evolved, Jacques Delors said 'that the overall philosophy behind what we proposed and even the structure of the Delors Report were very heavily influenced by the Werner Report.... The Delors Committee's report is a direct follow-on from the Werner Committee's report' (Werner papers, fn. 33; Danescu, 2016).

17 Jacques Delors memoires (Werner papers, fn. 32).

18 See Thatcher's nasty remarks reported in Eichengreen (2007: 353).

19 Commenting on this view, Issing (2008: 302) notes that, 'Alongside other fundamental weaknesses ... what argues against the view of the "monetarists" ... is the high risk of failure of such a "big-bang" with incalculable economic and political repercussions'.

20 See Giscard d'Estaing for the alternative suggestion of an ECB along the lines of the Federal Reserve.

21 None of these clauses were actually as binding as believed, as would become clear in the crisis. Art. 125 (the no-bail-out clause), actually stated that the Union and its member states 'shall not be liable for or assume the commitments' of other countries.

22 *One Market, One Money*, published by the Commission in 1990 (European Commission, 1990), presented the first detailed study of the costs and benefits of a common currency along these lines.

23 Ironically, both in the US and Europe the attempt to replace explicitly political decisions with technocracy and automatism eventually led, after drastic austerity measures, to the reappearance of politics in the guise of demagogy ('populism').

24   The fact that many peripheral countries (Spain and Ireland above all) were booming, fuelled by relatively cheap incoming financial flows from France and Germany, likely facilitated this misjudgement. The positive economic numbers made it easy for these governments to brush off domestic objections to full throated deregulation of the labour market, privatization and social spending cuts – always in the name of Europe.

(Costantini, 2015: 49)

25 Costantini (2015), quoting Blinder and Solow (1974: 8), recalls that in the 1960s the CAB was considered a convenient communication tool, rather than an engine of analysis:

The public seems to need a number, traditionally a budget deficit, to view with pride or alarm as the case may be. [Unfortunately,] whenever one attempts to reduce a multidimensional concept – like the influence of the Government on aggregate economic activity – to a single dimension, index number problems inevitably arise.... However, the political realities of the day seem to dictate settling on a single index to measure the overall expansionary or contractionary effect of any proposed tax and expenditure program.

(Costantini, 2015: 24)

26 The many ways to compute the CAB 'have been widely recognized to be weak and flimsy both theoretically and empirically by economists of different schools and traditions' (Costantini, 2015: 54).

27 See O'Connell (2016: 9):

the acute cycle in cross-border lending within the euro area by financial institutions based in its 'center' countries was funded in the rest of the world, most significantly by U.S. Money Market Funds. Thus euro area 'center' banks played a pivotal role in global finance, recycling funds across continents, part of it provided to their 'periphery' and huge amounts that returned to the U.S. in lending to the subprime mortgage market.

28 Following the transformation of the US financial markets, large global banks became increasingly dependent on wholesale markets for liquidity. Working in conditions of structural illiquidity, they came to rely on the continuous smooth functioning of the wholesale funding markets and on the Fed acting 'as a lender of first, rather than last resort' (De Cecco, 2010: 373; see also Goodhart and Perotti, 2015).

29 This title is taken from the heading of a section in Braun (2017).

30 Before the 2008 crisis there was a minimum rating of A−. In October 2008, it was reduced to BBB − and by July 2011 it was completely abolished in Greece, Ireland and Portugal. Finally, in November 2011 the ECB allowed seven national central banks to accept as collateral performing credit claims that did not satisfy ordinary eligibility criteria.

31 National central banks can provide Emergency Liquidity Assistance (ELA), at their own risk and at a higher interest rate, if their banks run out of acceptable collateral. With ELA, the role of Lender of Last Resort (LOLR) remains with the national central bank, that is, with the state and its taxpayers. The national central bank must inform the ECB within two working days. If the governing council, with a majority of two-thirds, decides that such support is at odds with 'the objectives and tasks' of the Eurosystem (the ECB together with the 19 national central banks), it can restrict the ELA.

32 Irish gross external debt in absolute levels was roughly the same as the Spanish one, and barely 12 per cent less than the Italian one. However, Ireland's GDP was only 18 and 12 per cent of the GDP of Spain and Italy respectively.

33 Based on the Bank of International Settlements (BIS) data on an 'ultimate risk basis'. The exposure of other Eurozone countries' banks was equally remarkable. Johnson (2010) reports that

British banks are owed $131 billion, or about 5 percent of Britain's G.D.P. French banks are owed $43.5 billion, which is approaching 2 percent of French G.D.P.... Belgium ... is owed $29 billion ... around 5 percent of G.D.P.

34 It has been estimated that '54% of the financial assistance provided to Greece was used to repay (foreign) debt, while another 21% was used to recapitalize Greek banks (some of which were owned by foreign institutions)' (Bortz, 2015: 1).

35 An emergency loan was unnecessarily delayed partly to avoid interference with a regional election in Germany, and as a consequence of the 'game of chicken' played between the ECB and the European Council over the creation of what became the European Financial Stability Facility (EFSF). The ECB's resistance was based on a moral hazard argument − the ECB was concerned that bond purchases would reduce 'the pressure on governments to establish the bailout fund' (Braun, 2017). Only after the creation of the EFSF, in May 2010, did the ECB launch the Securities Markets Programme (SMP), to purchase bonds of stressed sovereigns. Because of these delays, the programme had to be much larger than would have been the case if Europe had taken collective action more promptly.

36 Lorenzo Bini Smaghi (a member of the Executive Board) regularly gave speeches depicting a potential Greek default as provoking 'an economic meltdown'.

37 In December 2011 and February 2012, the ECB issued €1000 billion of cheap loans with a three-year maturity via two full-allotment tenders.

38 The Deauville compromise reaffirmed the differences between the German and French views on the appropriate economic policy that had been at the core of the EMU structure: Germany would loosen its approach to rules and make concessions to France if France would in return agree to 'an adequate participation of private creditors'.
39 The principle became definitive with Cyprus, before a Banking Union had become active.

References

Andreatta, B. (1978). Le conseguenze economiche del Sistema monetario europeo per l'Europa e per l'Italia. *Thema*, 2, 82–94.

Andreatta, B. (1991). Un divorzio per tutte le stagioni. *Il Sole 24 Ore*, 26 July.

Baffigi, L. (2016). *L'Economia del benessere alla sfida della tecnocrazia e del populismo: il pensiero democratico di Federico Caffè*. Mimeo, Banca d'Italia. https:// bancaditalia.academia.edu/ABaffigi [accessed 22 January 2017].

Banca d'Italia (1973). *Relazione Annuale sul 1972*. 31 May, Rome.

Barba, A. and Pivetti, M. (2016). *La scomparsa della sinistra in Europa*. Reggio Emilia: Imprimatur editore.

Bastasin, C. and Messori, M. (2017). A joint intervention for Italy: A non-punitive plan for investment and reform. *Luiss, Policy Brief No. 13*, February.

Bibow, J. (2015). The euro's savior? Assessing the ECB's crisis management performance and potential for crisis resolution. *IMK*, 42.

Blinder, A. S. and Solow, R. M. (1974). Analytical foundations of fiscal policy. In A. S. Blinder (ed.), *The Economics of Public Finance: Studies of Government Finance*. Washington, DC: The Brooking Institution, 3–115.

Bortz, P. G. (2015). The Greek 'rescue': Where did the money go? An analysis. *Ineteconomics Working Papers No. 29*. www.ineteconomics.org/uploads/papers/WP29-Bortz. pdf [accessed 29 September 2017].

Braun, B. (2017). Two sides of the same coin? Independence and accountability of the European Central Bank. http://transparency.eu/ecb/ [accessed 15 January 2017].

Brunnermeier, M. K., James, H. and Landau, J. P. (2016). *The Euro and the Battle of Ideas*. Princeton, NJ: Princeton University Press.

Bundesbank Archive (1978). Transcript of meeting of the Bundesbank Council, 30 November 1978. EMS: Bundesbank Council meeting with Chancellor Schmidt (assurances on operation of EMS). www.margaretthatcher.org/document/111554 [accessed 15 January 2017].

Caffè, F. (1979). I problemi della moneta europea. Reprinted in G. Amari and N. Rocchi (eds), *Stare in Europa: quali implicazioni per l'Italia*. Roma: Ediesse, 548–559.

Costantini, O. (2015). The cyclically adjusted budget: History and exegesis of a fateful estimate. *Ineteconomics Working Papers No. 24*.

Danescu, E. (2016). *A Rereading of the Werner Report of 8 October 1970 in the Light of the Pierre Werner Family Archives*. www.cvce.eu [accessed 25 February 2017].

Danescu, E. (2017). *The Werner Report of 1970 – a blueprint for EMU in the EU?*, May. www.eustudies.org/conference/papers/download/467 [accessed 25 February 2017].

De Cecco, M. (1992). *Monete in concorrenza: prospettive per l'integrazione monetaria europea*. Bologna: Il Mulino.

De Cecco, M. (2001). Sovranità monetaria: UME e movimenti internazionali dei capitali. In G. Corsetti, G. M. Rey and G. C. Romagnoli (eds), *Il future delle relazioni economiche internazionali*. Saggi in onore di Federico Caffè. Milano: Franco Angeli, 95–103.

De Cecco, M. (2010). La dinamica dei sistemi finanziari prima durante e dopo la crisi. In G. Bonifati and A. Simonazzi (eds), *Il ritorno dell'economia politica*. Saggi in ricordo di Fernando Vianello. Roma: Donzelli, 365–375.

De Grauwe, P. (2016). *Economics of Monetary Union* (11th edn). Oxford: Oxford University Press.

Dodig, N. and Herr, H. (2015). Current account imbalances in the EMU: An assessment of official policy responses. *Panoeconomicus*, 62(2), 193.

Dow, S. (2016). Ontology and theory for a redesign of European Monetary Union. *World Economic Review*, 6, 1–11.

Eichengreen, B. (2007). *The European Economy since 1945*. Princeton, NJ: Princeton University Press.

European Commission (1990). One market, one money: An evaluation of the potential benefits and costs of forming an economic and monetary union. *European Economy*, 44, October.

European Commission (2001). Public finances in EMU – 2001. *European Economy, Reports and studies, 3/2001*, Directorate General for economic and financial affairs, Brussels.

European Council (1989). Committee for the Study of Economic & Monetary Union. *Report on Economic and Monetary Union in the European Community*. Unipub.

Febrero, E., Uxó, J. and Bermejo, F. (2016). The financial crisis in the Euro Zone. A balance of payments crisis with a single currency? *UCLM*, DT 2016/1.

Giavazzi, F. and Spaventa, L. (1990). Il nuovo SME (con un poscritto). *Politica Economica*, 6(3), 417–447.

Ginzburg, A. and Simonazzi, A. (2011). Disinflation in industrial countries, foreign debt cycles and the costs of stability. In R. Ciccone, C. Gehrke and G. Mongiovi (eds), *Sraffa and Modern Economics*. London: Routledge, 269–296.

Goodhart, Charles A. (1998). The two concepts of money: Implications for the analysis of Optimal Currency Areas. *European Journal of Political Economy*, 14(3), 407–432.

Goodhart, C. A. (2007). Currency unions: Some lessons from the Euro-zone. *Atlantic Economic Journal*, 35(1), 1–21.

Goodhart, C. A. and Perotti, E. (2015). Maturity mismatch stretching: Banking has taken a wrong turn. *CEPR, Policy Insight No. 81*, May.

Gros, D. and Thygesen, N. (1992). *European Monetary Integration: From the European Monetary System Towards Monetary Union*. London: Longman.

Haldane, A. (2011). The big fish small pond problem. *Institute for New Economic Thinking Annual Conference*. Bretton Woods, NH.

Hopkin, J. (2015). The troubled southern periphery: The euro experience in Italy and Spain. In M. Matthijs and M. Blyth (eds), *The Future of the Euro*. Oxford: Oxford University Press, 161–184.

Houben, A. C. (2000). *The Evolution of Monetary Policy Strategies in Europe*. Boston, MA: Kluwer Academic Publisher.

Issing, O. (2008). *The Birth of the Euro*. Cambridge: Cambridge University Press.

Johnson, S. (2010). Will Ireland default? Ask Belgium. *The Baseline Scenario*, 25 November. https://baselinescenario.com/2010/11/25/will-ireland-default-ask-belgium/ [accessed 14 September 2017].

Kenen, P. (1969). *The Theory of Optimum Currency Areas: An Eclectic View. Monetary Problems of the International Economy*. Chicago: Peter Lang.

Keynes, J. M. [1923] (1971). *A Tract on Monetary Reform*. Vol. IV of *The Collected Writings of John Maynard Keynes*. London/Basingstoke: Macmillan, 65.

Keynes, J. M. (1936). *The General Theory of Money, Interest and Employment.* Reprinted in *The Collected Writings of John Maynard Keynes.* London: Macmillan/ Cambridge University Press.

Kruse, D. C. (1980). *Monetary Integration in Western Europe: EMU, EMS and Beyond.* London: Butterworth-Heinemann.

Lapavitsas, C., Mariolis, T. and Gavrielidis, C. (2017). The failure of the Eurozone and the role of German policies. *Il Ponte,* LXXIII, 5–6, 105–33.

MacDougall, D. (1977). *Report of the Study Group on the Role of Public Finance in European Integration.* EUR-OP.

Maes, I. and Verdun, A. (2005). Small states and the creation of EMU: Belgium and the Netherlands, pace-setters and gate-keepers. *JCMS: Journal of Common Market Studies,* 43(2), 327–348.

Masini, F. (2004). *SMEmorie della lira: gli economisti italiani e l'adesione al Sistema monetario europeo* (Vol. 48). Milano: Franco Angeli.

Matthijs, M. and Blyth, M. (2015). Introduction: The future of the euro and the politics of Embedded Currency Areas. In M. Matthijs and M. Blyth (eds), *The Future of the Euro.* Oxford: Oxford University Press, 1–17.

McKinnon, R. I. (1963). Optimum Currency Areas. *The American Economic Review,* 717–725.

McNamara, K. (1998). *The Currency of Ideas: Monetary Politics in the European Union.* Ithaca, NY: Cornell University Press.

McNamara, K. (2015). The forgotten problem of embeddedness: History lessons for the euro. In M. Matthijs and M. Blyth (eds), *The Future of the Euro.* Oxford: Oxford University Press, 21–43.

Meade, J. E. (1957). The balance-of-payments problems of a European free-trade area. *The Economic Journal,* 67(267), 379–396.

Modigliani, F. (1978). I pro e i contro per l'Italia. *Il Corriere della Sera,* 1 December.

Monti, M. (1978). Arduo con la nostra inflazione assumere vincoli di cambio. *Il Sole 24 Ore,* 5 December.

Mourlon-Druol, E. (2014). Don't blame the euro: Historical reflections on the roots of the Eurozone crisis. *West European Politics,* 37(6), 1282–1296.

Mundell, R. A. (1961). A theory of Optimum Currency Areas. *The American Economic Review,* 51(4), 657–665.

O'Connell, A. (2015). European crisis: A new tale of center–periphery relations in the world of financial liberalization/globalization? *International Journal of Political Economy,* 44(3), 174–195.

O'Connell, A. (2016). The EuroZone 'debt' crisis: Another 'center'-'periphery' crisis under financial globalization? *Ineteconomics Working Papers No. 51.* www.ineteconomics.org/uploads/papers/WP_51-O-Connell.pdf [accessed 29 September 2017].

Offe, C. (1984). Contradictions of the Welfare State. Cambridge: MIT Press.

Optica Report (1976). *Study Group on Optimum Currency Areas, Inflation and Exchange Rates: Evidence and Policy Guidelines for the European Community.* Report, EC Commission, D.G. II, Brussels.

Padoa-Schioppa, T. (1987). *Efficiency, Stability, and Equity: A Strategy for the Evolution of the Economic System of the European Community: A Report.* Oxford: Oxford University Press.

Padoa-Schioppa, T. (1994). *The Road to Monetary Union in Europe: The Emperor, the Kings, and the Genies.* Oxford: Clarendon Press.

Palayret, J.-M. (1994). Le Mouvement européen 1954–1969: Histoire d'un groupe de pression. In R. Girault and G. Bossuat (eds), *Europe brisée, Europe retrouvée*. Paris: Publications de la Sorbonne, 365–383.

Palumbo, A. (2013). Potential output and demand-led growth. In E. S. Levrero, A. Palumbo and A. Stirati (eds), *Sraffa and the Reconstruction of Economic Theory* (Vol. II). London: Palgrave Macmillan, 92–119.

Pivetti, M. (1992). Fixed exchange rates and free capital mobility: A note on Spaventa's 'change of regime'. *Economie Appliquée*, 45(3), 153–161.

Pivetti, M. (1998). Monetary versus political unification in Europe: On Maastricht as an exercise in 'vulgar' political economy. *Review of Political Economy*, 10(1), 5–26.

Rosenthal, G. G. (1975). *The Men Behind the Decisions: Cases in European Policy-making*. Lexington, MA: Lexington Books.

Schmidt, H. (1970). Germany in the era of negotiations. *Foreign Affairs*, October, 40–50.

Schmidt, V. A. (2015). The forgotten problem of democratic legitimacy. 'Governing by the rules' and 'ruling by the numbers'. In M. Matthjis and M. Blyth (eds), *The Future of the Euro*. Oxford: Oxford University Press, 90–114.

Scitovsky, T. (1957). The theory of the balance of payments and the problem of a common European currency. *Kyklos*, 10(1), 18–44.

Sen, A. (2012). Austerity is undermining Europe's grand vision. *Guardian*, 3 July. www.theguardian.com/commentisfree/2012/jul/03/austerity-europe-grand-vision-unity [accessed 14 September 2017].

Simonazzi, A. (2003). Innovation and growth: Supply and demand factors in the US expansion. *Cambridge Journal of Economics*, 27(5), 647–669.

Simonazzi, A. and Vianello, F. (1996). Credibility or 'exit speed'? Reflections prompted by the 1992 EMS crisis. *Rivista Italiana di Economia*, 1(1), 5–24.

Simonazzi, A. and Vianello, F. (2001). Financial liberalization, the European single currency and the problem of unemployment. In M. Franzini and F. R. Pizzuti (eds), *Globalization, Institutions and Social Cohesion*. Berlin, Heidelberg: Springer.

Spaventa, L. (1978). Il cambio è la più endogena delle variabili. Intervento alla Camera dei Deputati. Atti Parlamentari – Camera dei Deputati. VII Legislatura – Discussioni – Seduta del 12 Dicembre 1978, 24892–24899. http://legislature.camera.it/_dati/leg07/lavori/stenografici/sed0382/sed0382.pdf. Reprinted in G. Nardozzi (ed.) (1980). *I difficili anni '70*. Milano: Etas Libri, 20–30.

Spaventa, L. (1991). From the European Monetary System to the European Monetary Union: An uneasy transition. *Economie appliquée*, 44(3), 5–27.

The Economist (2015). What emergency liquidity assistance means. *The Economist*, 8 February. www.economist.com/blogs/economist-explains/2015/02/economist-explains-5 [accessed 29 September 2017].

Tsoukalis, L. (1977). The EEC and the Mediterranean: Is 'global' policy a misnomer? *International Affairs (Royal Institute of International Affairs)*, 1944, 422–438.

Ungerer, H. (1997). *A Concise History of European Monetary Integration: From EPU to EMU*. Westport, CT: Greenwood Publishing Group.

Vail, M. I. (2015). Europe's middle child: France's statist liberalism and the conflicted politics of the euro. In M. Matthijs and M. Blaug (eds), *The Future of the Euro*. Oxford: Oxford University Press, 136–160.

Verdun, A. (2000a). A history of European monetary integration. In A. Verdun, *European Responses to Globalization and Financial Market Integration*. Basingstoke: Palgrave Macmillan, 48–75.

Verdun, A. (2000b). From the EMS to EMU. In A. Verdun, *European Responses to Globalization and Financial Market Integration*. Basingstoke: Palgrave Macmillan, 76–102.

Verdun, A. (2002). *The Euro: European Integration Theory and Economic and Monetary Union*. Lanham, MD: Rowman & Littlefield.

Verdun, A. (2007). A historical institutionalist analysis of the road to Economic and Monetary Union: A journey with many crossroads. In S. Meunier and K. R. McNamara (eds), *Making History: European Integration and Institutional Change at Fifty*. Oxford: Oxford University Press, 195–209.

Vianello, F. [2009] (2013). La moneta unica europea. *Economia & Lavoro*, 47(1), 17–46.

Wallich, H. C. (1973). La crisi monetaria del 1971 e gli insegnamenti da trarne. *Bancaria No. 3*.

Werner, P. (1970). *Report to the Council and the Commission on the Realisation by Stages of Economic and Monetary Union in the Community – 'Werner Report' –* (definitive text) [8 October 1970]. Bulletin of the European Communities, Supplement 11/1970. [EU Council of the EU Document] http://aei.pitt.edu/1002/ [accessed 13 September 2017].

Whelan, K. (2013). Sovereign default and the euro. University College Dublin, Centre for Economic Policy Research, WP13/09. www.ucd.ie/t4cms/WP13_09.pdf [accessed 14 September 2017].

Wyplosz, C. (2006). European Monetary Union: The dark sides of a major success. *Economic Policy*, 21(46), 208–261.

Wyplosz, C. (2017). *Quo Vadis? Identity, Policy and the Future of the European Union*. Voxeu e-book. http://voxeu.org/system/files/epublication/QuoVadis_March2017_0.pdf [accessed 15 May 2017].

2 The European core-periphery divergent development before the crisis

1999–2008

1 Introduction

In 1999, the unemployment rate of the United States was approximately 4 per cent, half the European average. In particular, in the six European countries on which we focus (Table 2.1), the unemployment rate ranged between 5.1 per cent in Portugal, 11.2 in Greece and 11.9 per cent in Spain, with Germany, France and Italy between 7.7 and 10 per cent. As argued in Chapter 1, despite doubts and reservations, the formation of the single currency had nourished expectations of convergence in per capita incomes and unemployment rates. Moreover, according to most European economists, the better performance of the US in terms of unemployment had been achieved through measures of liberalization of goods and, above all, capitals, implemented by the Reagan administration (and the Thatcher government in the UK) since the 1980s, and usually identified as the starting point of the formation of global markets for goods and capital (globalization).

Expectations of convergence. The belief that the single currency would be a preliminary step of a process that would eventually lead automatically to polit-ical unification[1] was based on the idea, which found support in economic theory, that the European integration process had a self-sustaining dynamic: integration in one 'functional' area would tend to spill over into other areas. Proponents of this theory, called 'neo-functionalism' (Haas, 1958), pointed to the experience of the early years of the European integration. The creation of a common market in

Table 2.1 Unemployment rates in selected Eurozone economies (1999–2008)

	1999	2008
Germany	7.7	4.6
France	8.6	10.4
Italy	10.0	11.9
Spain	11.9	22.1
Portugal	5.1	12.6
Greece	11.2	24.9

Source: authors' elaboration on Eurostat data.

one sector – in 1951 it was the European Coal and Steel Community – led to the demand for the creation of a general Common Market, which in fact was established in 1957 as an area of free trade for all goods. In a less pragmatic vein, the belief in a smooth process leading to political unification was based on two presuppositions.

The first related to the expectations of income convergence among the countries joining the Monetary Union. This expectation relied on the idea,[2] based on the neoclassical theory, that even in a system characterized by full employment and no technical progress, the mobility of factors, in this case capital, would increase production and welfare. Following the elimination of trade barriers, capital would move in search of higher yields, that is, to countries where the initial relative scarcity of capital was associated with a higher marginal productivity. The reallocation of a given volume of investments, which responds to the principle of substitution with respect to relative prices, would rebalance capital endowments across countries, leading to the equalization of the factors' returns. These conclusions rest on the crucial assumption of the absence of demand constraints to the expansion of production. In addition, given the assumed plasticity of capital with respect to changes in relative prices, no damage can fall on the capital-recipient country, following sudden slowdowns or reversals in the direction of the flows of capital (sudden stops).

The second assumption was that the costs of transition towards the political union, entailed by the common monetary policy, would not be too high. This corresponds to assume that the structures of the various countries were not too dissimilar, and responded equally to external shocks. The theory of Optimum Currency Area proposed by Mundell, which provided the theoretical framework of the discussion on the Monetary Union (as discussed in Chapter 1), does not attach any weight to the diversity of production structures: the input price flexibility, especially labour, would be able to offset any initial difference. In this framework, the only structural difference relates to the flexibility of the labour market. In addition, even if events external to the area – such as a fall in world demand, changes in the dollar/euro exchange rate or massive inflows or outflows of capital – can have asymmetric effects across Europe, the latter are considered as 'country specific shocks', calling for fiscal policies to compensate for the absence of the exchange rate. In other words, the optimal area behaves as a closed system that does not take account of the relations with the rest of the world.

Core-periphery relations. The expected convergence did not occur or, when some convergence materialized, it worked as a veil covering the undercurrent and mounting structural divergence among Eurozone economies (Landesmann, 2015). In 2002–2007, the apparent convergence of real GDP diverted attention from the increasing divergence in terms of employment and current account balance. With the crisis, however, also the real GDP started diverging dramatically (see Figure 2.1). The unemployment rate, in turn, almost halved in Germany, but doubled or more than doubled in Greece, Spain and Portugal, and, starting from a relatively high level, it increased by about 2 percentage points in France

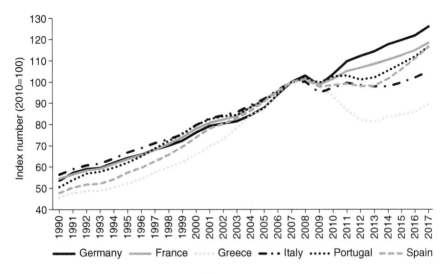

Figure 2.1 GDP per capita at constant prices (1990–2017).

Source: authors' elaboration on IMF-WEO data.

and Italy (Table 2.1). Germany's growing current account surplus was accompanied by increasing deficits in all other countries, particularly severe in the case of Greece and Spain. While Portugal already had a high deficit at the time of his entry into the EMU, France and Italy, which entered the EMU with a surplus, by 2008 recorded a current account deficit.

The disappointed expectations of convergence, specifically the widespread increase in the unemployment rates, have been attributed to lacking or insufficient reforms of the labour market and to the relatively higher wage rigidity of European countries compared to Germany, where the Hartz reforms introduced in 2003 would have enhanced the German firms' competitiveness. A detailed analysis of the major reforms carried out in the various peripheral countries (see Chapter 4), does not support this hypothesis.

Two aspects deserve to be emphasized before proceeding. First, the exclusive attention to the cost of labour (or unit labour costs), which corresponds to focus only on price competitiveness, is incompatible with the multidimensional complexity of change. The idea that a single variable (wage) can explain the whole trajectory of an economy strains credibility. Moreover, as Schumpeter strongly emphasized (Schumpeter, 1942), the process of transformation and innovation involves changes in products, production processes, markets, inputs supplies and organization. The failure of convergence invites to use a plurality of competitiveness indicators to account for the complexity of changes taking place in the age of globalization, characterized by a growing interdependence of economies, the international fragmentation of production processes and the cumulative interaction of innovations. Whenever this interaction is important, indicators such as the total factor productivity, which should capture the presence of technological and organizational change, or any decomposition based on the additive logic of growth accounting, are unreliable (Fagerberg, 1994: 1153; Felipe and McCombie, 2013).

The second aspect concerns the asymmetric interdependence between the European economies, which calls for the adoption of a centre-periphery perspective (we return to this issue in Chapter 9). One side effects of the economic crisis that began in 2007 is the rediscovery of these terms. We adopt this perspective, with a preliminary clarification of the terminology, since it is not free from ambiguity. To some of the authors who have applied dualistic variants of the 'varieties of capitalism' approach to Europe, centre-periphery simply denotes two macro-groups of countries, Northern and Southern Europe, considered as separate units of analysis. These studies contrast the German and the Latin, or Mediterranean, models, in the aggregate or in specific areas (e.g. welfare), often with normative intent. The focus is on the characteristics that are common to the countries belonging to the two groups and on their separate evolution, often disregarding their *relations*. Yet, the two terms – centre and periphery – refer to the dependency theory originally proposed in the 1950s by Latin American economists, which had the merit of focusing on the aspects of dependence in international relations. However, it had the weakness of attributing underdevelopment only to external circumstances, thereby exonerating national actors from any responsibility. Furthermore, the dependency relations were eminently static, lacking an analysis of the social configurations internal to the two groups of countries and of possible countertendencies to the dependency relations.[3] Trying to avoid these limitations, we consider the interaction of the processes of Europeanization and globalization in shaping the evolving relation between the centre and the European peripheries. We shall pay attention to the modifications occurring within the centre, namely the economic (and political) weakening of France with respect to Germany, and to the responsibilities of the governments of France and Southern Europe in adopting policies that ended up increasing their dependence on the core-country. In this context, the group of countries we identify as the Southern periphery (SP, hereafter) includes Greece, Italy, Portugal and Spain.

To understand the reasons of the divergence it is necessary to start from the reorganization of the German economy, which was accompanied by the formation of a strong current account surplus with the rest of the world and, more particularly, with France and the Southern European countries. Thus, this chapter deals with the discussion of the German model, leaving to the next two chapters the analysis of the French parabola and SP tribulations.

2   Germany: from Europe's sick man to export superstar

In the decade and a half following unification, Germany's economic performance was poor (in particular, between 1999 and 2005 the average growth rate was 1.1 per cent). In this period, as Carlin and Soskice (2008: 68) point out, the debate among domestic and international analysts focused on labour rigidities and the need for reforms 'with the objective of creating labour market flexibility in line with Anglo-American norms'. Two different supply-side reforms were implemented. In the manufacturing core the supply-side restructuring was carried out by the private sector 'using institutions of Germany's coordinated economy, including unions, work councils and blockholders owners' (ibid.). Conversely, 'orthodox' labour market and welfare state reforms created labour market flexibility especially in the lower end, less unionized segment of the market (i.e. services). The combination of these two supply-side developments resulted in an increase in labour market segmentation, with higher wage dispersion and greater incidence of low-paid workers. Carlin and Soskice observe that low GDP growth, high unemployment and low real wage growth relative to productivity recorded until 2005 are hard 'to reconcile with a supply-side causal mechanism'. 'Persistent domestic aggregate demand weakness'[4] played a role in explaining the pressure towards wage restraint and the increase in the profit share (see also Iversen *et al.*, 2016).

The poor economic performance of the beginnings, however, was rapidly reversed. Since the early 2000s, German exports skyrocketed and current account surpluses started mounting. At the aggregate level, the rise of the German current account surpluses after 2001 was associated with a sharp fall of domestic private investment as a share of GDP, accompanied by an increase in net capital outflows: net foreign direct investment driven by offshoring activities and loans to deficit countries. In the meanwhile, savings increased due to increased corporate profits, stagnating disposable income and possibly precautionary motives of households.

Figure 2.2 shows the intra-EU27 trade balance (in per cent of GDP) of the six countries under consideration (Germany, France and the SP) in the period 1999–2015. It is evident that the crisis (2007–2008) marks a watershed, reversing the trend of increasing deficits in the periphery, with the notable exception of France, which continues its downward trend. Focusing on the years before the crisis, besides the persistent and increasing German surplus, we can detect a certain degree of heterogeneity within the periphery. Greece and Portugal display the largest deficit (increasing since 2003). France and Spain record a less pronounced but rapidly increasing deficit. Italy is the only country to record a small current account deficit. The picture drastically changes when we consider each country's bilateral trade with Germany (Figure 2.3). The Italian position turns out to be far worse and deteriorating in time. As for the other peripheral countries, the deficits seem to be almost completely connected with the strong rise in imports of German goods, while, contrary to a widespread opinion, in the pre-crisis period the periphery's export performance did not show any substantial decline (see also Storm, 2016). Therefore, the current accounts deterioration does not seem to be related to an increase in unit labour cost differentials or, in more general terms, to a reduction in price competitiveness.[5] This evidence provides support, instead, to the thesis of the key role played by imports, 'as the driver of widening current account imbalances between 1999 and 2007' (Gaulier and Vicard, 2012).

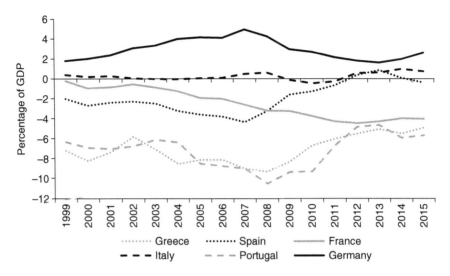

Figure 2.2 Current accounts of Germany, France and Southern European countries vis-à-vis EU27 (1999–2015) (% of GDP).

Source: authors' elaboration on Eurostat data.

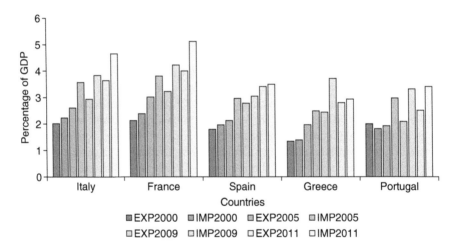

Figure 2.3 Bilateral trade relations with Germany: France and the SP exports and imports as a percentage of GDP (2000, 2005, 2009 and 2011).

Source: authors' elaboration on TIVA-OECD.

The export boom after 2005, credited by some authors exclusively to the wage moderation induced by the Hartz reforms introduced in 2003, could hardly be fully explained by the traditional cost determinant of price competiveness (Stahn, 2006), thus calling for interpretations of the long-term reorganization of the German economy based on both supply and demand factors. Danninger and Joutz (2007) show convincingly that the main determinants of the German export boom can be identified in four circumstances: (i) improved cost competitiveness through wage restraint; (ii) linkages with high-growth markets of emerging countries (especially China and India) through an appropriate mix of products or the use of established links; (iii) an increase in exports of capital goods in response to the increased investment in emerging countries; (iv) formation of a regionalized pattern of supply by relocating abroad (offshoring) part of the production. Although these explanations are not mutually exclusive, Danninger and Joutz attribute the majority of the export growth to the second and fourth items. In particular, they find that relative unit cost improvement accounted for less than 2 per cent of the German export growth.

Here, we add two more factors that can contribute to explain the export and current accounts boom. First, the increase in the incidence of temporary and part-time employment and low-paid workers, especially in the lower-end, less-unionized segment of the service sector, which affected the current account surplus in two ways. By affecting competitiveness, it indirectly contributed to exports. By sharply increasing income inequality and relative poverty in Germany, the fall in lower incomes is associated with a low level of imports of consumption goods.[6] Second, the de-synchronization of the German real estate cycle from the global real estate cycle of the years 1997–2012 that affected Germany's competitors. While the real estate bubble sustained imports, the fall of property prices which occurred in Germany since the beginning of the 2000s brought about a sharp drop in residential investment and complementary activities, and a decrease in household consumption, thus contributing to an improvement of the current balance also through reduced imports (Grjebine, 2014: 75) (see Section 4).

These six points establish a general framework that helps explain the persistent accumulation of German current account surpluses since the introduction of the euro. While the first point (wage restraint in manufacturing) and in part the fifth (wages in the lower end of the service sectors) may suggest the direct influence of labour costs on price competitiveness (internal devaluation), the others focus instead on lower costs embodied in increased imports of parts and components (point 4), income effects (impact on imports, points 1, 5 and 6), and non-price competitiveness of exports due to high specialization and product quality, especially of capital goods (points 2 and 3).

In the following sections, we discuss the role played by three aspects that differentiate the German economic system: the 'reforms' in the labour market, the structure of the housing market and of its finance system, and the spatial reorientation of German trade towards Eastern Europe and emerging Asia, especially China.

3 Wage moderation

The role played by wage moderation (and labour market reforms) in the formation of the huge German current account surplus since the start of the Monetary

Union has given rise to a lively debate. We briefly review the discussion, to stress our point on the multidimensional character of competitiveness.

Storm and Naastepad (2015a, 2015b) and Storm (2016) have recently taken up and extended Danninger and Joutz (2007)'s point on the role of non-wage factors in competitiveness. Their argument is based on two propositions: the low elasticity of German exports to changes in relative unit labour costs and the lack of evidence of a nominal wage squeeze on German workers. First, Storm (2016) estimates the export elasticity with respect to relative unit labour costs (ULCs) – that is, the product of the relative price elasticity of export demand and the price elasticity of output with respect to ULCs – for Germany and Greece, Italy, Portugal and Spain (Onaran and Galanis, 2012; Storm and Naastepad, 2015a, 2015b). The low value of these elasticities (0.20–0.25 in absolute value for most manufacturing sectors) leads Storm and Naastepad (2015a) to conclude that in the years 1996–2008 ULC changes did not affect in a statistically significant manner the growth of exports, imports and the trade balances. The low elasticity of export prices to ULCs is consistent with the observation that labour costs only make up 20–24 per cent of the gross output prices of Germany's tradable sectors, while the intermediate costs account for 67–68 per cent (reflecting, we may add, the expansion of outsourcing to the East).[7] It follows that if ULCs decline by 1 per cent, (relative) prices decline by 0.25 per cent if the cost pass-through is complete, or by only 0.125 per cent with a pass-through of 50 per cent, a figure consistent with the econometric evidence.[8] Next, Storm (2016) argues that

> there is no clear sign of a nominal wage squeeze on German workers.… It is true nevertheless that Germany's unit labour cost declined relative to those of the rest of the Eurozone … but this was not a result of wage restraint: *it was completely due to Germany's outstanding productivity performance*[9] … *it was German engineering ingenuity, not nominal wage restraint or the Hartz Reforms*, which reduced its unit labour costs.
>
> (Italics added)

This thesis is that Germany's surplus and Southern European countries' deficits are explained by the behaviour of exports and imports respectively. On the export side, the high correspondence between the German productive specialization – in particular high-tech, high-price products – and fast-growing markets and countries (BRIC), where the non-price, technology-based competition is greater (see also Diaz Sanchez and Varoudakis, 2013; Gabrisch and Staehr, 2014). On the import side, the crucial role of the sweeping capital flows from the core-countries, which fed a debt-led boom in the periphery. The ensuing trade deficit was more the result of an increase in imports due to a demand shock (income effect) than to a decrease in exports due to a price effect (see Gaulier and Vicard, 2012). Only later wages increased more than productivity giving rise to the widening differential in ULCs, which then was by no means the *primum movens* of the crisis.

These (convincing) considerations were used primarily to refute the mainstream thesis (see, for example, Sinn, 2014) that ULCs drive competition, and are the prime determinant of international competitiveness. The corollary is that the only way to a Eurozone recovery would be a reduction in ULCs in the periphery, to be obtained through 'structural reforms' consisting of additional doses of wage flexibility and/or worsening working conditions. Justifying the adoption of measures of wage restraint in a context of generalized austerity, this thesis has already produced a lot of damage without getting noticeable results in terms of growth and employment recovery. Yet, Storm and Naastepad (2015a, 2015b), to distance themselves from the mono-dimensional obsession of unit labour costs, risk falling into other mono-dimensionalities: finance as the only villain in the Southern European crisis, or the technological competitiveness as the only actor of the success of German exports. Emphasis on 'real factors such as relative unit labour costs' diverts attention from the main cause of imbalances: finance, the proximate determinant of imports fuelled by capital flows. The role of finance will be discussed at greater length in Chapter 4. Here we observe only that it is true that, in the short run, gross flows of capital and savings (achieved through the compression of wages and consumption) are determined by a variety of different circumstances. Yet, in the long term, in a situation of persistent surplus, current savings must find a counterpart in capital exports in order to avoid a pressure toward a revaluation of the real exchange rate that would lead to a reduction in the current account.

The role of wage moderation in the formation of the Eurozone current account imbalances deserves to be examined more in detail here. In Storm's (2016) effective synthesis, authors like Bofinger (2015) and Wren-Lewis (2015), and before them Lapavitsas *et al.* (2011), Stockhammer (2011) and Bofinger (2015), contended that 'Southern's cost competitiveness problem was created in Berlin'. This would have been achieved through a long-term policy of wage moderation based 'on a deliberate, voluntary tri-partite agreement between German employers, trade unions and government'. In fact, Storm and Naastepad counter, the German nominal wage relative to the Eurozone, Germany excluded, remained virtually unchanged between 1999 and 2007 (a reduction of 0.75 percentage points in eight years). High-quality products, not wage moderation, drove German exports.

The issue concerns the assessment of the continuity and change in the traditional German corporatist model. According to some authors (OECD, 2012; Bastasin, 2013; Ma and McCauley, 2013, cited in Storm and Naastepad, 2015a: 17), the German corporatist model – 'Modell Deutschland 1.0' – no longer exists:

> it has been radically transformed and superseded by something new, after a prolonged crisis in the 1980s and 1990s and under the combined influence of financial globalization, German reunification and European integration. In Modell 2.0, it is argued, social coordination and regulation have been replaced by market mechanisms.

Along the same lines are those authors (see Streeck and Thelen, 2005) who, following the labour market reforms initiated in the mid-1990s in the coordinated (corporatist) market economies, have questioned the usefulness of continuing to differentiate these economies from the (Anglo-Saxon) free-market ones, as initially proposed by the 'varieties of capitalism' approach (see Hall and Soskice, 2001).

Storm and Naastepad (2015a) contend that the substantial stability of employment, despite the strong initial fall in exports and the strong recovery in the following years, has shown that 'the crisis has actually strengthened Deutschland Model 1.0'. Their argument is not based only on the stability of the nominal wage in the crisis, but also on the behaviour of the State, the firms and the trade unions[10] during the crisis. The close cooperation of capital, finance, labour and Germany's entrepreneurial state in managing the crisis was based on the shared appreciation of the importance to protect core employment, technological capabilities and export competitiveness. Storm and Naastepad (2015a) emphasize that 'Germany's rebound is founded upon the strong technological competitiveness of its corporatist core – manufacturing – *not on the low wages in its sheltered non-traded sectors*. Germany's competitive core has … strong corporatist foundations' (p. 20, italics added).

Lehndorff (2015) arrives at partially similar conclusions with regard to the effects of the German government's policies on peripheral countries' deficits, but he emphasizes elements of strong discontinuity after 2008 with respect to the previous internal devaluation policies. Indeed, unlike Storm and Naastepad, Lehndorff argues that internal devaluation policies were systematically carried out in Germany before the crisis due to the weakening of the unions' bargaining power. He starts from the fact that the dynamics of wages, ULCs and inflation rates in Germany in the 2000s was most unusual. In particular, Germany emerges as the only country in the EU where real wages per employee fell on average over the period 2001–2009. While real wages fell by 6.2 per cent in Germany, in the remaining 26 European countries they increased at different rates. In particular, for the four countries of the periphery, the range varied from 13.4 per cent in Greece to 5.6 per cent in Portugal, and it was 8.4 per cent in France (Table 2.2). Distancing himself from those who associate the so-called 'wage moderation' with a form of 'corporate corporatism' (see Iversen *et al.*, 2016), he argues that it originated from the defeat of the unions on the ground of collective bargaining. Since the mid-1990s – thus well before the Hartz reforms – under the pressure of the employers' organization, the government introduced two structural breaks in the labour market. First, the erosion of the guideline on a minimum collectively agreed pay increase across sectors (defined as the inflation rate plus the average total productivity growth) widened the range of collectively agreed wages by sector, with a higher wage growth in the industrial sectors relative to the public sector and trade. Second, these measures contributed to produce a 'negative wage drift' between collectively agreed and actual wages. According to Unger *et al.* (2013) (quoted in Lehndorff, 2015: 173), the actual rise in nominal wages per employee was little more than half the rise in the nominal wages agreed in collective bargaining. This decline in the impact of collective bargaining on actual wages was associated with a strong decline in collective bargaining coverage: in 2013, only 49 per cent of all German workers were covered by sectoral agreements. The most important reason behind this decline was the weakening of trade unions: trade union density fell from around 30 per cent in the mid-1990s to 19 per cent in 2013.

Agenda 2010 (the Hartz Reforms) represented a third structural break in the employment system. It 'gave a particularly powerful boost to internal devaluation' (Lehndorff, 2016: 175). It put additional pressure on both collectively agreed and actual wages by eliminating previous restriction on temporary employment, promoting mini-jobs with pay of up to €450 without any reference to hours worked and pressuring to accept employment under the poorest terms as regards wages and employment conditions. The general 'success' of the reforms, apparently not limited to the so-called 'non-tradable sectors', is shown by 'the unusual stagnation of average real wages' during the 2005–2008 strong economic growth. Further, the rise of the low-wage sector led to a change in the overall pay structures: 'the lowest three deciles in the wage grid suffered from substantial losses over the 2000s, while hourly pay rose only in the top two deciles' (ibid.: 177). Internal devaluation supplemented the product and process strength of German manufacturing industry and supported the external surplus through its effects on imports (see Chapter 5).

Since wages in the private services sector are 'on average 20 per cent lower than industry ... many pre-services for industry are extremely cheap' (ibid.: 177). In industry, nominal unit labour costs fell up to 2008 much more than in any other country in the Eurozone, also due to the higher than average productivity growth. However, when competitors in the Eurozone increased their export prices, unit cost advantages were not reflected in falling prices, but in increased profits (as in the metal industry). The increase in profits was facilitated by the fact that 'from the founding of monetary union two-fifths of Germany's foreign trade no longer had to fear' (ibid.: 184) exchange rate adjustments by Eurozone economies experiencing rising unit labour costs and higher inflation.

The expansionary policy implemented during the crisis and the agreement with the unions to replace external flexibility with internal flexibility have managed to safeguard 'employment by reactivating precisely those elements of

Table 2.2 Change in real wages* per employee: Germany, France and the SP rates of change (2001–2009)

Germany	−6.2
France	8.4
Italy	10.7
Spain	6.4
Portugal	5.6
Greece	13.4

Source: Lehndorff (2015).

Note
* Nominal compensation divided by the national Harmonized Index of Consumer Prices (HICP).

the German social model that had survived the neo-liberally inspired zeal for demolition'. The expansionary measures, which move in the opposite direction of the policies carried out in the same period by most European countries, represent 'the first attempts at limiting the damage caused by [the] "structural reforms" on the German labour market'. Hence,

> the paradoxical situation which continues to dominate the European scene: the relatively positive employment trend in Germany has served as a political platform for the German government to push for a policy of internal devaluation approach in other countries, while the drivers behind this relatively positive development at home have been exactly those which are being forbidden to other countries.
>
> (Lehndorff, 2015: 189)

Lehndorff's thesis is that internal devaluation and high specialization and product quality are not incompatible but complementary phenomena. This implies that the formation of a vast low-wage sector, created through a series of measures to reform the labour market since the early 1990s and in-depth in the early 2000s, has exerted a moderating influence on wages and labour conditions not only in the sector 'non-core' (an aspect recognized by Storm and Naastepad) but also in the 'core' sector exposed to international competition. This occurred through two channels: an indirect influence through the provision of low-cost services to the manufacturing industry (producing for exports or in competition with imports) and to the core workers, and a direct influence through the extension of low wages – often associated with temporary work, fixed time employment, part-time employment or mini jobs – to segments of the manufacturing industry.

Also Hassel (2014: 22–23), like Storm and Naastepad (2015a) and Lehndorff (2016), argues that in the rapid recovery of the German economy after 2008 an important role must be attributed to the institutional foundations of the 'old' German model. She argues, however, that 'coordination and liberalization are not opposite or mutually exclusive but complementary processes: they can go hand in hand, leading to a segmented and dualist political economy'. Moreover, Hassel (2015: 3) observes that the formation of a large area of low wages occurred with the support of core industries and the tacit support of the work councils of core workers. The restructuring of the German industry, aimed at realizing strong cost cuts and productivity gains in response to globalization, took place

> exploiting existing patterns of plant-level cooperation. Intensified plant-level cooperation led to employment guarantees for core workers that insulated them from previous demands for strong social security provisions [to long-term unemployed]. In turn, persistent outsourcing to low cost countries and low cost service sectors has added to liberalization in other parts of the economy, particularly through the use of fringe workers ... liberalization

did not occur despite strong resistance by key beneficiaries of social policy, but rather was accepted and supported as a precondition for sustained coordination.

If coordination and liberalization appear complementary, resulting in a 'segmented and dualist political economy', also the relationships between the export-oriented high skilled industry and the fringe workers/fringe sectors are 'complementary and mutually dependent' (ibid.: 22). Germany's competitiveness in manufacturing sectors does not depend only on collaboration with works councils at the plant level, but also on the liberalization of the service economy that leads to cost-cutting in the services supplied, facilitating wage restraint and ULCs containment.

The formation of a dualistic and interdependent labour market highlights another distinctive feature of the dynamics of German wages with respect to the other Eurozone countries, besides the decrease in the real average wage growth in the years 2001–2008. Since the 1980s, in Germany (and Austria), the hourly wages of the sectors less exposed to foreign competition (retail and wholesale, hotels, personal services, real estate, finance and insurance) grew even less than the manufacturing hourly wages, despite the latter's persistent wage moderation policy. In the countries of the European periphery, instead, the opposite occurred: the wages of non-exposed sectors generally grew more than those exposed, thus providing, through the expansion of consumption, an outlet for the core-country's exports.

In conclusion, Hassel's analysis of the transformations of the German economic system since the mid-1990s provides support to the idea, already put forward by Carlin and Soskice (2008), of the importance of core producer coalitions in driving and shaping policy and institutional change, at a disadvantage of other producer groups. According to Carlin and Soskice, works councils representing skilled workers 'colluded' with the management on liberalizing reforms and supported low-level service labour markets for two reasons: cheaper services increased their real income, and their members would bear less the cost of long-term unemployment (Carlin and Soskice, 2008: 93; Hassel, 2014: 9–10). The concept of 'core producer coalitions' means that the transformation processes cannot be described as if they were dominated by the conflict of insiders and outsiders. It seems more appropriate to use the centre-periphery concept to explain the existing dualism within the same country (as long as one keeps in mind the mutual dependence and complementarity that provide relevant, though contingent, stability to the ensuing asymmetrical configuration). This is not a new concept. It recalls, on the one hand, the difficulties and tensions related to the integration process of East Germany with West Germany after 1989, and on the other, the concept of 'internal colonialism' used by Hechter (1975) to analyse the ethnic conflict in the United Kingdom. (Similar concepts were found before, in Hobson's analysis (1906) of the social stratification of English workers in the late 1800s, that is, in another era of globalization of goods and capital markets).

In any case, this configuration, based on core producer coalitions, does not lend itself to being described as Modell Deutschland 2.0 or Modell Deutschland 1.0. It makes us rethink the traditional dichotomist divisions of the varieties of capitalism approach and calls for a revision of the too heterogeneous character of the set of activities included in the 'non-core' or 'non-tradable' sector. In the next section, we focus on the financial-real estate complex, that has played a very important role not only in the relative performance of the German economy compared with the periphery countries, but also in the formation of its large current account surplus.

4 Housing: a 'non-tradable' sector?

One of the most important effects of domestic financial deregulation and international capital liberalisation starting in the early 1980s, is the appearance of *global* real estate cycles (Grjebine, 2014). The first cycle took place in the years 1985–1995, the second in the years 1997–2012. The second cycle was associated with the credit boom, which was triggered by the collapse of the dot.com bubble and the September 11th events that eventually overlapped with the events produced by the Monetary Union.

The synchronization of national cycles occurred for the joint action of two forces. First, domestic financial deregulation led to the abandonment of direct credit controls. The existence of specialized institutions having the monopoly of the financing of real estate, together with the practice of resorting to administrative measures rather than interest rates to regulate credit, meant that the magnitude of loans extended to real estate found a limit in these institutions' own resources. With domestic financial deregulation, credit limits disappeared and banks were allowed to compete with specialized agencies to fund real estate investment projects. The result was a growth in real estate credit and a sharp rise in house prices, generally well above the inflation rate, in many countries. Recent studies based on long-term longitudinal data (Jordà *et al.*, 2016) have shown that the driving force behind the financialization of advanced economies has been mortgage lending by banks. The share of mortgage loans in banks' total lending has roughly doubled over the course of the past century, to reach 60 per cent today. By contrast, non-bank mortgage lending as a percentage of GDP has remained stable over the last century. The liberalization of international capital movements compounded the effects of the internal financial deregulation: arbitrage operations across financial markets contributed to synchronize the national real estate cycles. In the ascending phase of the cycle, cross-border capital movements acted as a multiplier of the credit expansion triggered by financial innovations, such as mortgage-backed securities (MBS) and collateralized debt obligations (CDOs),[11] which derived their value from mortgage payments and ever-increasing housing prices.

The American subprime crisis spread across the world causing banking crises, state bail-outs, speculative attacks and deflationary measures. Germany was spared the costs associated with the boom and bust of the domestic real estate cycles. Indeed, Grjebine (2014) notes that the German real estate cycle was completely asynchronous and much attenuated compared to that of almost all OECD countries. He attributes this asynchrony to the fact that Germany had carried out only a partial financial deregulation, specifically, specialized institutions continued to provide loans within an unchanged regulatory framework. Actually, more than one factor helped to insulate the German economic system from both the expansive drive of real estate growth in the ascending phase, and the deflationary impulses in the downward phase of the cycle. Figure 2.4 displays the diverging dynamics of the real estate sector prices in Germany, France and in the SP.

We can identify the specific features of Germany's housing finance system by comparison with the main characteristics of a very different system, the Anglo-Saxon one. The latter is characterized by high levels of home ownership, easy mortgage refinancing, easy access to home equity and widespread securitization of mortgages (Schwartz, 2009: 35–42). Conversely, the German system has a low ownership rate associated with a large and well-regulated rental market. The interplay of home financing and rental sector regulations leads to prudential lending standards that contribute to the resilience of the housing sector (Voigtländer, 2014). The low ownership rate helps explain the relatively low ratio of outstanding mortgages in Germany (46.5 per cent of GDP compared with 85 per cent in the UK in 2010). The majority of mortgage loans are at fixed rates: 70 per cent of mortgages have a fixed rate for more than five years, only 0.5 per cent of all outstanding mortgages have floating interest rates. By contrast,

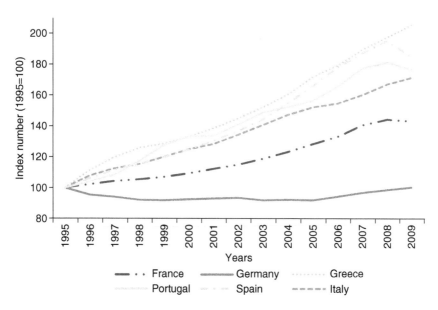

Figure 2.4 The dynamic of prices in the real estate sector (1995–2011) (1995=100).

Source: authors' elaboration on WIOD data.

in the UK, 72 per cent of all outstanding mortgages had floating rates. This implies that a change in interest rates will have a quick and important influence in the UK, while it will affect only the new loans or the requests of mortgage extensions in Germany.

The elasticity of mortgage rates to changes in monetary policy affects the effectiveness of the transmission of monetary policy on consumption, and therefore the relationship between house prices and consumption. The latter relies primarily on the important role played by the real estate as collateral, rather than on wealth effects. In Germany, although 55 per cent of all loans are secured by real estate, the correlation between house prices and consumption growth is much lower than in the UK.[12] This may be due to the higher difficulty to obtain a mortgage: the loan/value ratios (LTVs) are lower than in the UK, and the property valuation rules, based on the mortgage lending value instead of the market value as in the UK, are more restrictive and prudential. Moreover, in the German system it is not customary, although not formally prohibited, to use the increase in house prices to get an extension of a previous loan. Both the low home ownership ratio, which is associated with a low number of real estate transactions, and the prudential rules in granting loans, lead to mitigate the positive feedback of the sequence: lower interest rates, high demand for housing credit, high housing prices, high collateral value, high consumption and high housing prices. On the other hand, the peculiar characteristics of the German housing sector contribute reducing the probability of negative feedback during economic downturns: when the fall in consumption is associated with evictions, forced sales, falling house prices and bank losses. According to Voigtländer (2014), the presence of prudential rules – such as the low LTV, the virtual absence of equity withdrawal, the high downpayments, the high tax burden – deter low-income families from entering risky mortgages, encouraging them to turn to rent. The lower share of homeowners[13] depends not only on the higher financial and fiscal obstacles to house purchases but also on the presence of price caps in the rental market. In addition to reducing the variance of real house prices, this system eliminates the incentive to create a subprime market for families with low creditworthiness. The systemic risk associated with granting loans to debtors who, after the bubble bursts, may prove to be insolvent is then solved at its roots.

The particular German system of rents regulation and house financing has managed, so far,[14] to avoid the formation of property bubbles. However, a curious asymmetry is worth noting. On the one hand, the German banking system has not contributed to fuel real estate bubbles *within* the country. In fact, the German share of securitization issuance in total issuance in Europe is also still low (4.9 per cent in Germany compared with 14.4 per cent in Italy and 12.8 per cent in Spain), suggesting a financial system relatively less prone to 'financial innovations' compared with other countries that have made more resolute steps on the road of internal deregulation. On the other hand, German banks have participated very actively in fuelling financial bubbles *in other countries*, first as large purchasers of securities on the US subprime market, and subsequently participating, along with French banks, in the financing of credit bubbles in the SP.

The asynchrony of the German real estate cycle has important implications for the building up of external disequilibria. In fact, there is a strong inverse relationship between the current account and the real price of houses (nominal prices deflated by the consumer price index) (see Geerolf and Grjebine, 2013 for references). The traditional explanation links the rise in the real price of houses with increased financing capacity, and increases in consumption (with a corresponding reduction in savings) and investment, both in construction and in the rest of the economy. The excess of investment over savings results in a negative current account balance, which will be eliminated only with the bursting of the house price bubble. The increase in consumption and investment occurs through three channels: (i) a wealth effect (of which there is scarce evidence); (ii) a financing effect arising from equity withdrawals (which has been very important after 2000 in the US, UK and in some European countries such as the Netherlands, but absent in many others); (iii) and a financing effect operating through the increase in the value of collateral. While Jordà *et al.* (2016) emphasize the importance of mortgage lending for purchase of households' real estate, Chaney *et al.* (2012)[15] find a robust relation between real estate prices and investment, suggesting that estate property is used by firms as a collateral to finance investment projects.

In the two global real estate cycles, all major countries (excluding Germany) have recorded a credit boom accompanied by a real estate boom. On this evidence, Grjebine (2014) suggests an explanation of the formation of the German current surplus that is complementary to the traditional one based on the labour market effects of the Hartz reforms and on unit labour costs. According to this author, the slowdown in German house prices, which began in the early 2000s, would have caused a sharp fall in investment, especially in real estate, a reduction in household consumption and an improvement of the current account balance.

However, the German real estate cycle is not only asynchronous, but also highly attenuated compared to that of other countries and it does not seem capable of causing so significant effects. Moreover, as argued in the previous section, in the case of Germany the driving force is represented by exports. The widely held idea that we can interpret the external balance as the difference between savings and investment disregards the fact that we are dealing with an (ex post) accounting identity. It assumes that savings are given (for example, at the level associated with full employment income), so that a lower domestic absorption will inevitably result in a greater net use of the (given) product abroad. If we reject the hypothesis of a given income, the underlying dynamics may be different. In conditions of subdued domestic demand, the growth of German exports, in particular capital goods and high-quality durable consumer goods, generates large current account surpluses and enables large capital inflows in the European periphery. In the absence of a policy aimed at strengthening the industrial base of the receiving countries, capital finances mainly real estate business that provides the financial system with a collateral that is considered safer than the more uncertain alternative uses. The strong and sudden influx of capital to the peripheral countries is associated with a sharp increase in the price of real estate (the 'big fish small pond' metaphor, see Chapter 1, Section 6), and an increase in incomes directly and indirectly linked to the real estate and the financial sectors. The result is a sharp increase in imports, which provide support to German exports. This sequence is consistent with the interpretation suggested by Gaulier and Vicard (2012) and Storm and Naastepad (2015a). As we argued in Section 3, they could not find a significant relationship between the percentage change in exports and the percentage change in ULCs for peripheral countries in the period 1999–2007, but found instead a significant positive correlation between domestic demand growth and import growth. They concluded that there were no significant price effects.

We can move the analysis a step forward. As argued by Felipe and Kumar (2011), the aggregate ULC is not the weighted average of labour costs per unit of physical quantity of output of the various sectors: the price enters into the measure of ULCs, as deflator of the individual sectors' value added and as the deflator of GDP at the aggregate level. Thus, the variation in unit labour costs can be expressed as the product of the variation of the share of nominal wages in the nominal value added times the value added price deflator. That is, the ULC can be written as (Felipe and Kumar, 2011: 11):

$$ULC = \frac{w_n}{(VA_n/P)/L} = \left(\frac{w_n * L}{VA_n}\right) * P = \left(\frac{Total\ labour\ compensation}{VA_n}\right) * P$$

Where, w_n is the average money wage, VA_n is the value added in money terms, L is the number of workers and P is the value added deflator. By decomposing the variation in ULC in the wage share and in the 'price' index for the economy as a whole and for individual sectors, it appears that, in the peripheral countries, real estate and finance are the two sectors most responsible for the overall ULCs growth relative to Germany. Another important component of the output price, whose weight has been growing in Germany since the mid-1990s, is given by imported intermediate goods. Their effect on the final price is twofold: the increase in their weight reduces the impact of changes in ULCs; since the intermediate goods are imported from countries where labour costs are lower than in Germany, outsourcing tends to reduce the German output price compared to countries that have not carried out this relocation. In the next section we consider the effects of the Eastern relocation of parts of the German industry on the SP.

5 The construction of the Central European Manufacturing Core[16]

Since the mid-1990s the German trade has undergone substantial changes in its geographical breakdown and composition, with the Eastern European region and Emerging Asia, especially China, becoming important partners (see Chapter 6 for a detailed quantitative analysis). Many Eastern European countries have been given the opportunity to integrate into the supply chains of the EU countries.

This is reflected in the composition of trade: intermediate goods have been the most dynamic element of trade, with imports and exports of intermediate goods exceeding the equally dynamic expansion of trade in final goods.

The old EU members have differed in the extent and quality of their eastward expansion. Austria and Germany have been swift to take advantage of cultural ties and closer borders, though Italian firms have also been very active in creating supply chains in South-Eastern countries. Moreover, the pattern of German de-localization, based on keeping the final stages of production at home, differs from the Italian and French ones, which are based on the de-localization of the entire process, with obvious consequences on demand and growth (see Deutsche Bundesbank, 2011a, and Chapter 6, for an analysis of the automotive sector).

German industry in particular has invested heavily in the neighbouring countries, integrating the new industries into its value chain (the 'bazaar' economy). The progressive elimination of barriers to trade and investment, but not labour, has generated incentives to outsource only parts of manufacturing activity. De-localization of manufacturing to emerging Europe has actually helped to create jobs in the home country by sustaining productivity in manufacturing, while contributing to the sharp fall in Germany's relative ULCs (Marin, 2010b).[17]

The Eastward-oriented production network that Germany has built between the late 1990s and the early 2000s has affected the core-(Southern) periphery divergence. Lower production costs, particularly labour, good infrastructures and an extended pool of skilled and disciplined labour force characterize the former Socialist countries. In addition, Germany has profitably exploited the existing ties between former GDR companies and firms located in the economies now in the German network. In Chapter 6, we analyse in detail the consequences of the emergence of the German production network. Its relevance can be gauged by comparing the trade data of the two networks: the Germany–SP and the Germany–Eastern periphery (EP) networks exhibit very different dynamics. These data support the hypothesis of a redirection of trade away from the SP towards the EP. The key members of the Central European Manufacturing Core, in fact, tend to have a surplus in their bilateral trade with Germany (Figure 2.5), a result related to the offshoring and outsourcing of German productions in the Visegrad countries. Conversely, in the SP the change in trade flows has been larger for imports than for exports: consequently, before the crisis, the South accounted for one-third of Germany's total trade surplus.

Thus, Germany's closer ties with the East entailed a diversion of trade and a weakening of ties with the rest of Europe, and in particular with the SP, possibly contributing to an impoverishment of their matrix of production and trade network. This conclusion is supported by an authoritative source. In 2011, the Bundesbank highlighted the changing role of the various areas of the enlarged EU in the division of labour (Deutsche Bundesbank, 2011a). Investigating the impact of German growth on foreign economies, the Bundesbank detects an increasing cross-country heterogeneity, mirroring the diverse specialization patterns and the change in the relative positions within trade and production chains. In this respect, the demand for intermediate goods, which the German economy

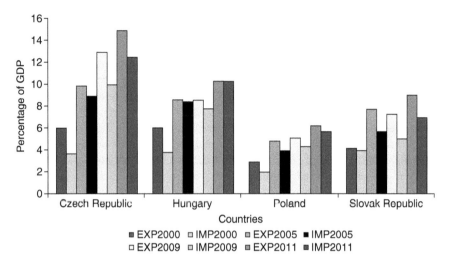

Figure 2.5 The German–EP bilateral trade relationships exports and imports as a percentage of GDP (2000, 2005, 2009 and 2011).

Source: authors' elaboration on TIVA-OECD data.

normally covers through imports, especially favours the neighbouring countries
of Central and Eastern Europe, which rely on the export of intermediate goods,
although the link with the East is strong also for capital goods.[18] Imports of intermediate goods from the EP have been boosted also because many suppliers
located there participate in the strong performances of German exporters, especially in the rapidly expanding Asian markets (Deutsche Bundesbank, 2011a,
2011b). Conversely,

> only with the Mediterranean countries is the interlinkage of the supply
> chains not very advanced so far.... The spill-over effects of German busi-
> ness activity tend to be weaker in countries which mainly deliver consumer
> goods to Germany and/or which are holiday destinations.
>
> (Deutsche Bundesbank, 2011a: 22)

This holds particularly for the Mediterranean countries. Far from demonstrating a
low activation potential of German growth, however, the Bundesbank's analysis
points to the relative importance of different demand components in supporting
growth: export-led growth is more intermediate inputs-intensive, thus resulting in
imports from both the East and the West, and much less from the South. Conversely, domestic demand gives greater impetus to more broadly geographically
based imports of consumption goods. In Chapter 5, we show that the quantity and
quality of the trade flows (and specifically of imports) can be affected also by the
distribution of income. The increasing number of low-income households in

Germany, in fact, has affected both the quantity and the quality of consumption, playing a role in the diversion of imports of consumer goods from high-price/high-quality SP's producers to low-price/low-quality producers (for example China). Leaving to Chapter 6 a more detailed examination of the factors affecting trade dynamics, we can conclude that the occurrence and magnitude of demand spill-overs on neighbouring countries depend on the pattern (intensity and quality) of German growth.

The export-led growth that followed the euro inception produced trade diversion, weakening of the SP and strengthening of the EP. A more buoyant internal demand in Germany, supported by greater income equality, would help economic rebalancing in deficit countries through the direct and indirect effects of an increase in German consumer goods imports. Nevertheless, this effect is larger the stronger the ties with the German economy. Therefore, small countries with close linkages with Germany (i.e. particularly, Austria, the Netherlands, Finland and Sweden) will gain the most from such an increase in internal demand. On the other hand, the industrial weakening of Southern Europe – which accelerated after the 2008 crisis – would significantly reduce the growth impact on the SP of an eventual rise in German imports.

6 Conclusions

The European integration was expected to encourage large inflows of foreign investment from the more developed to the less developed member countries: external imbalances would first widen, then narrow and eventually close as income levels would converge mainly because of export growth. This expectation, that shaped the institutional framework of the EMU, was rooted in an economic theory that does not attach any weight to the diversity of the production structures, disregarding all the effects stemming from unequal power relations and differentiated technological endowments.

The core-periphery divergence and the increasing disequilibria in the external accounts have been attributed to various causes: from the loss of competitiveness of the SP with regard to Germany to the inflationary demand in Southern Europe, sustained by huge capital inflows. Rather than selecting one single driver as the key culprit of current account imbalances, we emphasized the role of a complex set of drivers interacting with one another in determining the conditions for divergence and crisis. Specifically, we stressed the role played by 'non-tradable', an aspect that is not usually considered among the factors of competitiveness and net exports. We analysed the increasing segmentation of the German labour market and the asynchrony in the German house market cycle to highlight the connections between the 'non-tradable' sectors, export competitiveness and net exports. Given the relevance of 'non-tradable' services – as 'wage goods' for workers and as intermediate inputs for the firms of the exporting industries – neglecting their importance in explaining trade differentials means missing a key part of Europe's core-periphery divide. Moreover, as we argue in Chapter 4, the distinction between tradable and non-tradable introduces an artificial separation between all sectors related to welfare and the labour market. Contrasting welfare (non-tradable) to exchangeable goods paves the way to consider with a benevolent eye the austerity measures taken at the peak of the real estate cycle, diverting attention from their regressive effects on income distribution: the most affected sectors are aseptically defined as 'non-tradable', though they have a decisive role in protecting people's lives from market fluctuations. Finally, the attention paid to the formation of a dualistic and interdependent labour market responds to the risk of a monolithic distinction between core and periphery, uncovering the existence of structural, political and economic inequalities *within* both the core and the periphery, in mutual dependence and complementarity. The evolution of 'core producer' coalition, we argued, contributes to shape, and responds to, the formation of new (and the demise of old) peripheries.

Notes

1 It was only since the 1989 Delors Report that the notion that the single currency would be introduced *simultaneously* to the fiscal and political union, which had been generally accepted since the Werner Report (1970), was abandoned.
2 According to the traditional neoclassical theory, international capital flows are a direct reflection of (full employment) savings. Since 'the loan market directly reflects the supply and demand for saving', with capital mobility, a fraction of a country's *given* savings will be diverted to the acquisition of foreign bonds offering higher yields. The higher investment abroad will entail a lower domestic investment. The rise in net exports in the lending country will be the 'automatic' real counterpart of the transfer of international reserves to the receiving country. This theoretical perspective implies that 'there is no need to distinguish between the real and the money aspects of the phenomenon of free capital mobility'. For a critique of this position in the analysis of the current Eurozone crisis, see O'Connell (2015).
3 See Hirschman (1978) now in Hirschman (1981: 32).
4 In a large economy, such as Germany, internal demand is much more influential on growth than external demand. Cf. Carlin and Soskice (2008: 87).
5 In their analysis of price competitiveness across European countries, Bayoumi *et al.* (2011: 1) observed 'surprisingly wide divergences across alternative relative price measures' based on wholesale prices, consumer prices, unit labour costs and export unit values for intra and extra euro trade. Italy (and to a lesser extent Spain) provide an interesting puzzle, since the four indicators of the real exchange rate between 1995 and 2009 tell different stories: an enormous loss of competitiveness when using the indicator based on the unit values of exports and, to a lesser extent, the indicator of unit labour costs; only a slight appreciation when using the two indicators based on consumer prices and wholesale prices. This surprising divergence between the two groups of indicators (ranging between 70 and 30 percentage points by the end of the period) stems from the fact that Italy (and Spain) used the unit values of exports (an index that is affected by changes in the quality of products and by 'pricing to market' strategies that are widespread especially in the luxury goods industry), instead of an export price index as the other countries do. Since the export price indicator enters in the calculation of the value added deflator, it affects also the estimate of productivity and, ultimately, the ULC indicator.
6 On the quality composition of German imports of consumption goods, see Chapter 5.
7 On this point see also Deutsche Bundesbank (1988: 41–42).
8 Similarly low elasticities of export prices to ULC, and of exports to prices are found in a recent study on the determinants of German net exports (Horn *et al.*, 2017).

9 According to Storm (2016),

> during 1999–2007 average German labour productivity (per hour worked) increased by almost 8 percentage points compared to the rest of Eurozone, which accounts fully for the decline in Germany's relative unit costs by 7.8 percentage point in the same period.

10 As Storm and Naastepad (2015a: 20) remark, after two bail-out programmes for ailing banks and financially weakened companies (amounting to €595 billion), the state provided targeted support to the Mittelstand to reinforce its export strength. The stimulus program, amounting to 4 per cent of GDP, was the largest of all major European nations. The protection of core employment was provided through 'cash for clunkers programs', through the government offsetting a portion of the costs associated with temporary reductions in working hours and by extending support to part time. 'As a result, labour markets adjusted primarily through changes in hours worked per employee, rather than layoffs.... Layoffs predominantly hit workers with temporary contracts.'

11 Banks packaged risky credits into MBS and then dispersed pooled slices of them into CDO, transferring risks to CDO's subscribers.

12 According to Catte *et al.* (2004), the correlation between price changes and consumption is 0.24 in Germany and 0.85 in UK.

13 The diffusion of a wide rental market in Germany stems largely from the post-1945 reconstruction policies, when the authorities tackled house shortages by encouraging entrepreneurs to build for rent. Since then, an important incentive to rent instead of buying houses has been internal mobility.

14 Due to the rise in real house prices observed since 2010, concerns about the formation of a speculative house price bubble in the German market are rising. However, the empirical evidence on an overheating of the real estate market is still mixed.

15 Chaney *et al.*'s analysis is based on US data for the 1993–2007 period. They underline that in bank-oriented countries the role of the collateral should be even greater than in a market-based economy like the United States. They recall also that the severity of the Great Depression and the strong expansion of the Japanese economy at the end of the 1980s are often attributed to a 'collateral channel'.

16 The definition is taken from Stehrer and Stöllinger (2015). The countries identified as part of the German network are Poland, the Czech Republic, Hungary, the Slovak Republic and Slovenia.

17 According to Marin (2010a), outsourcing some activities to their EP's affiliates has helped Austrian and German firms to save between 65 and 80 per cent of their labour costs, helping them to stay competitive in an increasingly competitive environment.

18 In the case of capital goods, the regional structure is more concentrated. Switzerland and the Czech Republic specialize in supplying machinery and other equipment to German customers. The Slovak Republic has a higher weight in motor vehicles and motor vehicle parts followed some way behind by other Central and Eastern European countries and Spain.

References

Bastasin, C. (2013). Germany: A global miracle and a European challenge. *Global Economy & Development, Working Paper No. 62.* Washington, DC: Brookings Institution.

Bayoumi, M. T., Turunen, M. J. and Harmsen, M. R. T. (2011). Euro area export performance and competitiveness. *IMF Working Paper No. 11–140.*

Bofinger, P. (2015). German wage moderation and the Eurozone crisis. *Social Europe*, 1 December. www.socialeurope.eu/2015/12/german-wage-moderation-and-the-eurozone-crisis/ [accessed 23 September 2017].

Carlin, W. and Soskice, D. (2008). German economic performance: Disentangling the role of supply-side reforms, macroeconomic policy and coordinated economy institutions. *Socio-Economic Review*, 7(1), 67–99.

Catte, P., Girouard, N., Price, R. and André, C. (2004). The contribution of housing markets to cyclical resilience. *OECD Journal: Economic Studies*, 1, 125–156.

Chaney, T., Sraer, D. and Thesmar, D. (2012). The collateral channel: How real estate shocks affect corporate investment. *American Economic Review*, 102(6), October.

Danninger, S. and Joutz, F. (2007). What explains Germany's rebounding export market share? *IMF Working Paper WP/07/24*. Washington, DC: IMF.

Deutsche Bundesbank (1998). The indicator quality in different definitions of the real external value of the Deutsche Mark. *Monthly Report*, November, 39–52.

Deutsche Bundesbank (2011a). The transmission and regional distribution of the German economy's cyclical impulses within Europe. *Monthly Report*, March, 22–23.

Deutsche Bundesbank (2011b). Developments in the exports of the four largest euro-area member states since the launch of monetary union. *Monthly Report*, July, 15–34.

Diaz Sanchez, J. and Varoudakis, A. (2013). Growth and competitiveness as factors of Eurozone external imbalances: Evidence and policy implications. *WB Policy Research Working Paper No. 6732/2013*. Washington, DC: World Bank.

Fagerberg, J. (1994). Technology and international differences in growth rates. *Journal of Economic Literature*, 32(3), 1147–1175.

Felipe, J. and Kumar, U. (2011). Unit labour costs in the Eurozone: The competitiveness debate again. *Levy Economics Institute of Bard College Working Paper No. 651*.

Felipe, J. and McCombie, J. S. (2013). *The Aggregate Production Function and the Measurement of Technical Change: Not Even Wrong*. Cheltenham: Edward Elgar Publishing.

Gabrisch, H. and Staehr, K. (2014). The Euro plus pact. *Revue de l'OFCE*, (1), 287–325.

Gaulier, G. and Vicard, V. (2012). Current account imbalances in the Euro area: Competitiveness or demand shock? *Banque de France, Quarterly Selection of Articles*, 27, 5–26.

Geerolf, F. and Grjebine, T. (2013). House prices drive current accounts: Evidence from property tax variations. *CEPII Working Paper No. 2013–18*, June.

Grjebine, T. (2014). D'une crise a l'autre: 30 ans de globalisation des cycles immobilers. *La lettre du CEPII No. 342*, March.

Haas, E. B. (1958). *The Uniting of Europe: Political, Social, and Economic Forces, 1950–1957* (No. 42). Stanford, CA: Stanford University Press.

Hall, P. A. and Soskice, D. W. (2001). *Varieties of Capitalism: The Institutional Foundations of Comparative Advantage*. Oxford: Oxford University Press.

Hassel, A. (2014). The paradox of liberalization: Understanding dualism and the recovery of the German political economy. *British Journal of Industrial Relations*, 52(1), 57–81.

Hechter, M. (1975). *Internal Colonialism: The Celtic Fringe in British National Development*. Berkeley: University of California Press.

Hirschman, A. O. (1981). *Essays in Trespassing*. Cambridge: Cambridge University Press.

Hobson, J. A. (1906). *The Problem of the Unemployed* (3rd edn). London: Methuen, 79–80.

Horn, G. A., Lindner, F., Stephan, S. and Zwiener, R. (2017). The role of nominal wages in trade and current account surpluses. An econometric analysis for Germany. *IMK Report 125e*, June.

Iversen, T., Soskice, D. and Hope, D. (2016). The Eurozone and political economic institutions. *Annual Review of Political Science*, 19, 163–185.

Jordà, Ò., Schularick, M. and Taylor, A. M. (2016). The great mortgaging: Housing finance, crises and business cycles. *Economic Policy*, 31(85), 107–152.

Landesmann, M. (2015). The new north-south divide in Europe: Can the European convergence model be resuscitated? In J. Fagerberg, S. Laestedius and B. Martin (eds), *The Triple Challenge for Europe: Economic Development, Climate Change, and Governance*. Oxford: Oxford University Press.

Lapavitsas, C., Kaltenbrunner, A., Lindo, D. *et al.* (2011). Breaking up? A route out of the Eurozone crisis. *RMF Occasional Report 3*. November. Research on Money and Finance.

Lehndorff, S. (2015). *Divisive Integration: The Triumph of Failed Ideas in Europe – Revisited*. Brussels: European Trade Union Institute (ETUI).

Lehndorff, S. (2016). Internal devaluation and employment trends in Germany. In M. Myant, S. Theodoropoulou and A. Piasna (eds), *Unemployment, Internal Devaluation and Labour Market Deregulation in Europe*. Brussels: European Trade Union Institute (ETUI), 169–196.

Ma, G. and McCauley, R. N. (2013). Global and euro imbalances: China and Germany. *BIS Working Papers No. 424*. Basel: Bank for International Settlements.

Marin, D. (2010a). The opening up of Eastern Europe at 20: Jobs, skills, and 'reverse maquiladoras' in Austria and Germany. *Munich Discussion Paper 2010–14*. Munich: University of Munich.

Marin, D. (2010b). Germany's super competitiveness: A helping hand from Eastern Europe. *VoxEU.org*, 20 June. www.voxeu.org/index.php?q=node/5212 [accessed 10 January 2017].

O'Connell, A. (2015). European crisis: A new tale of center–periphery relations in the world of financial liberalization/globalization? *International Journal of Political Economy*, 44(3), 174–195.

OECD (2012). *Economic Survey of Germany 2012*. Paris: OECD.

Onaran, Ö. and Galanis, G. (2012). Is aggregate demand wage-led or profit-led: National and global effects. *ILO Conditions of Work and Employment Series*, (31).

Schumpeter, J. A. (1942). *Socialism, Capitalism and Democracy*. New York: Harper & Row.

Schwartz, H. M. (2009). Housing, global finance, and American hegemony: Building conservative politics one brick at a time. In H. Schwartz and L. Seabrooke (eds), *The Politics of Housing Booms and Busts*. New York: Palgrave Macmillan, 28–51.

Sinn, H.-W. (2014). Austerity, growth and inflation: Remarks on the Eurozone's unresolved competitiveness problem. *The World Economy*, 37(1), 1–13.

Stahn, K. (2006). Has the impact of key determinants of German exports changed? In O. de Bandt, H. Herrmann and G. Parigi (eds), *Convergence or Divergence in Europe?* Berlin, Heidelberg: Springer.

Stehrer, R. and Stöllinger, R. (2015). The Central European Manufacturing Core: What is driving regional production sharing? *FIW Research Reports No. 2014/15–02*.

Stockhammer, E. (2011). Peripheral Europe's debt and German wages: The role of wage policy in the Euro Area. *Research on Money and Finance Discussion Paper No. 29*.

Storm, S. (2016). German wage moderation and the eurozone crisis: A critical analysis. *Institute for New Economic Thinking*, 8 January. http://ineteconomics.org/ideas-papers/blog/german-wage-moderationand-the-eurozone-crisis-a-critical-analysis [accessed 14 September 2017].

Storm, S. and Naastepad, C. W. M. (2015a). Germany's recovery from crisis: The real lessons. *Structural Change and Economic Dynamics*, 32(1), 11–24. www.sciencedirect.com/science/article/pii/S0954349X15000028 [accessed 14 September 2017].

Storm, S. and Naastepad, C. W. M. (2015b). Europe's hunger games: Income distribution, cost competitiveness and crisis. *Cambridge Journal of Economics*, 39(3), 959–986.

Streeck, W. and Thelen, K. A. (eds) (2005). *Beyond Continuity: Institutional Change in Advanced Political Economies.* Oxford: Oxford University Press.

Unger, B., Bispinck, R., Pusch, T., Seils, E. and Spannagel, D. (2013). Verteilungsbericht 2013 – Trendwende noch nicht erreicht, *WSI-Report 10*, Düsseldorf.

Voigtländer, M. (2014). The stability of the German housing market. *Journal of Housing and the Built Environment*, 29(4), 583–594.

Werner, P. (1970). *Report to the Council and the Commission on the Realisation by Stages of Economic and Monetary Union in the Community – 'Werner Report' –* (definitive text) [8 October 1970]. Bulletin of the European Communities, Supplement 11/1970. [EU Council of the EU Document] http://aei.pitt.edu/1002/ [accessed 13 September 2017].

Wren-Lewis, S. (2015). Was German undercutting deliberate? *Social Europe*, 4 December. www.socialeurope.eu/2015/12/was-german-wage-undercutting-deliberate/ [accessed 14 September 2017].

3   France

The waning of a core country

1 Introduction

A thorough analysis of the evolution of the French economy after the formation
of the EMU is beyond the scope of this research. Indeed, because of its economic dimension, its political weight, besides its geographical location, France
pertains to the core. The French–German special relation represented the engine
of the European construction and shaped the EU institutions and rules. However,
French and German economies greatly diverged during the last two decades.
While Germany increased its competitiveness and strengthened its industrial
base, France's economic structure has come closer to that of Southern Europe
(Figure 3.1). Since the 1980s, and even more since the start of the EMU, France
has been affected by high unemployment, a decline in the rate of accumulation,
co-existence of public deficits and current account deficits and strong disparities
between the great metropolis and the smaller towns (Amable *et al.*, 2011). Thus,

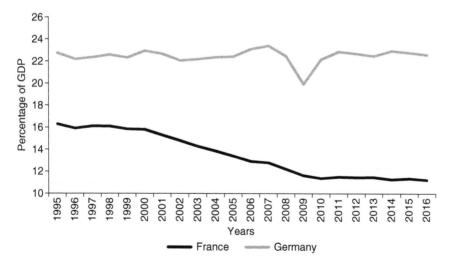

Figure 3.1 French and German manufacturing share (% of GDP, 1995–2016).

Source: authors' elaboration on World Bank data.

even if it would be difficult to include France among the countries of Southern Europe, its recent history presents some traits in common with those of the SP.

This relative weakening of a great country, which at the beginning of the projects of monetary integration was cultivating the ambition to reconcile, at the European political level, efficiency, equality and development, helps to explain the absence of a real French opposition, or alternative, to the economic policy guidance proposed by Germany. This absence eased the establishing of policies that led to the divergent development between Germany and the periphery (Figure 3.2). Yet, over the past 30 years, French governments undertook several measures aimed at encouraging the adjustments that were deemed necessary to meet the increased competition of the globalization era. We argue that France's weakness is partly explained by the ambiguity of its economic and political project, 'always somewhat uneasy with the monetarist "orthodoxy" enshrined in the Euro project, without which German approval was impossible' (Vail, 2015: 142), but incapable or unwilling to coordinate the forces on an alternative design.

The social and labour market programmes, oscillating between implementation of policies aimed at deregulating the labour market and defence of social policies, illustrate this ambiguity. From the mid-1990s, because of reforms of the system of industrial relations, aimed at introducing significant flexibility in the labour market, the French labour market experienced a gradual process of segmentation, which accelerated substantially after 2008.

The structural weakening of the French manufacturing sector (of which the automotive sector is paradigmatic) has been accompanied by the economic rise of finance. The French financial sector expanded and changed its 'nature' in line with the (neoliberal) regime change that unfolded from the 1980s onwards. Many of the banks that had been nationalized in the post-war period and during the Socialists' first years in office were privatized. No longer constrained by public control over allocation of resources, banks could focus on profitability. Meanwhile, 'the deregulation of financial markets, initiated in 1985, which enabled firms to raise funds by issuing equities, reduced their dependence on state-allocated credit' (Levy, 2008: 423).

In this chapter, we describe the evolution of the French economic policy, from 'dirigisme' to 'social anaesthesia', to 'liberal statism', highlighting the contradictions deriving from France's problematic partnership with Germany. We argue that France's ambition to strengthen its influence within the EU and on the international scene by playing the double role of countering German monetarist, highly deflationary rules and mediating between Germany and the SP was compromised because of two weaknesses: externally, its economic decline relative to Germany and, internally, the long-term legacy of the dismantling of the break of its dirigiste model in 1983. In Section 2, following Levy (2016), we observe the difficulty of returning to a statist revival in the field of industrial policies when most of the tools of statist industrial policy have been dismantled. The process of liberalization of the French labour market, the increasing segmentation of the labour market, together with the attempt to anaesthetize the social and economic

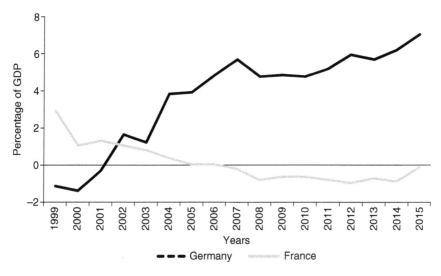

Figure 3.2 French and German current account balance (% of GDP, 1999–2015).
Source: authors' elaboration on Eurostat data.

consequences with a massive expansion of social expenditure are illustrated in Section 3. Finally, we explore the relative structural decline of France focusing on the weakening of a key manufacturing industry – automotive.

2 From dirigisme to statist liberalism

France's European policy was guided by the desire for political leadership within Europe. This was pursued by cultivating a special partnership with Germany, while preserving elements of its statist model. The growing discrepancy between French and German economic power convinced the French governments to trade their statist, pro-growth convictions, for political relevance. However, France's increasing economic weakness has undermined its 'effort to advance a substantive alternative to the German vision of a European economic future modelled on budgetary rigor, export competitiveness, and monetarism' (Vail, 2015: 139) and its ability to mediate between Northern and Southern Europe.

Mitterrand's 'turn to rigour'

For many years after the war, French and Japanese systems were similar as an example of state-led political economy (Levy, 2013). Through a number of industrial policy instruments (multiannual programming, selective protectionism, selective credit control) the state authorities had guided the strategies of firms choosing sectors to be promoted, favouring large corporations over small firms, protecting corporate profits through frequent devaluations and low direct and indirect labour costs. Despite some mistakes, the development policy of *grands projets* placed France at the top in industries such as high-speed trains, nuclear power and digital telecommunications switches. 'Within a generation', Levy (2013: 327) writes, 'under state guidance, France was transformed from a sleepy, backward, peasant economy to one of the world's most affluent and advanced industrial powers.'

In the 1970s in a rapidly changing environment and a period of intense international competition, this business guidance policy began to falter, also for the increased pressure to use industrial policy to bail out firms operating in the heavy industry sectors hit by the crisis.

A profound change took place in 1983, when the Mitterrand government, elected two years earlier with a strongly dirigiste electoral programme, carried out an expansive policy, in countertendency with the European cycle. The 1970s crisis – characterized by a halt in economic growth and a strong increase in unemployment – represented the background of such developments. The main pillars of the 1981 electoral programme – designed during the 1970s by a coalition including the French Communist and Socialist parties as well as the largest trade unions (Barba and Pivetti, 2016) – were: (i) a strong increase in public demand and investments; (ii) a rise of wages in the public sector; (iii) the nationalization of large firms operating in strategic sectors; (iv) tight controls on the financial sector; (v) the introduction of tariffs and other measures to reduce the dependence on foreign goods and spur domestic production (Amable *et al.*, 2011). The programme wanted to

> develop stepped-up industrial policies designed thoroughly to restructure the French economy while pursuing a 'rupture with capitalism'. This policy of 'redistributive Keynesianism' aimed to enact the left's electoral promises to create jobs, support consumption and incomes, and shelter workers from increasingly widespread economic dislocation.
>
> (Vail, 2015: 141)

It thus involved reorganizing the supply side of the economy, while stimulating demand, and conquering the domestic market.

The government started to implement the first three pillars of the programme, but the pillar on limitations on imports was not realized. Political as well as domestic and international economic pressures may have played a role in this choice (Barba and Pivetti, 2016). Without a parallel control of imports, the sudden demand boost (through rising wages and public investments) led to a heavy trade deficit. Under the pressure of the international speculation, the government made an abrupt U-turn, opting for budget cuts, macroeconomic deflationary policies, and a series of reforms that reversed the previous nationalizations and dismantled the institutions governing the interventionist policy. The option to remain in the EMS – which entailed three devaluations in two years to counter the increase in inflation – inaugurated a period of 'statist liberalism', a model that tried to keep together the state as the central guide of economic policy, responsible for equality, growth and job creation, with a neo-liberal approach to fiscal and monetary policy.[1] Under governments of different political orientation, industrial policy was virtually abandoned. Mitterrand's 'turn to rigour' succeeded in lowering inflation, but increased unemployment. Due to resolve to remain in the EMS, during this period, the French macro-economic policy remained focused on fighting inflation, to safeguard the nominal peg between the French franc and the Deutsche mark. This meant adopting a pro-cyclical stance, in spite of the recurring economic slowdowns (Amable *et al.*, 2011). As expected, the objective of low inflation and currency stabilization came at the price of persistently high unemployment rates. It also inaugurated a change in the French Left that, abandoning the alliance with the Communist party, started its shift to the centre (Amable *et al.*, 2011).

During the remaining of the 1980s and in the 1990s, successive French governments embarked on a remarkable process of market making. Most of the public enterprises were privatized, the financial system was liberalized, controls on capital movements were eliminated, and restrictions on layoffs, on part-time and temporary hires were reduced. 'Looking across the wealthy democracies', noted Levy (2013: 328), 'one would be hard-pressed to find any country that shifted so far away from its post-war economic strategy as the France of François Mitterrand and Jacques Chirac.' It was a 'liberalization by stealth' as Gordon and Meunier (2001) wrote, because the political discourse either maintained a 'voluntarist' attitude while conducting 'quietly, under the radar' liberalizing reforms, or tended to attribute responsibility to the European Commission.

Neoliberalism and social anaesthesia

Overall, French governments (particularly those of the centre-left) tried to strike a compromise between structural reforms, to ensure more freedom to capital, and the preservation of the French social model by strengthening welfare state and social protection, to overcome the strong opposition coming from both the centre-left and the centre-right blocs (Amable *et al.*, 2011).[2] Many of these liberalization measures had been taken, as Levy notes (2013: 331), in the belief that greater labour flexibility would quickly generate new jobs. This belief explains the decision to employ vast resources (which it was believed would be temporary) in the expansion of social and labour market programmes 'to cushion the blow to industrial workers and other groups made vulnerable by movement away from *dirigisme*' (ibid.: 328). These measures also reflect what Levy calls 'a social anaesthesia logic; that is, they sought to permit French firms to reorganize on a market-rational basis by pacifying and demobilizing the potential victims and opponents of economic liberalization' (ibid.: 328).

In fact, the liberalization measures of the labour market did not give the desired result: the continuing high levels of unemployment not only made it difficult to consider temporary measures (especially early retirement plans) taken to reduce social hardship, but rather demanded new massive injections of social

spending. In short, 'the "de-dirigisation" and the expansion of the social anaesthesia state were two sides of the same (very expensive) coin' (ibid.: 331). The
absorption of significant resources for social protection limited the scope for
public investment, preventing a reorientation of public intervention to cope with
the new tasks of enterprises guidance required by the changed situation. In conclusion, according to Levy, the hasty manner in which government implemented
the break with dirigisme in 1983 has limited the institutional, fiscal and political
resources needed to find a composition in the trilemma of liberalization, new
forms of public intervention and social protection. This introduced strong constraints to the decisions of all governments, of whatever political orientation,
which since then have followed. The persistent, unrealistic and inconclusive
oscillation between neo-interventionist and neo-liberal objectives even by the
same government reveals the absence of a sufficiently clear and coherent strategy
to be able to tackle the persistent legacies of the U-turn of 1983.

Overall, the labour market reforms undertaken in France since the 1990s have
contributed to generate a 'two-tier' system (Vlandas, 2017). The gradual liberalization of the use of fixed-term and/or non-standard employment contracts
favoured the segmentation between workers enrolled with open-ended contracts,
still enjoying strong protections, and precarious workers facing comparatively
more uncertain conditions with regard to job and income stability. The resultant
increase in job turnover and income inequality among workers could have hindered the process of human capital accumulation (Le Barbanchon and Malherbet, 2013),[3] thus contributing to weaken the rejuvenation of the French economy.
Despite its peculiar features, the French policies of flexibilization of the labour
market seem to have produced results not dissimilar from those observable in the
SP (Cirillo *et al.*, 2016; Guarascio and Simonazzi, 2016).

The European economic and monetary integration, and the French acceptance
of the institutional and practical rules required by Germany, are behind the
choices that Left governments put forth since the 'turn to rigour' in 1983. The
liberalization of capital movements,[4] in particular, coincided with a strategy
aimed at breaking with fiscal complacency and drastically and lastingly reducing
deficits. The restrictive monetary policy that followed was characterized by a
strong increase in real interest rates, justified by the need to adjust the French
fiscal and monetary systems to the requirements of the impending prospect of
European monetary union. The governments in charge along the 2000s tried to
push further the process of neoliberalization of the French economy.

A statist revival?

The 2008 economic crisis worsened this scenario: slow growth, long unemployment spells and rising public expenditure implying a growing public finance
problem, induced mostly by the operation of the automatic stabilizers and the
countercyclical interventions implemented between 2008 and 2010.

According to Levy (2016: 1), the financial meltdown prompted an apparent
revival of the statist economic model: 'French President, Nicholas Sarkozy

denounced laissez-faire capitalism, which he blamed for the crisis, and launched a series of industrial policy initiatives.' Moreover, he tried to mediate between continuing to pursue the neoliberal agenda while addressing the upheaval of those social groups losing more from the policies of liberalization and deregulation.[5] However, argues Levy (2016: 19),

> the government's neo-statist thrust ran up against long-standing developments in French economic policy, most notably the dismantling of most of the tools of statist industrial policy in the 1980s and early 1990s and the massive accompanying expansion of social and labor market programs that left little room for new public spending. Thus, even at a moment of crisis, French economic policy displayed a strong path-dependent character. The legacies of the movement from the dirigiste state to the social anaesthesia state in the mid-1980s essentially trumped President Sarkozy's neo-dirigiste aspirations a quarter-century later.

The attempt of reconciling deregulation with the preservation of a robust social protection system met with serious difficulties due to the increasing weakness of the French economy. Given the relatively high unemployment rate and the constraints on fiscal resources, the effectiveness of a 'French way' to labour market flexibility required a set of conditions hard to be met in the economic and financial conditions of France.[6]

The second problem concerns France's difficult partnership with Germany, and the obligations entailed to stand up to this special relation. The crisis-induced rise in public debt required a further move on the austerity and liberalization processes. At first, between 2008 and 2013, the French governments turned to Keynesian demand management and industrial policy, with stimulus packages and tax cuts heavily skewed toward business (Levy, 2016: 7). The attempt to return to a statist revival, however, soon ran counter to the worsening of the Eurozone financial crisis, the stiffening of the German stance and the tightening of the French fiscal constraints. By the end of his presidency, Sarkozy turned to fiscal orthodoxy. In spite of the anti-austerity promises of the electoral campaign, François Hollande's government continued the austerity agenda, though mitigated by a two-year deferral of the obligation to bring the deficit/GDP ratio down to 3 per cent, granted by the EC in May 2013. This gave France more leeway on fiscal policy, compared with the Southern countries' governments. Moreover, the new government aimed to shift the burden on the wealthiest sectors of the French society, so as not to erode the political consensus among the traditional centre-left voters (Cavero and Poinasamy, 2013).[7]

Also on the labour market the Hollande government continued a policy of flexibility, only slightly tempered by ever weaker social measures (Vlandas, 2017).[8] The key reforms introduced in France faced strong social opposition. The *Loi Travail*, finally approved in 2016,[9] can be considered the most pervasive flexibilization measure put in place in France since the outbreak of the crisis.

The rise (and fall) of finance

The liberalization of the financial markets within the EU and the neoliberal pro-gramme implemented by the French governments since the 1980s, which reduced the control of the state on the allocation of resources, favoured the rise of the financial sector. In this respect, Figures 3.3 and 3.4 report the dynamics of liabilities and equities held by French, German and Italian non-financial corpora-tion over the period 1995–2015. As the figures clearly display, both the indic-ators point to a significant financialization of the French economy. As Alvarez (2015: 450) underlines, 'over the past three decades, France has experienced one of the most intense liberalization and financialization processes of any OECD country'. The financialization of the French economy was driven by factors common to the other countries (see Chapter 7): the diffusion of corporate gov-ernance models aimed at maximizing shareholder value and financial profit-ability and the increasing participation of non-financial corporations in financial activities. The importance of financial investors in the management of non-financial corporations increased and the same occurred with respect to foreign penetration into French firms' stocks. Alvarez (2015: 451), for example, signals that during this period 'Anglo-Saxon institutional investors have acquired large equity stakes in French corporations, achieving a spectacular degree of foreign penetration.' All these factors contributed to increase the economic and political relevance of the financial sector.

Similarly to the dynamics illustrated by Krippner (2011) for the US case, such changes in corporate governance favour the passage from a management arrangement based on 'a strong control by the board of directors and managers

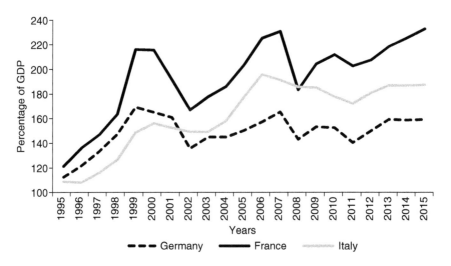

Figure 3.3 French, German and Italian non-financial corporations liabilities (% GDP, 1995–2015).

Source: authors' elaboration on Eurostat data.

to a shareholder model based on external control by liberalized financial markets' (Alvarez, 2015: 451). That is, managerial choices of French non-financial corporations are increasingly constrained by the need to maximize shareholder value, on one side; and by the pressure exerted by financial investors, on the other. The result has been higher pay-out ratios to capital markets, which skewed corporate profits towards investment in financial rather than real assets. Shifting managers' preferences towards short-term profits, financialization favoured a dynamics of underinvestment, providing an additional explanation for the drop in investments and gross fixed capital accumulation described by Levy (2008), as well as for the fall in competitiveness of manufacturing. Following Krippner (2011)'s conceptualization of the financialization process – measured by the increase in financial investments by non-financial corporations – Alvarez (2015) show how French non-financial corporations substantially increased their financial assets share. Between 1978 and 2013, the share of financial assets in the total assets of French non-financial corporations increased from 36.4 per cent to 59 per cent, among these stocks and loans to other non-financial corporations. As a consequence, we observe an astounding increase in financial income of non-financial corporations as a percentage of gross operating surplus: it increased from 5 per cent to 8 per cent during the 1950s and 1960s and jumped to 60 per cent in 2013 (Alvarez, 2015: 454).

The change in the financial choices of non-financial corporations was favoured by the deregulation of financial markets, which allowed to funds to be raised by issuing equities, thus reducing their dependence on state-allocated credit and on the banking sector. It was accompanied by a parallel change in the banking sector, which expanded and changed its 'nature' in line with the (neo-liberal) regime

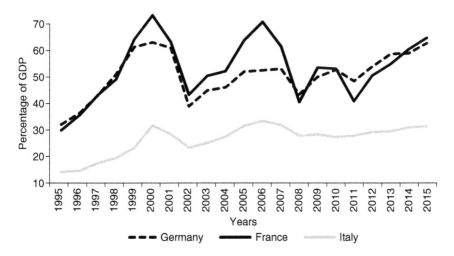

Figure 3.4 Equities held by French, German and Italian non-financial corporations (% GDP, 1995–2015).

Source: authors' elaboration on Eurostat data.

change that unfolded from the 1980s onwards. Many of the banks that had been nationalized in the post-war period and during the Socialists' first years in office were privatized. No longer constrained by public control over allocation of resources, banks could focus on profitability. The French financial system (together with the German one) plays an important role in fuelling the intra-EZ debit/credit relationships which unfolded after the euro inception (Veronese Passarella, 2014; O'Connell, 2015). German and French banks had the lion's share of the funds intermediated to the Southern periphery (SP) (Forster *et al.*, 2011). French banks were particularly aggressive: between 2001 and 2006, the amount of Greek, Irish, Italian, Portuguese and Spanish assets held by French financial institutions jumped from 10 per cent to more than 25 per cent of French GDP (Chen *et al.*, 2013: 105). Although an analogous trend is detectable for German–SP bilateral relationships, there is a relevant difference. Germany increased its net external position also with the rest of the EU, while France strengthened its position towards the SP but ran a net debt position with the rest of the world (ibid.: 101). When the financial crisis broke out, the greater exposure of the French banks to the periphery determined the greater weakness of the French financial system compared with the German one, notwithstanding the latter's exposure to the subprime losses.

To conclude, in the last decades leading to the formation of the European monetary union, France experienced a 'regime change', from a model based on strong state control on market forces to a neoliberal model characterized by deregulation and (gradual) labour market flexibilization. Several factors led to this evolution: the international constraints and the obligations connected with the implementation of the EMU project, the shift in the mindset of French élites and the need to adhere to the German monetary orthodoxy as a condition for France's special partnership with Germany. However, the French way to neo-liberalism proved to be a 'peculiar' one. The French governments tried to reconcile neoliberalism – meeting its strongholds: free movement of capital and goods and reduction of state interventionism – with the maintenance of the fundamental pillars of the French social protection system. This 'softer' liberalization, which differentiates France from its southern fellow countries, met with increasing difficulties after the 2008 crisis. The weakening of the French economy undermined its credibility as a counterweight to Germany, and compromised its ability to mediate between Germany and the European periphery.

3 The waning of a key sector: the automotive industry

In the previous section, we argued that the various governments, from the Left and from the Right, tried to combine German-style monetarism with interventions in the industrial and social fields. What explains then the increasing weakness of the French economy and industry compared with Germany? Did the Monetary Union affect French economic performance and its capacity to restructure its economy before and after the 2008 crisis? Undoubtedly, the European constraints on public deficits limited the resources that could be allocated to social protection and public investment, though these constraints were applied more flexibly in the case of France. Their strictness depends also on the rate of growth of the economy and on the parallel development of the external deficit.

In 1999, the budget deficit was 1.78 per cent of GDP and the current account showed a small surplus, but the unemployment rate was 10.4 per cent. Between 2002 and 2004, unemployment was only 1 per cent lower, but the public budget exceeded the 3 per cent limit set at Maastricht, which made difficult to sustain aggregate demand further through the public budget. Moreover, despite the reduced growth, the current account balance, and in particular the trade balance, showed a continuing deterioration. By 2008, the external deficit exceeded 4 per cent of GDP and the public deficit was 3.3 per cent of GDP. Without a coordinated action at the EU level, the presence of the twin deficits made it difficult to start the anti-cyclical policy that was needed to counteract the effects of the recession. The constraint did not come from an 'implicit finance constraint', signalled by the external deficit, that a well-functioning monetary union would a priori exclude, but from the enforcement of the Maastricht criteria on public budgets (though interpreted with some flexibility), which would leave only net exports to compensate for a persistent weakening of internal demand.

The trade balance deteriorated over time since the early 2000s, becoming negative since 2005. What caused this persistent deterioration? We do not claim to explain its absolute performance (since many factors combine to its determination), focusing instead on two aspects. The first concerns the analysis of the *different* performance of the import/export ratio for groups of products within the trade balance. The second aspect concerns the comparison of the French and German trade balances.

As for the first aspect, the sign reversal in the trade balance is significantly attributable to the performance of the car industry. The automotive balance showed a tendency to decline since the early 1970s to the mid-1980s, to stabilize in a positive area until the early 2000s (see Chapter 6 for an empirical exploration of these dynamics). Between 2004 and 2011 it turned from a surplus of €11 billion to a deficit of €8 billion (of which €7 billion was with Germany alone), dragging the French trade balance with it. The 2004–2011 decline in French car exports explains 32 per cent of the decline of the manufacturing trade balance and 17 per cent of the total trade balance. While the French trade balance has worsened uninterruptedly, in particular since 2004, the German trade balance has exhibited ever-higher surpluses. Also in the case of Germany, the auto industry significantly affects the trend of the overall trade balance (even more than in France). The car surplus rose from +€58 billion in 2004 to +€103 billion in 2011, accounting for two-thirds of the total German trade surplus in 2012. It should be noted that while imports of cars (including components) grew in the two countries (4.5 per cent in Germany and 3 per cent in France), exports grew by 5 per cent in Germany but decreased by 0.4 per cent in France. In 2011, German exports exceeded the level of 2007, while French exports were 20 per cent below.

The differential performance of the trade balance of the auto industry in France and Germany is puzzling, especially when considering the efforts spent by several French governments in support of the industry, deemed 'too big to fail' (Levy, 2016: 8).[10] In the year the French trade balance for cars turned into deficit, the share of cars manufactured abroad by French firms overtook the share manufactured domestically. This suggests that the offshoring strategies adopted by the automotive firms in the two countries can play a role in explaining the different performance. French manufacturers (Renault, PSA, former Peugeot-Citroen) have adopted a strategy of complete relocation of production abroad. This is reflected in the composition of imports of automotive products: 73 per cent cars, 27 per cent components. Conversely, the German firms (Volkswagen, BMW, Mercedes) have focused mainly on strategies of vertical integration, that is, the off-shoring of parts and components, which account for 41 per cent of total imports of car-related products, implying the maintenance domestically of the final assembly (as well as of strategic stages of the production process such as R&D). Indeed, among the most relevant factors that explain the exceptional growth of the German exports of cars is the outsourcing of the intermediate phases, along with the positioning of a high proportion of the production in the high range (relatively inelastic to price and elastic to income), and the high proportion destined to dynamic markets (i.e. China).

Given the high incidence of the sector in total exports (and in the overall balance), it is hardly surprising that the determinants of the performance of the German total exports (see Danninger and Joutz, 2007) overlap to a large extent to those of the automotive sectors. As demonstrated in Chapter 6, the offshoring strategies put in place by Germany, France (and Italy) are radically different. In the German case, the share of cars produced domestically in total production, albeit decreasing, remains much more stable than is the case for the other countries. The decline of the Italian share (due to the outsourcing strategy pursued by Fiat) precedes the decline of the French share, to finally converge with it.

Considering the product quality, the car market can be divided into three segments (high, medium and low). What seemed a different *strategy in the localization* of the same product, proves to be mostly a different *strategy of specialization* of products belonging to different segments. Of the German car production, 45 per cent falls into the medium and high range. Of this share, 30 per cent is produced inside and 15 per cent abroad. Of the remaining 52 per cent of the German production destined to the lower segment, 17 per cent is produced domestically and 35 per cent abroad. Conversely, 74 per cent of the French production belongs to the lower range, of which 21 per cent is produced domestically, a share not too different from the German share (17 per cent). Only 19 per cent of the French production is destined to the two top segments, the bulk of which (14 per cent) is produced abroad.

In conclusion, before the EMU, the major European car manufacturers adopted different strategies concerning both the range of products and the localization of their supply chains. The specific choices made by companies – sometimes, as in the case of Renault, with direct intervention by the state – have affected the trade balance (and employment) of the countries where their headquarters are located. The impact on trade balance was positive in Germany, negative in France (and in Italy).

What implications can we draw from this case? Trade deficits are often interpreted as an indicator of excess demand and/or inefficient use of resources, thus validating measures aimed to curb domestic demand in order to redirect the resources towards higher net exports. The costs deriving from the strategic choices of those companies who have resorted extensively to offshoring are doubly socialized: they entail the loss of industrial jobs due to relocation, and the loss of employment (and productive capacity) due to deflationary measures. Failing to recognize the 'micro' origin of the trade deficits, and by intervening at the aggregate level, these measures create new problems without offering solutions capable to solve the initial problem, which has do to with the impoverishment of the domestic productive structure. Germany, whose automakers specialized in relatively higher segments, while outsourcing intermediate products, has succeeded, thanks to the growth of net exports, to hold inside a larger share of sales and employment. However, this has also entailed significant social costs, both direct (due to the increase of outsourcing), and indirect, due to the formation of a two-tier labour market based on low wages and precarious work: two conditions associated with the stable achievement of large trade surpluses.

Our analysis of the change of economic relations between two core-countries, Germany and France, during the 2000s raises other two considerations. Changes in the market share of exports, in import penetration, or in trade deficits (or surpluses) are usually attributed to price competitiveness. Yet, it is difficult to admit that the internationalization strategy of companies has no influence on the performance of exports and imports of the sectors where they belong, and thus on the country's market shares and aggregate balances. Failure to take into account the influence of these strategies does not help in distinguishing *true* cases of loss of price competitiveness from the effects on exports and imports of strategies carried out in response to changing business conditions (price, cost, market, technology, etc.) and based on different forms of internationalization. If the latter result in the substitution of exports (or domestic production) with foreign production, they will cause – all things being equal, that is, if not compensated – a reduction of aggregate demand, of effective and potential output (through lower present and future investments), and thus of measured productivity. Both strategies – complete relocation and vertical integration – open the possibility of a fissure between the maintenance of a competitive edge by firms and by the country as a social system – interpreted as its ability to defend its residents' jobs and incomes. The existence of this gap can help explain the spread of temporary and underpaid jobs and the increase of the working poor, and the coexistence of high profits and industrial stagnation.

Finally, the diverging trade balances of France and Germany raise a more general problem concerning the unit of analysis. If the performance of a single sector (in our case the automotive sector), determined by the strategic choices of its firms, is able to explain a significant part of the performance of the aggregate (trade balance), the macroeconomic explanations (the exchange rate, the aggregate level of demand and/or supply, the regime and overall structure of the labour market) lose clout to the benefit of explanations that call into question other factors, such as the specific type of product (exclusive or mass consumption), market segmentation, 'make-or-buy' strategy, and the strength of domestic and foreign upstream and downstream linkages. All these aspects solicit, in case of crisis or the need to support the economy, industrial policy interventions. Exclusively macroeconomic interpretations lead to misdiagnosis and to equally erroneous therapies.[11]

4 Conclusions

The euro crisis accelerated the shift in the balance of power away from Paris towards Berlin. More and more, France looks like 'a core member state with periphery characteristics' (Matthijs and Blyth, 2015: 254). Despite its ambiguities, France's *dirigiste* and neo-Keynesian vision, stressing full employment, policy flexibility and solidarity had provided a (more or less effective) counterbalance to the German stance for stability, rules and fiscal restraint. The weakening of France's economic weight within the Eurozone leaves Germany as the one who decides. French leaders may feel compelled to follow the German quest for fiscal consolidation and structural reforms, thereby abdicating their ambition to mediate between the core and the SP. If this is the case, the Eurozone may be heading towards a Germanic setting with a technocratic edge (Legrain, 2014). As argued by Matthijs and Blyth (2015: 268), 'The major current risks to the euro stem from the attempt to make national-level austerity and structural reform superior objectives to restoring Eurozone growth and championing EU political reform.' Indeed, 'if the policy menu … is unending fiscal austerity, then quite apart from deflationary risks or GDP shrinkage, the sheer political sustainability of such policies comes into question' (ibid.: 266). Whether this will prove politically sustainable in the longer term or might provoke the Eurozone break-up is an open question.

Notes

1 This is when Jacques Delors enters the scene, reshaping the philosophy and contents of the French left government's programme. In particular, the use of extensive nationalizations and import controls as key industrial policy tools were turned back. Moreover, the political rise of Jacques Delors coincided with the substitution of the traditional Socialist objectives of equality and workers' empowerment with the idealization of the European integration as a sovra-ordinated political objective supposed to unify social classes beyond their naturally conflicting interests (for a discussion on this point, see Barba and Pivetti, 2016).

2   These changes were thus traded against extensions of employment protection, an increase in public employment and the 35-hours week, itself an ambiguous reform which decreased the duration of the legal working week while at the same time extending the flexibility of work organisation. The logic behind those reforms was the achievement of a transformation of the French model into a neoliberal/social hybrid model, whose stability is highly questionable if one considers the complementarity between institutions.…

(Amable *et al.*, 2011: 20)

3 By increasing job turnover, the diffusion of temporary employment may impact on both firms' and workers' decisions regarding training and education.
4 The full liberalization of capital movements in the EU was agreed in 1988 (Directive 88/361/EEC) and came into effect in 1990 for most member states, while for the rest specific transitional periods were agreed.

5   The search of a mediation led [the Sarkozy government] to follow two directions. The first one is the promise of a possible rise in purchasing power by an increase of the labour supply [to be achieved through] ... drop in taxes for overtime earnings and an easing of the regulation on overtime work ... emptying the 35-hour week regulation of its most social contents without actually abolishing it ... while at the same time keeping and even extending the work organisation flexibility measures. The second direction was the assurance that the way followed for the flexibilisation of the labour market would be a French-style flexicurity and not pure and simple Anglo-Saxon style flexibility ... a gentler neo-liberalisation ... or a 'rupture tranquille'.

(Amable *et al.*, 2011: 37)

6 An effective flexicurity system – implying high external flexibility (poor protection against lay-offs and various forms of temporary employment) accompanied by a strong safety net for workers losing their job – requires short unemployment spells, and generous compensation and adequate training for those losing their job.
7 The key measures included a tax rate of up to 75 per cent on earnings above €1 million per year, the elimination of fiscal incentives for large companies and €10 billion of cuts in public spending. Despite its progressive intentions, the austerity agenda ended up affecting the entire population. Also because of the measures adopted in 2014, when the French Parliament approved a new set of interventions aimed at saving €20 billion (including €5 billion in direct cuts from ministerial budgets). The VAT was raised from 19.6 per cent to 20 per cent.
8 With the 'Loi portant sur la sécurisation de l'emploi', the period in which the dismissal may be legally contested is reduced from 12 to three months, thus reducing the uncertainty (and the cost) faced by companies willing to dismiss part of their workforce. To soften the impact of such intervention, firms employing more than 50 workers are required to draft a 'social plan' to support the dismissed workers. In addition, the Hollande government reduced the 'prescription period', i.e. the period granted to a dismissed employee to contest the dismissal – from five to two years. On similar lines, the *Accord de maintien de l'emploi* allows companies declaring a state of 'economic difficulty' to negotiate with trade unions 'an "adjustment of wages/ working time for no longer than two years ... [specifying] that those who refuse can be dismissed under individual economic dismissals", which is easier than collective dismissals, thereby linking external with internal flexibility' (Vlandas, 2017: 192).
9 This Law allows firms to lay off workers if a drop in sales occurs; to change working time organization in case of demand fluctuations (both up and downward); and it allows to set overtime payments for hours worked beyond France's statutory 35-hour workweek below the level decided at the national/sectoral level.
10 Still in 2009 the Sarkozy administration intervened to help domestic manufacturers and their subcontractors with subsidized loans, besides the French version of the 'cash for clunkers' programme. France was not alone in supporting the French auto industry, other countries, Germany and the United States included, intervened to support their own industries (Levy, 2016).
11 Recent writings have highlighted the contribution of idiosyncratic shocks originated at the industry or enterprise level in generating aggregate fluctuations. Gabaix (2011: 734) argued that 'many economic fluctuations are attributable to the incompressible "grains" of economic activity, the large firms'. When, 'as in modern economies', the firm size distribution is extremely fat-tailed (the economy is 'granular') idiosyncratic

shocks to these firms will not average out (the law of large numbers does not apply) leading instead to not trivial aggregate movements. This direct effect is amplified across the economy through firms' linkages. See also Di Giovanni *et al.* (2014: 1305) who show that in more concentrated industries such as transport, petroleum and motor vehicles, firm-specific shocks contribute more to aggregate volatility than firm-specific shocks in less concentrated and less connected sectors. As Gabaix (2011) points out, these results do not depend in any way on the assumption that idiosyncratic shocks are related to productivity, whose exogeneity, contrary to what is generally claimed, is far from clear.

References

Alvarez, I. (2015). Financialization, non-financial corporations and income inequality: The case of France. *Socio-Economic Review*, 13(3), 449–475.

Amable, B., Guillaud, E. and Palombarini, S. (2011). The political economy of neo-liberalism in Italy and France. *Documents de travail du Centre d'Economie de la Sorbonne 2011.51* – ISSN: 1955–611X.

Barba, A. and Pivetti, M. (2016). *La scomparsa della sinistra in Europa*. Reggio Emilia: Imprimatur.

Cavero, T. and Poinasamy, K. (2013). A cautionary tale: The true cost of austerity and inequality in Europe. *Oxfam Briefing Paper No. 174*, Oxfam International.

Chen, R., Milesi-Ferretti, G. M. and Tressel, T. (2013). External imbalances in the euro-zone. *Economic Policy*, 28(73), 101–142.

Cirillo, V., Fana, M. and Guarascio, D. (2016). Labour market reforms in Italy: Evaluating the effects of the Jobs Act. *Economia Politica*, 1–22, online first article.

Danninger, S. and Joutz, F. (2007). What explains Germany's rebounding export market share? *IMF Working Paper WP/07/24*. Washington, DC: IMF.

Di Giovanni, J., Levchenko, A. A. and Méjean, I. (2014). Firms, destinations, and aggregate fluctuations. *Econometrica*, 82(4), 1303–1340.

Forster, K., Vasardani, M. A. and Ca'Zorzi, M. (2011). Euro area cross-border financial flows and the global financial crisis. *European Central Bank Occasional Paper No. 126*.

Gabaix, X. (2011). The granular origins of aggregate fluctuations. *Econometrica*, 79(3), 733–772.

Gordon, P. H. and Meunier, S. (2001). Globalization and French cultural identity. *French Politics, Culture & Society*, 19(1), 22–41.

Guarascio, D. and Simonazzi, A. (2016). A polarized country in a polarized Europe: An industrial policy for Italy's renaissance. *Economia e Politica Industriale*, 3(43), 315–322.

Krippner, G. R. (2011). *Capitalizing on Crisis*. Cambridge, MA: Harvard University Press.

Le Barbanchon, T. and Malherbet, F. (2013). An anatomy of the French labour market: Country case study on labour market segmentation. *ILO Employment Working Paper No. 142*.

Legrain, P. (2014). *How to Finish the Euro House*. CER (Centre for European Reform), June. www.cer.eu/sites/default/files/publications/attachments/pdf/2014/report_legrain_euro_house_june14-9111.pdf [accessed 16 June 2016].

Levy, J. D. (2008). From the dirigiste state to the social anaesthesia state: French economic policy in the longue durée. *Modern & Contemporary France*, 16(4), 417–435.

Levy, J. D. (2013). Directionless: French Economic policy in the twenty-first century. In D. Breznitz and J. Zysman (eds), *The Third Globalization: Can Wealthy Nations Stay Rich in the Twenty-First Century*. Oxford Scholarship Online, 323–349.

Levy, J. D. (2016). The return of the state? France's response to the financial and economic crisis. *Comparative European Politics*, 1–24. www.palgrave-journals.com/cep/ [accessed 14 September 2017].

Matthijs, M. and Blyth, M. (2015). Conclusion. The future of the euro: Possible futures, risks, and uncertainties. In M. Matthijs and M. Blyth (eds), *The Future of the Euro*. Oxford: Oxford University Press, 249–269.

O'Connell, A. (2015). European crisis: A new tale of center–periphery relations in the world of financial liberalization/globalization? *International Journal of Political Economy*, 44(3), 174–195.

Vail, M. I. (2015). Europe's middle child: France's statist liberalism and the conflicted politics of the euro. In M. Matthijs and M. Blaug (eds), *The Future of the Euro*. Oxford: Oxford University Press, 136–160.

Veronese Passarella, M. (2014). The process of financial integration of EU economies. *Financialisation, Economy, Society & Sustainable Development (FESSUD) Project*.

Vlandas, T. (2017). Labour market performance and deregulation in France during and after the crisis. In M. Myant and A. Pyasna (eds), *Myths of Employment Deregulation: How it Neither Creates Jobs Nor Reduces Labour Market Segmentation*. Brussels: ETUI books, 185–205.

4 The Eurozone's double-dip recession

Interpretations and policies

1 Introduction

After almost a decade since the start of the crisis, Southern European countries are still marred in stagnation, with high public debts and/or banking crises. Only a minority of the Eurozone member states recovered their pre-crisis production levels.

Europe's failure in recovering after the crisis has two main roots. The first concerns the growth model followed by the Eurozone before the crisis. We observe two divergent trajectories: the core countries' growth driven by exports of manufactured products and investments (in the Eastern periphery (EP)), aimed at consolidating the German production network; the Southern periphery (SP) relying mainly on debt-led consumption, sustained by financial and housing bubbles. Foreign capital plays a different role in the two peripheries. In the South, capital inflows finance real estate and consumption, leading to the accumulation of private debt, increasing current account deficits and greater fragility of the production structure. In the EP, FDI contributes to expand and modernize the productive base, strengthening the economy. The underlying increasing polarization of the productive structure affected the post-crisis *degree of resilience*.

The second root relates to the policies implemented in the crisis. The EZ lacked the countercyclical policies adopted by other industrial countries. In 2009, the expansive measures put in place by the US government – in coordination with the monetary policies activated by the Federal Reserve – have been impressive. An 847 billion dollar fiscal stimulus was accompanied by a huge expansion in the Fed's balance sheet. The American Recovery and Reinvestment Act of 2009 (ARRA), commonly referred to as *The Recovery Act*, responded to the 2008 crisis by saving and creating jobs, expanding unemployment benefits, providing temporary relief programmes for those most affected by the recession and pursuing public investments in infrastructure, education, health and renewable energy.[1]

In the EZ, there was no Europe-wide fiscal stimulus, due to the absence of an (adequate) common budget, nor coordination with the ECB, due to its independent status. After a brief 'Keynesian' spell, starting from 2009, all the EZ member states turned to fiscal austerity in order to reduce public debts and deficits, which had been increased by the bank bail-outs. After a first expansion of liquidity to avoid a financial meltdown, the ECB contracted its balance sheet and increased interest rates twice, in 2008 and in 2011.[2] The austerity agenda contributed to deepen and prolong the recession, especially in the South. The double-dip recession was a peculiarly European phenomenon. Between 2010 and 2014, the Eurozone countries implemented a huge contractionary policy

> equal to four percentage points of the monetary union's economy.... The GIIPS [Greece, Ireland, Italy, Portugal and Spain] accounted for 48% of the fiscal swing, even though they accounted for only a third of EZ's GDP. Eurozone core nations decided that they too had to embrace fiscal rectitude. As the monetary union's largest economy, tightening by Germany accounted for 32% of the Eurozone's overall fiscal tightening. France's austerity amounted to 13% of the Eurozone total.
>
> (CEPR, 2015: 10–11)

Owing to these austerity policies, only a few EZ nations have recovered their pre-crisis growth and employment rates, while socio-economic conditions worsened dramatically. The sovereign debt crisis has been averted (or, perhaps, magnified) by a rigorously deflationary fiscal policy that has been implemented without interruption since 2010. After July 2012, this was accompanied by a belated commitment on the part of the ECB to break the vicious circle of expectations that, in the absence of a debt-buyer of last resort, encouraged a massive liquidation of sovereign debt.

The crisis has differed across the EZ in characteristics, intensity and length, reflecting the asymmetries that divide core and periphery. In the SP, the crisis evolved in a strong and lengthy recession: a sharp drop in consumption, investments and GDP and a rapid rise in unemployment. Conversely, Germany (and the EP) showed a remarkable resilience: after the first two years of crisis, Germany and its production network started to grow again. The main driver has been the reorientation of exports from the stagnant SP's markets to the still rampant Asian ones. While the SP's productive capacity collapsed, with a reduction of 25 per cent in Italy and Spain and more than 30 per cent in Greece, the core maintained and in some cases increased its productive capacity – particularly in the manufacturing sector. Overall, the crisis seems to have fuelled opposite dynamics: de-industrialization in the Southern periphery and re-industrialization (or strengthening of the existing productive base) in the core (Cirillo and Guarascio, 2015; Dosi *et al.*, 2017). Similar dynamics characterize the labour market: the core recovered rapidly its pre-crisis employment levels; in the periphery, youth unemployment reached dramatic levels – 40 per cent in Italy, close to 50 per cent in Spain and Greece – and South–North migration of all kinds of workers – high and low skilled, as well as highly educated – restarted in great numbers.

If the crisis has accelerated the core-periphery divergence within the Eurozone – a process that is deepening the *structural* nature of the divide – its extent and duration is producing similar effects within the periphery (and possibly within the core too). The regional divides that characterize most peripheral economies – with a concentration of industry, jobs, infrastructure, networks, in their core[3] (see Chapter 5) – are increased by the structural effects of the crisis, magnifying the fragility of the SP's economies.

With households, corporations and governments simultaneously reducing expenditure, income and production have dropped and unemployment has soared, with youth and long-term unemployment and inactivity rates at record levels. Several years of harsh austerity have also taken their toll in terms of inequality and poverty, and have cancelled a significant part of the gains in living standards achieved by low-income households over the past 20 years. Welfare provisions have been cut everywhere: the European Union's ambitious targets for combating poverty and achieving social inclusion are self-delusive because of the constraints faced by the member states on the periphery, which were hardest hit during the crisis and are no longer in a position to ensure even a minimum level of social inclusion (Arpe *et al.*, 2015). The destruction of productive capacity, skill capabilities and welfare protection will take years to redress. Meanwhile, the euro area is churning out the world's largest current account surplus in value terms (approximately 3.0 per cent of GDP in 2015). The bulk of this is accounted for by Germany (7.9 per cent of GDP) and the Netherlands (10.6 per cent), but also the former deficit countries are now recording balanced or surplus positions. The austerity measures opened up a process of alignment with Germany also for other economic indicators of the peripheral countries: since 2010, the European periphery has achieved a significant reduction in unit labour costs compared with Germany and EU27 (Cirillo and Guarascio, 2015: 5).

In this chapter, we first review the interpretations that have been offered on the causes of the crisis. Interpreted as a balance of payments crisis due to debtor countries' 'reckless spending', this view overlooks the role played by the 'reckless lending' (O'Connell, 2015) of international capital and surplus countries' creditors, thus missing the concatenation of events that transform what had previously appeared to be a local sudden stop narrative into a broader, worldwide narrative of contagion (Section 2). Similarly, the interpretation of the Eurozone crisis as a balance of payments crisis tends to conceal the role played by the faulty institutional framework of the EMU (Section 3 on the Target2 discussion). Section 4 provides an overview of the austerity policies that have been implemented in the SP since the beginning of the crisis, which found a partial justification in the interpretation of the crisis and in the EMU's institutions, while Section 5 illustrates the consequences of these policies on the SP's industrial fabric.

2   A standard balance of payments crisis?

The first recession of the EZ (a cumulative drop of 3.7 percentage points of GDP in the years 2008–2009) was provoked by the fall in European exports (–11.7 per cent) due to the direct and indirect effects of the fall of US GDP. In the US, the crisis was triggered by the credit restriction implemented by the Federal Reserve, which burst the subprime housing market bubble, and it was compounded by two other deflationary channels: the fall in commodity prices and the sharp fall in the demand for manufactured goods following the drying up of credit caused by the failure of Lehman Brothers. It was a 'sudden, severe and synchronized collapse' (Baldwin, 2009: 79) of world trade,[4] of an extent comparable to that of the Great Depression of the 1930s, though much faster (it reached the trough in nine months instead of the 24 that it took in the 1930s). It differed also for the rapid reaction of the economic policy, in particular the expansionary fiscal policy of the US, which, thanks to the strong support of China's growth, made for a much shorter duration of the recession. The most affected sectors were those linked to export trade, while those tied to domestic demand were less affected. The opposite happened in the second recession, which began in 2010 and involved almost solely the EZ countries. The recession lasted much longer and hit especially the countries of Southern Europe (and to some extent France), thus deepening the gap in per capita income between Northern and Southern Europe. In addition, within each country, the sectors more affected were those more dependent on domestic demand, and, among these, the firms and the social segments located in the poorest areas and more dependent on the public budget for support.

The fact that the two crises have been described with two different names (the subprime crisis and the sovereign debt crisis) and have produced different outcomes in different countries could lead to underestimate the link of the second crisis with the first. This artificial separation gave rise to misleading interpretations (see the CEPR, 2015 document that will be examined below).

Before the crisis, none of the peripheral European countries, except Greece, showed the characteristics of public budget profligacy. This definitely disproves the idea that the so-called sovereign debt crisis was due in general to the presence of states that, after joining the Monetary Union, systematically lived beyond their means. Therefore, it would be more appropriate to define the crisis that hit the European countries in 2010 as a crisis of sovereign bonds markets. In both crises, the root cause was a *banking crisis* that required public intervention to avert dramatic systemic effects. In both situations, the presence of 'financial innovations', such as the securitization of bonds, allowed the banks to transfer the credit risk – by splitting and hiding it through special purpose vehicles – to non-bank holders of securities. Given the lack of loan loss provisions, these operations increased banks' ability to lend and the financial leverage. Hence, it is more correct to speak of 'private finance profligacy'. When the bubble burst, the systemic risk associated with the fall in the price of assets (house prices in the first crisis, government bonds in the second) and the drying up of credit required a strong public intervention, both in the US and in Europe, to stabilize banks' balance sheets, allowing the deleveraging and eventually the resumption of lending.

The United States did not experience a 'double-dip' recession – there, the recession took on the appearance of a V, not of a W. Why did apparently similar public interventions produce such different results? It is by now widely acknowledged that, in the US, the public policies prevented the transmission of the banking crisis to the securities market. In the Eurozone, instead, the bank risk was allowed to turn into a sovereign default risk. At that point, never reached in the United States, the austerity measures of the Eurozone governments blocked the expectations of default but, because of the fall in demand, at the price of a further fall in corporate loans.

The different outcomes of the crisis were influenced by differences both between the US and Europe, and within Europe. Among the latter were the strategies of the banks, the constraints on actors' behaviour imposed by public institutions, macroeconomic policies, the timing and size of the interventions, and the structural conditions of the economic systems in which these interventions were implemented. With regard to the differences between the US and Europe, banks' financial leverage at the beginning of the crisis (and therefore their different strategy following the deregulation of capital markets) has an important role. Before the crisis, the major European banks had a lower capital/assets ratio (the proportion of a bank Tier 1 capital to its total risk-weighted assets) than the US banks. The higher total assets/equity capital ratio exposed them to a greater risk of bankruptcy, and implied a higher potential cost to rescue them (see Cafruny, 2015). In the first crisis, the Fed quickly expanded the liquidity, a move accompanied by an equally rapid fiscal expansion. We know from Chapter 1 that institutional constraints reduced the freedom of action of the ECB; however, this does not explain the delay of the ECB in abandoning the thesis that labour market reforms, together with restrictive fiscal policies, would be necessary and sufficient to restore the stability of the financial system. Eventually, institutional and cultural constraints prevented the Eurozone from adopting an expansionary fiscal policy. Since synchronized austerity policies across the Eurozone reduced all the components of the aggregate demand except exports, only those countries (and regions) with a sufficiently broad export base – especially if directed to extra-EZ markets – managed to reduce the effects of the second crisis.

In November 2015, a conspicuous number of prestigious economists[5] signed a document entitled 'Rebooting the Eurozone: Step 1 – Agreeing a crisis narrative' (CEPR, 2015). Though claiming to come from different backgrounds, the authors found it 'surprisingly easy to agree upon a narrative and a list of the main causes of the EZ Crisis'. The key terms in their accounts are 'excessive intra-EZ capital flows' and 'sudden stop'. The crisis is interpreted as a standard balance of payments crisis that can be analysed using models previously applied to developing countries. A country's membership of a monetary union is considered irrelevant except for the greater opacity in signalling the risks involved in the formation of large capital flows imbalances. 'EZ also mattered since the incomplete institutional infrastructure [no lender of last resort, impossibility of devaluation] *amplified* the initial loss of trust in the deficit nations' (italics added). The main message, which assigns blame and transmits recipes for the future, is that 'All the nations stricken by the Crisis were running current account deficits. None of those running current account surpluses were hit.'

The paper contains three striking omissions, a number of unconvincing or contradictory statements, and an important admission. The first significant omission is the absence of any reference to the complementary relationship between the formation of persistent, growing current account surpluses by the core countries (in particular Germany) after 1999 and the corresponding deficits of the peripheral European countries with respect to Germany. Trade surpluses lead to debt imbalances. By definition, a current account deficit entails net capital inflows. Germany's large current account surpluses fuelled German banks' lending to the SP. The 'consensus narrative' of the causes of the crisis tends to neglect the surplus aspect (which could have prompted expansionary fantasies or, even worse, criticism of the export-led model), arguing that the crisis was triggered unilaterally by excessive foreign indebtedness on the part of the peripheral countries. Huge capital flows were drawn from the core to the periphery, facilitated by the monetary union and its regulatory framework.[6] Figure 4.1 reports the exposure of Northern European banks towards the SP before the crisis while Figure 4.2 shows the rise and fall of corporate loans in the SP.

Moreover, the CEPR (2015) narrative overlooks altogether that the major impact of foreign indebtedness, as discussed in Chapter 2, was on rising imports rather than on declining exports, suggesting the prevalence of income effects over price effects in explaining the deterioration of the SP's current accounts. The crisis started – we read in the CEPR document and see in Figure 4.1 – with a 'sudden stop' in cross-border lending: the EZ institutions and short-sighted governments' choices combined to trigger a vicious cycle between banks and their governments that amplified and spread the crisis. The term 'sudden stop' had previously been used in the literature to describe a sudden slowdown in private capital flows to emerging market economies after the formation of large current account deficits. It was usually followed by a sharp fall in demand, production and employment, and by drastic exchange rate depreciation. The assignment of a central role in the EZ crisis to a phenomenon observed in emerging markets is worth noting because the entire institutional architecture of the Monetary Union had been based instead on the assumption that countries that met the Maastricht criteria for accession were all on a level playing field.

As for the second important omission of the 'consensus narrative': what circumstances led to the 'sudden stop'? The CEPR document accepts the conventional story that the trigger was the newly elected Greek government's revelation that previous governments had concealed the size of the budget deficit. However, by examining the data on foreign debts held by credit institutions published by the Bank for International Settlements (BIS), Lindner (2013) has been able to trace the dual role that German and French investors, particularly banks, played at the start of the Eurozone crisis. This aspect is by now fairly well known, and we have anticipated it in Chapter 1. However, it is important to recall it here because this dual role connects the subprime crisis in the US with the Eurozone crisis that hit the European periphery: a concatenation of events transforms what had previously appeared to be a local sudden stop

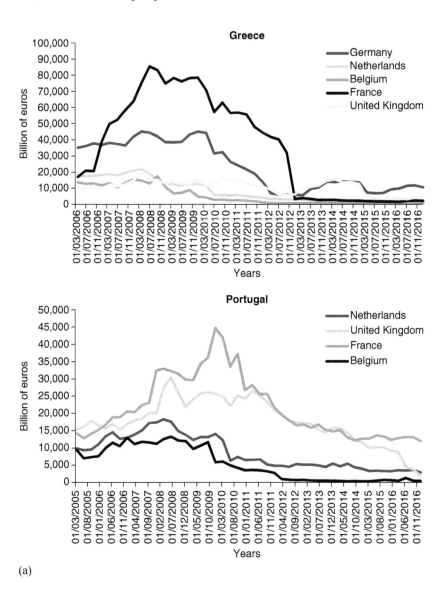

Figure 4.1 SP liabilities (all sectors) held by Belgian, Dutch, French, German and UK
banks (absolute values (billion of euro) – 2006–2016).

narrative into a broader, worldwide narrative of contagion. Lindner recalls that
before the Lehman Brothers' collapse (September 2008), French and German
financial institutions held almost a quarter of the debt that the US owed to
foreign banks. European banks had accumulated speculative positions buying
securitized US mortgages through off-balance-sheet Special Purpose Investment
Vehicles.

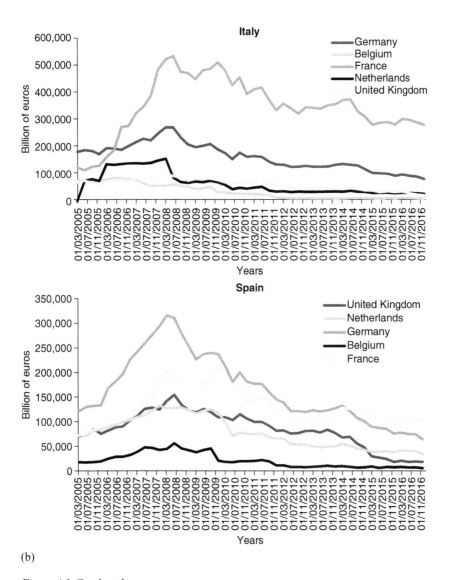

(b)

Figure 4.1 Continued

As we mentioned before, these lightly regulated 'shadow banks' need only a small amount of capital, and as a result have a high level of debt. As shown, in the middle of 2008, French and German financial institutions were also the largest creditors of the countries of the SP. At that time, French and German financial institutions accounted for 60 per cent of the amounts owed by Italy, 45 per cent in the case of Spain, 42 per cent in the case of Greece, 37 per cent in the case of Ireland and 33 per cent in the case of Portugal.[7] As a consequence of the US subprime crisis,

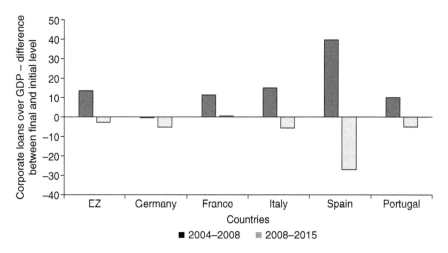

Figure 4.2 Corporate loans over GDP: EZ, Germany, France, Italy, Spain and Portugal: difference between final and initial level (2004–2008 and 2008–2015).

Source: authors' elaboration on Eurostat data.

Note
Between 2004 and 2008 the amount of corporate loans over GDP passed from 58 per cent to 71.5 per cent in the EZ; from 45.7 per cent and 45.2 per cent in Germany; from 59.6 per cent to 48.3 per cent in France; from 56 per cent to 70.6 per cent in Italy; from 73.6 per cent to 112.1 per cent in Spain; and from 80 per cent to 90 per cent in Portugal. Between 2008 and 2015, in turn, the indicator moved in the opposite direction passing from 71.5 per cent to 68.7 per cent in the EZ; from 45.2 per cent to 39.9 per cent in Germany; from 59.6 per cent to 60 per cent in France; from 70.6 per cent to 65.2 per cent in Italy; from 112.1 per cent to 85.5 per cent in Spain; and from 90 per cent to 84.9 per cent in Portugal.

which began in 2007, German and French financial institutions suffered large losses that have come to light only later, and in a partial and opaque way.[8]

In fact, the German banking system, supposedly more protectionist and conservative, recorded much higher losses than the more liberalized French system (Hardie and Howarth, 2009: 1018). Both systems have been internationalized, but while the French banks focused on the trading of lower-risk retail activities, the German banks have turned mainly to trading highly risky foreign assets as derivatives and investment in highly complex securities. During the years 2000–2007, compared to most OECD countries, the German banks showed a higher leverage (lower capital to asset ratio) and a relatively higher capital-to-risk-weighted assets ratio, signalling a higher under-pricing of credit risk, which explains their greater vulnerability.

At the base of an excessive risk taking is the lower profitability of German banks, which manifested itself already in the 1990s (Hüfner, 2010: 12–13). It stems more from lower non-interest income than from lower interest margins or higher operating costs. With regard to the first pillar of the German banking system, the commercial banks, a progressive distancing of large industrial enterprises from bank funding may have contributed to the banks' urgent search for alternative uses abroad. However, this occurred in even more striking form for the banks belonging to the second pillar, which includes public sector banks (Landesbanken, mostly owned by the states and municipalities, and Sparkassen, savings banks, mostly owned by local governments). In the past, Landesbanken enjoyed a state guarantee on their loans; they mainly provided services for the savings banks paying scant attention to profitability. Since 2002, the European Commission asked to eliminate the public guarantee on Landesbanken refinancing. However, 'a generous phasing-out period until 2005 allowed the banks to enter liabilities with government guarantee at a maximum duration until 2015' (ibid.: 9). At the same time, public institutions were increasing their pressure on Landesbanken to push them increasing profitability. Between 2005 and 2008, Landesbanken increased 'the volume of their capital market refinancing sharply, accumulating large funding reserves, as refinancing costs would rise sharply once the state guarantees vanished' (ibid.: 10).[9]

Overall, the crisis highlighted deficiencies in both banking regulation and supervision. In Germany, in particular, the German Financial Supervisory Authority (Bundesanstalt für die Finanzdiensleinstungsaufsicht, BaFin) did not issue early warnings on the risks associated with the build-up of large liquidity stocks during the phasing out of government guarantees. As Hüfner (2010: 17) points out,

> interference with the business models of some state-owned banks may have been delicate for BaFin as it is working under the legal and technical oversight of the Ministry of Finance, which itself has representatives on the supervisory boards of the supervised banks.

In the progression of the crisis (August 2007), the French bank BNP Paribas had suspended two funds involved in the US mortgage market. Other French banks were having difficulties securing funds in the interbank markets. In July 2007, the German IKB, which had dealt substantially in US mortgage securities, announced that it had been severely affected by the subprime crisis. IKB has been rescued twice. First, in 2007, through bail-outs organized, on the first occasion, by KfW (Kreditanstalt für Wiederaufbau, a government-owned development bank). Second, in 2008, by the German Government itself. In order to rebuild their capital, financial institutions called in the loans they had made to what in retrospect are considered 'crisis countries'. As Lindner (2013) says, 'In this way, through the banks, the subprime crisis contributed very significantly to the Euro crisis.' The expansion of the bank crisis into a Eurozone crisis was helped, Lindner adds, by the instructions the European Commission gave in 2009 to all the banks that needed to be rescued by their national governments: they were obliged to reduce the credit they were providing. Between the second quarter of 2008 and the fourth quarter of 2012, the banks covered by the BIS survey reduced the debt held in the Euro-crisis countries by 42 per cent, creating massive financing problems. French and German financial institutions accounted for half of this cut in lending. These events are recalled here to set out the context in which the first bail-out of Greece took place in May 2010. Its failure is crucial because it lies at the origin of a chain of crises in Greece and a contagion effect in the other peripheral countries.

In the CEPR document, the figures documenting the financial exposure of 'core' countries vis-à-vis peripheral countries are followed by some important remarks that hint at mismanagement of the crisis. It is worth quoting them in full:

> This interlinkage between core-nation banks and periphery-nation borrowers created one of the fragilities that made the Crisis politically difficult to manage. It meant restructuring the debt of Crisis-stricken nations like Greece would have forced the problem back onto banks in nations leading the bail-out. In other words, the obvious solution of writing down Greek debt might well have increased the risk of classic bank-solvency crises in France and Germany. Indeed, this is exactly what happened to Cyprus when investors were eventually forced to take a haircut on Greek debt.
>
> (CEPR, 2015: 7)

The document goes further arguing that 'political "conflicts of interest"' inhibited 'some natural solutions: such as the writing down of Greek government debt in the early days of the Crisis' (pp. 13–14).

The unusually outspoken tone of these sentences (and, indeed, the contrast between a 'natural' and a 'political' solution of the crisis[10]) recall the analysis of the first Greek bail-out carried out by Orphanides (2015: 550), who served as Governor of the Central Bank of Cyprus between 2007 and 2012. He recalls that when Greece sought IMF assistance, one of the criteria for an IMF loan was that 'a rigorous and systematic analysis indicates that there is a high probability that the member's debt would remain sustainable in the medium term'. Since sustainability could not be proved, on the insistence of the German and French Governments the IMF introduced an exemption to the established procedures and proceeded with a programme that by ruling out debt restructuring was doomed to failure. 'Systemic' reasons, namely the fear of contagion-induced losses associated with restructuring, were invoked to justify this exemption, which ended up with Greece having to bear additional costs. As Orphanides recalls, that the risk to restructuring might ignite contagion in the EZ whole area could not be easily dismissed at the time. 'The banking system in a number of euro area member states, Germany importantly, remained fragile in the aftermath of the global financial crisis' (ibid.: 551). As mentioned above, because Chancellor Merkel's government had bailed out several German banks since 2007, new losses would have put her in a difficult political position.[11] This had a decisive influence on the Troika's decision to launch a rescue plan without debt restructuring, even though everyone knew it would fail. According to

Orphanides, a solution should have been found that would compensate Greece for the higher costs associated with the decision to avoid restructuring. Instead, fiscal tightening pushed the Greek economy into deep recession, triggering a financial panic that soon engulfed the other debtor nations. 'The result was unfortunate but predictable: massive destruction in some member states, and a considerably higher total cost for Europe as a whole' (ibid.: 537).

The CEPR (2015) document makes a third omission: the role of house prices in fuelling the financial crisis (see Chapters 2 and 8). We have argued in Chapter 2 that Germany avoided the global real estate cycles by virtue of a series of administrative and banking regulations. Since 1945, these norms contributed to the construction of a well-regulated market for rents that discouraged the spread of home ownership. Further, these norms helped to break the link between increases in bank credit and house prices. This vicious circle was the main fuel of the housing bubbles that involved in varying degrees almost all other European countries with the exception of Germany.[12] When it is recognized that an important aspect of the welfare state concerns the introduction of benefits in kind or items of income independent from market forces or by the property (see Crouch, 2011), all of these norms can be considered, in a broad sense, part of the welfare state at the disposal of German workers in the years considered. These regulations are meant to shelter basic 'subsistence' goods' (in this case the use of the house) from the unpredictable vagaries of the market, of the economic cycle and of the insecurity of property ownership. The dismantling of these protections, which results from the commodification of essential goods and services, is the most disastrous long-term legacy of the cuts of public services and the liberalization of their prices, which have been implemented in the SP to finance the deleveraging of local and international banks after the outbreak of the housing bubble.

Was the ECB responsible for creating the housing bubbles? Kannan *et al.* (2012) have shown that the real estate bubbles are not preceded by particular patterns of monetary policies and price dynamics. They are associated, instead, with the simultaneous occurrence of four conditions: acceleration of credit and current account deficits, increase in the share of residential investments on GDP and in house prices. However, De Grauwe (2011: 16–17) recalled that the ECB is not only responsible for price stability but also for financial stability. Given that

> the financial crisis in the Eurozone that erupted in 2010 had its origin in a limited number of countries it is important … that the ECB focuses not only on system-wide aggregates, but also on what happens in individual countries.

He categorically contests the objection that the ECB 'does not have the instruments to deal with excessive bank credit in parts of the Eurozone', arguing that 'The Eurosystem has the technical ability to restrict bank credit in some countries more than in others by applying [as stabilizing instruments at the national level] differential minimum reserve requirements or by imposing anti-cyclical capital ratios.' These forms of 'selective credit guidance' could be seen as tools aimed at the prevention of the formation of real estate bubble, that are alternative to the institutional regulation of the house rental market (though less effective from the point of view of solving the problem of housing).

3 The Target2 debate: a stealth bail-out?

The interpretation of the financial crisis of the Eurozone as a balance of payments crisis has initiated a debate on the role of the automatic 'financing' provided by the Target2 system. In the Eurozone, the Target system of payments was devised to provide the smooth settlement of credit and debit positions within countries: the central bank settlement creates a credit in the balance sheet of the national central bank to which the payment flows, and a debt in the balance sheet of the national central bank from which the payment originates. Paraphrasing the ECB's words:

> The Eurosystem implements its monetary policy in a decentralised manner, whereby the aggregate Eurosystem liquidity provision via its NCBs corresponds to the aggregate liquidity needs of the euro area banking sector. Liquidity can be redistributed across banking sectors through the euro area interbank market.
>
> (Moutot *et al.*, 2008: 39)

According to Sinn and Wollmershäuser (2012), expanding credit in the deficit countries and contracting it in the surplus countries, in particular in Germany, the Target2 mechanism stops the rules of the game from operating. In their view, the EMU worked like a fixed exchange rate system with destabilizing capital flows and external structural imbalances between non-homogeneous countries. In this context, Target2 and the ECB's Outright Monetary Transactions (OMT) impeded a dramatic increase in redenomination risk, which is a classical balance of payments (or currency) crisis. Thus, the Eurozone crisis has strong similarities with financial crises in emerging markets, with a convertibility risk and a moral hazard problem. Excessive borrowing and lending among member states have been accommodated by the Target2 system. When the reversal of capital flows occurred, Target2 allowed a stealth bail-out of the debtor countries by the ECB (see Cesaratto, 2017 for a discussion). The two authors conclude that Target2 has deprived the German economy of capital and savings.

This conclusion, that refers to the 'loanable-fund theory', has been rebuked among other, by O'Connell (2015), who argues that 'centre' creditor institutions largely fund themselves in international financial markets so that their lending – providing purchasing power to finance spending – has little to do with country-to-country transfers of savings. When the 'sudden stop' arrives, the problem therefore is not that of returning savings to the poor depositors in those institutions but of extricating them from their large exposure to borrowers in difficulties in the 'periphery'. Thus, in no way did savings from the core fund mean more spending in the periphery (see Chapter 7). On the contrary, the expansion of the periphery consented the creation of the 'excess savings' in the core of the EZ.

Much of the discussion turns around the problem of the institutional setting devised for the functioning of the EMU. A 'currency area', Barba and De Vivo (2013: 74) claim,

> is viable if it allows persistent imbalances to take place in the current account of the regions of which it is composed. In other words, a viable currency area is an area within which there is no binding balance of payments constraint.

The US system provides the most obvious example of a viable monetary union. Thus, comparison of similarities and differences can provide clues on the EMU problems.

In the US, Federal Reserve (Fed) districts do not coincide and have no fiscal connection with the states that they serve; there are 12 District Banks (DBs) serving 50 states. The DBs are separate from the states, and have a unique relation with the Fed, which must guarantee the value of the currency. The Fed takes responsibility for the Treasury securities, and, ultimately, for the public debt. The states' budget must be balanced. Their bonds are not used for settlement between DBs and their prices can (and do) vary. Their participation in the monetary union is never questioned. Balance of payments and state solvency are separate. There are no 'balance of payments' problems, but 'the only effect (which is never officially recorded) is that residents of deficit states either run down their existing asset holdings or build up obligations to residents of surplus states' (Palley, 1997: 153). 'There might be a problem with the quality of the loans that have been granted by the banks, or with the size of the government debt, but that as such has nothing directly to do with a balance-of-payments problem' (Lavoie, 2015: 158). An analogous situation would apply for EMU member countries in a well-behaved monetary union.

Final settlement is achieved through shifts in holdings of the System Open Market Account (SOMA).[13] The SOMA portfolio consists largely of US Treasury securities acquired by the Federal Reserve System via open market operations (though since QE1 and 2 many more securities have been involved), and the regulation between different federal districts takes place by 'shifting' public debt securities held in the Fed SOMA portfolio from a district central bank to another. In case of a run on the banks of a district, rediscount from other district banks would replenish reserves (voluntarily, or by law, on request by the Fed board, that could do it itself) (Bindseil *et al.*, 2012). In fact, should one DB run out of SOMA securities, it and its banks would be cut off from credit and their securities/credits would sell at a discount, that is, a dollar in this district would be worth less than a dollar in the rest of the US. Since the Fed must guarantee the par value, it would step in, either allowing overdraft or providing liquidity itself. Looking at the history of the US system, Eichengreen *et al.* (2014) find that cooperation between regional reserve banks has been essential for the cohesion of the US monetary union. They mutualized their individual gold reserves in emergency situations, creating gold flows from districts with payment surpluses to those with deficits.

> That mutual assistance between Reserve Banks was common during liquidity crises and bank runs suggests that the increase in TARGET2 balances since the outbreak of the global economic and financial crisis is an intrinsic part of the adjustment mechanism in a cohesive monetary union.
>
> (Eichengreen *et al.*, 2014)

As Bindseil and Winkler (2013: 37) argue, 'the unlimited and unconditional character of TARGET2 balances is at the very heart of monetary union. The ability of banks to transfer deposits across national central banks constitutes the genuine single currency.'

Differently from the ECB, the Fed does not have its own balance sheet and capital. There is no 'Fed as a whole', but only DBs. This explains a large difference between the Target2 mechanism and the Interdistrict Settlement Account (ISA). Target2 liabilities are ultimately claims on the ECB, and a claim on the ECB is ultimately a claim on each government according to the ECB's capital key. In fact, the ECB is owned pro-quota by the various countries.[14] Conversely, ISA liabilities are not claims on the Fed, since there is no parent institution. They are bilateral claims on other district Reserve banks (Bindseil *et al.*, 2012). In the Eurozone, these credits and debits are guaranteed and cleared by the central bank. This last point has re-ignited the dispute on the costs of the Target2 system in case of a member country exit.

Also the architecture of the European System of Central Banks is different, as noted above. There is a one-by-one correspondence between states and CBs. Each country has its own independent CB. However, the separation between the state and 'its' CB is incomplete. The state cannot rely on the CB for monetary financing, but it is responsible for the solvency of its CB (at least until the creation of the Banking Union). The Emergency Liquidity Assistance (ELA) is the responsibility of the national CBs, meaning that any costs of, and the risks arising from, the provision of ELA are incurred by the relevant NCBs and, eventually, by their state.

We mentioned above that the states' budgets must be balanced. This is made possible by the existence of a centralized fiscal (transfer) policy. If poorer states are no longer able to finance their debt by issuing local bonds, they have to adjust. That is, they cannot issue their own money, nor are their bonds accepted for the settlement of district central banks' disequilibria. However, looking at historically viable currency unions, Barba and De Vivo (2013: 75) observe that 'persistent real imbalances are accepted by surplus regions and are made sustainable by financial transfers revolving around the system of taxes and transfers and the public debt'. At the federal level, deficit spending can provide substantial automatic transfers from richer to poorer states through the automatic stabilizers, as well as overall support to the economy. The federal budget can sustain the purchasing power of the population living in poorer regions, indirectly also partly relieving their public budget. The issue of 'fiscal transfers' has to do with the economic and social cohesion of a monetary union – having given up other forms of intervention at the nation state level (sovereignty on monetary and fiscal policy, variation of the exchange rate) – not, strictly speaking, with the viability of a currency union.[15] The EMU was built instead on the premise that private capital flows could be relied upon to provide the equalization, so that no fiscal transfers at the European level were needed nor were desirable.

In conclusion, a 'political' limit came to operate when the crisis burst. 'Redenomination risk did not materialize in the foreign exchange market – which by definition does not exist in a CU – but in the sovereign bonds market' (Lavoie, 2015: 151).[16] Target2 imbalances and refinancing operations go hand in hand and cannot be separated when the interbank money market does not distribute adequately a given amount of reserves if the ECB aims to implement a single monetary policy for all its members. However, the Euro system lacks a security, like the US Treasury securities, that can be used to settle the imbalances, that is, it lacks a 'federal state'. Without such a safety cushion, national banking industries and sovereigns can default. The increasing spread on public debt affects the whole yield curve, including the companies' cost of capital as well as the solvency of the banking system. When, taking up a more active role in support of the state's securities, the ECB accumulated deficit countries' balances, it started to be perceived as subject to the risk of insolvency.

> For a US federal district, whether reserves are created through credit towards another district or through normal open market operations is equally acceptable. For the creditor countries in the Euro area it is not, and in fact they are showing increasing unwillingness to see their credit balances increase. The BoP view holds because the EZ misses the mechanisms, existing in standalone countries, to restore the equilibrium in troubled countries: in essence, a supranational fiscal authority able to make transfers amongst regions and a centralized bank resolution mechanism. If these mechanisms were present in the EZ we would not be talking about a BoP crisis.
>
> (Vernengo, 2015)

The recent re-opening of Target2 imbalances, occurring despite the return to surplus of all the peripheral countries' current accounts, has nothing to do with a 'classic' balance of payments problem, but is a reflection of the difficulties in which the mismanagement of the crisis and the austerity measures have thrown the debtor countries. The risk of a country exiting the monetary union poses the problem of how to settle the negative balances. Paradoxically, this issue was raised by Draghi[17] himself, who, responding to a query by two members of parliament, bluntly said that the exiting country should repay its Target2 balance with the ECB.

This brief review help to assess the solution, suggested by Henning and Kessler (2012), that national governments agree to self-impose running balanced budgets, like states in the US, in order to avoid irresponsible indebtedness. Yet, this happens because the US federal government provides fiscal support to states when required, and there is a centralized mechanism (which depends on the Treasury and the Fed) able to manage the resolution of a banking crisis and to provide bank deposit insurance in cooperation with the federal fiscal authority. The sudden stop and the capital reversal observed since 2009 are the consequence of the EMU's institutional set-up.

4 The unfolding of the crisis and the role of austerity

Between 2010 and 2014, the Eurozone countries implemented a huge contractionary policy. Due to these policies, the SP's economies experienced a dramatic downturn. The sovereign debt crisis has been averted by a rigorously deflationary fiscal policy that has been implemented without interruption since 2010. Only after July 2012, was this accompanied by a belated commitment on the part of the ECB to break the vicious circle of expectations that, in the absence of a debt-buyer of last resort, encouraged a massive liquidation of sovereign debt.

The consequences of the two crises on the GDP of our selected countries are depicted in Figure 4.3. After a deep plunge in 2008–2009, a second fall occurs, with different intensity, in 2010–2011. Only Germany and France succeed in recording small, positive growth. The SP continues in the negative until 2013, the feeble recovery being insufficient to regain the pre-crisis production levels. Between 2007 (just before the crisis explosion and at the peak of the debt-led growth phase developing until that point) and 2015, the SP loses (on average) 10.3 per cent of its real

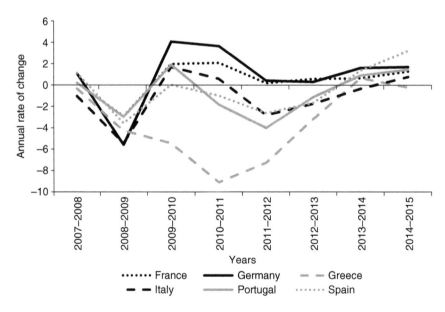

Figure 4.3 Rate of change of real GDP: Germany, France and the SP (2007–2015).

Source: authors' elaboration on Eurostat data.

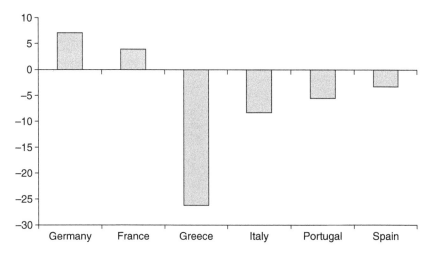

Figure 4.4 Cumulative change of real GDP: Germany, France and the SP (2007–2015).
Source: authors' elaboration on Eurostat data.

GDP, with Greece posting a staggering –26.2 per cent. Contrarily, Germany and France post a positive cumulative growth (Figure 4.4). Of course, the drop in GDP is mirrored by unemployment dynamics. All across the SP, youth and long-term unemployment mounts with impressive peaks in Greece and Spain (Table 4.1).

An element is worth emphasizing here. On the eve of the crisis, the SP's public debt was not alarming (with the exception of Greece) while the opposite is true with respect to private debt (see Table 4.2 reporting Germany, France and the SP's public and private debt in 1999 and in 2007, just before the crisis explosion). Despite an unimpressive growth since the inception of the EMU, even Italy had succeeded in reducing its public debt/GDP ratio. The unfolding of the sovereign crisis, epitomized by the hike in the spreads of the interest rates with the German Bund, represented the 'emergency background' providing the justification for the *austerity agenda*.[18] Three key features characterize the latter period: (i) the adoption of the austerity agenda across the periphery; (ii) the (temporary) relapse in capital flights and convergence of the spread after the massive ECB interventions; (iii) the adoption of 'rescue programmes' featuring conditionality.

Three countries – Greece, Portugal and Spain – had to sign Reform Programmes (RPs).[19] Italy is the only SP country where austerity was introduced without the enforcement of an RP. Actually, in the fiscal field, austerity policies started before the obligation attached to the RP, although the latter added zest.

Conditionality went well beyond balancing the budget. The blueprint of austerity policies, the same for all the SP's countries, consists of three main pillars: (i) cuts in public expenditure and increase in taxation to reduce public debt and deficits; (ii) privatization of public assets, not only finalized at reducing the public debt, but also meant to increase overall efficiency; (iii) structural reforms

Table 4.1 The unemployment rate of selected categories of workers in the SP (2007, 2011, 2015)

		2007	2011	2015
Greece	Unemployment	8.4	17.9	24.9
	Youth unemployment	22.7	44.7	49.8
	Long-term unemployment	33.9	30.2	68.9
Italy	Unemployment	6.1	8.4	11.9
	Youth unemployment	20.4	29.2	40.3
	Long-term unemployment	33.7	38.4	49.4
Spain	Unemployment	8.2	21.4	22.1
	Youth unemployment	18.1	46.2	48.3
	Long-term unemployment	11.1	34.8	45.9
Portugal	Unemployment	8.1	12.9	12.6
	Youth unemployment	16.7	30.3	32.0
	Long-term unemployment	NA	NA	56.8

Source: authors' elaboration on Eurostat data.

Note
Long-term unemployed are those individuals remaining unemployed for more than one year.

Table 4.2 Private and public sector debt: Germany, France and the SP (1999–2007)

	Private sector consolidated debt		Public debt	
	% GDP	% GDP	% GDP	% GDP
	1999	2007	1999	2007
Germany	120.3	110.7	60.0	63.6
France	94.7	115.6	60.2	64.4
Greece	44.1	101.9	98.6	103.1
Spain	93.6	191.2	60.9	35.5
Italy	71.8	109.7	109.6	99.7
Portugal	124.5	185.0	51.0	68.4

Source: adaptation from Bogliacino and Guarascio (2016).

– making labour and product markets more flexible in order to stimulate price competitiveness, boost exports and balance the current account. A thorough list of the key measures and a detailed year-by-year chronicle of the SP's austerity path is provided in the Appendix.

The labour market represents a privileged objective of conditionality. Identifying labour market 'rigidities' – namely, strong trade unions, generous social benefits, high minimum wages, powerful insiders and firing restrictions – as the main causes of inefficient factors' allocation, mismatch between labour demand and supply, weak competitiveness and, ultimately, persistent unemployment

(Cirillo *et al.*, 2016: 2),[20] the 'reforms' pursued two fundamental goals: increase flexibility and favour decentralized bargaining. Greater flexibility (freedom of entry and exit) targets 'insiders' – that is, *security in employment* (protection against dismissals) and *security in unemployment* (protection against income losses provided by unemployment benefits – mostly by reducing costs and legal constraints to workers' dismissals. All the countries of the SP (but, as we saw, partly also Germany) have substantially downsized protection against dismissals and assistance to the unemployed (Moreira *et al.*, 2015).

The second goal of labour market reforms is to reduce coverage and relevance of sectoral/national level of bargaining in favour of decentralized, individual/firm level of bargaining. Southern European labour markets were characterized by high levels of collective bargaining coverage (80–90 per cent), backed by *erga omnes* regulations and extensions of collective agreements. By 2014, with the exception of Italy, collective bargaining coverage had decreased across the SP (Schulten and Müller, 2014) (Table 4.3). The conditionality of the RP triggered a process of *disorganized decentralization*, whereby single-employer bargaining processes became the dominant mode of determining wages. This transfer of regulatory capacity, imposed by law, considerably weakens the wage-setting power of trade unions. Italy – the only peripheral country not passing through a formalized RP – faced continuous difficulties in respecting the EC's requirements, which meant that 'structural reforms' were on

Table 4.3 Collective agreements and collective bargaining coverage in Greece, Portugal and Spain (2008–2013)

	2008	2009	2010	2011	2012	2013
Greece						
Sectoral agreements	202	103	91	55	31	14
Company-level agreements	462	347	352	241	978	408
Portugal						
Sectoral agreements	200	164	166	115	46	
Company-level agreements	95	87	64	55	39	
Coll. agreements (total)	295	251	230	170	85	
Number of extension of coll. agreements	137	102	116	17	12	
Employees covered by coll. agreements (in millions)	1.9	1.4	1.4	1.2	0.3	
Spain						
Sectoral agreements	1.448	1.366	1.265	1.163	982	543
Company-level agreements	4.539	4.539	3.802	3.422	2.781	1.281
Coll. agreements (total)	5.987	5.689	5.067	4.585	3.763	1.824
Employees covered by coll. agreements (in millions)	12	11.6	10.8	10.7	9.1	5.7

Source: Schulten and Müller (2014: 105).

Note
In 2013 data on Portugal were not available.

the agenda in any negotiations and EC recommendations. Thus, similarly to the other SP economies, Italy continued a trend of deregulation which had been under way well before the beginning of the crisis (Cirillo *et al.*, 2016). Implemented with the partial involvement of the trade unions, Italy followed a pattern of *organized decentralization*.

The design of these 'structural reforms' has been formulated directly by the European Commission's DG ECFIN. The official document on country-specific 'recommendations' – reported under the heading 'employment-friendly reforms' – provides the following list: decrease statutory and contractual minimum wages; decrease the bargaining coverage; decrease (automatic) extension of collective agreements; reform the bargaining system in a less centralized way; introduce or extend the possibility to derogate from higher level agreements or to negotiate company-level agreements (European Commission, 2012: 103–104).

Not surprisingly, the austerity agenda in the field of labour market resulted in: (i) increase in the diffusion of company-level agreements and parallel reduction of the coverage of collective agreements; (ii) derogation from collective bargaining: company-level agreements can undermine standards defined by sectoral agreements;[21] (iii) reduction in collective agreements' 'after-effect', that is weakening of the criteria for the extension of collective agreements; (iv) enhanced opportunities for non-union groups of employees to negotiate and conclude company-level agreements (Schulten and Müller, 2014).

The brief country-by-country chronicle provided below highlights two factors: the absolute similarity of the policies that have been recommended across the board, irrespective of institutional and structural differences and the strong public opposition, also in response of the evidence of the largely damaging short-run effects of these measures (Monastiriotis *et al.*, 2013), leading to a devastating political instability.

Greece

Between 2010 and 2016, Greece has gone through 12 austerity packages. We have described how the crisis started and got out of control. Already, in May 2010, a Memorandum of Understanding was signed between the Greek centre-left government of Georgos Papandreu, elected in 2009, and the *Troika* – the European Commission, the European Central Bank and the IMF. It provided financial assistance in exchange of the implementation of a harsh austerity programme, a structure that will characterize all the following RPs. The measures are the standard ones that we shall find in the other Memoranda: cuts in wages and in the number of public employees, increase in indirect (VAT) and other taxes, pension reforms (extension of retirement age, reduction of pensions), privatizations, labour market reforms, reduction in minimum wages (Monastiriotis *et al.*, 2013, Varoufakis and Tserkezis, 2014). The programme was expected to raise up to €50 billion by 2015.

The political turmoil raised by these measures led to the resignation of the PASOK government, in November 2011, replaced by the 'technocratic' government of the former ECB vice-president Lucas Papademos. A second bail-out was negotiated and a set of new austerity measures introduced, expected to realize 41 billion dollars in budget savings (Matsaganis, 2013).[22] New elections in May 2012 brought to power a 'large coalition', led by the centre-right MP Antonis Samaras. New measures reducing the protection in the labour market and new cuts in public services were introduced in 2013 (Karamessini, 2015). Finally, in January 2015, a new political reshuffle occurs: the Syriza left-wing government wins the elections on the basis of a programme which rejected further austerity packages. After barely one year of resistance, it capitulates: a new bail-out agreement is signed and further doses of the same medicine approved: VAT and other taxes increase, retirement age is further extended. A new set of interventions is approved by the parliament by the end of 2015 and at the beginning of 2016. Taxes are raised in the agricultural sector – both fuel taxes and farmers' income tax are augmented; private-school taxation is introduced (23 per cent); taxes on the shipping industry are also increased.

As largely anticipated, these programmes have failed to achieve their main goals, producing quite the opposite effect: GDP and employment dropped dramatically, public debt exploded. Labour market policies and austerity have worsened workers' conditions, spending cuts have savaged welfare institutions, and the generalized crisis has decimated the industrial structure. Tax avoidance is an endemic problem in Southern economies; however, the fiscal measures imposed under emergency conditions were not apt to tackle this problem. They ended up in hitting the most vulnerable, resulting in worsening the problem of tax collection, while greatly exacerbating inequality and poverty.

Portugal

> With a record of dismal GDP growth since 2000, high levels of indebtedness of both firms and households, a gradual increase in public debt until 2008 and a rapid one thereafter, the Portuguese economy was particularly vulnerable to the speculative attacks against sovereign bonds in the euro zone which started in late 2009.
>
> (Lagoa *et al.*, 2014: 39)

The impact of the financial crisis was substantial (Santos and Fernandes, 2015), although 'the adjustment programme implemented in Portugal between May 2011 and May 2014 did not represent a dramatic break with the recent past with regard to the measures relating to public finances' (Lagoa *et al.*, 2014: 63). As in the other countries, the adjustment programme was based on restrictive budgetary and financial measures that were expected to lead to the consolidation of public finances, to economic recovery and to job creation. The strategy of internal devaluation, implemented in common with a reform of the labour market, aimed at increasing flexibility and, thus, fostering job creation.[23] These changes were negotiated at the national level with the social partners, and led to the conclusion – in January 2012 – of a tripartite agreement aimed at fostering growth, competitiveness and employment (Santos and Fernandes, 2015: 10).[24]

The New Labour Code of 2012 introduced several novelties. The severance payments were reduced from 30 to 20 days per year and the amount of benefit received was capped at a maximum of 12 times the employee's monthly wage or 240 times the minimum wage (Moreira *et al.*, 2015).

As in the Greek case, the first destination of the resources stemming from the RP was the banking sector. The Portuguese government allocated €12 billion of the total loan to bank recapitalization, without reserving any decision-making power to the state in the board of the rescued banks. The state received non-voting shares, while the management was elected by the old shareholders (Monastiriotis *et al.*, 2013).[25] Various synthetic indicators, produced by the OECD and the World Bank, suggest that these reforms have made Portugal a more flexible economy and a more attractive investment location (European Commission, 2014).[26] However, the assessment of the macroeconomic adjustment programme in terms of employment is disappointing. The unemployment rate reached 17.5 per cent in the first quarter of 2013 (compared with a peak of 12.4 per cent in 2012 forecasted in the RP). The increase in the number of unemployed people was combined with a drop in employment and in wages (in both the public and the private sector).

Was domestic devaluation successful? Santos and Fernandes (2015: 13–14) argue that it did nothing to improve 'the structural weaknesses of the Portuguese economy'. Weaknesses fuelled by the low level of formal education, as well as by a sectoral specialization based on low and medium-low technology intensity sectors. 'In the last four years, there has been no change in the economy's specialisation profile, the technology intensity of exports or labour productivity.' As in the other RP countries, the internal devaluation process had a huge impact on the decrease in household income, with a negative effect on domestic demand and imports, but little impact on external competitiveness. In the Portuguese case, exports are 'below the levels observed before the macroeconomic adjustment programme'. Furthermore, Portugal's innovative capacity has decreased to the levels of 2007. 'Portugal', Santos and Fernandes conclude,

> needs a new medium-term strategy focused on public policies that support innovation, workforce qualification, the promotion of knowledge and changes in the specialisation profile of the economy towards higher added value activities. In brief, a new generation of public policies is needed in order to promote sustainable growth, consolidate public finances and create more and better jobs.

In November 2015, a coalition of left parties (the Bloco de Esquerda, formed by Communists of the PCP, the Greens and the *Partito animalista*, Pan) voted down the centre-right government, which had won the October elections without obtaining the absolute majority in Parliament. Antonio Costa, Secretary General of the Socialist Party, formed the government of the 'geringonça',[27] on an anti-austerity programme. The first measures concerned a gradual increase in the minimum monthly income (from €557 in 2017 to €600 by the end of the term in

2019), increase in pensions and public employees' wages, reduction in VAT on some services, block on privatization of public transport, and, most important, resumption of public investment, especially in health and education, which had been slashed in the previous years.[28]

The first results were encouraging: for the first time in years the public deficit decreased, growth picked up and the unemployment rate fell to 10.5 per cent. However, Portugal still has a huge public debt (about 133 per cent of GDP). In its latest report, the IMF warned that,

> The modest growth outlook, high public and private indebtedness and weaknesses in the banking system are mutually reinforcing. As banks continue to struggle with a large stock of non-performing loans (NPLs), low profitability, and high operating costs, they are unable to provide adequate lending for new investment. Weaker growth, in turn, makes it more difficult for banks to address NPLs and improve profitability, while hampering fiscal consolidation efforts.
>
> (IMF, 2017)

The Commission, on its part, warned against Portugal's excessive imbalances. Both institutions reiterate their recipe: reinvigorating macro-critical structural reforms remains essential to boost the economy's competitiveness, growth potential, and resilience to shocks.

They encouraged the authorities to proceed with reforms in labour and product markets, with a particular focus on tackling labour market segmentation, improving education and skills, and enhancing public sector efficiency. They noted that it would be important to ensure that increases in the minimum wage do not impair labour competitiveness and undermine prospects for new entrants to the labour force. 'Removing regulatory barriers, strengthening institutional capacity and addressing other supply bottlenecks are also considered critical reforms' (IMF, 2017: 2). It is obvious that the Portuguese experiment of 'Keynesianism in one country' is heavily dependent on 'the volatile market sentiment' and the external environment (such as the ECB's QE, the EZ and world rate of growth), and can easily be nipped in the bud by the continuation of the EU macro-policies.[29] As argued by Santos and Fernandes (2015: 1),

> Portugal needs a new medium-term strategy focused on public policies that support innovation, workforce qualification, the promotion of knowledge and changes in the specialisation profile of the economy towards higher added value activities. In brief, a new generation of public policies is needed in order to promote sustainable growth, consolidate public finances and create more and better jobs.

Spain

'At the beginning of the Great Recession (2008–2009)', Uxó and Álvarez (2017: 1001) recall,

> the Spanish government implemented an economic policy aimed at the recovery of domestic demand, through an expansive fiscal programme. Actually, the Spanish package of fiscal stimulus was one of the most expansive in the world (2.3% of GDP in 2009), because Spain had a large fiscal space (public balance and public debt were 2% and 36% of GDP in 2007). Of course, one of the outcomes of the crisis itself and of this expansive policy was the increase in fiscal deficit and public debt (–11.1% and 53.1% of GDP in 2009). Then, the government curbed public spending in 2010, and the stance of Spanish budgetary policy became strongly restrictive and procyclical between 2010 and 2013.

The negative impact on GDP and employment are as much the result of the burst of the real estate bubble, as the consequence of a mistaken macroeconomic policy. Specifically, the combination of fiscal austerity and wage devaluation had strong restrictive effects on domestic demand between 2011 and 2013, triggering a second recession with severe effects on employment. Economic authorities argued initially that fiscal consolidation could be associated with an expansion in private domestic demand through some 'non-Keynesian effects'. However, while fiscal austerity and internal devaluation had a strong depressing effect on internal demand, they did not trigger an expansion in exports sufficient to sustain the recovery of growth and employment.

Most of the fiscal adjustment has been due to reductions in public expenditure. The sum of public consumption and public investment was, in real terms, 16.5 per cent lower in 2014 than in 2009.[30] The Spanish authorities also raised some taxes (direct taxes on income, but above all indirect taxes such as VAT), but, as in the case of the other programme countries, the increase in public revenue has been systematically lower than forecasted, precisely because of the strong negative impact on effective demand of these decisions. The negative contribution to growth of public demand explains 40 per cent of the total drop in domestic demand in this period, even neglecting its multiplier effects. The government intervened also on the labour market.[31] Since 2010, all Spanish governments operated to broaden the possibility for employers to dismiss employees for economic reasons. In 2010, the government introduced the possibility of firing workers in case of persistent falls in sales or revenues, extended in 2011 to include technological or organizational change. In 2012, this measure was revised to reduce the judicial controversies that had exploded after the introduction of the law: the employer must demonstrate actual or expected falls in sales or revenues for three consecutive quarters (Moreira *et al.*, 2015).

Despite the policy of cutbacks, Spain has failed to reduce public deficit in line with established targets. Instead, poverty and inequality have increased. Nor did wage devaluation policy turn out useful to guarantee a current account balance. The surplus was due mostly to the fall in imports, while the increase in exports was limited, since the pattern of industrial specialization in sectors of medium value and low productivity was unchanged. Different policies are required to promote changes in the industrial structure, for example, fostering investment in renewable energies. Expansionary fiscal policy and structural reforms to modernize the economy and reduce external dependence go hand in hand. The consequence of this policy is that, if recovery resumes, the Spanish economy will have to rely, as in the past decades, on external borrowing.

Since the last quarter of 2013, Spain has been experiencing a strong recovery. This raises the question: has austerity finally worked in Spain? Rosnick and Weibstrot (2015) argue that the data do not support the thesis that the current economic recovery is the result of a return of market, consumer and investor confidence due to fiscal consolidation. Much of Spain's economic recovery could be explained by the government's loosening of fiscal policy,[32] in addition to 'tailwinds', noted by the IMF, which include falling oil prices, a depreciating euro and the ECB's quantitative easing. Uxó and Álvarez (2017: 1003) note that,

> The gradual fall in the rate of household saving has had a positive impact on private consumption and, in addition, the government has significantly relaxed the pace of austerity over the past year. In fact, net primary expenditure (without financial aid to the banking system) rose 1.9 billion in 2014, and public consumption grew by 2.5% in 2015. If public final consumption and investment were making a negative contribution to growth between mid-2010 and the end of 2013, they began to make a positive contribution in 2014.

However, 'austerity has not been abandoned, but merely softened'. Relying on continued 'growth-friendly fiscal consolidation' – as the IMF recommends – as well as pursuing efficiency gains from further labour market or other reforms, is unlikely to move the economy toward reasonable levels of employment in the foreseeable future. Uxó and Álvarez (2017: 1010) conclude that a strategy of fiscal stimulus and public investment, combined with revenue increases that maintain a sustainable debt burden, present a much more effective alternative.

Italy

Since the 1980s, the Italian economic scene has been dominated by the public debt. The debt/GDP ratio reached a peak of 120 per cent in the aftermath of the 1992 currency crisis. Fiscal austerity in the second half of the 1990s and declining interest rates in the first years of the EMU lowered it to 103 per cent of GDP just before the crisis, and shot up again to 133 per cent in 2013, because of the fall in national income and rising interest rates. Debt servicing remained above 10 per cent of GDP between 1990 and 1997, hovering around 5 per cent of GDP for most of the past decade (5.4 per cent in 2013). The debt and its servicing have represented the main – perverse – channel of income redistribution, eating away the primary surpluses that had to be squeezed out of the economy even in the depths of the crisis because of the Fiscal Compact.

Italy is the only peripheral country that did not sign a RP. However, the size of its public debt, both in absolute value and in per cent of GDP, represents such a serious threat to the financial stability of the Eurozone to make Italy a closely monitored member. At the outset of the crisis, the weakness of its fiscal position made it difficult to counteract the effects of the crisis with an expansionary fiscal policy: according to IMF estimates, Italy's fiscal stimulus over 2008–2010 amounted to 0.3 per cent of GDP, compared with an average of 3.4 per cent for the main advanced economies. The stimulus was achieved mainly by changing the composition of the budget, leaving the balance unchanged. In spite of this prudence, the depth of the economic crisis took a heavy toll on the public finances: in two years, the debt/GDP ratio increased by 13 percentage points (from 103 per cent in 2007 to 116 per cent in 2009). Thus, when in 2010 the worst seemed to be over, the efforts aimed at reducing the deficit were resumed, mainly through cuts in expenditure (Simonazzi, 2015: 350).

The policies implemented in the crisis mark a continuity with the reforms implemented in the two previous decades in the fields of welfare and labour. In the years of 'low taxes for all' (Mr Berlusconi's slogan) social spending – education, research, social services, social investment and capital expenditure – were at the forefront of any financial law aimed at coping with the umpteenth financial crisis. The deepening of the crisis brought further cuts in social investment and social expenditure, privatization and higher co-payments for social services, unfair tax and pension reforms, more labour market flexibility, changes in social dialogue and weakening of national collective bargaining. The collapse in families' incomes and in employment opportunities has made the lack of a universal safety net socially unbearable. Hence, the increase in poverty among lower income families and the impoverishment of the middle class.

When the sovereign debt crisis eventually hit Italy, on 5 August 2011, ECB President Jean-Claude Trichet and Bank of Italy Governor Mario Draghi sent a confidential letter to the Italian prime minister, demanding fiscal tightening and sweeping reforms before the ECB stepped into the market to ease mounting pressure on Italian bonds. Adopting an unusually clear and explicit language, Trichet and Draghi urged Prime Minister Silvio Berlusconi to make deep reforms, including opening up public services, toughening deficit cuts (for example, reducing the number of public employees and cutting their wages), overhauling rules on the collective bargaining system, fostering and prioritizing company-level agreements, and reforming hiring and firing rules (Simonazzi and Fiorani, 2017: 234). The Berlusconi government started, and then the new Monti government duly complied, passing bills that contained measures of exceptional magnitude (see Table A4.1 in the Appendix). It was mainly regional governments that bore the brunt of spending cuts in the first period: the 2011 financial law drastically cut financial transfers to regions and municipalities, compelling local authorities to divert funds from other items, to outsource social services or to increase local taxes in order not to cut service provisions.

Major changes overhauled also the Italian pension system and the labour market. At the peak of the crisis, the Monti government implemented a pension reform that increased the minimum retirement age to 66 years, eliminating all forms of flexibility. Having fixed the calculation of pension benefits strictly according to contributions paid, it introduced an unnecessary rigidity with regard to retirement age. Precipitously and rigidly applied to respond to the urgent need to reduce spending and appease the financial markets (and the EU and German authorities), this reform left several short-term and long-term problems open. If, according to international assessments after the Fornero–Monti reform the Italian pension system had become the most rigorous of EU systems, it was also the least adequate in terms of pension level and the most ineffectual with respect to the broader objectives of productivity, growth and employment. First, by increasing the retirement age among older workers, the reform had a negative effect on youth unemployment. By slowing down the substitution between workers of different ages, this might have had an impact also on productivity, if young workers are more attuned to new technologies. Second, by allowing atypical workers with low pay and fragmented work careers to be inadequately covered, the new contribution-based system set in motion a 'pension time bomb' ready to explode when these people reach retirement age.

The labour market legislation aimed to increase flexibility through liberalization of a wide range of atypical contracts, first, and then to reduce 'dualism' in the labour market by reducing the firing costs of open-ended contracts, while trying both to regulate and promote non-standard forms of employment. A wide-ranging enabling law (the so-called Jobs Act, Law 183/2014) involved the regulation governing dismissals, simplification of contracts and labour law procedures, reformed unemployment benefits and active and passive labour market policies, and improved reconciliation between work and family life. The Jobs Act abolished workers' reinstatement rights in case of dismissal (except for discriminatory reasons), replacing them with monetary compensation amounting to two months' pay per year of work, reduced to half for firms with fewer than 15 employees. It introduced a new standard open-ended contract for new hires, which reduces the level and uncertainty of firing costs for all new permanent contracts in firms with at least 15 employees (the 'contratto a tutele crescenti', or 'graded security contract').[33] At the same time, the government is favouring the shift to a decentralized bargained structure.

As a result of the crisis and the measures implemented, Italy's economic growth continues to stagnate, the debt/GDP ratio has increased, and inequality and poverty is one of the highest. The devastation of its industrial network of small-medium size firms has dragged the banking system with it. Italy now has to deal with a huge public debt, a banking crisis and the tax fatigue of its over-burdened tax-payers.

5 The structural impact of the crisis

The crisis and the austerity measures implemented in the crisis widened the divides between and within the EU: between core and periphery, within the core and the periphery, and between peripheries. As for the latter, while the EP, closely linked to the German economy, recovered at a relatively fast pace, the SP remained trapped in low growth and suffered a destruction of productive capacity.

The austerity measures determined a dramatic fall in the production for the domestic market. The long crisis pushed many firms out of the market, shrinking the productive capacity of the Southern economies. The allocative efficiency hypothesis assumes that resources made available by dying (less efficient) firms are allocated to most efficient uses, ensuring the full utilization of resources and the increase in aggregate productivity. It is true that firms are different: productivity varies greatly across firms even within a narrowly defined sector because of internal and external factors (for instance, the organization of production, or the role of the firm in the value chain). If firms' heterogeneity is part of the competitive process, it is not true, that the resources set free by the firms that exit the market are 'automatically' transferred to ones that are more efficient (Bottazzi *et al.*, 2010). Moreover, firms that are not at the productivity frontier play an important role: seedbed of entrepreneurial spirit; source of income and employment; part of the value chains.

Because of the devastation caused by the crisis, the SP's productive base is now too narrow to sustain decent growth and employment, and it export base is too narrow to sustain a development driven only by external demand. Moreover, the inquiry on the complexity of factors that combine to determine one country's competitiveness (see Chapter 2) suggests caution in using the 'tradable-non tradable' distinction as an indicator of competitiveness.[34] We showed that the (right) investment in 'services' has important effects on competition and welfare.

The increasingly important role played by the EP as part of the German manufacturing core (Stehrer and Stöllinger, 2015) combined with Germany's success in re-orienting its exports towards growing markets, triggered a 'disconnection' of core and SP economic trajectories, further accelerating the process of structural divergence between the two areas. The different SP–EP resilience to the crisis may also be related to the different offshoring strategies of the SP economies, characterized by a comparatively lower preservation of domestic productions compared to Germany (see Chapter 6). The diverging trend between the SP (plus France), on one side, and the EP plus Germany, on the other, is stunning: regardless of the indicator of industrial production selected – aggregate production or capital goods (Figures 4.5 and 4.6), medium- or high-tech sectors (Figures 4.7 and 4.8) – Germany and the EP emerge as the undisputed leaders. After a severe, brief drop in 2008–2009, they have resumed growth. There is no double dip in the trend of industrial production, but only a brief, gentle decline in the rate of growth, with only one, noteworthy exception. In the high-tech sector the EP exhibits a remarkable fall, which is not accompanied by a similar fall in Germany's production. Given the tight link between the German and eastern European productive structures, this suggests a policy of flexible organization in the allocation of production within the value chain by German firms. Equally remarkable is France's performance, which is not doing better than the SP, especially in the period before the crisis. Conversely, and not surprisingly, Greece experiences a collapse in production.

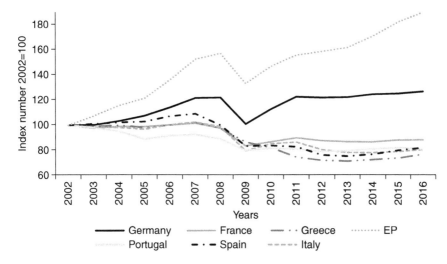

Figure 4.5 Industrial production: Germany, France, the SP and the EP (2002–2016) (2002 = 100).

Source: authors' elaboration on Eurostat data.

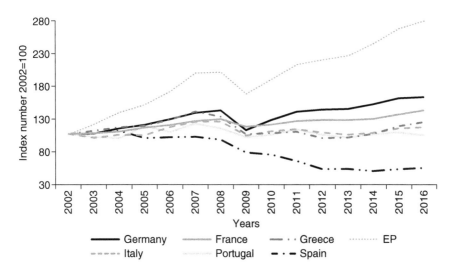

Figure 4.6 Production of capital goods: Germany, France, the SP and the EP (2002–2016) (2002 = 100).

Source: authors' elaboration on Eurostat data.

To conclude, the emergence of the German manufacturing network contributed to reshape the geography of industrial production in Europe. The EP's economies have emerged from the crisis with a broader productive base. Moreover, they have succeeded in strengthening their industrial structure from a

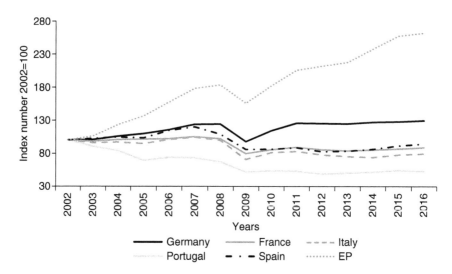

Figure 4.7 Industrial production: medium-tech sectors (selected countries) (2002–2016) (2002 = 100).

Source: authors' elaboration on Eurostat data.

Note:
Data on Greece are not available for the reference period.

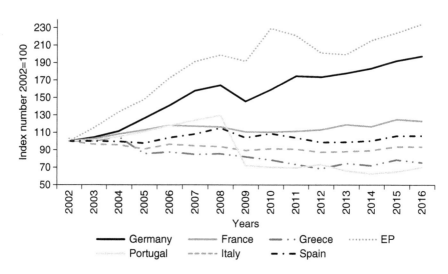

Figure 4.8 The dynamics of industrial production: high-tech sectors (selected countries) (2002–2016) (2002 = 100).

Source: authors' elaboration on Eurostat data.

technological point of view, as the evolution of medium- and high-tech productions testifies. In this context, the crisis has exacerbated a trend that was already under way at least since the early 2000s. The destruction of production and productive capacity and the related disappearance of jobs and work opportunities (Cirillo and Guarascio, 2015) has caused a huge increase in unemployment and inactivity. As already shown in Table 4.1, if the rate of total unemployment varies across countries, the rate of youth and long-term unemployment is despairing across the board. Migratory flows from the Southern to Northern Europe have resumed *en masse*. Though, according to Lafleur *et al.* (2017), their size is not yet comparable to the flows observed in the 20 years following the Second World War,[35] they now involve mostly youths and people with medium and high education, thus depriving the SP of essential skills.

6 Conclusions

The rationale underlying the macroeconomic adjustment programmes is that the SP countries have suffered a major loss of competitiveness over the past decade, purportedly due to the higher increase in unit labour costs there than in its euro area partners, possibly worsened by huge capital inflows that further swelled the non-tradable prices. In order to restore national competitiveness, with adjustment of the nominal exchange rate no longer an option for the euro area member states, the macroeconomic adjustment programme rested on an internal devaluation strategy focused on the downward adjustment of unit labour costs and/or prices.

This strategy has utterly failed, precipitating the countries in a vortex of falling incomes and swelling public and private debts. The claim that the pain was a necessary step towards a more sustainable long-term growth did not prove right. The weakening of their trade links with the core and the destruction of their productive capacity has seriously mortgaged their future.

Appendix

A1 Classification of 'structural reforms'

In what follows, we list the set of structural reforms characterizing the agenda implemented in the SP both before and (more intensively) after the 2008 crisis. An analogous list can be found in OECD (2013).

Tax reforms

Tax reforms include: (i) elimination or reduction of a number of deductions from personal income tax (Greece, Ireland and Portugal) and increase of the value added tax (VAT) (all peripheral countries); (ii) tax shifting aiming to lower labour costs (all peripheral countries); (iii) increasing or introducing property taxation (Greece, Italy and Portugal); and (iv) enhancing tax compliance.

Table A4.1 The SP's structural reforms chronicle (2010–2015)

Country	2010	2011	2012	2013	2014	2015
Italy	*First austerity package ($41 billion):* • Increase in healthcare expenditures • Cuts to regional subsidies • Cuts in family tax benefit; • Cuts in the pensions of high earners	*'Salva Italia' Decree:* • Introduction of the local housing tax (3.5 billion euro fiscal revenue per year expected) • VAT tax: +2% • New property tax (IMU – affecting particularly first houses and lacking any safety net for low incomes) and tax on yachts and luxury goods • Petrol tax is increased • Universalization of the contributive pension system • Retirement age raised (from 67 to 70 for men and 62 for women) • Partial stop at pensions indicization and public sector wages are frozen • Reduction of fiscal burden for firms (IRPEF)	*Constitutional Law 1/2012:* • Introduction of the principle of the balanced budget (Art. 81) *Legge 92/2012 (Legge Fornero):* • Reduction of legal constraints on firms lay-offs • Reorganization of temporary contract and unemployment benefits system *Spending Review Decree (94/2012):* • Reduction of public expenditures • Reduction of public employees • Sale and privatization of public assets *Reform of professional services:* • Removes some restrictions on fees and access by abolishing all references to minimum, maximum and recommended tariffs in all regulated professions	*Budgetary Law 2014:* • Reduction of corporate tax • Reduction of house tax	*Budgetary Law 2014:* • Tax reduction for firms hiring with permanent contracts or transforming existing contracts in permanent ones *Decreto Poletti (Law 78/2014):* • Increased to five the number of extensions to the use of temporary contracts	*Jobs Act (Law):* 1 Abolishment of all previous protections against unfair lay-offs 2 Abolishment of previous cap on the use of temporary contracts 3 Firms allowed to monitor workers by means of electronic devices 4 Softening of the tenure-based wages progression mechanism 5 Reduction of the constraints for the use of 'voucher contracts' – job-on-call contracts not providing any protection in case of illness, vacation or unemployment

Greece	1st Rescue programme:	2nd Rescue program:	2nd Rescue program (continuing):	2nd Rescue program (continuing):	2nd Rescue program (continuing):	3rd Rescue program:
	• VAT Tax: +4% • Tax on imported cars: + 10% • 3% cut in public sector wages and cap on the summer and Christmas bonuses • 10% cut in public wages bonus • Freeze in public sector recruitment • Weakening of EPL legislation: reduction in notice periods, rise in the lawful redundancy rate, softening of unfair dismissal rules and a drastic cut in severance pay entitlements • Retirement age raised from 60 to 65 and gender equalization introduced • Replacement rates for new retirees capped at 65% and all final salary schemes abolished • Privatization of public assets (50 billion euro)	• Increase in income tax • Continuation of the privatization program (50 billion euro) • Further weakening of EPL legislation	• Minimum wage reduced by 22% • Full decentralization of the wage bargaining system • Lay-off of 15,000 public servants • Life-tenure rule abolished in large parts of the public sector • Unemployment insurance benefits reduced by 22% • Reduction in social benefits • Increase in fuel taxes • Complete abolition of the summer and Christmas bonuses • Spending cuts and public assets privatization (expected revenues)	• Reduction of the notice period for workers dismissals (from a maximum of 24 to a maximum of 4 months) • Reduction of the severance pay period for unemployed: 2–24 months to 1–6 months (with prior notice) or 2–12 months (without prior notice) • Reduction of the severance pay for workers with more than 17 years of service (from 24 to 12 months' wages) – The Greek Public Broadcasting Service ERT is shut down	• Public wages and pensions are frozen until 2018 • New cuts to public services • Further privatization of public assets	• Extension of the range of products charged with the 23% VAT tax • Abolition of the VAT discount of 30% for islands • Solidarity tax on incomes over 50,000 euro • Pensioners' health contribution raised from 4% to 6% • Retirement age moved from 65 to 67 years • Increase in agricultural sector tax (fuel taxes and farmers' income tax); private-school taxation is introduced (23%) • Taxes on the shipping industry are also increased

Table A4.1 Continued

Country	2010	2011	2012	2013	2014	2015
Spain	*1st Adjustment plan (2010–2011):* • VAT tax: general rate increases from 16% to 18% and reduced rate from 7% to 8% • Increase in excise taxes • Withdrawal of personal income tax credit of 400 euro • Increase in taxation on saving • 5% cut in public sector staff remuneration • (Law 35/2010 of 17 September)	*Continuation of the 1st Adjustment plan:* • Elimination of the deduction for purchase of main residence • Freeze of public sector wages • Reduction of pharmaceutical cost • Implementation of 10% replacement rate for all public sector staff • Reduction of public investments	*2nd Adjustment plan:* • Supplementary levy on personal income tax • Reduced deductions on corporate tax • VAT tax: general rate increased from 18% to 21% and reduced rate from 8% to 10% • Tax on property • Increase in the transfer from local communities to the central government • Reintroduction and re-elimination of the deduction for purchase of main residence • Cuts in education and healthcare (0.4% GDP) • Law 3/2012: priority of firm-level agreement over national/regional ones	Additional labour market reforms following up and implementing Law 3/2012: • Firms are allowed to opt out from collective agreements, even in the absence of consensus between the two sides of industry, for reasons of an economic, technical, production-related or organisational nature • Firms are allowed to introduce unilateral changes to working conditions, such as working hours or wages • August 2013: measures to limit the competence of the courts to reverse collective dismissals in order to reduce the insecurity of firms resorting to the new measures (Horwitz and Myant, 2015)	Additional interventions following up and implementing the 2010–2013 reforms	Additional interventions following up and implementing the 2010–2013 reforms

Portugal		Portugal rescue program:	Portugal rescue program (continuing):	Portugal rescue program (continuing):	Portugal rescue program (continuing):	Additional interventions following up and implementing the 2010–2013 reforms
	• VAT tax increase (+2%) • Increase in income and corporate tax • Public sector wages reduced by 5%	• VAT tax increased from 21% to 23% • Increase in the work week of public employees (42 hours) without extra pay • Reduction of public sector wages (−5% cut for top public sector wage earners) • Civil servants and pensioners holiday-related and year-end bonuses are eliminated • Generalized cuts in health, welfare and education spending	• Cuts further over the level and the duration of unemployment benefits (the cap on unemployment insurance benefits passes from 1257 euro per month to 1048.10 euro) • Further cuts on employment benefits (end of the year) by 10%	• New labour code: • Severance payments are reduced from 30 to 20 days per year and the amount of benefit received is cap at a maximum of 12 times the employee's monthly wage or 240 times the minimum wage • Cases identified as fair dismissals (weak legal constraints for firms) are increased	• Reduction of public workers' wages (between 3.5 and 10% – wages below 1500 euro a month exempted by a Constitutional court ruling) • Reduction in supplementary pensions in the public enterprise sector	

Sources: Monatiriotis *et al.* (2013); Karger (2014); European Commission (2014); Moreira *et al.* (2015); Horwitz and Myant (2015); Cirillo *et al.* (2016).

Pension, welfare and labour market reforms

Pension reforms include: (i) increasing the legal and/or minimum retirement ages and lengthening the contribution periods required for a full pension (all peripheral countries); (ii) reducing the generosity of pension – directly or blocking the indexing to inflation (Greece and Italy); (iii) reducing early retirement via reducing benefits and revising the list of arduous occupations (Greece and Italy); and (iv) introducing a mechanism to index the retirement age to life expectancy (all peripheral countries)

Welfare and labour market reforms include: (i) reducing unemployment benefit rates (Ireland and Portugal) and duration (Portugal), introducing means-tested benefits (Greece); (ii) cutting welfare payments such as child benefits (Greece); (iii) reducing legal constraints and costs (for firms) of workers lay-offs (all peripheral countries); (iv) favouring the use of temporary and flexible contracts (all peripheral countries); and (v) incentives to favour decentralized (firm level) bargaining systems in place of sectoral/national ones (all peripheral countries).

Product market reforms

Product market reforms include: (i) privatization programmes – primarily aimed at raising public revenues – in various energy and transport sectors (all peripheral countries) and launch of public-private partnerships and concessions to develop some state-owned immovable assets (Greece); (ii) strengthening the power, independence or effectiveness of the competition authority (Greece and Portugal); (iii) reducing the number of steps required to start a new business (Greece) and the complexity of licensing procedures (Greece and Portugal); (iv) increasing competition in transport and network industries by reducing barriers to entry in road and maritime cruises (Greece) and phasing out regulated tariffs in electricity and gas (Greece and Portugal); and (v) increasing competition in retail trade (Portugal) and reducing barriers to entry in professional services (Greece and Portugal).

Public sector reforms

Public sector reforms include: (i) reorganizing local and central government (Greece and Portugal); (ii) rationalizing the public remuneration system (Greece); (iii) rationalizing management and improving efficiency and governance of state-owned enterprises (Greece and Portugal); (iv) public healthcare sector measures, including strengthening and better monitoring of prescription rules and rationalising procurement procedures (Greece and Portugal), increasing co-payments (Portugal) and enhancing cost-accountability in the hospital sector (Greece and Portugal).

Notes

1 The US has attempted to maximize the impact of its government spending through a strategy of domestic procurement (so-called 'Buy American', according to which the government is allowed to purchase only domestically produced goods and services). The EU does not have any such policy, at least officially.

2 The radical differences dividing the US and Europe in terms of anti-crisis actions are reflected in the (harsh) exchange between the former US President Obama and the German Finance Minister Schauble late in 2011. To Obama who, speaking in California, claimed: 'the Europeans' inaction facing the crisis is scaring the world … they are fuelling a new financial crisis', Schauble replied: 'I don't think Europe is the greatest American problem … it is always easier giving advice to others rather than solving [one's] own problems' (see Da Rold, 2011).

3 The Italian case is paradigmatic. Italy's divergent trend from the European core is mirrored by a North–South increasing divide. The Italian Mezzogiorno is caught in two traps: the trap of regional under-development within the 'medium income country' trap (Viesti, 2015). As argued in Chapter 5, the length of the recession, the reduction in public resources and the fall in domestic demand all contributed to weaken an already fragile structure (Svimez, 2015).

4 Exports of machinery and motor equipment were hit particularly hard: they fell by 11.4 per cent in the US and by 14 per cent in Germany (Baldwin, 2009: 104, 91 and 175).

5 They include R. Baldwin, T. Beck, A. Bénassy-Quéré, O. Blanchard, G. Corsetti, P. de Grauwe, W. den Haan, F. Giavazzi, D. Gros, S. Kalemli-Oczan, S. Micossi, E. Papaioannou, P. Pesenti, C. Pissarides, G. Tabellini and B. Weder di Mauro.

6 Orphanides (2015: 546) observes: 'The regulatory framework that had been created by the governments treated all euro area sovereigns as zero-risk-weight assets, from a capital requirement perspective, and exempted them from regulations regarding large exposures.' The author suggests that these rules might have induced the financial markets to assume away the country risk.

7 Acharya and Steffen (2015) have shown that profits and losses of the EZ core countries' banks may be understood as the outcome of a 'carry trade' strategy. With access to short-term funding in the wholesale markets of the US financial system, European banks have undertaken long peripheral sovereign bond positions.

> On the upside, the trade would pocket the 'carry', the spread between the long term peripheral sovereign bonds and banks' short-term funding costs. On the downside … the spreads between the two legs of the trade diverged even further resulting in significant losses for banks.
>
> (Ibid.: 1)

Thus doubts were cast on their solvency. For evidence on core EZ banks' funding in foreign financial markets and re-lending to the European periphery, see Hale and Obstfeld (2014) and O'Connell (2015). Shin (2011) pointed out that before the sub-prime crisis European global banks sustained the 'shadow banking system' (not subject to regulatory control) in the US by drawing on dollar funding in the wholesale markets to lend to US residents through the purchase of securitized claims on US borrowers.

8 In 2007, a peak year for production of CDOs, Deutsche Bank created about 42.5 billion dollars worth of them, compared with 25 billion dollars by Goldman Sachs. Deutsche Bank played a double role in the mortgage market: while creating and selling mortgage securities to some of its clients, it was betting the other way (Wall Street Journal, 2010).

9 According to Mediobanca-R&S (2015: 94–95), in the years 2008–2009 the Landesbanks (banks owned by the German Länder) registered losses amounting to €14 billion,

writing down more than one-third of their net worth. Large losses were due to specula-tion in financial derivatives.

10 See also Orphanides (2014). In his research work, he argued against output-gap-based policy rules, favouring non-activist rules drawing on K. Wicksell and M. Friedman.

11 Orphanides reports a 'startling and controversial' statement given by the former Gov-ernor of the Bundesbank, Karl Otto Pöhl, in an interview published by *Der Spiegel* on 18 May 2010, just one week after the Troika programme had been decided: 'It was about protecting German banks, but especially the French banks, from debt write-offs' (quoted in Reuter, 2010). On that occasion, he argued that Greek debt should have been restructured to reduce it by one-third.

12 As mentioned, German banks have implemented elsewhere those real estate specula-tive financing operations that were hindered at home by stricter administrative regulations.

13 A DB cannot buy securities on the open market paying them by creating money. Only the Federal Open Market Committee (FOMC) is permitted to purchase or sell securi-ties and decides how to allocate them among the various DBs. So in the end, what relaxes the constraints on inter-district flows is not district open market operations, but the Board's decision to change settlement procedures so as to protect the integrity of the system as a whole.

14 The argument that a CB does not need capital in order to function effectively is prin-cipally correct up to a point and especially for the case of a sovereign state fiscally backing its own national central bank in the conduct of monetary policy. However, the EMU is not a sovereign state or fiscal union (Bibow, 2015: 37).

15 Already in 1977 the MacDougall Report (MacDougall, 1977: 60) stressed that dire consequences could be envisaged for a monetary union that does not contemplate measures of compensatory financing.

16 In 1999, Simonazzi and Vianello (p. 276) observed that

> Monetary unification eliminates one of the two causes of interest rate spreads, that is, the exchange rate risk, but not the other, linked to trustworthiness of debtors.... Financial speculation, unable to target exchange rates, concentrates on the sover-eign bond market, determining a fall in bond prices, making servicing of debt unsustainable and exposing the country to a risk of insolvency. The opinion then beginning to circulate in the markets that it is better for the country to abandon the monetary union and seek escape from its woes in inflation will aggravate the crisis further, and aggravated crisis will reinforce the opinion.

17 Mario Draghi has served as President of the European Central Bank since November 2011.

18 The theoretical support rested in the mainstream approach that argued that austerity measures stimulate growth by: lowering interest rates and encouraging investment; and stimulating consumption through the reduced expectations of further fiscal adjust-ments (on this point, see Alesina and Ardagna, 2009).

19 Ireland had also to sign a Memorandum in 2010.

20 The SP's labour markets were described as segmented labour markets (Meardi, 2012; Schulten and Müller, 2014 and Cirillo *et al.*, 2016), with high levels of employment protection for 'insiders' and a large number of atypical workers with very low levels of security. Sectoral/national level bargaining ensured a large coverage of workers.

21 There is still a high degree of heterogeneity across the periphery: in Greece and Spain company agreements are now roughly prevailing; in Italy and Portugal, the possibility to derogate from sectoral standards still needs the agreement of the bargaining parties at the sectoral level.

22 We refer to Table A4.1 in the Appendix for a summary of the measures agreed in the various austerity packages.

23 The Portuguese rescue programme moves along three main lines: (i) a fiscal consolidation strategy, including cuts of public expenditures, a raise of both income and consumption based taxes and a 'better control of Public-Private-Partnerships (PPPs) and state-owned enterprises (SOEs) aimed at breaking the increase in the gross public debt-to-GDP ratio'; (ii) a state-backed procedure to ease deleveraging and reinforcement of banks capitalization; and (iii) 'deep and frontloaded structural reforms' directed at introducing further flexibility in the labour market, reorganizing the judicial system and the housing and services sectors. The financial package envisaged €78 billion for possible fiscal financing needs and support to the banking system (European Commission, 2014: 3).

24 In 2013, the Constitutional Court declared unconstitutional a policy meant to weaken the discipline lay-offs, requiring new legislation. According to the new rules, there are no constraints to lay-offs, but firms must follow a ranking: individuals with the lowest performance assessment, lowest qualifications, highest costs to the company, lowest level of experience and fewest number of years in the company (in that order).

25 Following the RP, a number of new measures have been put in place (see Table A4.1). In 2012, the Conservative government cut further the level and duration of unemployment benefits (the cap on unemployment insurance benefits passed from €1257 to €1048.10 per month). An additional cut on employment benefits (−10 per cent) was implemented at the end of the year.

26 For an in-depth critique of the indicators adopted by World Bank and OECD to evaluate structural reforms effectiveness, see Zenezini (2014).

27 A Portuguese word that indicates a thing poorly constructed and unsound and at the same time a jargon or an incomprehensible language. It was so defined by Vasco Pulido Valente, historian and former columnist of the daily newspaper *Público*.

28 In only one year, in 2016 Portugal jumped from the 20th to the 14th position in the European health systems. Important progress has been made in education, with the introduction of free textbooks in primary schools, creation of new scholarships and reduction of college tuition, and finally the decision not to finance private schools.

29 Overall, the Commission concludes that Portugal has made limited progress in addressing macroeconomic imbalances and structural reforms covered by the 2016 country-specific recommendations.

30 In 2013, public spending was reduced in total by €29 billion compared to 2009. And if we deduct from public spending direct aid to financial institutions (€50 billion in the period 2011–2013) and interest payments (which increased by €16 billion between 2009 and 2013), the total nominal reduction was €52 billion. Between 2009 and 2013, the amount devoted to education and healthcare has been reduced by €18 billion, and public investment by €33 billion (from 5.1 per cent to 2.1 per cent of GDP) (Uxó and Álvarez, 2017).

31 The cohort of individuals eligible for the 'Contrato de Fomento del Empleo' – a type of contract providing lower compensation in case of dismissal, 33 days per year as opposed to the 45 under standard contracts, and imposing no advance notice to firms proceeding to a dismissal – is significantly extended. Originally, only people up to 30 years old were eligible, after the reform all people up to age 44 became eligible (Monastiriotis *et al.*, 2013: 24). The severance pay is reduced to 20 days per year of tenure, with a maximum of 12 times the Spanish minimum monthly wage. In addition, after six months on benefit, the unemployed would get only 50 per cent of their previous wage – before they were entitled to have 60 per cent (Moreira *et al.*, 2015). Furthermore, the discipline on collective dismissals has been changed deeply. From 2012 onwards, the latter are no longer dependent on authorization from national, regional or local authorities; and the period between notice and dismissals is reduced.

32 Indeed, the European Commission estimates that Spain's government missed its net fiscal consolidation targets by 2.8 percent of GDP for the years 2013–2015 indicate that the government's fiscal consolidation may have been significantly less than reported (Rosnick and Weibstrot, 2015).

33 The Jobs Act was complemented by a measure, passed in the 2015 Budget Law, which provides a sizable temporary rebate of non-wage labour costs (up to €8060 per year for three years) to new permanent hiring of workers who, in the previous semester, did not hold an open-ended position. These incentives are not targeted to specific groups of workers, nor are they contingent upon firm-level net job creation; that is, firms can use the subsidy to convert a temporary contract into a permanent one.
34 See, for instance, Stöllinger (2016) who finds a negative relationship between increasing specialization in the production of non-tradable output and export capacity. He concludes that the sectoral specialization matters to explain export performances and, ultimately, current accounts divergent patterns. Thus, an economy's relative international position is closely related to the tradability of output it produces.
35 According to Lafleur *et al.* (2017) formal and informal measures of welfare – such as provision of unemployment benefits or other kind of public services and financial assistance by families to their unemployed children – played a role in reducing the flows, by providing a safety net which was lacking in the post-Second World War period..

References

Acharya, V. V. and Steffen, S. (2015). The 'greatest' carry trade ever? Understanding eurozone bank risks. *Journal of Financial Economics*, 115(2), 215–236. ISO 690.
Alesina, A. and Ardagna, S. (2009). Large changes in fiscal policy: Taxes versus spending. *NBER Working Paper No. 15438*, October.
Arpe, J., Milio, S. and Stuchlik, A. (eds) (2015). *Social Policy Reforms in the EU: A Cross-national Comparison*. Bertelsmann Stiftung. www.bertelsmann-stiftung.de/file-admin/files/user_upload/Study_EZ_SIM_Europe_Reformbarometer_2015.pdf [accessed 14 September 2017].
Baldwin, R. E. (ed.) (2009). *The Great Trade Collapse: Causes, Consequences and Prospects*. London: CEPR books.
Barba, A. and De Vivo, G. (2013). Flawed currency areas and viable currency areas: External imbalances and public finance in the time of the euro. *Contributions to Political Economy*, 32(1), 73–96.
Bibow, J. (2015). Making the euro viable: The Euro Treasury Plan. *Levy Economics Institute of Bard College Working Paper Series No. 842/2015*.
Bindseil, U. and Winkler, A. (2013). Dual liquidity crises: A financial accounts framework. *Review of International Economics*, 21(1), 151–163.
Bindseil, U., Cour-Thimann, P. and König, P. (2012). Target2 and cross-border interbank payments during the financial crisis. *CESifo Forum*, 13, 83. Institut für Wirtschaftsforschung (Ifo).
Bogliacino, F. and Guarascio, D. (2016). La natura del processo di integrazione monetaria e i destini dello stato sociale europeo. *La Rivista delle Politiche Sociali*, 3–4, 367–382. Ediesse.
Bottazzi, G., Dosi, G., Jacoby, N., Secchi, A. and Tamagni, F. (2010). Corporate performances and market selection: Some comparative evidence. *Industrial and Corporate Change*, 19(6), 1953–1996.
Cafruny, A. W. (2015). European integration studies, European Monetary Union, and resilience of austerity in Europe: Post-mortem on a crisis foretold. *Competition & Change*, 19(2), 161–177.
CEPR (2015). Rebooting the Eurozone: Step 1 – Agreeing a Crisis narrative. *Voxeu.org*, 19 November. http://voxeu.org/epubs/cepr-reports/rebooting-eurozone-step-1-agreeing-crisis-narrative [accessed 15 September 2017].

Cesaratto, S. (2017). Alternative interpretations of a stateless currency crisis. *Cambridge Journal of Economics*, 41, 977–998.

Cirillo, V. and Guarascio, D. (2015). Jobs and competitiveness in a polarised Europe. *Intereconomics*, 50(3), 156–160.

Cirillo, V., Fana, M. and Guarascio, D. (2016). Labour market reforms in Italy: Evaluating the effects of the Jobs Act. *Economia Politica*, 1–22.

Crouch, C. (2011). *The Strange Non-death of Neoliberalism*. Cambridge: Polity Press.

Da Rold, V. (2011). 'Obama's lesson on the euro crisis is overpowering, arrogant, and absurd': Obama's allegations enrage the Germans ['La lezione di Obama sulla crisi dell'euro è prepotente, arrogante e assurda': le accuse di Obama fanno infuriare i tedeschi]. *Il Sole 24 Ore*, 29 September. www.ilsole24ore.com/art/notizie/2011-09-29/lezione-obama-crisi-euro-160902_PRN.shtml [accessed 14 September 2017].

De Grauwe, P. (2011). Only a more active ECB can solve the Eurozone crisis. *CEPS Working Papers*, 4 August. www.ceps.eu/publications/only-more-active-ecb-can-solve-euro-crisis accessed 14 September 2017].

Dosi, G., Guarascio, D., Mazzucato, M. and Roventini, A. (2017). Investing out of the crisis. *ISIGrowth Policy Brief*, 7 March. www.isigrowth.eu/wp-content/uploads/2017/04/ISIGrowth_policybrief1.pdf.

Eichengreen, B., Mehl, A., Chiţu, L. and Richardson, G. (2014). Mutual assistance between federal reserve banks, 1913–1960 as prolegomena to the TARGET2 debate. *NBER Working Paper No. 20267*, June.

European Commission (2012). *Labour Market Developments in Europe 2012*. Brussels: European Commission.

European Commission (2014). The economic adjustment programme for Portugal 2011–2014. *Occasional Paper 202*, October.

Hale, G. and Obstfeld, M. (2014). The Euro and the geography of international debt flows. *NBER Working Paper No. 20033*.

Hardie, I. and Howarth, D. (2009). Die Krise but not La Crise? The financial crisis and the transformation of German and French banking systems. *Journal of Common Market Studies*, 47(5), 1017–1039.

Henning, C. R. and Kessler, M. (2012). Fiscal federalism: US history for architects of Europe's fiscal union. *Brueghel*, 10 January. http://bruegel.org/2012/01/fiscal-federalism-us-history-for-architects-of-europes-fiscal-union/ [accessed 14 September 2017].

Horwitz, L. and Myant, M. (2015). Spain's labour market reforms: The road to employment – or to unemployment? *ETUI WP 2015/3*.

Hüfner, F. (2010). The German banking system: Lessons from the financial crisis. *OECD, Economic Department WP No. 788*.

IMF (2017). Portugal. *IMF Country Report No. 17/58*, February. www.imf.org/en/Publications/CR/Issues/2017/02/22/Portugal-Fifth-Post-Program-Monitoring-Discussions-Press-Release-Staff-Report-and-Statement-44674 accessed 14 September 2017].

Kannan, P., Rabanal, P. and Scott, A. M. (2012). Monetary and macroprudential policy rules in a model with house price booms. *The BE Journal of Macroeconomics*, 12(1).

Karamessini, M. (2015). The Greek social model: Towards a deregulated labour market and residual social protection. In Daniel Vaughan-Whitehead (ed.), *The European Social Model in Crisis: Is Europe Losing Its Soul?* Cheltenham: Edward Elgar, 230–288.

Karger, H. (2014). Bitter pill: Austerity, debt, and the attack on Europe's welfare states. *The Journal of Sociology and Social Welfare*, 41, 33.

Lafleur, J. M., Stanek, M. and Veira, A. (2017). South-North labour migration within the crisis-affected European Union: New patterns, new contexts and new challenges. In J. M. Lafleur and M. Stanek (eds), *South–North Migration of EU Citizens in Times of Crisis*. Dordrecht: Springer, 193–214.

Lagoa, S., Leão, E., Mamede, R. P. and Barradas, R. (2014). Financialisation and the financial and economic crises: The case of Portugal. *FESSUD, Studies in Financial Systems No. 24*. http://fessud.eu/wp-content/uploads/2012/08/FESSUD-STUDY-WP3-Country-study-Portugal-final-study-24.pdf [accessed 14 September 2017].

Lavoie, M. (2015). The Eurozone: Similarities to and differences from Keynes's Plan. *International Journal of Political Economy*, 44(1), 3–17.

Lindner, F. (2013). Banken treiben Eurokrise [Banks drive the Euro crisis]. *IMK Report 82*, June.

MacDougall, D. (1977). Report of the Study Group on the role of public finance in European integration. EUR-OP.

Matsaganis, M. (2013). *The Greek Crisis: Social Impact and Policy Responses.* Friedrich Ebert Stiftung. http://library.fes.de/pdf-files/id/10314.pdf [accessed 14 September 2017].

Meardi, G. (2012). Employment relations under external pressure: Italian and Spanish reforms in 2010–12. In *International Labour Process Conference*, Stockholm, 27–29.

Mediobanca-R&S (2015). *Indagine annuale*. Dati cumulativi delle principali banche internazionali e piani di stabilizzazione finanziaria, Milan.

Monastiriotis, V., Hardiman, N., Regan, A., Goretti, C., Landi, L., Conde-Ruiz, J. I., Marin, C. and Cabral, R. (2013). Austerity measures in crisis countries: Results and impact on mid-term development. *Intereconomics*, 48(1), 4–32.

Moreira, A., Domínguez, Á. A., Antunes, C., Karamessini, M., Raitano, M. and Glatzer, M. (2015). Austerity-driven labour market reforms in Southern Europe: Eroding the security of labour market insiders. *European Journal of Social Security*, 17(2), 202–225.

Moutot, P., Jung, A. and Mongelli, F. P. (2008). The working of the eurosystem: Monetary policy preparations and decision-making-selected issues. *European Central Bank occasional papers No. 79/2008.*

O'Connell, A. (2015). European crisis: A new tale of center–periphery relations in the world of financial liberalization/globalization? *International Journal of Political Economy*, 44(3), 174–195.

OECD (2013). *Economic Policy Reforms: Going for Growth 2013*. www.oecd-ilibrary.org/economics/economic-policy-reforms-2013_growth-2013-en [accessed 14 September 2017].

Orphanides, A. (2014). The euro area crisis: Politics over economics. *MIT Sloan School Working Paper No. 5091–14.*

Orphanides, A. (2015). The euro area crisis five years after the original sin. *Credit and Capital Markets–Kredit und Kapital*, 48(4), 535–565.

Palley, T. I. (1997). The institutionalization of deflationary policy bias. In H. Hagerman and A. Cohen (eds), *Advances in Monetary Theory*. Boston: Kluwer Academic Publisher.

Reuter, W. (2010). Former Central Bank Head Karl Otto Pöhl bailout plan is all about rescuing banks and rich Greeks. *Spiegel*, 18 May. www.spiegel.de/international/germany/former-central-bank-head-karl-otto-poehl-bailout-plan-is-all-about-rescuing-banks-and-rich-greeks-a-695245.html [accessed 14 September 2017].

Rosnick, D. and Weibstrot, M. (2015). Has austerity worked in Spain? *Center for Economic and Policy Research*. http://cepr.net/documents/Spain-2015-12.pdf [accessed 14 September 2017]

Santos, A. B. and Fernandes, S. (2015). Internal devaluation and unemployment: The case of Portugal. *The Jacques Delors Institute, Policy Paper No. 154*, December.

Schulten, T. and Müller, T. (2014). Wages and collective bargaining during the European economic crisis: Developments in European manufacturing industry. *Report for the industriAll Collective Bargaining and Social Policy Conference*, Vienna, 12–13.

Shin, H. S. (2011). Global banking glut and loan risk premium. *Mundell Fleming Lecture*. www.imf.org/external/np/res/seminars/2011/arc/pdf/hss.pdf [accessed 14 September 2017].

Simonazzi, A. (2015). Italy: Continuity and change in welfare state retrenchment. In D. Vaughan-Whitehead (ed.), *The European Social Model in Crisis – Is Europe Losing its Soul?* Cheltenham: Edward Elgar, 339–385.

Simonazzi, A. and Fiorani, G. (2017). Italy: Industrial relations and inequality in a recessionary environment. In D. Vaughan-Whitehead (ed.), *Inequalities and the World of Work: What Role for Industrial Relations and Social Dialogue?* Geneva: ILO, 227–264.

Simonazzi, A. and Vianello, F. (1999). Financial liberalization, the European single currency and the problem of unemployment. In M. Franzini and F. R. Pizzuti (eds), *Globalization, Institutions and Social Cohesion*. Berlin, Heidelberg: Springer, 257–282.

Sinn, H. W. and Wollmershäuser, T. (2012). Target loans, current account balances and capital flows: The ECB's rescue facility. *International Tax and Public Finance*, 19(4), 468–508.

Stehrer, R. and Stöllinger, R. (2015). The Central European Manufacturing Core: What is driving regional production sharing? *WIIW-FIW Research Reports No. 2014/15–02.*

Stöllinger, R. (2016). Structural change and global value chains in the EU. *Empirica*, 43(4), 801–829.

Svimez (2015). *Report on the Economy of Southern Italy*. Bologna: Il Mulino.

Uxó, J. and Álvarez, I. (2017). Is the end of fiscal austerity feasible in Spain? An alternative plan to the current Stability Programme (2015–2018). *Cambridge Journal of Economics*, 41(4), 999–1020.

Varoufakis, Y. and Tserkezis, L. (2014). Financialization and the financial and economic crises: The case of Greece. *Studies in Financial Systems No. 25*. http://fessud.eu/wp-content/uploads/2012/08/FESSUD_studies-in-financial-systems_Greece_final_Study25.pdf [accessed 15 September 2017].

Vernengo, M. (2015). Greece on the verge, blog entry. nakedkeynesianism.blogspot.com.es/2015/06/greece-on-verge.html, 30 June [accessed 29 September 2017].

Viesti, G. (2015). For the industrialization of Southern Italy: The recent transformation, the national framework and the international experiences. *Research Report of the Cerpem per la Fondazione Mezzogiorno Tirrenico*. http://profgviesti.it/wp-content/uploads/2013/04/VIESTISINTESIECONCLUSIONI.pdf [accessed 29 September 2017].

Wall Street Journal (2010). Dual role in housing deals puts spotlight on Deutsche. 3 August. www.wsj.com/articles/SB10001424052748703900004575325232441982598 [accessed 14 September 2017].

Zenezini, M. (2014). Riforme economiche e crescita: una nota critica. *Economia & lavoro*, 48(3), 99–128.

5 Inequality, poverty and imports

Core, periphery and beyond

1 Introduction

This chapter goes beyond the core-periphery divide to consider the socio-economic divisions within the core and the peripheral countries. We look specifically at the relation between income distribution and imports as an example of how social and economic developments retro-acted on the core-periphery relations.

First, we focus on the formation, in Germany, of a dualistic labour market, which resulted in an increasing share of the German population living in poverty. In the second chapter of this book, we paid attention to the 'supply-side' effects of a dualistic and interdependent labour market: the direct and indirect influence on export price competitiveness of lower labour costs in non-tradable services. The aspect we wish to focus upon here is the 'demand side' influence of the devaluation of labour, specifically, the income effects of the casualization of labour and its impact on imports. The increasing proportion of temporary, part-time and underpaid workers (working poor) led to a fall in workers' incomes, constraining spending on consumption goods and limiting imports of such goods, with the result of boosting Germany's balance of trade surplus. Reduction in the value of imports is not to be interpreted solely in terms of volume of imports, but also as a reduction in the quality of the goods acquired abroad, reflected in the prices. We will argue that the point is by no means insignificant, for it involves substantial changes in the geographical composition of German imports, entailing a displacement of SP's exports to Germany. Thus, the internal vicissitudes of employment, wage and income conditions in Germany had important repercussions on the rest of the Eurozone not solely through the effects of wage restraint on export competitiveness, but also through the connections between falling real incomes, the quality of imports and their geographical composition.

Second, we explore the evolution of economic and social conditions in the SP. As in Germany, the SP's labour markets went through a process of profound segmentation, which started well before the crisis. Unlike Germany, however, the casualization of the labour market occurred within a generalized worsening of economic and social conditions that accelerated as from 2008, with rising unemployment rates, mounting income inequalities and poverty. This is particularly true of countries like Greece and Portugal, where the consequences of the 2008 crisis were most severe. While the crisis contributed to exacerbating the geographical asymmetries within the SP countries, here too the general impoverishment of their population led to an increase in low-quality, low-cost imports, epitomized by China. Thus, we observe the paradox of countries that can no longer afford their own production of 'quality' goods. Here, we shall argue, lies the difference in the macroeconomic effects of the import penetration of cheap consumption goods in the two cases of Germany and the Southern European countries. In fact, the consumer goods industries of the South came to lose the support of their domestic markets, besides suffering the displacement of their exports in their main European market.

The increasing fragmentation of the periphery corresponds to a worsening of the regional divide within each single country. In the final part of this chapter, we focus on the North–South divide in Italy. It will be shown how the pattern of European integration and, in particular, the abandonment of industrial policies in favour of a market-oriented agenda (see Chapters 8 and 9) have exerted their more damaging effects on the least developed regions of the South, contributing to increasing also internal (within-country) socio-economic disparities.

2 Rich Germany, poor Germans

The German welfare state created after the Second World War guaranteed the vast majority of the population universalist coverage of the major economic and social risks (such as unemployment, illness, accidents, old age, etc.). This was combined with an inclusive system of wage determination, based on the principle of equal pay for equal work, and social services and stable living standards over time equal throughout the various parts of the country. Up until the mid-1990s the system had guaranteed that the differences in status and income were effectively mitigated, and levels of poverty remained low. In fact, before reunification, the proportion of low-wage employment in Germany – the low-wage threshold standing at two-thirds of the national median of gross hourly wages – was essentially stable or declining.

In the course of the 1990s, these conditions started to change. As from the middle of the decade, the proportion of low wages began to grow. In the three-year period 2003–2005 (the years that saw implementation of the Hartz plan), it reached nearly 23 per cent – a rate close to that of the United States (25 per cent), the country with the highest share of low-wage workers among the OECD countries (Bosch, 2009).

Setting out to examine what lies behind this reversal in trend, the first point to consider is that the change started ten years before implementation of the Hartz reforms, which therefore cannot be blamed as its *primum movens*, although they contributed greatly to the further growth and consolidation of Germany's share of low-wage workers. Basically, the reasons are to be seen in: (i) the decline of the unions' bargaining power subsequent to the collapse of East Germany's economic system and the consequent increases in unemployment rates, together with the difficulty of exporting West Germany's collective bargaining system into less productive East Germany (Bosch and Kalina, 2016); (ii) a change in the behaviour of German entrepreneurs who, taking advantage of the high level of unemployment and the weakness of the unions, broke free from the collective agreements and, indeed, from their representative associations; (iii) transference of the supply of numerous public services to private concerns, which, unrestrained by collective agreements, competed with the public enterprises through wage dumping (Bosch, 2014). Figure 5.1 illustrates the sectoral segmentation of the German labour market that followed the weakening of the institutional foundations of the old corporatist model, with the services sectors recording nominal wage growth well below the rate of inflation.

Essentially, the Hartz reforms stepped up the process of labour market deregulation embarked upon in the 1990s and, in the rising phase of the German cycle – in the period 2005–2008 (and also subsequently, during the crisis) – prevented economic expansion from playing a part in reducing the proportion of low-wage employment. Indeed, the latter continued to grow in Germany, reaching about 24 per cent by 2011. That same year saw 6.1 million German workers being paid below the minimum hourly wage of €8.50 called for by the DGB (the

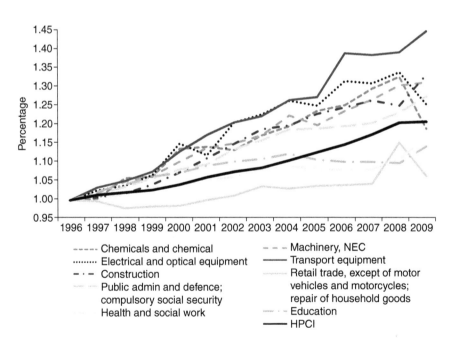

Figure 5.1 Growth in nominal wages by sector and inflation in Germany (1996–2009).

Source: authors' elaboration on WIOD-SEA data.

Note
The bold line reports the evolution of the German Household Consumer Price Index (HCPI).

German Union Confederation), while 2.9 million were earning less than €6 an hour (Kalina and Weinkopf, 2013).

The Hartz reforms questioned some basic principles of the German welfare state: (i) the principle of investment in training for the unemployed was replaced with placing in employment at all costs, even in underpaid jobs (with wages down to only 30 per cent of the customary local wage); (ii) the principle of basing unemployment benefit on the wage previously received was no longer applied, and the maximum duration of the benefit was reduced for elderly workers; (iii) deregulation measures were brought in both in the case of the so-called mini-jobs, with exemption from income tax and social insurance contributions, and for temporary jobs, with the elimination of the time limit for the firms' use of this type of employment, as well as exceptions to the principle of 'same pay for same work' in collective contracts. In the case of mini-jobs and temporary employment, the result was a very appreciable increase in the proportion of these types of employment in the German labour market. The number of temporary workers had risen from the 300,000 of 2003 to 900,000 by 2013, while the number employed in mini-jobs rose from five million to 7.5 million in the same period (Bosch, 2014). Considering that 71 per cent of the mini-jobs and 67 per cent of the temporary workers represent low-wage employment (Kalina and Weinkopf, 2013), the labour market liberalization policies embarked upon in the last decade can be said to have contributed to the increasing share of the working poor in Germany's socio-economic fabric, and to the risk of falling into poverty for ample strata of the population. Between 1995 and 2013 the share of workers receiving gross hourly wages below the poverty threshold (60 per cent of the median wage) rose by just over 13 per cent to about 18 per cent of overall employment. The increasing inequalities in the distribution of income in Germany over the last two decades is reflected in the dwindling of the middle class: the proportion of German households in the middle income class[1] fell from about 57 per cent in 1992 to 48 per cent in 2013. According to Bosch and Kalina (2016), the fall is not to be attributed to demographic factors,[2] nor to a decline in the level of workers' qualifications. Rather, it is to be ascribed to unequal distribution of hours of work amongst the households and the proliferation of insecure low-wage jobs.

The paradox of poverty amidst plenty – the image of macroeconomic success of the German model and the microeconomic failure in spreading the fruits of this success more equally among its people – though insufficiently emphasized, has not gone totally unnoticed. *Rich Germany, Poor Germans: The Dark Side of Welfare* is the title of the book published in Italy in 2014 by an Austrian journalist and anchorwoman, Patricia Szarvas (2014). The statistical evidence of the increase in Germany's poverty rates is undeniable. We need only peruse the Eurostat database on income and living conditions in the European Union (EU-SILC survey) to see Germany's unfavourable position in comparison with the Eurozone. To give only a few examples, in 2014 almost a quarter of Germany's single-person households were considered at permanent risk of poverty as against 17 per cent in the Eurozone as a whole (see Figure 5.2). In 2015, 17 per

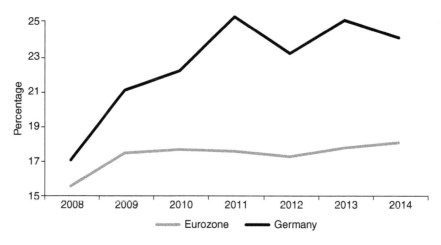

Figure 5.2 Single-person households at persistent risk of poverty: Germany and Euro-zone (2008–2014).

Source: authors' elaboration on EU-SILC data.

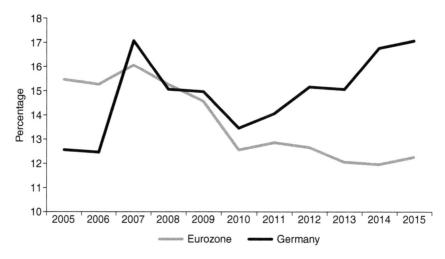

Figure 5.3 Share of retired persons at risk of poverty: Germany and Eurozone (2005–2015).

Source: authors' elaboration on EU-SILC data.

cent of German pensioners were at risk of poverty as compared with 12 percent in the Eurozone (Figure 5.3), and 13 per cent of German employees aged between 16 and 29 were considered at risk of poverty compared with 10 per cent in the Eurozone (Figure 5.4). The latter figures are remarkable when considering the excellent reputation of the German apprenticeship system.

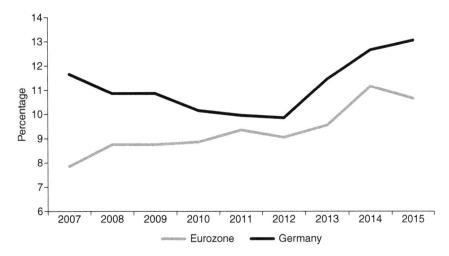

Figure 5.4 Share of employed persons (16–29 years) at risk of poverty: Germany and
     Eurozone (2007–2015).

Source: authors' elaboration on EU-SILC data.

Poverty rates and imports in Germany

We have already discussed the effects of the casualization of the labour market
on German export competitiveness in Chapter 2. If it is true, as argued by Lehndorff (2015), that in the rapid recovery of the German economy after 2008 an
important role must be attributed to the institutional foundations of the 'old'
German model, it is equally true that, as maintained by Hassel (2015), coordination and deregulation are not opposite or mutually exclusive, but complementary processes. They can go hand in hand, leading to a segmented and
dualist political economy. While the coexistence of regulation in the export
industries and liberalization in the services sectors may be seen as a combination
of factors favouring German exports, income effects, through their influence on
the volume and composition of imports, have also played a major role in shaping
Germany's foreign trade surplus. The growth of low-wage employment, the
increasing risk of falling into poverty of ample strata of the German population,
and the sharply increased inequality have affected consumption. In the period
2000–2008 the growth in German households' expenditure on consumption
goods has proved systematically lower than that of the Eurozone as a whole
(Figure 5.5). In turn, the level and composition of consumption have influenced
the volume and quality of German imports of consumption goods, bringing
about appreciable changes in their geographical composition.

The theoretical and empirical literature investigating the connection between
the labour market and international trade has mainly focused on the impact of
trade on employment composition (*skilled versus unskilled*) and pay, with the

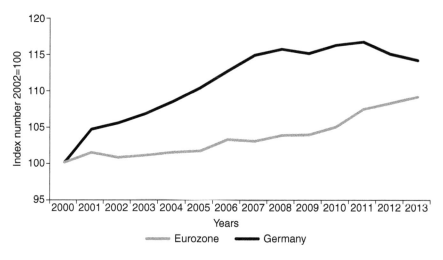

Figure 5.5 Final consumption expenditure of households: Germany and Eurozone (2000–2013) (2000 = 100).

Source: authors' elaboration on Eurostat data.

causal link running from international trade to the labour market.[3] The inverse link, running from labour market and income distribution to trade flows, has focused mostly on export competitiveness, while rather less investigation has gone into the link with imports and their quality. A number of recent studies have taken this latter approach (Adam *et al.*, 2011; Fajgelbaum *et al.*, 2011; Bernasconi and Wuergler, 2013). In these models, advanced countries are net exporters of high-quality goods and net importers of products of lower quality, while the less advanced countries show the opposite pattern of trade. These models find a significant relation between inequality in income distribution and imports,[4] with international trade mitigating the disadvantage of households on relatively low incomes in the advanced countries (while favouring households with relatively high incomes in the less advanced countries).[5]

These models seem to grasp well (with one important qualification reported below) the link between the stylized facts outlined above regarding the trend of income distribution and imports of consumer goods in Germany. Figure 5.6 shows that in the period 2000–2009 German imports of consumption goods from China increased significantly, above all at the level of the low-quality product segment, which increased from 2.5 billion dollars in 2000 to 13 billion in 2009.[6] The availability of cheap consumption goods from China may be seen as complementary to the labour devaluation policies culminating with the Hartz reforms. The geographical reorientation of imports of consumption goods towards cheap suppliers represents an alternative model to the one pursued by Germany until the establishment of the Monetary Union, when appreciation in the exchange rate allowed for reductions in the prices of imported raw materials, consumer goods and intermediate goods, thus helping curb the increase in domestic prices and safeguard the social pact upon which the system of industrial relations rested.

(Simonazzi and Vianello, 1999: 264) (see Chapter 8)

Meanwhile, the progressive upgrading in China's exports,[7] evident in Figure 5.6, shows that as from 2010 the intermediate quality range became predominant in Chinese exports to Germany, with the high-quality segment also showing significant growth.

The increase in Germany's imports from China is reflected in the change in the geographical composition of Germany's imports of consumption goods. Figure 5.7 shows that from 2001 to 2009 China took an increasingly appreciable share in Germany's consumption good imports, above all in the low-quality segment; by 2009 it had exceeded both the share held by the SP and that of the EP. However, it was above all the countries of Central-Eastern Europe that boosted their share in German consumption good imports, with significant upgrading to the medium- and high-quality segments.[8] As for the countries of Southern Europe, their share was in decline over the entire period, with evident reduction in the area of high-quality goods.

On the whole, therefore, focusing on Germany's imports of consumption goods and their geographical composition, three main facts emerge: (i) an appreciable increase in low-quality goods imported above all from China in the period 2000–2009, which accompanied the process of segmentation and casualization of Germany's labour market; (ii) steady growth in the share held by the EPs in

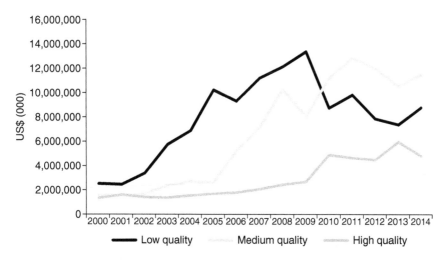

Figure 5.6 Germany's imports of consumption goods from China by quality (2000–2014).

Source: authors' elaboration on CEPII data.

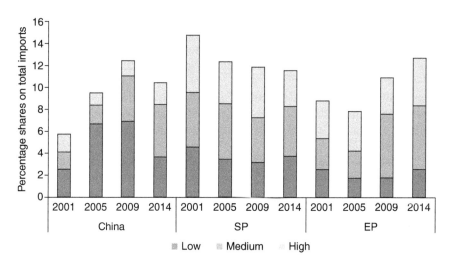

Figure 5.7 Germany's imports of consumption goods from China, the SP and the EP by
quality (2001–2014).

Source: authors' elaboration on CEPII data.

the period 2005–2014, especially strong in the medium- and high-quality segments; (iii)[9] a significant drop in the share held by the SP especially in the high
range. By the end of the period the Southern European countries, which had held
the strongest position at the beginning of the period, were registering approximately the same share of China and the EP.

3 Poor Southern Europe, poor Southern Europeans

Inequality had been on the rise in the Southern European countries long before
the crisis: labour market reforms led to a polarization of the labour market that
the lack of a universal safety net made socially unbearable.[10] The crisis exposed the
problems that the pattern of development of the Southern economies had left
unsolved. The destruction of production capacity, the rise in unemployment, the
worsening in income and working conditions proved far more dramatic in the
peripheral countries of Southern Europe than in the rest of the European Union.
Ample strata of the population have come close or actually succumbed to
poverty, with heavy repercussions on the socio-economic fabric.

A recent Eurofound report (Eurofound, 2017) offers evidence that the crisis
has marked a radical change in the dynamics of income distribution in Europe,
not only widening the gap between centre and periphery but also bringing about
divergences amongst the peripheral countries themselves. While the decade preceding the 2008 crisis saw a certain convergence of 'between-countries'
incomes, thanks above all to the Central-Eastern European countries, the years

following immediately upon 2008 saw an abrupt halt to the process of convergence, with decline in the relative incomes due mainly to the SP (plus the Baltic countries and Ireland) and income resilience in the core countries. However, while the Baltic countries and the EP, involved in Germany's value chain, returned to growth after 2011, the countries of Southern Europe experienced a further decline in incomes. The Eurofound analysis also reveals that, subsequent to 2008, not only has the process of convergence between countries come to a halt, but also the within-countries inequalities have shown dramatic increase, above all due to the high rates of unemployment registered in some countries (mainly the SP).

While studies regarding the few decades preceding the great recession of 2008 attributed the major responsibility for the increasing inequality to wage gaps (OECD, 2011), subsequent to 2008 the main explicative factor behind the growing divergence in incomes lies in the dramatic rise in unemployment rates. These have been particularly high in the countries of Southern Europe, where, lacking a proper welfare state, the traditional mechanism tending to smooth out individual inequalities, based on the sharing of family resources, has practically ground down to a halt given the increase in families devoid of incomes and the dwindling dimensions of the families. Thus, the dramatic aggravation of the economic situation faced by the countries of Southern Europe subsequent to 2008 has had heavy repercussions on the socio-economic fabric of these countries. Figure 5.8 shows that the inequality and socio-economic distress indicators (risk of poverty, severe material deprivation, inability to bear unforeseen expenses) have proved systematically higher in the countries of Southern Europe than in Germany or indeed the entire Eurozone.

As in Germany, the Southern European countries have also seen the rise of China as a main exporter of low price/quality consumption goods, albeit to different degrees in the various countries. Italy shows a certain similarity with Germany in terms of trends in consumption good imports from China: a marked increase in the low-quality segment from 2000 to 2008, and growth also in the other two qualitative components thereafter, although low-range imports continued to predominate in 2014 (Figure 5.9).[11] Spain, Portugal and Greece show a different picture. In these countries, while the low quality/price range increased rapidly since the early 2000s, peaking around 2008–2012, medium- and high-range consumption good imports from China remained decidedly limited throughout the period 2000–2014. The dramatic increase in unemployment and falling wages, above all in the period subsequent to the 2008 crisis, transformed these countries into 'low-quality buyers'.[12]

Thus, the increasing income inequality in the Eurozone produced asymmetric effects between core and periphery. More specialized in capital goods, the core can compensate the impoverishment of a part of its population with imports of cheaper consumer goods. Conversely, the SP countries, producers of medium-high quality consumption goods, suffer a twofold displacement of their markets. The increasing import penetration of cheap consumer goods in the SP markets compounds the negative effects deriving from the redirection of German imports

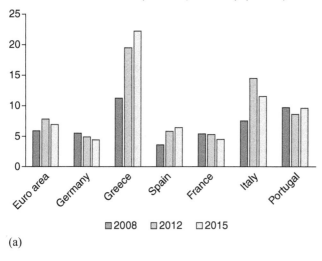

(a)

Figure 5.8 Indicators of inequality and socio-economic distress in selected European countries (2008–2015).

Source: authors' elaboration on Eurostat data.

towards cheaper/lower quality producers. By assuming continuous full employment, the theoretical models that investigate the effects of income distribution on imports and welfare (Adam *et al.*, 2011) miss the negative effects on production, employment and income caused by the loss of domestic demand.

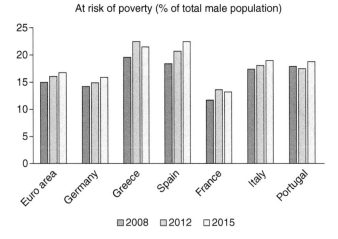

At risk of poverty (% of total male population)

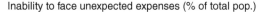

■2008   □2012   □2015

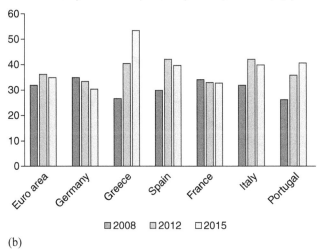

Inability to face unexpected expenses (% of total pop.)

■2008   □2012   □2015

(b)

Figure 5.8 Continued

To conclude, the SP suffered a twofold displacement of its exports to Germany. Just as Germany's increasing productive complementarities with the countries of Central-Eastern Europe entailed a diversion of trade and a weakening of the SP's ties with the core, the dualization of Germany's labour market and the impoverishment of a large part of its population contributed, through their effects on the quality of imports, to divert Germany's imports of consumption goods away from the countries of Southern Europe towards the relatively cheaper goods of the countries of Asia, in the first place China.

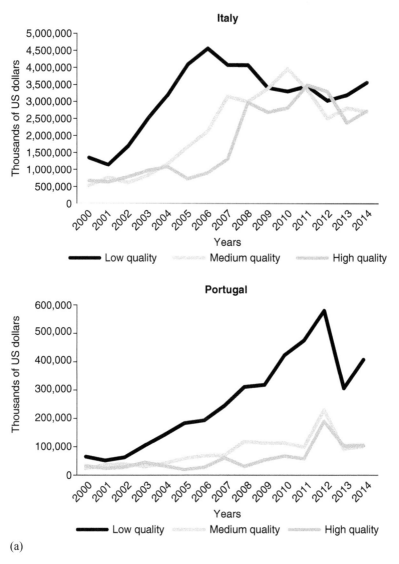

(a)

Figure 5.9 SP's imports of consumption goods from China by quality (2000–2014) (values in US dollars, '000).

Source: authors' elaboration on CEPII data.

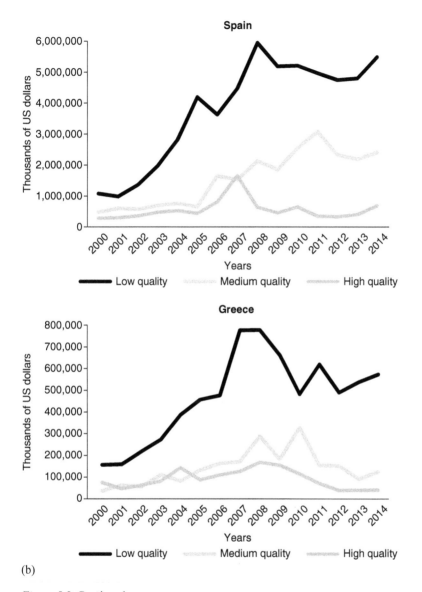

(b)

Figure 5.9 Continued

4 South of South: the case of the Italian Mezzogiorno

The centre-periphery lens can be applied to sharpen the focus on various scales and situations of polarization and dependence. As we have seen, centre-periphery relations can also set in within core countries through the dynamics of labour market segmentation and polarization. These in turn interact with foreign trade, generating repercussions on the economic and social scenario of the other countries. We have also seen that deterioration in wage conditions and income distribution occurred at an even greater degree in the periphery countries (SP), which, above all as from 2008, have seen a dramatic rise in unemployment and poverty. Figures 5.8 and 5.9 reveal wide differences between the peripheral countries in terms of worsening socio-economic conditions. But this is not all, for within each of the peripheral countries the crisis shows differentiated effects, penalizing above all certain productive sectors or structurally weaker regions.

Without any pretence of being exhaustive, having analysed the features of dualism and fragility emerging within the core country, we will close this chapter by describing the increasing internal divide in a country in Southern Europe. Italy has continued to exhibit the features of a two-track country from its foundation as a unified state (1861) to the present day, the North being endowed with a substantial industrial base and export capacity, the Mezzogiorno (Southern Italy) showing a weaker and more dependent productive structure. In particular, we present an interpretative framework to study the widening of the gap between the Mezzogiorno and the rest of the country under way in the last few years, and increasingly aggravated by the differentiated impact of the crisis.

The latest Svimez reports[13] (Svimez, 2016) paint a disheartening picture of the economic situation in the Mezzogiorno, showing that almost all the relevant macroeconomic indicators point to an ever greater gap with the rest of the country. From 2008 to the present day, the fall in the GDP of the South has proved twice that of the Centre-North. The decline in investment and employment has also been more marked in the South, resulting in further shrinking of the manufacturing sector, rising poverty rates and heavy streams of migration from the Mezzogiorno (Svimez, 2016). The situation is not new. For over a decade, year after year, the figures presented in the Svimez – as well as reports and warnings about an economic situation that can only be defined as dramatic – are met with a sort of cynical inurement and resignation. In part, this is due to the fact that structural interventions in favour of Italy's southern regions have practically been reduced to zero over the last decades, no longer enjoying the political (and cultural) consensus necessary for their implementation. And yet, looking at the historical trend of the gap between the Mezzogiorno and the rest of the country, the only significant phase of relative convergence occurred between the early 1950s and the first oil shock,[14] precisely in the period that saw extraordinary intervention in favour of the southern regions by the Cassa per il Mezzogiorno at its height (see Chapter 8).[15] However, after the repeated oil shocks of the 1970s which coincided with the slowdown in Italy's economic growth and an even more marked decline in the development of the southern regions, in the following decades every dirigiste and structuralist approach to the problem of the Mezzogiorno was abandoned. It gave way to a more nuanced, ramified approach aiming, on the one hand, to enhance the economic components of a self-propelling, decentralized development, emulating the successes of the industrial districts of the Centre-North[16] and, on the other hand, to highlight the importance of and need for upgrading of the institutions and social fabric in order to tackle the ills typical of southern and Mediterranean societies: lack of civic sense, scant endowment with social capital, corruption, organized crime, etc.[17]

Initially this turn of the tide in the approach to development of the Mezzogiorno represented a positive advance beyond the 'questione meridionale' (Southern issue) which had by then crystallized in a claim-making pattern with the southern ruling classes relieved of responsibility on the grounds of economic exploitation of the South by the North. However, as time went by this new course failed to deliver the goods in terms of narrowing the gap, in part because the excessive importance attributed to the 'local development agents', social capital and institutional factors entailed losing sight of some important structural changes under way in the economy, also associated with processes of internationalization, which eventually contributed to widening the gap. Effectively, while the New Regional Planning (NPR) – inaugurated at the end of the 1990s by the then Treasury Minister, Ciampi – brought in an innovative approach aimed at building social capital through concerted, place-based planning, it has also shown all its limitations in terms of both support of macroeconomic growth in southern regions and institutional efficiency. The excessive fragmentation of interventions produced through the mediation of the local actors ultimately led once again to the formation of patronage networks and squandering of public resources.[18] Thus, the prevalent idea in the last few years has been to step up on ordinary national policy over the short term, backing down on interventions to restore the geographical balance, given the inefficiency of the local administrations in the South, their exposure to patronage (and often to criminal relations) and the lack of social capital.[19] As a result, structural interventions have been severely reduced.

In the meantime, from the end of the 1980s the trends towards internationalization and their asymmetric effects on the development of Italy's regions were also playing a part in widening the North–South gap.[20] The vertical disintegration of firms – achieved as a reaction to trade union struggles of the late-1960s through decentralization of production (*decentramento produttivo*) – had remained contained within the country up until the 1980s. Although most of the productive complementarities between firms were located in the Centre-North, some subcontracting was also extended to a number of southern firms, above all in the textile/clothing and footwear sectors. As the 1980s came to an end, however, the situation changed and the process of productive fragmentation took on different characteristics. In a scenario that saw the competitive pressure of the emerging countries gaining ground, with an exchange rate no longer susceptible to competitive adjustments as in the past, and a pervasive spread of new information technologies creating new opportunities for the spatial coordination of productive activities, Italian firms set about further restructuring and reorganization of the division of labour, this time also involving internationalization of production.[21]

The results of this internationalization process have been examined in some recent contributions assessing, besides exports, the impact of outgoing foreign direct investment and international outsourcing on the productive performance and employment of Italian firms. Most of these studies point to an increase in productivity and employment as well as upgrading of the composition of employment in the firms that internationalize. However, the geographical dummies introduced in the econometric estimations almost always show that this virtuous link between internationalization and corporate performance applies above all to the Centre-North, rather than the Mezzogiorno. In a study taking the territorial dimension into consideration, for instance, Giunta *et al.* (2012) analyse the intensification of subcontracting relations between Italian firms in the 1990s. They find that although the enhancement of vertical relations between firms can be observed throughout Italy, in the case of the Mezzogiorno, unlike the Centre-North, it is not accompanied by advance in terms of technological innovation, export propensity and growing profitability/productivity for the subcontracting firms.

The southern firms appear to be unable to pull away from the stage of captive supplier, remaining subordinate and vulnerable to competitive pressures. But this is not all, for the internationalization processes involving northern firms contribute to weakening the links of productive complementarity with the southern firms: the extension of the value chain to the international dimension achieved by the firms of North Italy is tending progressively to undermine the subcontracting connections in place with the southern plants. In turn, this contributes to weakening yet further the productive fabric of the Mezzogiorno. This dynamic of polarization and widening of the gap within a peripheral country subsequent to internationalization processes suggests analogies with the processes behind the divergence of areas in the core country:[22] the de-industrialization brought under way in East Germany following upon reunification continued in the successive decades, also in consequence of the West German firms' relocation of production to the countries of Central-Eastern Europe.[23]

Studies of the Italian productive system carried out at the eve of the crisis reveal significant differentiation in the resilience of firms at the territorial level (Bank of Italy, 2009; Bugamelli *et al.*, 2009; Accetturo *et al.*, 2011; Bronzini *et al.*, 2013).[24] These studies evidence that while a great many firms in the Centre-North have found efficient inclusion in the international production chains, very few southern firms are involved in global value chains, while also showing weaker bargaining power. These findings also suggest that while the firms of the Centre-North faced up to the crisis implementing strategies of productive restructuring and greater efficiency, with reduction of costs, diversification of markets and qualitative enhancement of products, the southern firms – typically of smaller dimensions, with limited access to credit and weak bargaining power in subcontracting relations – limited their efforts to squeezing profit margins.

Clearly, this rather different response to crisis contributes to compromising the southern firms' prospects for growth, confining them in marginal conditions and widening yet further the gap with the Centre-North. Even the empirical studies analysing the impact of the crisis on the Italian productive system at firm level paint a picture in which it is all too easy to detect a yet deeper reach in the productive gap between Italy's North and South.

Substantial convergence has been achieved, instead, in one fundamental sector: education. The last few decades have seen an improvement in Italy's educational levels in both North and South alike. Our reference here is not to specific indicators like dropout rates or Programme for International Student Assessment (PISA), but to scholastic-educational levels. We may say that over a considerable span of time an upward North–South convergence has been under way in the educational levels of the workforce, which has not translated, however, into higher qualification of the labour incorporated in southern production (Celi and Sportelli, 2004). Rather, it would appear that the upward convergence in levels of education and the divergence in productive structure have combined to swell the migratory flows of the qualified workforce from the Mezzogiorno to the Centre-North (Celi, 2013). Effectively, after a fall in internal mobility, which began in the 1970s and lasted for two decades,[25] as from the 1990s there has been a marked upturn in internal migration: between 1990 and 2009, 2,350,000 people moved from the Mezzogiorno to the Centre-North (Svimez, 2012). However, in contrast with the internal migration that occurred in the period of the Italian 'economic miracle', when a great mass of southern workforce with low educational levels flooded the factories of the 'Italian industrial triangle',[26] recent migratory flows from the Mezzogiorno are accounted for mainly by people with high levels of education (Mocetti and Porello, 2010). Thus, aggravating the processes of structural polarization between the southern regions and the rest of Italy came the effects of a brain drain – a drain of human resources rich in knowledge, creativity, skills and productive potential that would be crucial for the future economic and civil development of the Mezzogiorno.

The South of Italy is suffering from the consequences of a twofold displacement: the growing distance from the North of Italy, and Italy's growing gap with the European core. Clearly, given the interpretative framework we have outlined, lacking measures to restore the regional and industrial balance, the processes of globalization and Europeanization will contribute to widening the structural gap between the Mezzogiorno and the Centre-North. Vigorous intervention is needed to reinforce and requalify the productive structure of the Mezzogiorno, alongside policies to enhance the 'human' and 'social' capital of the South. Otherwise, these latter policies alone would, paradoxically, prove counter-productive, with the risk of perpetuating the drain on the highly qualified workforce of the southern regions, thereby jeopardizing development in the Mezzogiorno over the long period.

However, the trend over the last few years has been to abandon any significant measure for structural revival of the Mezzogiorno. Even the studies produced by the Bank of Italy, while denouncing the backwardness of the productive structure and the dramatic draining of resources, paradoxically continue to propose futile market-based development policies. For example:

> It is largely a matter of actions not specifically targeting industry, but rather the productive system in general, and enhancing civil life: determination in fighting crime and corruption, which obstruct competition and thwart the chances of the most deserving companies; improvement in the efficiency and quality of public services, far from adequate in the South.
>
> (Bronzini *et al.*, 2013: 8)

The prevalent approach continues to elude the need for a long-term industrial policy (see Chapter 9 and Ginzburg and Simonazzi, 2017). The paradox in public intervention is that abandonment of industrial policy does not mean a reduction in state intervention, for maintenance of acceptable standards of consumption and income in the Mezzogiorno, as indeed in the Länder of East Germany, has entailed massive transfers of state resources (Giacchè, 2014). This paradox will continue to hold if industrial policy and, in general, the role of the state as entrepreneur continue to be eluded.

5 Conclusions

The widening gap between the core and the periphery of Europe involved the creation or the expansion of more inequalities within the core and the periphery alike. In the same way as the countries of the periphery, characterized by historical internal divides, even the core was not spared polarization and divergence. The dark side of Germany's economic success hides the increasing segmentation of the German labour market: high-skilled manufacturing workers employed in the export sector benefiting from protection and high wages and the more fragile components of the labour market, namely low-paid workers, precarious labourers and working poor employed prevalently in the services sector. The increasing wage inequality and the impoverishment of a significant part of the German population shed new light on the sources of the German trade surplus. In fact, the increase in the share of low-wage employment went hand in hand with a remarkable rise in the incidence of low-quality consumption goods in German imports. This evidence has two important implications. On the one hand, it highlights the relevance of 'income effects', besides internal devaluation, in generating the German trade surplus. On the other hand, it contributes to explain the change in Germany's trade network, specifically, the diversion of German imports from the 'luxury' goods produced by the SP to the low-quality, cheaper consumption goods of China. We shall return to this problem in the next chapter.

Increasing inequalities are to be seen also within the peripheral countries. Focusing on the North–South divide in Italy, we showed how the asymmetric involvement of Italian regions in the process of internationalization – further intensified over the last two decades – contributed to widening the socio-economic

distance between the Italian Mezzogiorno and the rest of the country. The abandonment of the industrial policy in favour of a market-oriented agenda and the
differential impact of the 2008 crisis caused the enlargement of the gap. Since
2008, the fall in southern GDP has been twice that of the Centre-North, with
more marked decline in investment, employment and productive capacity in the
South. The dramatic fall in incomes and jobs have caused a significant revival in
internal migration from the South to the Centre-North which, unlike in the past,
is made up of highly educated young people, a circumstance that penalizes even
further the future development of the Mezzogiorno.

Notes

1   The middle class is defined as the percentage remaining after eliminating incomes
    below 60 per cent and above 200 per cent of the median value.
2   Enste *et al.* (2011), for example, attribute the growth in the proportion of the low
    brackets in Germany's income distribution to the increase in single-person households
    resulting from the separation of couples.
3   For a review of the ample literature on the effects of international trade on the labour
    market, see Greenaway and Nelson (2001) and, for an updating, Greenaway *et al.*
    (2008).
4   In particular, surveying a panel of 59 countries in the period 1970–1997, Adam *et al.*
    (2011) find that the relation shows a positive sign in the case of the developed coun-
    tries, but negative in the developing countries. When income inequality increases in
    the advanced countries – when, that is, income increases for households enjoying high
    incomes and decreases for households on low incomes – the latter shift their demand
    towards low-quality goods, and thus the volume of imports increases. Conversely, in
    the case of the developing countries increasing income inequality shifts the demand
    of the lower income households towards low-quality products of domestic production,
    and the volume of imports consequently falls.
5   In the model proposed by Fajgelbaum *et al.* (2011), the international specialization of
    the country is accounted for with a Linder mechanism based on a 'home-market'
    effect: the country tends to export goods that loom larger in its domestic demand
    structure; thus the rich countries tend to export goods of higher quality for which there
    is strong domestic demand. Moreover, in the rich countries international trade favours
    the lower income groups insofar as it extends the range of low-quality products avail-
    able to them and so channels income to them from the groups consuming a greater
    proportion of high-quality/price goods.
6   This evidence is in line with Gaulier *et al.* (2012), who analyse the growth in weight
    of the emerging economies in EU-15 trade in the period 1995–2008, finding that
    European imports from Asia were mainly of Chinese origin (70 per cent in 2007), and
    concentrated in the low-quality segment. Furthermore, the authors demonstrate that
    the specifically high-tech European imports from Asia were also greatly concentrated
    in the lower range in terms of price/quality (about 60 per cent in 2007).
7   The data on international trade show that a positive correlation exists between export
    unit values and the degree of development of the exporting countries (Schott, 2004;
    Hummels and Klenow, 2005; Hallak and Schott, 2011). It is therefore hardly surpris-
    ing to find progressive upgrading in the quality/prices of the goods exported as the
    exporting country improves its position in terms of per capita income, as in the case
    of China. However, Ito and Okubo (2016) question the impression many authors (for
    example, Rodrik, 2006) convey of an alleged qualitative upgrading of Chinese exports
    over the last few years. In particular, analysing the eight-digit unit values in bilateral
    intra-industry trade between China and Germany, Ito and Okubo demonstrate that the

price/quality gap between the two countries has not narrowed over the last two decades, but remains wide. By contrast, the same analysis conducted on Germany–EP bilateral intra-industry trade reveals that the price/quality gap between Germany and the countries of Central-Eastern Europe has significantly narrowed. Nevertheless, as explained in the following note, this finding may be conditioned by the strong incidence of vertical trade in Germany–EP trading relations.

8 In an article of 1997, Murphy and Shleifer started from the observation that trade between West Europe and Eastern Europe was limited, growth being thwarted by the low quality of eastern production and due to the fact that eastern consumers could not afford the high prices of western consumption goods. It was impossible to approach this situation with an analytic scheme à la Heckscher-Ohlin, and the two authors therefore proposed an alternative model entailing trade between countries with similar levels of development. This offered a key to interpret the case of the scant trade with the countries of Eastern Europe, which 'have nothing to sell to the West' (p. 1). Surprisingly enough, after only two decades the pattern of trade between Western Europe and Central-Eastern Europe has proved completely different from that anticipated by Murphy and Shleifer (1997). Not only has East–West trade grown appreciably, but the exports of the EP have also shown significant qualitative upgrading, as evidenced by trade with Germany. As we argued in Chapter 2, a considerable part of this trade derives from involvement of the Central-Eastern European countries in the German value chain. Thus, it is not surprising to observe the high unit values of EP exports to Germany if we bear in mind that, in many cases, it is a matter of German production exported to the EP to be processed and subsequently reimported by Germany.

9 This trend was not limited to consumption goods alone. As pointed out above, and as will also be seen in the following chapter, in the intermediate goods, too, the EP achieved significant growth in the exports to Germany, above all in the medium- and high-quality segments, while the SP (in particular Italy) consolidated their role as exporters of low-quality intermediate goods.

10 See the issue of *Economia & Lavoro* (2014) for a review of the evolution of the European social models before and in the crisis.

11 Unlike the other countries of Southern Europe, Italy probably saw a preference effect, based on the characteristics of the domestic market, favouring the progressive qualitative upgrading of consumption goods imported from China. In any case, the growth in the number of discount stores in Italy (above all in the southern regions) and the significant increase in their market share in terms of sales of daily consumer goods are indicative of the degree to which the severity of the crisis has increased the proportion of low-price/quality goods in the demand of ample ranges of Italian consumers (Scarci, 2016).

12 This pattern is to be seen not only in the countries of Southern Europe but on an appreciably broader scale. In fact, some recent studies, analysing the characteristics of the slump in world trade subsequent to the 2008 crisis, point to a 'flight from quality' in the imports of certain countries and in certain sectors provoked by falling incomes. See Chen and Juvenal (2016), in the case of Argentina's wine exports; Bems and Di Giovanni (2016), in the case of Latvia; Berthou and Emlinger (2010), in the case of the European Union (EU15).

13 Svimez, 'Associazione per lo sviluppo dell'industria nel Mezzogiorno' (Association for the development of industry in southern Italy), is a research centre instituted in 1946 with the aim of studying the economy of the Mezzogiorno and proposing to the central government and local administrations projects for development in the southern regions. As from 1974, every year Svimez has published a report on the economic situation of the Mezzogiorno.

14 The per capita GDP of the Mezzogiorno in proportion to that of the rest of the country had fallen to the historical low of 47 per cent by 1951. In the only phase of convergence of the southern economy with that of the Centre-North, in the period spanning

from the 1950s to the eve of the first oil shock, in 1973, the relative per capita GDP peaked at 66 per cent. In the following decades, the per capita income in the South never exceeded the threshold of 60 per cent of that of the Centre-North and the gap persists even now: the figure for 2015 (55.8 per cent) is practically identical with that of 1940 (Daniele and Malanima, 2007: tab. 4).

15 The Cassa per il Mezzogiorno ('Fund for extraordinary works of public interest in Southern Italy') was instituted in 1950 by the sixth De Gasperi Government to fund infrastructural works and industrial activities in the southern regions of Italy with the aim of closing the gap between these and the northern regions. According to the original plan, the Cassa per il Mezzogiorno (Casmez) was to fulfil its task within a time span of ten years (1950–1960), but successive legislative extensions prolonged its mandate until 1984, when it was closed. Nevertheless, 1986 saw the institution of the 'Agenzia per la promozione e lo sviluppo del Mezzogiorno' (Agency for promotion and development of the Mezzogiorno), with the same functions and objectives as the Casmez. The Agency was dissolved in 1992.

16 An optimistic view of the dynamics of the southern productive system in the 1990s emerged in contributions by Cersosimo and Donzelli (2000), Viesti (2000) and, only partially, in Sarno (2002). In these studies, the intensification of subcontracting relations between the southern firms was seen as a positive trend towards the creation of industrial districts, industrial-system areas and local productive systems.

17 At the end of the 1950s, Banfield (1958) pointed to 'amoral familism' as central to the inefficiency of the institutions and the backwardness of civil society in the Mezzogiorno, referring to the tendency to give the immediate interests of own family priority over those of the community. Two decades later, Putnam (1993) traced the differential in 'civic sense' between the two areas of the country to the different historical vicissitudes of the Centre-North and the South of Italy. According to Putnam, while the establishment of the commune system encouraged citizens to take part in public affairs in the Centre-North, the creation of the absolute state by the Norman monarchy favoured hierarchical relations, leaving the subjects no room for political participation. Banfield and Putnam's ideas were recently taken up once again to account for the gap between Centre-North and southern Italy in terms of 'social capital' differential. For example, Alesina and Ichino (2009) placed great stress on the lack of social capital and civic sense as the main cause of the backwardness of the Mezzogiorno, proposing four 'micro-interventions' designed to reconstruct the social capital (even involving the education of southern Italian children in primary school). Recent 'non-economic' explanations of the gap between the Mezzogiorno and the rest of Italy do not confine attention to the social capital but even go as far as dusting off and dragging out Lombrosian and racist approaches. In an essay published in 2010, Richard Lynn (University of Ulster) opines that the differences between the North and the Mezzogiorno in the population's IQ (intelligence quotients) underlie the differences in income, education, infantile mortality and stature (in southern Italy genetic mixing with immigrants from North Africa and the Middle East played a part in this, according to Lynn).

18 For an evaluation of the development policies for the Mezzogiorno, cf. Cannari *et al.* (2009) and Franzini (2010). For discussion of the limitations of the new regional planning, see Giunta (2010) and Prota and Viesti (2012).

19 This opinion is argued by Rossi (2006).

20 Actually, some scholars studying economic development in Italy, including Bonelli (1978) and Cafagna (1989), had already noted that even before the unification of Italy the fundamental element differentiating North and South lay above all in the different degrees of international integration. While the northern regions were able to export in the agro-industrial sector (silk thread) with consequent positive fallout, extending the industrial base, the southern regions, once able to export agricultural produce, became mired down in the backwardness of relations in the large estate system (*latifondo*) and

geographical isolation. Thus, the difference in export propensity between northern and southern Italy had already set in before the unification of the country and is now universally recognized, albeit neglected (with rare exceptions, such as the recent contribution of A'Hearn and Venables, 2013). In a recent book, Felice (2013) argues that the incapacity of the South to supersede the large estate system depended upon the 'extractive' proclivity (extracting rent, in accordance with the definition by Acemoglu and Robinson, 2012) of the southern ruling classes, as well as the low level of literacy shown by the lower classes.

21 The evolution of Italy's productive system in the changed international competitive scenario marked by the three features referred to in the text is described in Brandolini and Bugamelli (2009). Specific analysis of the impact of the euro on the restructure of Italian firms can be found in the study by Bugamelli *et al.* (2008), who note that it is the firms that depended on devaluation of the lira in the past that are most involved in restructure processes. These processes have also entailed a sharp reduction of the manual labour component of the workforce.

22 Boltho *et al.* (1997), drawing a – not particularly convincing – parallel between southern Italy and East Germany, argue that the greater 'social capability' enjoyed by the latter would ward off any repetition of a 'Mezzogiorno' scenario for this area. A far more interesting comparison between Italy's Mezzogiorno and East Germany, approached through broader and more detailed discussion of German unification, is to be seen in Giacchè (2014).

23 A complementary explanation of this trend in East–West divide in Germany after reunification is provided by Coniglio *et al.* (2011). According to the authors, the slowdown in productivity convergence between East and West Germany has been affected by the growth in productivity in western Länder due to the upgrading in skill composition of employment occurred in western firms after relocation of activities in Central-Eastern European countries.

24 *Indagine sulle imprese industriali e dei servizi* (Survey of industrial firms and services), published by the Bank of Italy in various years, includes the regional aspects.

25 On the basic reasons for the halt in migratory flows from southern Italy to the Centre-North from the early 1970s to 1994, despite the increasing unemployment differentials between the two areas, see Faini *et al.* (1997).

26 Milan, Turin and Genoa are the cities in Italy's North-West forming the vertices of the triangle.

References

A'Hearn, B. and Venables, A. (2013). Regional disparities: Internal geography and external trade. In G. Toniolo (ed.), *The Oxford Handbook of the Italian Economy since Unification*. Oxford: Oxford University Press.

Accetturo, A., Giunta, A. and Rossi, S. (2011). The Italian firms between crisis and new globalization. *L'industria*, 32(1), 145–164.

Acemoglu, D. and Robinson, J. (2012). *The Origins of Power, Prosperity, and Poverty: Why Nations Fail*. New York: Crown Business.

Adam, A., Katsimi, M. and Moutos, T. (2011). Inequality and the import demand function. *Oxford Economic Papers*, 64(4), 675–701.

Alesina, A. and Ichino, A. (2009). Sud e Isole: far crescere il capitale sociale. *Il Sole24 ore*, 22 December. www.ilsole24ore.com/art/SoleOnLine4/dossier/Italia/2009/commenti-sole-24-ore/22-dicembre-2009/giovani-sud-crescita-capitale-sociale_PRN.shtml [accessed 22 December 2009].

Banfield, E. (1958). *The Moral Basis of a Backward Society*. Glencoe, IL: The Free Press.

Bank of Italy (2009). Survey of industrial and service firms. Year 2008. Supplement to the *Statistical Bulletin, New Series*, XIX(38).

Bems, R. and Di Giovanni, J. (2016). Income-induced expenditure switching. *American Economic Review*, 106(12), 3898–3931.

Bernasconi, C. and Wuergler, T. (2013). *Per capita income and the quality and variety of imports*. Mimeo, University of Zurich.

Berthou, A. and Emlinger, C. (2010). Crises and the collapse of world trade: The shift to lower quality. *CEPII Working Papers No. 2010–07*.

Boltho, A., Carlin, W. and Scaramozzino, P. (1997). Will East Germany become a new Mezzogiorno? *Journal of Comparative Economics*, 24(3), 241–264.

Bonelli, F. (1978). Il capitalismo italiano. Linee generali di interpretazione. In *Storia d'Italia. Annali 1. Dal feudalesimo al capitalismo*. Turin: Einaudi.

Bosch, G. (2009). Low-wage work in five European countries and the United States. *International Labour Review*, 148(4), 337–356.

Bosch, G. (2014). Reconstructing the German social model. *Economia & Lavoro*, 48(2), 31–48.

Bosch, G. and Kalina, T. (2016). The German middle class from a labour market perspective. *Economia & Lavoro*, 50(2), 25–38.

Brandolini, A. and Bugamelli, M. (2009). Reports on trends on the Italian productive system. *Questioni di Economia e Finanza, Bank of Italy Occasional Papers No. 45*.

Bronzini, R., Cannari, L., Staderini, A. and Santioni, R. (2013). L'industria meridionale e la crisi (Industry in the south of Italy and the crisis). *Questioni di Economia e Finanza, Bank of Italy Occasional Papers No. 194*.

Bugamelli, M., Schivardi, F. and Zizza, R. (2008). The euro and firm restructuring. *NBER Working Paper No. 14454*.

Bugamelli, M., Cristadoro, R. and Zevi, G. (2009). The international crisis and the Italian productive system: A firm-level study. *Bank of Italy Occasional Papers No. 58*.

Cafagna, L. (1989). *Dualismo e sviluppo nella storia d'Italia*. Venice: Marsilio.

Cannari, L., Magnani, M. and Pellegrini, G. (2009). What policies do we need for Southern Italy? The role of national and regional policies in the last decade. *Questioni di Economia e Finanza, Bank of Italy Occasional Papers No. 50*.

Celi, G. (2013). Globalization and native internal mobility in a dualistic economy. *Économie appliquée*, LXVI(4), 57–78.

Celi, G. and Sportelli, M. (2004). Internazionalizzazione, mercato del lavoro e capitale umano in Italia. *Economia e società regionale*, 2004(3), 105–128.

Cersosimo, D. and Donzelli, C. (2000). *Mezzogiorno. Realtà e rappresentazioni delle tendenze del cambiamento territorial*. Rome: Donzelli.

Chen, N. and Juvenal, L. (2016). Quality and the great trade collapse. *IMF Working Paper WP/16/30*.

Coniglio, N., Prota, F. and Viesti, G. (2011). Note sui processi di convergenza regionale in Germania e in Spagna. *Rivista economica del Mezzogiorno*, (1–2), 91–128.

Daniele, V. and Malanima, P. (2007). The product of the Regions and the North-South divide in Italy (1861–2004). *Rivista di politica economica*, 97(3–4), 267–315.

Economia & Lavoro (2014). Growing diverse? European social models in turbulent times, No. 2.

Enste, H., Erdmann, V. and Kleineberg, T. (2011). Mythen über die Mittelschicht. *Roman Herzog Institut. Information*, 2011(9).

Eurofound (2017). *Income Inequality and Employment Patterns in Europe Before and After the Great Recession*. Luxembourg: Publication Office of the European Union.

Faini, R., Galli, G., Gennari, P. and Rossi, F. (1997). An empirical puzzle: Falling migration and growing unemployment differentials among Italian regions. *European Economic Review*, 41(3–5), 571–579.

Fajgelbaum, P., Grossman, G. and Helpman, E. (2011). Income distribution, product quality, and international trade. *Journal of Political Economy*, 119(4), 721–765.

Felice, E. (2013). *Perché il Sud è rimasto indietro*. Bologna: Il Mulino.

Franzini, M. (2010). Le politiche per il Mezzogiorno e i limiti della politica. *QA-Rivista dell'Associazione Rossi-Doria*, (2), 169–174.

Gaulier, G., Lemoine, F. and Ünal, D. (2012). The rise of emerging economies in the EU15 trade. *The European Journal of Comparative Economics*, 9(1), 133–175.

Giacchè, V. (2014). *Anschluss. L'annessione. L'unificazione della Germania e il futuro dell'Europa*. Reggio Emilia: Imprimatur.

Ginzburg, A. and Simonazzi, A. (2017). Out of the crisis: A radical change of strategy for the Eurozone. *The European Journal of Comparative Economics*, 14(1), 13–37.

Giunta, A. (2010). L'incoerenza attuativa della Nuova politica regionale. *QA-Rivista dell'Associazione Rossi Doria*, (2), 159–168.

Giunta, A., Nifo, A. and Scalera, D. (2012). Subcontracting in Italian industry: Labour division, firm growth and the North-South divide. *Regional Studies*, 46(8), 1067–1083.

Greenaway, D. and Nelson, D. (2001). Globalisation and labour markets: A review of the literature. In D. Greenaway and D. Nelson (eds), *Globalisation and Labour Markets Vols. I and II*. Cheltenham: Edward Elgar.

Greenaway, D., Upward, R. and Wright, P. (eds) (2008). *Globalization and Labour Market Adjustment*. London: Palgrave Macmillan.

Hallak, J. and Schott, P. (2011). Estimating cross-country differences in product quality. *The Quarterly Journal of Economics*, 126(1), 417–474.

Hassel, A. (2015). The German model in transition. In B. Unger (ed.), *The German Model: Seen by its Neighbours*. London: SE Publishing, 105–133.

Hummels, D. and Klenow, P. (2005). The variety and quality of a nation's exports. *The American Economic Review*, 95(3), 704–723.

Ito, T. and Okubo, T. (2016). Product quality and intra-industry trade. *The Singapore Economic Review*, 61(04), 1550106.

Kalina, T. and Weinkopf, C. (2013). Niedriglohnbeschäftigung 2011: Weiterhin arbeitet fast ein Viertel der Beschäftigten. In *Deutschland für einen Niedriglohn*. IAQ-Report 2013–01, Duisburg: Universität Duisburg-Essen.

Lehndorff, S. (2016). Internal devaluation and employment trends in Germany. In M. Myant, S. Theodoropoulou and A. Piasna (eds), *Unemployment, Internal Devaluation and Labour Market Deregulation in Europe*. Brussels: ETUI, 169–196.

Lynn, R. (2010). In Italy, north–south differences in IQ predict differences in income, education, infant mortality, stature, and literacy. *Intelligence*, 38(1), 93–100.

Mocetti, S. and Porello, C. (2010). Labour mobility in Italy: New evidence on migration trends. *Questioni di Economia e Finanza, Bank of Italy Occasional Papers No. 6*.

Murphy, K. and Shleifer, A. (1997). Quality and trade. *Journal of Development Economics*, 53(1), 1–15.

OECD (2011). *Divided We Stand: Why Inequality Keeps Rising*. Paris: OECD Publishing.

Prota, F. and Viesti, G. (2012). *Senza cassa: le politiche di sviluppo del Mezzogiorno dopo l'intervento straordinario*. Bologna: Il Mulino.

Putnam, R. (1993). *Making Democracy Work: Civic Traditions in Modern Italy*. Princeton, NJ: Princeton University Press.

Rodrik, D. (2006). What's so special about China's exports? *China & World Economy*, 14(5), 1–19.

Rossi, N. (2006). *Mediterraneo del Nord. Un'altra idea del Mezzogiorno*. Bari: Laterza.

Sarno, D. (2002). *Le piccole e medie imprese nel Mezzogiorno*. Soveria Mannelli: Rubbettino.

Scarci, E. (2016). I discount in Italia superano quota 5 mila. *Il Sole24ore*, 23 September. www.ilsole24ore.com/art/impresa-e-territori/2016-09-22/i-discount-italia-superano-quota-5mila-152938.shtml?uuid=ADyNoMPB [accessed 23 September 2016].

Schott, P. (2004). Across-product versus within-product specialization in international trade. *The Quarterly Journal of Economics*, 119(2), 647–678.

Simonazzi, A. and Vianello, F. (1999). Financial liberalization, the European single currency and the problem of unemployment. In M. Franzini and F. R. Pizzuti (eds), *Globalization, Institutions and Social Cohesion*. Berlin: Springer, 257–282.

Svimez (2012). *Rapporto Svimez 2012 sull'Economia del Mezzogiorno*. Bologna: Il Mulino.

Svimez (2016). *Rapporto Svimez 2016 sull'Economia del Mezzogiorno*. Bologna: Il Mulino.

Szarvas, P. (2014). *Ricca Germania, poveri tedeschi: il lato oscuro del benessere*. Milano: Egea.

Viesti, G. (2000). *Mezzogiorno dei distretti*. Rome: Donzelli.

6 The network of European trade between core and periphery

1 Introduction

In Chapters 1 and 2, we investigated the structural and institutional elements at the basis of the core/periphery divide in Europe. We argued that the hierarchical reorganization of the European industrial fabric fostered the emergence of two peripheries: the SP (Southern periphery) and the EP (Eastern periphery). Here, we provide a representation of this reorganization. We focus on its key drivers, in particular the role played by the German manufacturing sector in its evolving relations with the two peripheries.

Since the euro's inception, the SP has experienced a weakening of its industrial base and an increasing dependence on foreign financial flows. Conversely, as the result of entering as a key partner in what Stehrer and Stöllinger (2015) call the 'Central European Manufacturing Core' (CEMC), the EP has dramatically enlarged and strengthened its manufacturing base (see Chapter 4). Manufacturing productions – closely connected with German-based firms' activities – proliferate in the EP, partly crowding out suppliers located in the SP (see Chapter 2 and Simonazzi et al., 2013). Besides the two peripheries, there is an incipient third one formed by the set of Eastern economies that have recently joined the EU but have little or no involvement in the German production network – i.e. Bulgaria, Croatia, Estonia, Latvia, Lithuania and Romania. As opposed to the countries more strongly linked to the German economy, this group has weaker growth dynamics, particularly in regard to exports, and no comparable increase in its manufacturing base (Lefilleur, 2008). Within this reorganization process, France is undergoing relative economic and political decline; a decline that, as will emerge in what follows, is clearly detectable from its trade relations (on this point, see also Chapter 3).

This chapter illustrates the hierarchical reorganization of the European economy from different perspectives. Section 2 describes the evolving structure of the network of trade among Germany, France, SP, EP and key international partners. It documents the rise of Germany's trade leadership since the introduction of the euro in 1999, the resizing of the SP and the increasing relevance of the EP. Section 3 considers the structural relations, taking into account the international fragmentation of production and the different offshoring strategies.[1]

Section 4 documents the development of core-periphery relations by considering the evolution of the key automotive sector

2 The European trade networks

The decade following the introduction of the euro coincides with the emergence of Germany as the European trade leader. The consolidation of German economic leadership and the accompanying industrial reorganization gave rise to a more general reshuffling of the various areas directly or indirectly connected with the German economy. In what follows, we explore two distinct networks of trade. The first network (N1, hereafter) considers the changing relations between Germany and its Southern partners and includes Germany, Greece, Italy, Spain, Portugal and France. The second network (N2, hereafter) encompasses the entire EZ, the near and far Eastern countries, as well as Germany, France, the clusters of countries belonging to the SP and the EP, the remaining Euro-9 – i.e. Austria, Belgium, Cyprus, Finland, Ireland, Luxembourg, Malta, Netherlands and Slovenia – and China.

We analyse the evolving shapes of networks 1 and 2 for the years 1999, 2008 and 2014. This time span covers the European trade relations before and after the euro's introduction, and before and after the crisis. Figure 6.1 shows the N1 in 1999. The arrows start from the surplus countries and point to the deficit ones. The small boxes in the middle of each arrow report the amount of bilateral exports. Following the arrows' direction, the first box reports the value of exports of the surplus country (in billion dollars) while the second box reports the value of exports of the deficit country (that is, the surplus country's imports from the deficit country).[2] Thus, in the case of the Germany–Italy bilateral relation as reported in N1, the arrow starts from Germany and points to Italy, indicating that the former has a surplus vis-à-vis the latter. The figures in the boxes show that, in 1999, trade between the two countries was almost balanced. In fact, Germany's surplus with respect to Italy amounted to 950 million dollars, significantly less than German surpluses vis-à-vis all the remaining countries of N1. Overall, the N1 exhibits a clear hierarchical ordering. Germany has a surplus with all the countries considered, followed by Italy, which, in turn, with the exception of its very small deficit vis-à-vis Germany, records a surplus with all the remaining countries. France has a trade surplus with Greece, Spain and Portugal. Thus, two countries – i.e. Germany (with a total surplus of 28.55 billion dollars) and Italy (with a total surplus of 13.68 billion dollars) – have a surplus with respect to the rest of the network. The bilateral surpluses of France with the rest of the network are not sufficient to compensate for its heavy deficit with Germany (and Italy). Spain shows the largest overall deficit (12.84 billion dollars), only slightly offset by a large bilateral surplus with Portugal.

Figure 6.2 depicts how the N1 changed in 2008, eight years after the euro introduction. The most striking figure regards the German surplus, which exploded vis-à-vis all other countries: four times higher than in 1999 with respect to France and Spain, significantly greater with respect to Greece, Italy and Portugal. Italy has

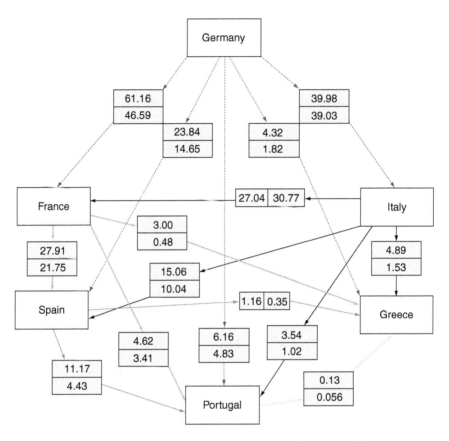

Figure 6.1 Network 1 (1999): France, Germany, Greece, Italy, Spain and Portugal.

Source: authors' elaboration on COMTRADE data.

managed to more than compensate its huge deficit with Germany by means of its overall surplus with all the rest of the network (scoring an overall surplus of 6.71 billion dollars). The economic decline of France, as delineated in Chapter 3, is reflected in the evolution of its bilateral trade balances: a huge deficit with Germany, an increased deficit with Italy and a surplus turned into deficit with Spain. Spain's increased surpluses with Greece, France and Portugal are not enough to compensate the explosive deficit with Germany and, to a more limited extent, with Italy. While Greece records increasing deficits with all the network members, its deficits with Germany and Italy shoot up. The hierarchical structure appears to be reinforced: while bilateral flows double, Germany's surpluses treble. Italy manages to retain its net surplus position, while Spain's improved surplus with France, Portugal and Greece cannot compensate its huge deficit with Germany. If Germany is the undisputed leader, France emerges as the true loser in this period. The effects of six years of crisis, reported in Figure 6.3, radically change the picture.

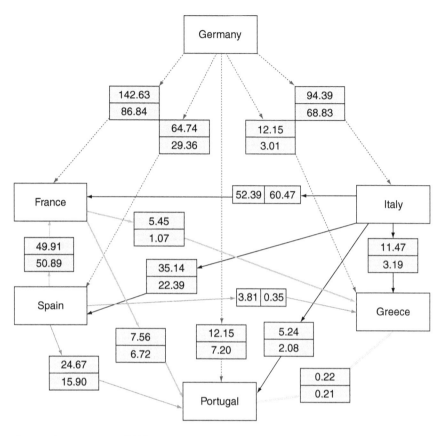

Figure 6.2 Network 1 (2008): France, Germany, Greece, Italy, Spain and Portugal.
Source: authors' elaboration on COMTRADE data.

Between 2008 and 2014, the value of total trade within the network greatly diminished. This reduction is explained by a sizeable drop in the imports of all countries but Germany, only partly compensated by an increase in German imports from all partners, except for Italy and Greece. In particular, German total exports to the network in 2014 were 18 per cent below their 2008 value (a fall of 58.35 billion dollars), leading to a significant erosion of German surpluses. The crisis of the SP also hit France, whose exports to the area, excluding Germany, declined by 22.5 per cent (26 billion dollars), only partially compensated by an increase in exports to Germany (+8 per cent). The French deficit towards the rest of the N1 increased more than it fell vis-à-vis Germany, so that its overall deficit increased to 64.50 billion dollars. The adjustment in Spain's imports was particularly severe: –28.6 per cent in imports from Germany, and –21.3 per cent from the rest of the area; a total adjustment of –24.1 per cent, which turned the Spanish external deficit into a surplus. Thus, the deflationary

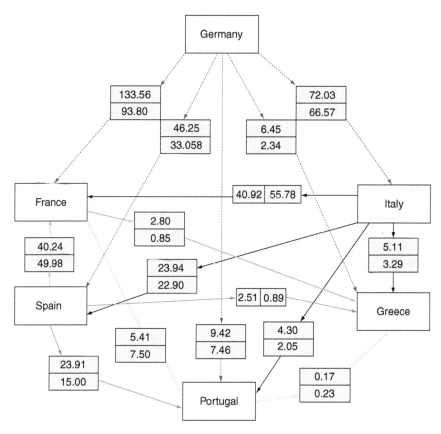

Figure 6.3 Network 1 (2014): France, Germany, Greece, Italy, Spain and Portugal.

Source: authors' elaboration on COMTRADE data.

impulses transmitted through the external trade multiplier exerted their effects on the economies of the area without sparing the traditional surplus countries, Germany and Italy. Italy, in particular, was the only country (except Greece) not increasing its exports to Germany, being able to increase its bilateral balance with France only thanks to an exceptional decrease in its imports. The disruptive effects of the crisis in the SP did not change the hierarchical structure of trade. However, they were sufficiently important to induce core-based exporters to reorganize their foreign markets in search of new outlets for their surpluses. Such reorganization was facilitated by the ongoing process of globalization and regionalization of world trade and, in the last period, by the spectacular growth of the Chinese economy. The N2 allows the change in European trade relationships to be contextualized within these broader processes.

In 1999, the N2 was still focused on Europe (Figure 6.4). Germany was no longer a net-exporter vis-à-vis all partners, as in N1. It compensated its deficit

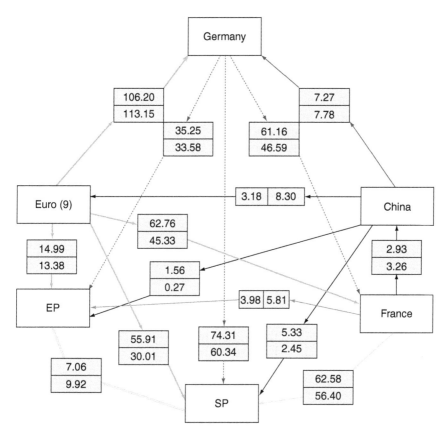

Figure 6.4 Network 2 (1999): China, France, Germany, the SP (Greece, Italy, Spain and Portugal), the EP (Czech Republic, Hungary, Poland and Slovak Republic) and the EZ (Austria, Belgium, Cyprus, Finland, Ireland, Luxemburg, Malta, Netherlands and Slovenia).

Source: authors' elaboration on COMTRADE data.

with the Euro-9, which was its most important partner in terms of volume of trade, with a surplus towards France and the SP. The volume of trade with the EP and China was still relatively small, resulting in a small surplus with the EP and a deficit with China. Overall, Germany ran a surplus of 23.67 billion dollars. The Euro-9 group, in turn, displayed a surplus with all partners but China. Notice that, however, the Euro-9 surpluses – particularly the one vis-à-vis Germany – are likely to have been influenced by the so-called 'Rotterdam effect', that is, by the role of world trade hub played by the Netherlands: serving as transit area, particularly through the port of Rotterdam, the Netherlands import goods produced in other countries and then re-export them. Though recording surpluses with all countries or groups of countries except France,

China was in 1999 still a minor player in terms of trade volumes, and its surpluses were equally small. The SP had strong trade relations with all the other EU countries, and ran deficits with all of them, with the exception of the EP. The latter had weak trade relationships with all the network except Germany. The picture was very different nine years later. In 2008 (Figure 6.5), Chinese exports to the N2's partners were ten times higher than in 1999. A less pronounced, though significant, growth characterized Chinese imports, with Germany exhibiting the highest value of exports and the smallest bilateral deficit. The rise of China in world trade is reflected in the generalized strengthening of Chinese trade ties – both imports and exports – with almost all partners.

Germany's trade relations present two main features: all its bilateral flows show a remarkable increase, but while German trade with the Euro-9 and the EP is fairly balanced, Germany records huge surpluses with the SP and France.

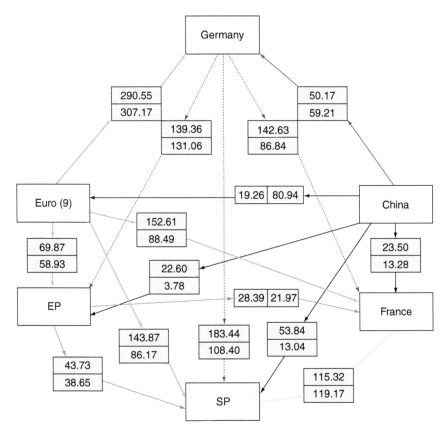

Figure 6.5 Network 2 (2008): China, France, Germany, the SP (Greece, Italy, Spain and Portugal), the EP (Czech Republic, Hungary, Poland and Slovak Republic) and the EZ (Austria, Belgium, Cyprus, Finland, Ireland, Luxemburg, Malta, Netherlands and Slovenia).

Source: authors' elaboration on COMTRADE data.

Moreover, the dramatic rise of trade volumes between Germany and the EP between 1999 and 2008 highlights the creation of a dense network of trade and production relationships (see Chapter 2). The value of EP's exports (of intermediate goods) to Germany overtook the value of exports of the SP, signalling the relative weakening of Germany–SP's relations and the crowding out of SP suppliers within the German manufacturing value chains (VCs). Though running a net deficit towards N2 partners (amounting to 45.99 billion dollars), the EP became a net exporter vis-à-vis France and the SP, which, in turn, ran deficits vis-à-vis all the N2 partners (139.96 billion dollars in the case of France). The process of hierarchical reorganization taking place within Europe interwove with the global trends, and specifically with the rise of China.

The 2008 crisis reshaped the N2 (Figure 6.6). The key changes concerned the Germany–EP–China triangle. Germany is now in surplus with China and in

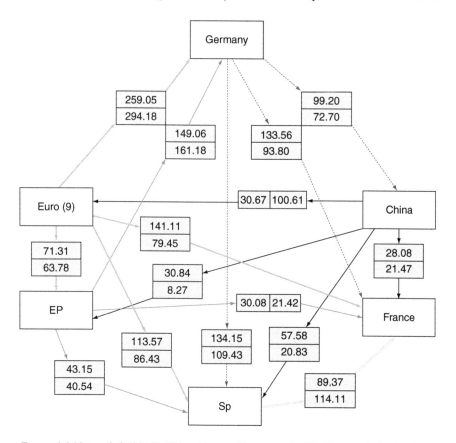

Figure 6.6 Network 2 (2014): China, France, Germany, the SP (Greece, Italy, Spain and Portugal), the EP (Czech Republic, Hungary, Poland and Slovak Republic) and the EZ (Austria, Belgium, Cyprus, Finland, Ireland, Luxemburg, Malta, Netherlands and Slovenia).

Source: authors' elaboration on COMTRADE data.

deficit with the EP, while the latter increases its deficit with China. The consolidation of this triangle seems to match two distinct trends related to the unfolding of the crisis. First, following the sharp drop in the SP's imports, Germany is partially able to reorient its exports to China. Second, the increased importance of the EP is now reflected in the surplus that this area had with Germany. The weak French trade position worsens in 2014.

3 The structure of trade

N1 and N2 depict the hierarchical reorganization of trade relations within the EU and the EMU. This process is driven by the consolidation of the German leadership, which seems to unfold through a twofold strategy: a regional one of expanding and strengthening the Eastern commercial network; and a global one based on the establishment of an increasingly close connection with China. We argued above that the crisis strenghtened the German–Chinese trade partnership and favoured the reorientation of German exports to the US and the UK. Moreover, the consolidation of the German–EP manufacturing network coincided with the weakening of the SP as a destination of German intermediate goods, testifying to the weakening of the supply chains linkages between the two areas. To test these hypotheses, we analyse the shift in the relative importance of Germany's export markets and the composition of German trade. The developments in the production organization have changed the way in which firms organize production and compete on domestic and international markets. The international fragmentation of production means that looking at aggregate export data may lead to wrong interpretations of countries' relative competitiveness. Gross export market shares are no longer an unambiguous measure of competitiveness, which is more properly measured by the value added accruing to each economy according to its participation and positioning within global value chains (GVCs). This is all the more true in the case of the EP, which is host to many subsidiaries of German firms. If mostly low-value added productions are processed in the EP, gross figures of production and exports may overestimate its international performance. When properly measured, the amount of value added generated by the international trade activities, and the employment created by trade, may be drastically reduced. Therefore, we examine both gross exports and their value added content to obtain a reliable assessment of the countries' relative performances.

The reorientation of German trade

Between 2000 and 2014 the relative importance of various countries and areas as markets for German exports changed considerably. In Figure 6.7 we show the market shares of a number of destinations over total German exports between 2000 and 2014. The data testify the rising importance of EP and China, and the fall of the SP. Within the SP, the pattern, which differed across countries before the crisis, becomes more homogeneous thereafter: the share of the region drops

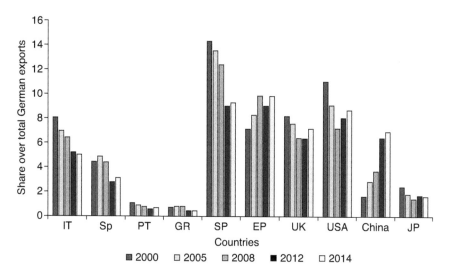

Figure 6.7 The dynamics of German exports by destination, selected countries – country shares over total German exports (2008–2014).

Source: authors' elaboration on CEPII data.

dramatically from 12.6 per cent to 9.3 per cent, to be replaced by China, the UK and the US. Conversely, after a temporary drop in 2012, the EP's share returns to the 2008 level.

The diverging patterns between EP and SP and the increasing relevance of China as a German partner find further evidence when we distinguish the bilateral trade by type of good. Figures 6.8 and 6.9 report the change in the shares of each selected destination in total German exports of final and intermediate goods before and after the crisis (the periods 2000–2008 and 2008–2014). The following points are to be noted. Despite the import boom documented in Section 2, between 2000 and 2008 the SP's share of German exports of final goods slightly decreased, with only Greece and Spain increasing their shares. Compared with an average annual growth rate of 13.2 per cent, Germany's exports of final goods to Greece and Spain increased by 17.8 per cent and 15.1 per cent respectively, testifying to the role of these countries in the build-up of trade imbalances in the pre-crisis phase. After 2008, a drastic drop in the SP's share of German exports of final goods coincided with the consolidation of the links among Germany, the EP and China, and the increase in the shares of the US, the UK and Japan.

The change in the market shares of intermediate goods reflects the drastic relocation occurring among the SP, EP and China. The SP share fell considerably also in the period before the crisis, with Italy experiencing the strongest reduction. As mentioned above, this evidence seems to support the view of the

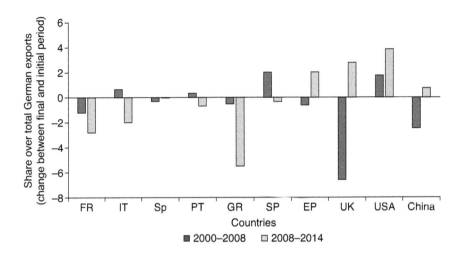

Figure 6.8 The dynamics of German exports by countries' relative shares, final goods – selected countries (change between 2000–2008 and 2008–2014).

Source: authors' elaboration on CEPII data.

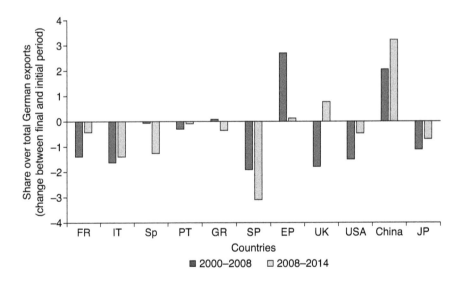

Figure 6.9 The dynamics of relative shares over total German exports, intermediate goods – selected countries (change between 2000–2008 and 2008–2014).

Source: authors' elaboration on CEPII data.

crowding out of Italian suppliers due to the emergence of the Germany–EP manufacturing hub (see Chapter 2 and Simonazzi *et al.*, 2013). Since the crisis, the strong increase in the Chinese share highlights the intensification of the German–Chinese relationship.

The changing relations of the German economy with its EP and SP are reflected in the employment impact of exports. We use the World Input Output Database (WIOD)[3] to calculate the direct and indirect employment impact of German, Italian and French exports (Figures 6.10, 6.11 and 6.12).[4] Considering the effects of the fragmentation of production in the various countries, the employment impact is calculated as the share of employment generated in country j (France, Germany, Greece, Italy, Portugal, Spain and the EP countries as a whole) by the exports of country i (France, Germany and Italy) in the total EU employment associated with country i's exports. Since 2000, the employment activated by German exports (Figure 6.10) is increasingly localized in the EP; the share of jobs activated in Italy and Spain falls or stagnates, while no clear trends emerge as regards France. In the case of the employment activated by French exports (Figure 6.11), there is a substantial increase in the share of jobs generated in Germany and in the EP, while the SP shares stagnate. An analogous pattern emerges for the employment impact of Italian exports (Figure 6.12): employment shares rise in Germany and in the EP and decrease in France and in the SP.

To complete the picture, we report the evolution of the export-related employment generated domestically in France, Germany and Italy. Between 2000 and 2008, Germany was the only country where the share of employment activated domestically in the total employment generated in the EU remained almost

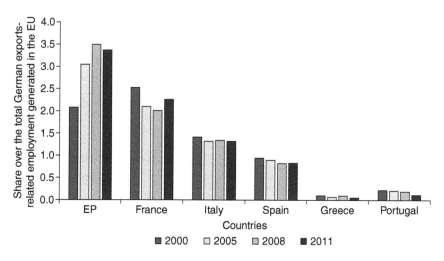

Figure 6.10 The employment impact of German exports – selected countries (share over total employment generated in the EU 2000–2011).

Source: authors' elaboration on WIOD data.

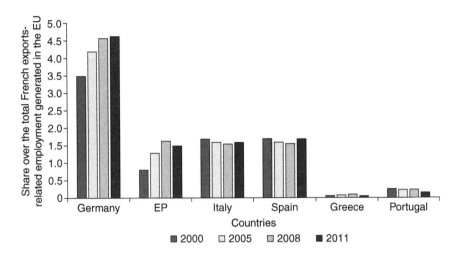

Figure 6.11 The employment impact of French exports – selected countries (share over total employment generated in the EU 2000–2011).

Source: authors' elaboration on WIOD data.

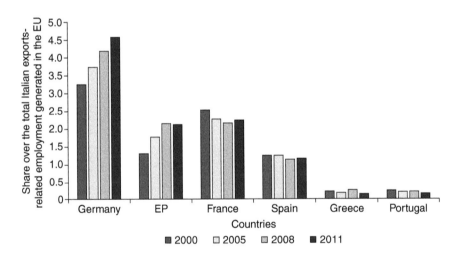

Figure 6.12 The employment impact of Italian exports – selected countries (share over total employment generated in the EU 2000–2011).

Source: authors' elaboration on WIOD data.

constant (the domestic share moved from 83.7 per cent to 83.4 per cent), while both France and Italy recorded a reduction in their domestic shares (from 84.6 to 83.1 per cent and from 86 to 84.6 per cent respectively). These figures support our thesis of a process of structural impoverishment which occurred outside the Central European Manufacturing Core. We suggest two explanations for this heterogeneous dynamic. The first, which we have already mentioned above, refers to the substitution of SP suppliers with EP-based competitors within the German manufacturing network,[5] resulting in an increasing dependence of French, Italian and Spanish exporting firms on components produced in Germany and in the EP. A second explanation relates to the adoption of different offshoring strategies in Germany and in the rest of Europe. As argued in Simonazzi *et al.* (2013) and in Chapter 2, German firms' offshoring to the EP was part of a broader competitive strategy involving business organizations, unions and the Federal Government. Specifically, the involvement of the trade unions of the manufacturing sectors – with the purpose of paying particular attention to specialized manufacturing workers and high-valued productions – contributed to preserve domestic employment. As argued by Chiappini (2012), the German–EP network is the result of a process of *vertical specialization*. That is, the German firms offshored the production of specific components of a product chain keeping the final production stages (as well as the more value added intensive components of the production process) at home and exporting the final good.[6] Conversely, the French and Italian companies relied more on strategies implying the offshoring of entire productions.[7] Consequently, the offshoring-related job destruction occurring in France and Italy has been significantly stronger than in Germany. This helps to explain, on the one hand, the resizing of the French and Italian manufacturing bases; on the other, the different evolution of the employment intensity of exports. Overall, both strategies favoured a generalized enlargement of the EP's manufacturing base. In addition, the German vertical specialization strategy favoured the technological upgrading of the EP's manufacturing base. As we show in Chapter 4, since the early 2000s the share of medium- and high-tech productions carried out in the EP has increased constantly, while the opposite has occurred in France and in the SP.

Gross export shares and value added creation

The evolution of gross export shares from the common market's early stages – in 1995 – to the years after the 2008 crisis (Figures 6.13 and 6.14) confirms the results of the analysis of N1 and N2. German trade performance contrasts with the French and SP's loss of market shares. France suffers losses in both final and intermediate goods, while the SP performs slightly better in intermediate goods. Conversely, the EP displays the higher increase in gross export shares, both final and intermediate goods.

However, we argued at the beginning of this section that a reliable assessment of a country's relative performance requires examination of both gross exports and their value added content. Recent efforts to build data sets that make it possible to track intermediate inputs flows and 'trade-in-value-added' dynamics have provided new valuable statistical sources. The data capture the value added created domestically by foreign demand, both directly through exports of final goods and services, and indirectly via exports of intermediates embodied in foreign final demand. Thus, the measure reflects how domestic industries

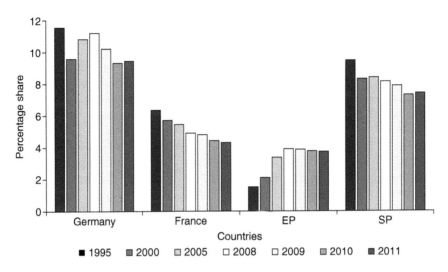

Figure 6.13 World export market shares – manufacturing sector, final goods.
Source: authors' elaboration on TIVA-OECD data.

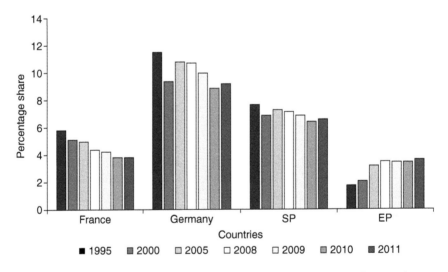

Figure 6.14 World export market shares – manufacturing sector, intermediate goods.
Source: authors' elaboration on TIVA-OECD data.

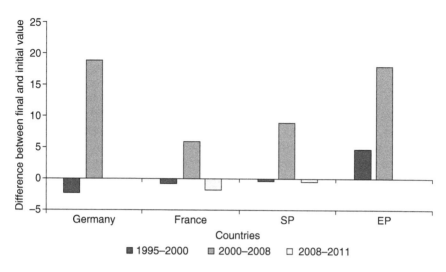

Figure 6.15 Domestic value added content of final demand – manufacturing sector (%).
Source: authors' elaboration on TIVA-OECD data.

(upstream in VCs) are connected to consumers in other countries, even where no direct trade relationship exists. As the OECD suggests, this measure can be interpreted as 'exports of value added'. Therefore, it is a proxy for the economic benefits that a country obtains from its participation in highly fragmented GVCs.

When using this variable, the data confirm the trends observed for gross exports (Figure 6.15). That is, even when the fragmentation of production is explicitly accounted for, Germany and the EP clearly outperform France and the SP. Not only does the EP increase the domestic value added associated with the final demand activated in foreign countries, but, between 2000 and 2008, the growth of value added activated in Germany and EP by foreign demand is more than twice the rates recorded in France and the SP. This evidence is in line with the dynamics of employment directly and indirectly activated in Germany and the EP by French and SP exports.

4 The evolution of the automotive industry in Europe

Analysis of the evolution of key sectors can enhance our understanding of the changes in the relative international positionings and hierarchical relationships among countries. The automotive industry plays a pivotal role in European manufacturing (see Chapter 3).[8] Its importance is related to a number of factors. First, its weight in terms of employment, production – direct and indirect linkages with the rest of the economy – and technological intensity – the companies operating in this industry are responsible for a very large share of R&D investments and patents.

Second, this industry is traditionally led by few oligopolistic firms capable of influencing with their decisions a large number of markets and economic actors. Third, the automotive industry is characterized by highly fragmented production processes with leading firms governing long chains extending through several areas and countries (Amighini and Gorgoni, 2014). Fourth, there is a rigid technological hierarchy along the VCs: leading companies develop and own key technologies, while peripheral suppliers operate in a sort of technological subordination. Since the hierarchical distribution of power along the VCs shapes the localization of important technological and institutional capabilities, the international performance is related to the distribution of power along the VCs, which is concentrated where the relevant decisions and the more crucial part of the production process are undertaken (Timmer *et al.*, 2013). In this section, we focus on the automotive sector in order to observe in more detail the creation of a central-European enlarged core and the competing peripheries' divide.

We start by looking at the evolution of motor vehicles' production in Germany, France, Italy, Spain and the EP from 2001 to 2015 (Figure 6.16). The industry trends mirror the aggregate trade dynamics shown above. Three key facts stand out. First, after 2001 the EP became a location of the utmost importance for the production of motor vehicles. Since the mid-1990s, the largest share of FDI flowing from Western Europe to the EP has concerned automobile and motor vehicle equipment manufacturing. The latter represents nearly 20 per cent of the region's aggregate FDI and is now the dominant industry in the EP (Lefilleur, 2008). Second, despite an intense process of de-localization, Germany

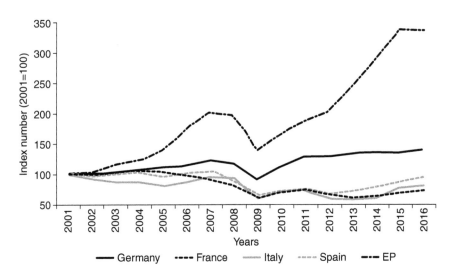

Figure 6.16 Production in the automotive industry, index of production (2001 = 100).

Source: authors' elaboration on Eurostat-STBS data.

Note
Calendar and seasonally adjusted data.

shows an increase in domestic production. Third, production declines in France, Italy and Spain, with the contraction growing worse since the crisis.

Labour cost differentials are one of the major drivers of the German eastward expansion, with German companies relocating labour-intensive segments while keeping R&D intensive activities in Germany (Nunnenkamp and Spatz, 2002; Nunnenkamp, 2005; Leaman, 2009). Leaman (2009: 145) finds that in 2002 'the major locations for German FDI in the region – the Czech Republic, Hungary, Poland and Slovakia – had total hourly wage costs of between one-quarter and one-fifth of those in East Germany'. Differentials in corporate taxation and, more broadly, the business-friendly tax system characterizing the EP represent a second driver. The generous fiscal subsidies offered to the German manufacturing corporations by the Republic of Slovakia, for example, 'have succeeded in attracting firstly Volkswagen and subsequently Hyundai, Kia and Peugeot with both tax breaks and direct grants' (Leaman, 2009: 149).[9] Leaman provides evidence of the diversion of production from Southern European suppliers in favour of the German–EP's manufacturing network. In 2002, for instance, the Volkswagen Group decided to move 10 per cent of the SEAT Ibiza production from the Martorell plant (Catalonia) to Bratislava, following the failure of negotiations with Spanish trade unions over flexible work. On that occasion, Volkswagen managers decided that, should demand fall, it would be the Spanish plant reducing production.

The diverse offshoring strategies adopted by German, French and Italian companies represent a most important driver of divergence. In fact, differently from the French and Italian strategies, which have offshored the entire production, including final assembly and exporting, to foreign countries, the German automotive companies have tended to implement a vertical specialization strategy, keeping high-value/high-tech production stages at home. Consequently, despite being one of the main actors in the process of offshoring to the EP, German firms have preserved a larger share of domestic production than the French and Italian ones. In the mid-1990s, the foreign share of total automotive production[10] was 27, 23 and 26 per cent respectively in France, Germany and Italy. Ten years later, the figures were 35, 30 and 30 per cent (Chiappini, 2012: 332).[11] While recognizing the relative infrequency of the relocation of entire car model productions from Germany to the EP,[12] Krzywdzinski (2014) emphasizes that the key point is the pattern of the Germany–EP division of labour. In this respect, the production of low price, small, and compact cars has been shifted gradually to Eastern Europe.

This development has strengthened the German automotive industry's specialization in quality products and in the high-value parts of the production process; in doing so the companies simultaneously profit from those components produced under low-wage conditions in Central and Eastern Europe. Thus, the production of premium brands – for example, Audi, Porsche and Mercedes – has increased continuously in Germany over the last 20 years, while the brands traditionally characterized by low quality and low technology have decreased.[13] By contrast, the offshoring strategy undertaken by French and Italian automotive firms has resulted in a relative weakening of the domestic productive base and technological intensity (Chiappini, 2012). It should be noted that German car production units located in the EP differ significantly from the other overseas units (Leaman, 2009: 148). In fact, production units located in China (140 plants), Latin America and North America (over 300 plants) serve mostly local markets. Conversely, EP producers are strongly integrated into the German manufacturing network and export a large part of their production back to the core country. German automotive multinational enterprises (MNEs) have adopted the strategy of creating a large integrated components network in the EP, with direct ownership of plants producing intermediate components – as in the case of Audi and Opel in Hungary – or the promotion of local supply networks for German subsidiaries – like Volkswagen in the Czech Republic in relation to Skoda.[14]

Innovation-related indicators confirm the divide between European producers. Between 2013 and 2016, the German automotive companies increased their R&D investments by 8.6 per cent, compared with the 1.4 and –1.5 per cent of the French and Italian firms. In 2015–2016, the German companies made 74 per cent of the total EU automotive R&D investments, while French and Italian firms accounted for 12 and 10 per cent respectively (Table 6.1). The ranking of the first ten EU automotive R&D performers (Table 6.2) comprises six German companies, two French, one Italian and one UK-based firm.[15] Between 2012 and 2014 German companies filed about 2000 patents, compared with 800 and 300 patents filed by their French and Italian competitors (Lucarelli and Romano 2016). This 'technological divide' accelerated after the introduction of the euro, widening the distance between the German companies and their French and Italian counterparts. According to OECD data, between 2001 and 2008 German R&D expenditure in the automotive industry grew by 3.5 per cent per year, compared with 2.4 and 1.4 per cent for France and Italy.

Although key activities are kept close to the headquarters, the integration between German and EP automotive industries is increasing production and technological intensity in both areas. Automotive firms located in the EP are experiencing a significant technological upgrading, as indicated by the evolution of the composition of their automotive trade. Lefilleur (2008) finds that the EP's exports are increasingly characterized by skill-intensive goods, with a corresponding significant fall in the share of labour-intensive goods. Meanwhile, a regional core-periphery divide is unfolding in the Eastern European area. In fact, while the economies that we include in the EP and that participate in the CEMC – i.e. Czech Republic, Hungary, Poland and Slovakia – display both a dimensional and a technological upgrading of their manufacturing base, countries such as Bulgaria, Croatia, Estonia, Latvia, Lithuania and Romania show no sign of quantitative and qualitative upgrading. On the contrary, they seem to experience a slight qualitative downgrading.

The European and worldwide automotive industry has undergone deep structural changes. The rise of producers located in China and in the EP has reshaped auto production, allowing the leading producers – Germany, Japan and the US – to act 'as the core of a more hierarchical international division of labour than a decade ago' (Amighini and Gorgoni, 2014: 926). Within this reorganization

Table 6.1 German, French and Italian automotive companies R&D expenditure and employment dynamics (2013–2016)

	R&D expenditure (2015–2016)	Share over total EU (%)	R&D growth (2015–2016) (%)	R&D growth (2013–2016) (%)	Employment growth (2015–2016) (%)	Employment growth (2013–2016) (%)
Germany	37,046.6	73.6	8.2	8.6	14.0	6.5
France	6171.0	12.2	3.5	1.4	3.1	0.5
Italy	5050.6	10.0	4.2	−1.5	−2.2	−0.6

Source: authors' elaboration on European Commission-JRC data.

Note
Data in the first column are in million euro while growth rates between 2013 and 2016 are computed as compound average annual growth rates.

Table 6.2 European automotive companies ranked by R&D expenditure intensity and growth (2015–2016)

Company	Country	R&D expenditure (2015/2016) (€m)	R&D expenditure (%)	R&D expenditure (3 yrs, %)
Volkswagen	Germany	13,612	3.8	12.7
Daimler	Germany	6529	15.6	5.0
Robert Bosch	Germany	5202	3.2	1.8
BMW	Germany	5169	13.2	9.4
Fiat Chrysler Automobiles	Italy	4108	12.1	7.5
Continental	Germany	2528	15.2	11.4
Peugeot (PSA)	France	2244	−0.7	−3.3
Renault	France	2243	18.7	5.9
ZF	Germany	1350	55.9	17.9
Delphi	UK	1102	−7.7	0.0

Source: European Commission-JRC data.

process, Germany has succeeded in gaining market shares in both final goods and components (GTAI, 2017). Although all Western European economies increased their involvement in the EP from the late 1990s onwards, 'German companies stand out as the dominant actors commanding between around one-fifth and one-quarter of all foreign owned assets in the 2004 EU accession countries' (Leaman, 2009: 145), and in 2000 they controlled 12 of the 40 largest foreign affiliates in the EP, accounting for 35 per cent of the turnover. It is now the largest European automotive producer, accounting for 30 per cent of all passenger cars manufactured and hosting the largest concentration of Original Equipment Manufacturers (OEM)'s plants in Europe: 41 OEM sites are located in Germany, with a European market share above 51 per cent.[16]

The consolidation of the German leadership goes along with a tightening of the auto production networks. Suppliers of key components – electrical, miscellaneous and rubber parts and engines – are increasingly linked to only one or a few single major destinations, while showing weak or no relationships with other supplying countries.[17] In such a context, the process of regionalization giving rise to the Germany–EP network assumes the form of a paradigmatic transformation. By increasing their importance within German-led VCs, the EP's component producers have taken the opportunity to increase their market shares exponentially, becoming at the same time strongly dependent on German-based OEM operations.

The trade in intermediate inputs well documents the effects of the emergence of the German–EP production network in the transport sector (Figure 6.17). Until the inception of the euro, German industry made intense use of French, Italian and Spanish intermediate inputs. Since then, however, the geographical origin of German intermediate suppliers has changed rapidly. Between 1998 and 2010, the share of intermediates imported from the EP in total German domestic intermediates skyrocketed – rising from 6 to 20 per cent, while the shares of France, Italy and Spain declined from 12.6 to 9.6 per cent, from 6.2 to 4.6 per cent and from 6 to 3 per cent respectively. Not only do these countries suffer crowding out from the EP, but they also experience a weakening of their ties and an increase in the amount of imported intermediates produced in the EP. Thus, in line with the results on the domestic employment activated by their total exports (see Figures 6.11 and 6.12), the automotive sector reduces the dimension of its domestic production while increasing its dependence on the EP's intermediate flows. The employment activated by the automotive sector moves in line with domestic value added. Germany recorded positive

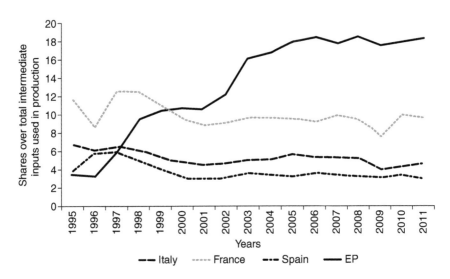

Figure 6.17 Imported intermediate inputs by sourcing countries: Germany – transport sector (1995–2011) (shares over total intermediate inputs used in production).

Source: authors' elaboration on WIOD data.

and substantial increases in employment (an average growth rate of 6.5 per cent between 2013 and 2016 and 14 per cent between 2015 and 2016) compared with much smaller growth for France (0.5 and 3.1 per cent) and negative rates for Italy.

Between 2000 and 2008, only Germany and the EP increased their world market shares of automotive final and components goods. Figures 6.18 and 6.19

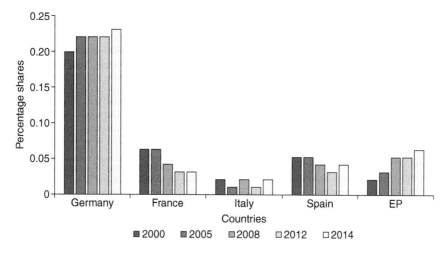

Figure 6.18 World market shares – automotive sector, final goods shares (2000–2014).
Source: authors' elaboration on CEPII data.

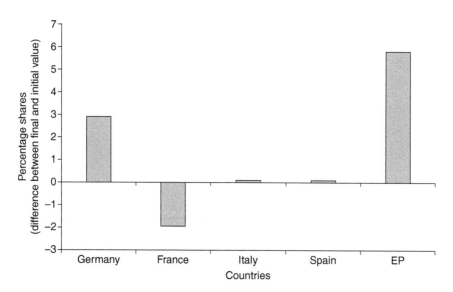

Figure 6.19 World market shares – automotive sector, components change in world market share (2000–2008).
Source: authors' elaboration on CEPII data.

show the divergent paths followed by France and SP, on the one hand, and the EP on the other: Germany and, in particular, EP increase their shares; Italy and Spain stagnate; and France falls.

Finally, as we emphasized above, the hierarchical distribution of power along the VCs shapes the localization of important technological and institutional capabilities, and the geographical distribution of the more crucial parts of the production process. Germany's dominant position, and its international de-localization strategy, is reflected in the evolution of market shares of the high-quality segment (Figure 6.20). Its share of high-quality cars rose from 36 per cent in 2000 to 51 per cent in 2008, and remained at that level until 2014. While France, Italy and Spain showed a much weaker increase in their market shares (from 2 per cent to 4 per cent), the EP, starting from a lower level, seemed to gradually gain ground.

5 Conclusions

This chapter has provided an empirical overview of the hierarchical reorganization of the European industrial fabric. Trade, production and R&D data confirm the role of Germany as the undisputed leader of the European economy; a leadership which has consolidated substantially during the past 20 years, resulting in the impressive surpluses reported in networks 1 and 2 (Figures 6.3 and 6.6). The data also confirm that Europe is deeply polarized. The EP has gained increasing importance in terms of volume of trade and production ties. Conversely, France and the SP have recorded a much poorer performance: increased deficits, reduced markets shares, weakened production bases and sluggish R&D dynamics. The structural

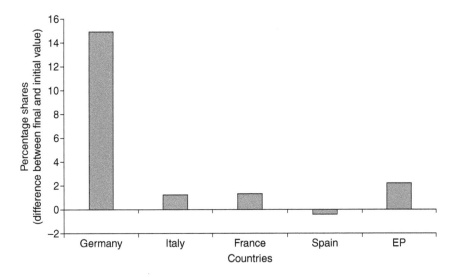

Figure 6.20 World market shares – automotive sector, high-quality segment – final goods change in world market share (2000–2014).

Source: authors' elaboration on CEPII data.

weakening of France and the SP is reflected in the declining employment intensity of their exports (taking into account the direct and indirect production linkages): domestic employment activated by exports decreases in the SP, increases in Germany and in the EP. We have argued that this result can be partly explained by the diverse offshoring strategies pursued by German companies, on the one hand, and by French and Italian ones on the other. In fact, German firms have adopted a vertical specialization strategy, keeping the more high-value/tech productions internally, thus benefiting from the inflow of low-cost intermediate inputs from the EP, while preserving a solid manufacturing base at home. France and the SP, on the contrary, have followed a more cost-driven strategy by de-localizing entire productions abroad. As shown by the evolution of N1 and N2, this strategy has resulted in lower trade benefits and structural weakening.

The 2008 crisis exacerbated the polarization between European economies. While France and the SP hardly recovered their pre-crisis production levels and continued to stagnate, Germany managed to reorient its exports to China, the UK and the US. By preserving its export volumes, Germany succeeded in reducing the negative impact of the SP's collapse in demand caused by the adoption of austerity policies. Due to the crowding out of SP's suppliers within the German manufacturing network, the post-2008 increase (and diversification) of German trade flows almost exclusively benefited Germany and the EP. These macro-trends are evident also at the industry level. We selected the automotive sector as paradigmatic of the hierarchical reorganization of European industry. The rise of the German–EP production network is apparent in all domains: increasing market shares of both total exports and quality products, increasing trade in car components, higher R&D and innovation dynamics, ever stronger German–EP production ties.

Notes

1 On this point, see also Bramucci *et al.* (2017). The term 'offshoring' is used to denote the outsourcing of parts of the production process (Feenstra and Hanson, 1996).
2 We use the value of exports f.o.b. (COMTRADE data) for both exports and imports; therefore, country A's imports from country B are measured by country B's exports f.o.b. to country A.
3 The employment impact of exports is calculated using Input-Output techniques allowing to account for both direct and indirect intermediate input flows.
4 Lefilleur (2008) terms these two groups of countries the 'core' and 'periphery' of the Central and Eastern European Economies cluster.
5 The dynamics of export-related Spanish employment are very similar to the French and Italian ones.
6 Chiappini (2012: 5) cites the example of Audi. The company produces its cars at Ingolstadt, in Germany. Since 1993, Audi has outsourced the production of engines to Györ in Hungary. As a result, it imports engines from Hungary and finishes the production in Ingolstadt, from where it exports a large part of its final products. This coincides with a strategy of vertical specialization as defined by Hummels *et al.* (2001).
7 In the French case, Chiappini (2012) reports the example of PSA, which offshored the entire production of some vehicles to the Czech Republic. On this point, see also Chapter 3.

8 See also Lefilleur (2008), who notes that the automotive sector contributes more than 12 per cent of European trade revenues. With nearly 30 per cent of world production, Europe ranks first, ahead of Japan and the US.

9 The Siemens-controlled Osram in Slovakia producing car lightbulbs received a direct grant of €153.2 million from the Slovak government (Leaman, 2009: 149).

10 Chiappini (2012) measures the foreign content of production as the ratio of the production of automotive products carried out abroad for country i to the total production of automotive products of country i.

11 Overall, the automotive sector plays a fundamental role in explaining the dynamics of German FDI towards the EP. In this regard, Leaman (2009: 147) underlines that

> whereas at the beginning of the 1990s there was limited overseas production by German car companies (the exception being Latin America), major FDI programs in the Czech Republic, Hungary, Poland and Slovakia produced a situation where, in 2003, German subsidiaries in central and Eastern Europe were producing almost three quarters of a million vehicles a year, of which over a third were imported back into Germany and exports to central Europe.

12 Krzywdzinski (2014) mentions the episodes of GM (Opel) moving the Opel Zafira production from Bochum (Germany) to Gliwice (Poland); the offshoring of large part of the Astra production from Rüsselsheim to Poland; or Volkswagen moving Polo (sub-compact), Golf (compact) and Passat (middle class) to Slovakia.

13 This specialization pattern, moreover, is not limited to the premium brands. Building on previous studies exploring Volkswagen utility vehicles production, Krzywdzinski (2014) shows that the German Hanover plant is now specialized in labour-intensive high-quality product; while the Polish plant in Poznań concentrates on standard low-quality products.

14 According to Leaman (2009: 148), at the time of writing Volkswagen employed over 20,000 workers in Poland, Slovakia and Hungary and 23,400 in the Czech Republic.

15 To give an example, between 2015 and 2016, Volkswagen invested €13 billion in R&D, more than all the French and Italian car producers included in the European Commission scoreboard (13 companies, among which were Renault, PSA and Fiat, investing €11 billion).

16 In 2015, German automobile manufacturers produced over 15 million vehicles – equivalent to more than 19 per cent of total global production. Of the world's 100 top automotive suppliers, 21 are German companies. Germany is the European production leader: some 5.7 million passenger cars – and 325,200 trucks and buses – were manufactured in German plants (GTAI, 2017).

17 In 2000, a number of newcomers, notably China, Czech Republic, Poland and Hungary, became important suppliers of electrical components, a sector where the German–EP production network consolidated substantially, while France, Italy and, to a lesser extent, Spain reduced their weight in terms of both volume of trade and number of ties. Germany was the largest exporter also of miscellaneous parts and components, and it operated as the coordinator of several complex production networks in Europe, increasing its production sharing with the EP, particularly the Czech Republic and Hungary. Unlike the electrical components network, however, production and trade of miscellaneous parts are more globalized, with China and other Asian producers increasing their importance. Finally, the production of engines is the only network showing a weakening of regional clusters even in Europe, probably due to the role played by economies of scale. However, here too Germany is the largest exporter, followed by Japan and the US and, between 2000 and 2008, the EP showed a dramatic increase in market shares, with the Czech Republic and Poland displaying the strongest increase.

References

Amighini, A. and Gorgoni, S. (2014). The international reorganisation of auto production. *The World Economy*, 37(7), 923–952.

Bramucci, A., Cirillo, V., Evangelista, R. and Guarascio, D. (2017). Offshoring, industry heterogeneity and employment. *Working Paper, Institute for International Political Economy Berlin No. 88/2017.*

Chiappini, R. (2012). Offshoring and export performance in the European automotive industry. *Competition & Change*, 16(4), 323–342.

Feenstra, R. C. and Hanson, G. H. (1996). Globalization, outsourcing, and wage inequality. *NBER Working Paper No. 5424.*

GTAI (2016). The automotive industry in Germany. www.gtai.de/GTAI/Navigation/EN/ Invest/Service/Publications/industry-specific-information,t=the-automotive-industry-in-germany--,did=371926.html [Accessed 30 September 2017].

Hummels, D., Ishii, J. and Yi, K. M. (2001). The nature and growth of vertical specialization in world trade. *Journal of International Economics*, 54(1), 75–96.

Krzywdzinski, M. (2014). How the EU's eastern enlargement changed the German productive model: The case of the automotive industry. *Revue de la régulation. Capitalisme, institutions, pouvoirs*, (15).

Leaman, J. (2009). *The Political Economy of Germany Under Chancellors Kohl and Schröder: Decline of the German Model?* (Vol. 29). New York and Oxford: Berghahn Books.

Lefilleur, J. (2008). Geographic reorganization of the European automobile sector: What role for the Central and East European countries in an enlarged European Union? An empirical approach. *Eastern European Economics*, 46(5), 69–91.

Lucarelli, S. and Romano, R. (2016). *Politiche, innovazioni e tendenze dell'automotive in Italia e nel mondo*. Mimeo, University of Bergamo.

Nunnenkamp, P. (2005). The German automobile industry and Central Europe's integration into the international division of labor: Foreign production, intraindustry trade, and labor market repercussions. *Papeles del Este 9/2005*.

Nunnenkamp, P. and Spatz, J. (2002). Globalization of the automobile industry: Traditional locations under pressure? *Aussenwirtschaft*, 57(4), 469–493.

Simonazzi, A., Ginzburg, A. and Nocella, G. (2013). Economic relations between Germany and southern Europe. *Cambridge Journal of Economics*, 37(3), 653–675.

Stehrer, R. and Stöllinger, R. (2015). The Central European Manufacturing Core: What is driving regional production sharing? *FIW Research Reports No. 2014/15–02*.

Timmer, M., Dietzenbacher, E., Los, B., Stehrer, R. and De Vries, G. (2013). The construction of world input–output tables in the WIOD project. *Economic Systems Research*, 25(1), 71–98.

Part II

European de-industrialization processes in a long-term perspective

7 The weakening of the European growth engine

1 Introduction

In the preceding chapters, the attention was focused on the euro crisis and the divergent development paths between centre and periphery since the start of the Monetary Union. This periodization can be useful to highlight the recent aspects of the European crisis, but it neglects underlying trends involving the main drivers of growth, the different forms of public intervention in the economy, the diversity of production structures and their transformations. Most of the analyses that have recognized the need for a long period perspective to interpret the current crisis focused on the (unexplained) slowdown of productivity since the early 1970s. However, productivity is an elusive concept and an endogenous variable: it depends on the degree of capacity utilization, as well as on many other circumstances (Ginzburg, 2012). Thus, we prefer to start our analysis from the interweaving between globalization and Europeanization,[1] that is the specific way in which the globalization process, which originated in the US, was translated into Europe through the formation of the European Union and the Monetary Union. We argue that, since the beginning of the 1970s, the European countries were immersed in two different forms of deregulation, the global and the European ones. This chapter aims at highlighting similarities, differences and interactions between the two processes of globalization and Europeanization.

Indeed, Europeanization can be interpreted as the EU-wide application of a policy of deregulation of goods and capitals similar to the Anglo-Saxon one, for example the abolition of controls on capital movements by all European countries between 1985 and 1990, the elimination of non-tariff barriers and the establishment of the single market in 1993 and the supra-national regulation of competition. However, the project of European integration exhibits significant differences with respect to the deregulation scheme implemented in the Anglo-Saxon countries. First, one of the aims of European integration was to counter the US hegemony by speaking with one voice in all the places where the rules of the game are made (Chapter 1). Interpreted as an attempt to acquire more bargaining power against external interests and stronger protection of domestic interests within the European area, the Europeanization process was in contrast with the 'unfettered' action of competition resulting from market liberalization.

Second, it is often argued that the European policy had the task of safeguarding and improving the so-called 'European social model', considered a distinctive feature of the European system, compared to the Anglo-Saxon one. Despite wide differences across countries, its common traits were said to include employment support, social protection, social inclusion and democracy.

So vaguely defined, these traits are susceptible to hiding behind rhetorical arguments, a reality that moves in the opposite direction. In fact, there is a contrast between the scope of the policies designed to expand, sustain and defend the European social model, however defined, and the distinctive features of the institutions built around the establishment of the euro. As seen in Chapter 1, the latter do not consider budgetary and fiscal unification, and thus the formation of a collective policy designed by a collective actor, to be an essential prerequisite of the single currency. The decision to abolish the controls on capital movements, to centralize monetary policy (entrusted with the sole task of ensuring price stability), to exclude the monetary financing of public deficits without establishing a centralized system of public finance, but on the contrary introducing upper limits to the member states' budget deficits, are tantamount to deprive communitarian institutions – with the exception of the government of money, and even here with limitations – of the major tools of economic policy, in particular those designed to boost employment. When joining the euro, the member states relinquished their national management tools without any supra-national governance to take their place: the tacit, underlying premise was the ideological preconception that markets are self-equilibrating through price competition.

Moreover, the priority attached to the promotion of exports has led to describe many economic activities related to the European social model by negation, as 'non-tradables' (or as public expenditure, therefore susceptible to be cut). As we argued in Chapter 2, this classification, that reflects a narrow view of welfare, led to ignore the important indirect macroeconomic effects of different modes of regulation and financing of services of crucial importance for well-being.

In the following, we first review the interpretations of the factors leading to the decline of growth and the rise of financialization (Section 2), and how the heterodox and orthodox theories have explained the 'secular stagnation' (Sections 3 and 4). We then see how these global changes, and specifically the process of financialization, have been transferred to the countries of the periphery. The US neoliberal model, intermediated by the European construction, institutions and norms, shaped in conformity with the German model, has modelled the structure and affected the functioning of their economies, substantially weakening their resilience.

2 The fading of the golden age

Two engines of growth

In the three decades after the Second World War, the major industrial countries were committed, domestically, to the implementation of policies supporting domestic demand and, internationally, to the progressive dismantling of the barriers to foreign trade inherited from the inter-war period. The memory was still fresh of the competitive devaluations and the destabilizing speculative capital movements that led to the spread of protectionist practices. The Bretton Woods Agreement, establishing a regime of fixed but adjustable exchange rates (with the dollar convertible in gold at a fixed price), envisaged full convertibility with regard to the current account, but introduced limitations for the capital account (in particular for short-term capital flows).

Various factors combined to favour growth, among these the undisputed socio-economic, technological and military hegemony of the United States, the presence of a large pool of unemployed labour in the European countries engaged in post-war reconstruction, the availability of cheap and stable energy supply. Two engines sustained the growth process, according to the sequence: investment-income-imports (i.e. other countries' exports). High domestic demand in the US (and in the other industrialized countries) resulted in high world demand, prompting world export growth that was transmitted to the capital goods sector. The high import content reinforced the expansion of the world market through the foreign trade multiplier. The relatively simultaneous growth across the developed countries favoured the parallel expansion of production and productive capacity.

The smooth functioning of this international transmission of income growth through the Keynesian multiplier requires a financial mechanism to provide deficit countries with internationally accepted means of payment. For two decades, the deficit of the US balance of payments provided the European countries (that were gradually becoming net exporters to the US) with the dollar reserves necessary for growth, without raising recriminations.

In the late 1960s, the conditions that had ensured a vigorous growth ran out of steam. While tensions developed in many areas, the two engines that had supported growth in the previous period – investment and exports – began to splutter. Both in the US and in Europe, the leading role of investment tended to wane. Left to rely on the sole engine of exports (see Figure 7.1), in the subsequent 40 years growth proceeded in a faltering way. It will be occasionally supplemented by private consumption, with unsustainable effects in the long run, since, given the stagnation of wages, the growth in consumption was financed with private debt. What are, then, the circumstances that led to the weakening of the investment engine?

First, the erosion of the US competitive supremacy resulted in heightened conflicts on market shares, particularly with German, French and Japanese firms. As we discuss in detail in Chapter 8, in the mid-1970s the markets of consumer durables – that, in combination with the related investments, including the necessary infrastructure (e.g. motor vehicles), had driven growth in the golden age – reached saturation (given the existing distribution of income). Second, in the currency field, given persistent US trade deficits, the 'exorbitant privilege' of the only country whose national currency was also the global currency was increasingly called into question. Currency instability was simultaneously cause and

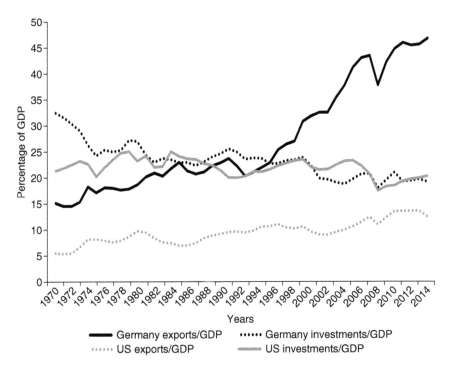

Figure 7.1 Investment and exports: US and Germany as a percentage of GDP (1970–2014).

Source: authors' elaboration on World Bank data.

effect of increasing speculative capital flows. Third, in the social field, the absorption of a large part of unemployment was associated with sharp struggles over income distribution and a more inclusive development model. Social strife was transferred on prices: the result was higher inflation. When, on 15 August 1971, the US devalued the dollar (declaring its inconvertibility into gold and implicitly the end of the Bretton Woods system), inflation involved the commodities market, which is quoted in dollars. The devaluation of the dollar worsened the terms of trade of oil-producing countries, urging them to unite to negotiate higher prices. The outcome of the negotiation, a quadrupling of oil prices, affected the various countries differently, on the basis of their degree of dependence on oil, but provided new fuel to international inflation.

Discontinuities: depoliticization, financialization, investments

The great inflation of the 1970s, associated with political and social tensions, opens the way to three fundamental, intertwined discontinuities in the mode of operation of western capitalist countries. The first discontinuity is associated with the transition from a 'politicized' management of economic policy based on discretionality (albeit confined to well-defined areas of the macroeconomic level, as in Keynesian public intervention), to a 'depoliticised' management based on the automatism of rules (Burnham, 2001; Krippner, 2011). Depoliticization should not be understood as 'the removal of politics ... [but] ... as the reorganization of the boundary between the political and the economic so as to allow policymakers to govern the economy "at one remove"' (Burnham, 2001: 128, quoted in Krippner, 2011: 145). The second discontinuity is the passage from the inflation phase of the 1970s to the next phase, that of 'financialization', defined as a process in which financial activities become increasingly more important in the formation of the profits of the economy (Krippner, 2011: 17).[2] The third discontinuity is the slowdown of capital accumulation and its delinking from exports, the latter remaining the main driving force of domestic growth.

The depoliticization of the economic policy can take many forms. In general, if

> to be 'political' means that [something] ... is subject to human manipulation and control, then the most fundamental form of depoliticization is to remove some question from the realm of active decision to the realm of fate where the exercise of human agency is neither possible nor desirable.
>
> (Krippner, 2011: 145)

For our purposes, we highlight two specific forms of depoliticization. The first includes

> "the transfer of a given problem from the direct control of elected officials to non-elected officials" as in the case of the creation of an independent central bank, but also the attribution to private corporations of "responsibilities formerly assumed by government".
>
> (Ibid.: 145 and 199)

In both cases, the decisions are no more subject to 'public scrutiny and deliberation'. A second dimension of depoliticization refers to the content of decisions, that is, the attribution of objective and 'thus higher' knowledge to 'technocratic expertise', which presupposes the creation of a social distance between public decisions, that it would be inefficient not to delegate to the experts, and the non-delegable decisions of the private sphere.[3]

All these forms of depoliticization have a common trait. They exonerate, at least until the outbreak of a crisis, policymakers from the responsibility to operate transparent, difficult choices on income distribution that could alienate the support of broad social groups. For this reason, Krippner sees an analogy (and a continuity) between the phase of 'inflation' and the next phase of 'financialization'. In the 1970s, 'inflation could serve as a solvent for social conflict avoiding more direct forms of confrontation between social groups and also making it difficult to determine who was ahead and who was behind at any given point of time' (ibid.: 17). In the same way as inflation, the financialization of the American economy, which began in the 1970s, offered, according to Krippner, an unexpected and temporary solution to three crises that plagued the US economy in the age of globalization: a social crisis, a fiscal crisis and a crisis of state legitimacy. 'Paradoxically', Krippner adds (ibid.: 144), 'this resolution was possible not because policymakers successfully transferred the task of disciplining unrestrained social wants to the market, but rather because the market *failed* to impose the discipline that policymakers sought' (italics in the original).

In Europe, the formation of the Monetary Union was accompanied by the intention to import 'Germanic' market discipline in France and in the peripheral countries, plagued by high inflation and strong social tensions. Here too, as it was later discovered, the success in reducing inflation and nominal interest rates following the formation of the Monetary Union was not associated with market discipline and full employment, as described in mainstream textbooks, but with the unsustainable increase in financial resources and asset prices. As in the US, the financialization associated with the liberalization of financial markets initially attenuates the political conflicts, apparently 'depoliticizing' them, except for making them more acute in the next austerity phase. These attempts at depoliticizing economic policy choices are important because liberalization and depoliticization lead to financialization.

It is customary to attribute the processes of financialization to two circumstances, the political choices made in the early 1980s by Reagan in the US and by Thatcher in the UK, and the replacement of Keynesian ideas with a monetarist doctrine. This attribution, that contains elements of truth, does not take into account some unwanted consequences of previous decisions that opened the way to financialization. Already in the 1970s, persistent inflation and banks' pressure had led to the elimination of administrative instruments (credit rationing, interest rate ceilings, segmented and specialized credit supply) born with the New Deal. Paradoxically, even some associations of consumers urged to move to the deregulation of interest rates, which occurred gradually in the US during Carter's presidency. In their opinion, variable rate mortgages would have ensured adequate returns on savers' deposits (only to discover later that, as consumers, the rise in mortgage rates was no longer followed by an adjustment of wages, making it difficult to pay the loan instalments). We should also not forget that it was the democratic Carter who, seeking re-election, appointed Volcker as head of the Federal Reserve. Volcker promptly raised the federal funds rate from 11 per cent to 20 per cent, provoking a precipitous fall of inflation and a parallel drastic increase in unemployment.

Monetarist predominance

We may recall that in the 1970s there were structural, socio-political bases for a 'new' ideology as an antidote to the Keynesian view of the government's autonomy in the conduct of economic policy. As Bhaduri and Steindl (1983: 3) observed, the rise of monetarism to worldwide eminence was preceded by a continuous shift of power from industry to banks,[4] favoured by the latter's great expansion of their international activities. This expansion was due to the creation of the Eurodollar market in the late 1960s, followed, in the 1970s, by the huge increase of financial transactions related to the recycling of oil revenues. The expansion of international operations provided banks with 'a certain degree of independence both from the national government and from the domestic public sector'. It so happened that a high interest rate policy benefited[5] the banks, because it was associated with high interest margins, without affecting their international operations (while hurting the domestic industries).

Banks and financiers have always supported restrictive policies. However, why, in Europe, did political leaders and economists of progressive persuasion, who did not consider themselves monetarists, come to favour restrictive monetary and fiscal policies strongly oriented by the monetarist doctrine?[6] As we argued in Chapter 1, according to a conception of the political effects of economic integration that nowadays seems rudimentary and naïve, European integration would have had the function to temper and correct old national vices, otherwise considered incorrigible, and bring the deviant countries into line. Capital markets would have operated as a threat or as a punishment for profligate behaviours. As in the neo-functionalist approach, the expectation was that economic integration would have brought about benefits for the common good, through automatic and linear progressions and *without relevant drawbacks*. Ironically, both in the US and in Europe, the attempt to replace explicit political decisions with technocracy and automatism eventually led, after drastic austerity measures, to the reappearance of politics in the guise of demagogy ('populism').

The attraction of monetarism – we argued in Chapter 1 – resided also in its offering (wrong) answers to two important issues that progressive policymakers tended to underestimate. The first is the issue of inflation. Monetarism is not the only scheme capable of offering solutions, nor are its solutions the correct ones. In fact, according to monetarism, inflation is always a purely monetary phenomenon. Thus, a cost-push effect such as the oil price boost is explained by underlying monetary disorder and arguments in favour of a price stabilization policy are based upon a peculiar theoretical position that assumes a long-run vertical Phillips curve. The acceptance of these two premises is equivalent to starting on the wrong foot.

The second issue relates to the exhaustion of Keynesian inward-looking policies in the 1970s and 1980s. The effectiveness of those policies, on which welfare policies were based, relied on the possibility to control the main variables (from raw materials to interest rates, to capital movements, to investment embodied technical progress). The exhaustion of the hegemonic capacity of Keynesian policies, and of the social contract upon which they were founded, cannot be explained only by the monetarist offensive, but must also be attributed to the need to cope with the changes in the post-war overall picture that had made these policies possible. Both in dealing with the inflation problem and in addressing the issue of the need to adjust Keynesian policies in an outward-looking direction in ways compatible with the preservation of the welfare state, recourse to monetarism was certainly not the only choice.

3 Heterodox explanations of the fall in investment: industry and finance

Both in the US and in Europe the deregulation of interest rates in the 1970s was a prelude to the diffusion of financialization. However, it was only in the early 1980s that in the US the combination of high interest rates and strong fiscal expansion (largely attributable to military spending) created a favourable environment for the full deployment of financialization, that spread all over the world. 'Extraordinarily high interest rates with short-term rates climbing as high as 20 percent in the early 1980s – [raising the hurdle rate] created punishing conditions for productive investment' (Krippner, 2011: 87; see also Stockhammer, 2004 and Orhangazi, 2008). At the same time, the high interest rates and subsequently, between the second half of the 1990s and 2000, the relatively higher growth rates of the US economy, attracted large capital inflows that strengthened the process of financialization.

There are two theses on the relations between investment and financialization: (i) in an environment of falling rate of profits, investment decisions were increasingly diverted towards the higher returns obtainable from finance; (ii) organizational changes in the finance domain increasingly inhibited non-financial investment since finance absorbed funds that could have been allocated to non-financial investment.

According to the first interpretation (Magdoff and Sweezy, 1987; Foster, 2007), since the 1970s a tendency to the fall of the US rate of profit in the non-financial sector was associated with a stagnation of the productive system. This tendency, due to income inequality and under-consumption or to the exhaustion of profitable outlets, would be temporarily buffered by the state through financial concessions and deregulations, but at the price of recurring asset bubbles. A variant of this position (Arrighi, 1994, 2007) puts the long-term stagnation thesis of the US within the historical alternations in the leadership of the world system.[7]

The second interpretation (Lazonick and O'Sullivan, 2000; Lazonick, 2011) does not refer to the fall of the rate of profits, but attributes all the investment slowdown to finance. It is argued that, in the phase of financialization that corresponds to the introduction of new business models based on ICT (information and communication technologies), the companies have set themselves the goal of shareholder value maximization, with two important consequences. The first is the dominance of short time horizons ('short-termism', with important consequences on jobs' instability and insecurity). The second is the granting to managers of compensations in the form of stock options (the source of huge and increasing inequalities in income distribution). In both cases, the shareholder value goal has increased the propensity to divert resources from long-term innovative investment to purely short-term financial transactions, designed to support artificially the value of the shares (through stock buybacks and M&A operations for speculative purposes).

The definition of financialization adopted by Krippner (measured, as mentioned above, by the share of profits arising from financial assets) allows to distinguish between incomes from financial assets of non-financial companies (in particular industry and large retailers) from financial assets of financial companies. The former includes dividends, capital gains and, in greater proportion, interests: the relationship between these revenues and the total income of these companies tended to rise mildly in the 1970s and accelerated in the 1980s, when it reached a level equal to *five* times the level registered after the war. This trend highlights an important structural change in the US economy, parallel to the, not unexpected, sharp increase in the share of financial companies' income (Krippner, 2011: 35). How to interpret these data? Krippner reads them as providing a specific instance of the diversion of corporate funds from industrial to financial investments, because of their higher returns, and confirming that the growth of finance has been driven by corporations based in the 'real' economy.

A complementary interpretation, that will be explored in the next chapter, points to the possibility that part of the financial income of non-financial companies reflects a transformation of the modalities of competition occurred since the early 1970s. The saturation of the main mass consumer goods markets urged the enterprises, at this point operating largely in a replacement market, to increase the number of product variants and engage in intense vertical market segmentation. The accentuation of competition based more on quality than on price meant that industrial companies entered increasingly non-industrial activities, such as instalment credit, rental and maintenance services, post-production assistance, etc. An extensive literature (see Froud *et al.*, 2006, cited by Krippner, 2011: 29) has documented the spread of 'captive finance' of industrial firms: activities that were originally intended to support consumers' purchases of manufactured products ' "by offering instalments financing ... eventually became financial behemoths that overshadowed the manufacturing or retailing activities of the parent firm'. The creation of forward linkages related to sales promotion, and not simply the outsourcing of services previously carried out within the company, is a novelty of the accumulation pattern of larger non-financial companies. It contributes to blur not only the traditional distinction between industry and services, but also the division between industry and finance. At the same time, the new pattern widens the distance in the practices of competition between firms of different sizes, and between the firms that serve the retail market and the intermediate goods producers. As the minimum efficient size of the firms serving the retail market increases, financial constraints limit the peripheral countries' success in maintaining a specialization in phases that include the final market. As a result, after each crises, the periphery's specialization appears ever more confined to smaller-scale productions belonging to the intermediate stages.

4 Orthodox explanations of the fall in investment: secular stagnation

The two views on the relation between investment and financialization are not mutually exclusive. While for the first position the growth of finance stems from unresolved problems of the 'real' economy, for the second, it is the internal logic of finance that exogenously contributes to the decline of innovative accumulation and to the crisis of the 'real' economy. However, the numerous examples of endogenous financialization of non-financial enterprises show that the distinction between 'real' and 'financial' aspects can be artificial. Both views focus on the long-run tendency to stagnation that is associated with a weakening of capital accumulation in the western capitalist countries and may be connected with the 'break' in the association of investment and exports that characterized the 'golden age'.

Both views stand in sharp contrast with the most common interpretations of the declining rate of growth that focus instead on circumstances calling for 'structural reforms', such as increased wage and labour flexibility, productivity increases, correction of public deficit imbalances. Only recently, in Europe, after the implementation of substantial labour market reforms, drastic cuts in public expenditure and non-conventional monetary policies, recognition of their failure is eventually leading to acceptance of the need to combine fiscal expansion and monetary easing. Due to hysteresis effects, the delay in acting has caused a *permanent* reduction in production capacity and employment. It is therefore important to analyse the reasons for this delay, and to assess whether a simple, short-term fiscal expansion would suffice to reduce the income disparities exacerbated by the crisis and restart growth.

Since the mid-1970s, the principle gradually came to prevail, endorsed by central banks and the banking system alike, that private investment should be supported *indirectly* through monetary policy, rather than through direct interventions. The theoretical basis of this approach is to be found in Solow's neoclassical model, which denies any long-term influence of aggregate demand, in particular of investment, on growth. In a well-behaved production function with diminishing returns, the only way to support growth is a technical progress which allows saving of the fixed factors (in particular, a disembodied technical progress that falls on the economy as manna from heaven). Hence, in a layman's version of this theory, the harsh attack on the importance given to investment, considered as an expression of 'capital fundamentalism', in favour of intangible incentives that produce innovation – in practice tax relief to households and businesses.

The fundamental assumption of the neoclassical model is that it is always possible to undertake investments equal to full employment savings, thus keeping the economy in steady state equilibrium. The existence and stability of equilibrium – where the warranted rate that ensures the equality between full employment savings and investments is equal to the sum of the rate of increase of population and the exogenous rate of technical progress – is given by the capital/labour substitution, that will ensure the capital/output flexibility required to reduce any divergence between the above-mentioned rates. Although the mechanism that guarantees the equality between savings and investment is generally not specified (see for example the Solow model), it is implicitly assumed that there is an underlying *financial* mechanism that leads to equilibrium also the rate of interest corresponding to full employment savings and the rate of profits on investment (augmented for a risk premium).

It is to *a dysfunction in this financial mechanism* that several interpretations today (Summers, 2013, 2014, but see also Blanchard *et al.*, 2014 and Krugman, 2014) attribute the tendency towards stagnation. Following Summers, the theoretical framework originally proposed by Wicksell has been renamed 'secular stagnation theory', an expression proposed, in another context and with different meaning, by Alvin Hansen. For Summers and the other authors, as in Wicksell, the loanable funds theory, where demand and supply of bank credit is added to demand and supply of savings, provides the equilibrating financial mechanism. It was upon reflection on the 'Great Depression' of the last two decades of the nineteenth century that Wicksell set out to advance an original interpretation of the positive correlation between prices and interest rates observed in that period. He pointed out that anyone seeking to explain this correlation on the basis of the theory then accredited – the quantity theory of money – would face 'contradictions'. The expectations of the theory 'that rising prices are due to an excess of money, falling prices to scarcity' did not accord with observed movements: 'when prices are falling there is a continual *fall* in rates of interest' (Wicksell, 1898a: 167, italics in the original). It was precisely to settle these contradictions (and at the same time reject the interpretation previously proposed by Thomas Tooke, funded on the determination of prices based on production costs) that Wicksell came out with the ingenious idea of the *short run* divergence between the money rate of interest and a non-observable magnitude (of which 'nothing is really known at all', or 'practically an unknown' (Wicksell, [1898b] 1958: 85), namely the natural rate of interest, associated with prices finally stable and the equality of investment and savings. In Wicksell's version, the fall of investment for any given level of the interest rate leads to a decline in the natural interest rate below the monetary interest rate. Since the banks contrast a reduction in the monetary interest rate, for *routinier* habit or to safeguard their profits, they sell bonds withdrawing money, thus causing a deflation of the price level that will cease only when the monetary interest rate is realigned to the lower natural rate.

In the modern reformulation, the shocks that destabilize the loanable funds market and lead to a fall in the natural rate may be various (Teulings and Baldwin, 2014): an investment fall or a savings increase (to repay loans or other losses), a higher demand for safe assets due to an increase in risk and uncertainty, or an increase in income inequality that would increase savings. The underlying idea is that, as in the neoclassical description of the labour market, *some rigidity* is preventing the achievement of the equilibrium (in this case of savings and investments) that otherwise would be at hand. Whatever the cause of this rigidity, the negative real interest rates that would be required to equate full employment saving and investment, cannot be achieved because of a zero lower bound on nominal interest rates in a low inflation regime. Hence, the stagnation that nominal rigidity, if persistent in a low-inflation regime, would make 'secular'. The terminology is Keynesian,[8] the policy implications are those of a short-term expansionary fiscal policy, but the apparatus is neoclassical. Adopting this theoretical framework, the issue of the investment inelasticity to interest rate is accurately avoided, and the effectiveness of monetary policy reaffirmed.[9]

In line with its assumptions, this approach attributed to the monetary instrument alone the merit of the significantly reduced output volatility in the so-called Great Moderation, from the mid-1980s to 2007. This interpretative scheme proved too simplified to be able to take into account subsequent developments: the Great Moderation was only the gateway to the Great Recession.

5 Financialization and Europeanization

The 'Great Moderation' is a synthesis of the central message of monetarism, which is sharply opposed to the Keynesian vision. For Keynes (and Polanyi), the instability of the private sector requires the stabilizing action of public intervention. For monetarists à la Friedman the private sector is self-regulating and government intervention always destabilizing (because it is always late, overextended and inefficient). The task of monetary policy is to smooth the cycle, keeping the path of the economy within the 'natural' corridor of the growth trend. In this perspective, price stability is both a means and an end. The misleading importance attributed to the evidence of a decline over time of the volatility of output and prices[10] contributes to explain the events that preceded and followed the construction of the European Monetary Union.

Describing the phase of 'Great Moderation', Bernanke stressed the role played by structural changes in increasing macroeconomic flexibility and stability. These changes included 'the increased depth and sophistication of financial markets, deregulation in many industries, the shift away from manufacturing toward services' with important developments in technology and 'increased openness to trade and international capital flows' (Bernanke, 2004: 1). However, his main argument was that the decline in volatility was obtained through an improvement in the effectiveness of monetary policy, the direct and indirect impact of a low inflation environment and stable expectations on the economic structure and on the sensitivity to external shocks.

Bernanke's interpretation of the economic situation in 2004 was far from perceiving the storm that was coming.[11] It is by now well known that the period of the Great Moderation was associated with a huge rise of household indebtedness. Since 2000, home mortgages accounted for an increasing percentage of household debts, also thanks to growing mortgage equity withdrawals (that were used to finance all kind of consumer goods). As Barba and Pivetti (2008) remarked, rising household debt should be considered as 'the response to falling and stagnant real wages and salaries'. In the context of conspicuous redistribution of income, of financial deregulation and of an easing of financial constraints on low- and middle-income households, the long-run process of substitution of loans for wages sustained aggregate demand and output, replacing higher private investment and higher public debt. Clearly, this model was unsustainable in the long run. The rhetoric of the Great Moderation and of 'financial innovations', that ignored the continuous hikes in asset prices, may have been instrumental in inducing banks to extend credit to the more risky, low-income segments. When interest rates finally rose, the fall in demand (and prices) hit especially hard the owners of cheaper properties, the major victims of speculative and Ponzi finance (Leamer, 2007).

The US crisis shows that, given an unsustainable growth path, today's fall in volatility is fully compatible with future instability.[12]

The US as a role model

Since the mid-1970s, the monetarist conceptions in the US and in Europe start to converge, albeit with partially different outcomes. It would be wrong to attribute only to the evolution of the ideas (as opposed to 'facts') the responsibility of policy choices that have been made in the US and in Europe. However, since 'facts' were increasingly interpreted with monetarist categories, a vicious circle arose: monetarist interpretations of facts (which also implied a schematic caricature of the positions subject to criticism) seemed to validate and strengthen the monetarist doctrine, thus facilitating its penetration and hegemony. The transition to supply-side policies well epitomizes this process. It was facilitated by the idea that the stagflation associated with the increase in oil prices and the simultaneous deflationary response of the major economies was a *new* phenomenon that required relinquishing Keynesian ideas. This conclusion was based on several assumptions. First, the proposition that every inflation has a monetary origin, ignoring the traditional distinction between cost-push and demand-pull inflation. Second, a confusion between the *key* principle of Keynesian theory – namely the principle of effective demand, based on the independence, in a capitalist economy, of investment and savings decisions – and the *particular* policy of undifferentiated increase in aggregate demand through public budget expansion, generally defined (not by Keynes) 'Keynesian policy'. Third, the belief that the only possible form of greater international integration was an unrestrained liberalization. From the wrong diagnosis of the stagflation of the 1970s derives the wrong diagnosis of the stagdeflation of the 2000s, the long delay in recognizing the danger and the influence of deflationary cost factors, and the failure of the Central Bank to achieve, through monetary expansion, its 2 per cent inflation target.

Was there an alternative? From a policy perspective, the cost push/demand pull distinction shifts the focus on the degree of capacity utilization and on supply bottlenecks, on the possibility of incomes policies (not only wage policies), on long-term agreements with producer countries, on international agreements for the stabilization of commodity prices. In 1960, Myrdal discussed with foresight problems that will emerge more clearly only in the following decade. He affirmed that in the developed countries the battle for public intervention and for the welfare state had been won, but at the cost of a widening gap between developed and underdeveloped countries. Exploiting this argument, he wrote, the opponents of the welfare state (i.e. 'of equalitarism') would urge to 'return to a system of greater international automatism, where the individual national economies would have to adjust themselves to changes in the world around them, even though this would sometimes be exacting and occasionally cause unemployment and business losses' (p. 122). To defend the achievements obtained thus far would require an effort of greater international integration that Myrdal indicated in the formation of complementary relations in the productive structures of the various countries. Instead of automatisms, that push the developed countries to adapt to the external pressures of the market with heavy job losses, he advocated a state 'driven' structural adjustment, aimed to 'make room' for the industrial exports that the developing countries will be prepared to produce. In the 1970s, the forces of the automatisms prevailed, though the reason is not the absence of alternatives. Myrdal's proposals involved a type and a degree of public intervention – and of public-private cooperation – to which the majority of governments were not willing to commit, preferring depoliticization and automatism instead.

Germany as a role model

Given the heterogeneity of productive structures, institutions, policies and economic cultures in the European countries in the 1970s, it was by no means obvious that the political elites would accept to converge on what has been defined a 'neoliberal consensus' that served as a basis for the creation of the Monetary Union. Among the main factors that led to this outcome are the 'lesson' on the impossibility to adopt 'Keynesian policies', at the time of the first oil crisis, and the progressive affirmation, in Europe, of a 'pragmatic' version of monetarism. In the US, the end of Bretton Woods led to the adoption of flexible exchange rates (due also to the reduced international opening of the economy) in a regime of capital liberalization. Conversely, in Europe the process of liberalization of capital movements, fully completed by 1990, was associated, even before the EMU, with schemes of monetary cooperation based on fixed exchange rates – the Snake (1973–1978) and EMS (1979–1998) – rejected by the monetarism à la Friedman (Chapter 1). Remembering the irreconcilable Mundell–Fleming trilemma, it follows that, unlike the US, the European countries agreed to give up their monetary autonomy (although framing the mission and the prerogatives of the European Central Bank strictly in line with the monetarist dogma).

What prompted the European member states to make those choices, to place monetary union before political union (and hence fiscal and banking union) against the recommendations of the MacDougall report (and the Werner Report before it), and a large number of economists? The lessons learned from the first oil crisis and the existence of monetarism as an alternative paradigm to Keynesianism – argued McNamara – would not have had the same influence on the policies adopted in Europe in the 1980s and 1990s had not the German economic policy been considered a model to follow. Even countries situated at a much lower level of development and economic diversification looked at the German success, measured, however, by indicators that did not include any structural data. Macroeconomic data in the post-1973 period showed that Germany had passed the test of the two oil crises with a very restrictive monetary policy, associated with inflation and *unemployment* rates much lower than those of the other European countries. Its growth rate was on average lower in the years 1974–1985, but it appeared slightly higher in the following decade (when all countries suffered a decline).

As with the 'Great Moderation' of the US in the period 1985–2007, also in Europe the 'facts' appeared at first glance to agree with the framework offered by the academic monetarism. The alleged absence of a trade-off between inflation and unemployment seemed to confirm the existence of a natural rate of unemployment where inflation is not accelerating (the NAIRU, or Non-Accelerating Inflation Rate of Unemployment, is the equivalent in the labour market of the Wicksellian natural rate of interest in the loanable funds market). This allowed to shift the attention from growth and employment to monetary objectives (and instruments) of stability. Comparing the period of the Snake with that of the EMS, in which, following Germany's example, a greater number of countries adopted restrictive monetary measures, results appeared, from the stability point of view, satisfactory: lower volatility and better monetary cooperation, measured by fewer defections.[13] Up to the 1992 crisis.

As we argue in Chapter 1, in the process of building a European 'neoliberal consensus', the shift towards austerity in France was decisive. The policies initially promoted by Giscard d'Estaing and Barre in the late 1970s, briefly interrupted during the 'Mitterrand experiment', were resumed by Mitterrand himself and by governments of different persuasion. The direct application in France of Modell Deutschland was facilitated by the weakening of the labour movement as a result of the growth in unemployment in the mid-1970s, and the absence of an alternative programme after the failure – with Chirac in 1975–1976 and Mitterrand in 1983 – of unilateral and undifferentiated expansionary policies. In a 1978 interview, Giscard made clear that 'the French leadership wished to restructure the French economy along German lines so that France could better compete with Germany, thus ensuring that the two countries carried equal weight in the EC'. While Giscard justified the adoption of the German model with the *political* argument that it was necessary in order not to lose ground in Europe – a proposition that was quickly picked up by the political leaders in Italy, Spain, Holland, Belgium – the prime minister Barre was responsible for arranging its *economic* translation. Price stabilization through monetary tightening and strengthening of the currency became the primary targets that subsumed all the others (in particular price competitiveness); administrative controls over prices were eliminated, based on the argument that Germany had reduced inflation without recourse to them.

The Italian government, for the first time supported by the Communist Party with an abstention vote, adhered between 1976 and 1978 to an austerity programme based on the stabilization of the exchange rate and wage restraint. The result was a strong current account surplus, which was used not to expand investment but – when the Communist Party had already taken away its support – to buttress the participation to the EMS under the conditions imposed by Germany. The agreement did not include any clear commitment to a symmetrical adjustment of external accounts, to financial support for countries at a lower level of development. There was no mention of 'a fiscal policy for the Community', as proposed by the MacDougall Report. Italy's accession to the EMS was followed by a sharp acceleration in the monetarist direction. In his speech in Parliament to justify the EMS membership, senator Andreatta, who in the following year would take an important government post, argued that 'in this age of largely open economies, the exchange rate [is] a monetary variable which affects very little the real terms of trade, the movement of goods and services, and instead affects the price level'. In 1981, as Minister of the Treasury, Andreatta, in consultation with the Governor of the Bank of Italy (Azeglio Ciampi), signed the 'divorce' between the Treasury and the Bank of Italy, exempting the central bank from the obligation to underwrite government securities not subscribed by private investors at the auction. Giving autonomy to the monetary policy, Andreatta believed that the increase in the real cost of debt, due to higher interest rates, would impose an overhaul of the fiscal policy in the direction of greater financial rigor. This retrenchment occurred only *11* years later, after the currency crisis of 1992. In the meanwhile, fiscal laxity, particularly on tax revenues, and the higher cost of funding the debt sent the debt/GDP ratio from 58 to 120 per cent.

The common sentiment in Europe in the second half of the 1970s is well summarized by Lord Robbins: 'The example of German policy is in my opinion a lesson for us all and perhaps a hope for the world' (quoted in McNamara and Jones, 1996). Many years later, in 1989 – after the 1984 austerity policies implemented by the Socialist Fabius in continuity with those launched by Giscard–Barre – a Spanish banker, Luiz Martinez Arévalo, stated that the Spanish entry into the EMS had been decided in the hope of achieving the '*desinflation à la française* ... following the example of the Fabius Government in the mid-eighties, whose motto might well have been "squeeze them and blame the Bundesbank" '.

Germany's two models

The 'analysis of the German political economy', argued Dyson (2002: 138), 'has suffered from a tendency to reification of the German model and, as a consequence, from a failure to capture processes of change'. The German model is not monolithic and unified but is 'a complex, tense and changing process of antagonism and accommodation between two different domestic "advocacy" coalitions, ordoliberalism and "managed capitalism"'. While 'managed capitalism' is a legacy from the early stages of industrialization and stresses the need for pragmatism and coordinated actions, ordoliberalism is profoundly distrustful of coordination and has a theoretical basis in academic economics. It is a 'legal variant' of neoclassical theory associated since the 1930s with the names of Walter Eucken, Franz Böhm and Alfred Müller-Armack of the Freiburg School. It gives primacy to the discipline of monetary policy and market-based adjustment but, in contrast to the *laissez faire* doctrine that mandates a minimum state, it advocates a strong state to provide the most suitable legal framework to facilitate competition. Ordoliberalism and managed capitalism are thus 'the two faces of the German model' that exhibits over time 'subtle shifts in its centre of gravity' (Dyson, 2002: 138–139) depending on the particular situation and on which coalition is ascendant on particular issues.[14]

Very different conclusions on the causes of the German success would have been drawn had the analysis been broadened beyond the monetarist scheme to include the changes that occurred in those years in the German economy. First, in the years 1970–1976 the strong compression of investment was accompanied by a greater relative increase of foreign direct investment. Reacting to the revaluation of the Mark in 1969 and 1971 and to the trade union conflicts (in particular expressed by the immigrant workforce), even before the first oil crisis the German system had begun a restructuring process aimed at increasing its presence in international markets and regained competitiveness by reducing employment in the more labour-intensive production phases or sectors, often laying off immigrant workers. Between 1973 and 1978 the total labour force decreased by 0.8 million, 0.6 million of which were foreigners, and employment declined by 1.6 per cent per year. For extension and continuity 'the phenomenon has no comparison in other industrial countries' (Ciocca and Vito Colonna, 1981: 102). The reduction of the profits share in manufacturing was followed, in the early 1970s, by industrial restructuring, investments in non-manufacturing sectors (services including finance) and abroad. In 1975, 60 per cent of the total profits came from the services sector. Domestic investment and much of the FDI had moved towards higher value added sectors. The location of FDI, mostly concentrated in the US, was designed to exploit the demand and cost advantages in high-end productions, while labour- and energy-intensive sectors or stages of production had been transferred to other countries. In the course of a few years, West Germany was transformed from a capital- and labour-importing country into a capital exporter, with an increasing share of its labour force abroad. In addition, it moved from a highly industrial to a highly tertiarized country (when measured in terms of the share of sectorial profits to total profits).

The high current account surpluses that were recorded in those years were the result of a number of circumstances (see Chapter 2). The contribution of exports – attributable to the quality of the products (in particular investment goods) – was associated with a slowdown in domestic demand, and therefore in imports. Wage moderation – which presupposes the conclusion of a renewed 'political exchange' with the unions in terms of employment and welfare security – and the redirection of part of the investments abroad contributed to the decline of domestic demand.

Reviewing the reasons for the low growth of the German economy in the 1970s, Ciocca and Vito Colonna (1981: 133) argued that the reason for the stronger restraint of domestic demand (compared with other countries) was not to be searched in alleged structural stagnation trends or in the objective to contain inflation but 'in the purpose – exclusive, predominant or parallel with respect to the price stabilization – to achieve an active balance' in the current accounts. It translates into an accumulation of potential international credit that can be used for different purposes, economic or political, but anyway reached through economic conditioning. The goal of accumulating credit potential is defined by the authors as a 'neo-mercantilist' policy. While this *financial* aspect is definitely significant to interpret also the events of the following years, if taken in isolation, it risks overshadowing the industrial restructuring of the German economic system, at home and abroad: in Germany the two aspects are often, though not always, welded together. The process of internationalization and internal restructuring, begun in the 1970s, continued in a much more significant way after the unification of Germany, in the phases that preceded and followed the formation of the Monetary Union.

The political leaders of the European countries, who wanted to imitate Germany, seized only the neoclassical aspects without paying attention to the complex tensions between the two faces of the German model. It is not surprising that the results of a restrictive policy in the other European countries gave results very different, in terms of exports, output and unemployment, from those in Germany.

6 Conclusions

An implication of the experience of the three decades that separate the demise of Bretton Woods from the birth of the EMU is that while, in general, a restrictive monetary policy leads to a divergence of interests between bank and industry, as Bhadury and Steindl observed, some variants are possible. The case of Germany of the 1970s–1990s suggests that one can have a 'Rhenish monetarism', in which internal monetary restriction provides the framework within which an internationalization/restructuring process of both industry and finance takes place, with industry retaining a primary role. The case of the US and the UK in the post-1980s phase can be defined instead as a case of 'financial monetarism', in which finance dominates industry (which in turn becomes a participant of financial roles). The case of the peripheral European countries is still different. It can be defined as an example of 'subaltern monetarism': it suffers passively both the forces that push towards deindustrialization, without undertaking policies for a renovation/upgrading of their production structures, and the destabilizing effects of capital inflows/outflows. Thus, inflows are not addressed to remove the bottlenecks or to open the way to long-term development objectives. The practical consequence of this 'subaltern monetarism' has been the hollowing out of public capabilities that makes the exit from the current crisis even more difficult.

In the following chapter, we trace the specific consequences of the weakening of the investment engine for the countries of the European periphery since the mid-1970s.

Notes

1 Ladrech (1994: 84) defined Europeanization as 'an incremental process of re-orienting the direction and shape of politics to the extent that EC political and economic dynamics become part of the organisational logic of national politics and policy-making'.

2 The standard representation of structural change is in terms of employment shares. If we look at the profit shares, the picture that emerges

> is nearly the mirror image, with the relative position of services and FIRE [Finance, Insurance and Real Estate] inverted.… Rather than post-industrialism [i.e. tertiarization], it is financialization that comes sharply into view when profit data rather than employment or GDP are the focus of the analysis.
>
> (Krippner, 2011: 32–33)

See also, for the UK, Bhaduri and Steindl (1983: 5, Table 2).

3 This point recalls the objections raised by Federico Caffè in the debate on Italy's participation to the EMS, reported in Chapter 1.

4 Conversely, according to Kalecki as reported by Steindl (Bhaduri and Steindl, 1983: 2), the events in Britain around 1931/1932 can be interpreted in terms of a shift of power from the City to industry. The decline in the international status of the City after the abandonment of the Gold Standard 'provided the necessary socio-political base for the acceptance of Keynesian policies'.

5 However, as Bhaduri and Steindl pointed out (1983: 2 and 15), a high interest rate policy benefits the banks 'under normal circumstances i.e. as long as they do not become the victims of a financial crisis'. In the crisis, 'the reverse side of the monetarist medal had become visible' and

> the position (and the point of view) of the banks has undergone a fundamental change: their interest is now in easier money, because they want more liquidity, so that their customers, threatened with insolvency and forced to borrow, can at least service their debt service.

6 In this context, we mean by monetarism a doctrine that looks at the economic system as the spontaneous result of a competitive equilibrium based on supply and demand. Moreover, attempts by economic policy authorities to push the effective rate of unemployment below the natural rate can be successful only in the short term and in the presence of agents' forecast errors. While the first aspect applies to all theoretical positions inspired by the neoclassical theory, the second aspect differentiates the monetarist position from the neoclassical synthesis of the 1950s and 1960s.

7 According to Arrighi, the capitalist development occurs through the alternation of two phases. A phase of 'material expansion' in which the profits of the hegemonic country are mainly derived from the exchange of goods and international trade, and a phase of 'financial expansion' in which, in a situation of declining profit opportunities on 'material' activities, the origin of the profits is transferred, within the same country, from goods to finance. The second phase corresponds, according to Arrighi, to the passing on of the world hegemony to another country that, thanks to innovative forms, enters the 'material expansion' phase.

8 Krugman (1998), for example, improperly describes as a 'liquidity trap' the presence of an absolute nominal limit equal to zero to the rate of interest.

9 The investment function may be such that no level of the real rate of interest is capable of eliciting a sustainable investment level (that is, free from bubbles) and adequate to absorb the available labour force. The inelasticity of investment with respect to interest rate emerges from a plurality of observations, both recent and older. Its recognition would seriously undermine the fundamental justification of the supply-side policies. Proposed in the early 1980s, these policies were believed to boost private investment by reducing taxes on profits. However, as noted by Mazzucato (2013), they have had little effect on investment, and thus on growth, but major regressive effects on income distribution. The recognition of the failure of a policy based solely on incentives regardless of the level of demand, compared to a direct intervention policy, calls into question the theoretical foundation of the supply-side policies, namely the existence of a demand function for factors of production elastic

to their real rate of remuneration. Highlighting the high probability that monetary policy may prove ineffective for the purpose of triggering a recovery in investment, Keynes had written (1936, 173): 'If … we are tempted to assert that money is the drink which stimulates the system to activity, we must remind ourselves that there may be several slips between the cup and the lip.' The absence of the expected expansionary effect of an increase in the money supply may result from contemporaneous counter-forces that simple interpretative schemes, based on the assumptions of the absence of uncertainty, high elasticity of investment and *coeteris paribus*, were unable to take into account.

10 In Bernanke's opinion, after the mid-1980s, lower output volatility was associated with less frequent and milder recessions, with more stable employment and a reduction of uncertainty, while lower inflation volatility improved the working of the markets and the ordered scheduling of economic decisions. We may observe that, at this point, the target of stability is replacing the time-honoured targets of unemployment reduction and fostering growth.

11 He concluded that 'improved monetary policy has likely made an important contribution not only to the reduced volatility of inflation (which is not particularly controversial) but to the reduced volatility of output as well'.

12 As shown in Leamer's data (Table 1, p. 159), in the period from 1985 to 2006 all components of demand showed a fall in volatility, measured by the standard deviation, with residential investment – which proved to be the weakest link of the chain – showing the *largest relative drop*.

13 In May 2008, Cabanillas and Ruscher (2008) provided 'a euro area view of the Great Moderation process', assessing the member states' output volatility and its determinants. The authors concluded that, given the considerably worse initial conditions, 'improvements in the conduct of monetary policies have been much larger in several member states than in the US over the past three decades, bringing larger gains in terms of output stability'.

14 As Dyson (2002, 140) points out, while ordoliberals embraced with enthusiasm globalization, the single European market, EMU and capital mobility, at the same time, especially in the version accepted by the Bundesbank, they gave pre-eminence to price stability over financial liberalization when the latter could jeopardize an effective monetary policy. This reluctance to embrace regulatory change may help to explain why the German banking system had to turn abroad to realize those speculative profits that were hindered in their homeland.

References

Arrighi, G. (1994). *The Long Twentieth Century: Money, Power, and the Origins of Our Times*. London: Verso.

Arrighi, G. (2007). *Adam Smith in Beijing: Lineages of the Twenty-first Century (Vol. 3)*. London: Verso.

Barba, A. and Pivetti, M. (2008). Rising household debt: Its causes and macroeconomic implications – a long-period analysis. *Cambridge Journal of Economics*, 33(1), 113–137.

Bernanke, B. (2004). *The Great Moderation*. Washington, DC: Eastern Economic Association.

Bhaduri, A. and Steindl, J. (1983). The rise of monetarism as a social doctrine. *Thames Papers in Political Economy*.

Blanchard, O., Furceri, D. and Pescatori, A. (2014). A prolonged period of low real interest rates? In C. Teulings and R. Baldwin, *Secular Stagnation: Facts, Causes and Cures*, 15 August. http://voxeu.org/content/secular-stagnation-facts-causes-and-cures [accessed 21 September 2017].

Burnham, P. (2001). New Labour and the politics of depoliticisation. *The British Journal of Politics & International Relations*, 3(2), 127–149.

Cabanillas, L. G. and Ruscher, E. (2008). *The Great Moderation in the Euro Area: What Role Have Macroeconomic Policies Played?* (No. 331). Directorate General Economic and Financial Affairs (DG ECFIN), European Commission.

Ciocca, P. and Vito Colonna, O. (1981). La politica economica della Germania Federale e i suoi riflessi internazionali (1969–79). In S. Alessandrini and V. Valli (eds), *L'Economia tedesca: la Germania federale verso l'egemonia economica in Europa (Vol. 8)*. Milano: Etas Kompas.

Dyson, K. H. (ed.) (2002). *European States and the Euro: Europeanization, Variation, and Convergence*. Oxford: Oxford University Press.

Foster, J. B. (2007). The financialization of capitalism. *Monthly Review*, 58(11), 1.

Froud, J., Johal, S., Leaver, A. and Williams, K. (2006). *Financialization and Strategy: Narrative and Numbers*. London: Routledge.

Ginzburg, A. (2012). Sviluppo trainato dalla produttività o dalle connessioni: due diverse prospettive di analisi e di intervento pubblico nella realtà economica italiana. *Economia & Lavoro*, 46(2), 67–80.

Keynes, J. M. (1936). *The General Theory of Money, Interest and Employment*. Reprinted in *The Collected Writings of John Maynard Keynes*. London: Macmillan/Cambridge University Press, 7.

Krippner, G. R. (2011). *Capitalizing on Crisis*. Cambridge, MA: Harvard University Press.

Krugman, P. (1998). It's baaack: Japan's slump and the return of the liquidity trap. *Brookings Papers on Economic Activity*, 29(2), 137–206.

Krugman, P. (2014). Four observations on secular stagnation. In C. Teulings and R. Baldwin, *Secular Stagnation: Facts, Causes and Cures*, 15 August. http://voxeu.org/content/secular-stagnation-facts-causes-and-cures [accessed 21 September 2017].

Ladrech, R. (1994). Europeanization of domestic politics and institutions: The case of France. *JCMS: Journal of Common Market Studies*, 32(1), 69–88.

Lazonick, W. (2011). From innovation to financialization: How shareholder value ideology is destroying the US Economy. In M. H. Wolfson and G. A. Epstein (eds), *The Handbook of the Political Economy of Financial Crises*. Oxford: Oxford University Press, 491–511.

Lazonick, W. and O'Sullivan, M. (2000). Maximizing shareholder value: A new ideology for corporate governance. *Economy and Society*, 29(1), 13–35.

Leamer, E. E. (2007). Housing is the business cycle. *National Bureau of Economic Research No. w13428*.

Magdoff, H. and Sweezy, P. M. (1987). *Stagnation and the Financial Explosion*. New York: Monthly Review Press.

Mazzucato, M. (2013). *The Entrepreneurial State: Debunking Private vs. Public Sector Myths*. London: Anthem.

McNamara, K. R. and Jones, E. (1996). The clash of institutions: Germany in European monetary affairs. *German Politics & Society*, 14(3), 5–30.

Myrdal, G. (1960). *Beyond the Welfare State: Economic Planning and its International Implications*. London: Taylor & Francis.

Orhangazi, Ö. (2008). Financialisation and capital accumulation in the non-financial corporate sector: A theoretical and empirical investigation on the US economy: 1973–2003. *Cambridge Journal of Economics*, 32(6), 863–886.

Stockhammer, E. (2004). Financialisation and the slowdown of accumulation. *Cambridge Journal of Economics*, 28(5), 719–741.

Summers, L. H. (2013). Speech at the 14th Annual Research Conference in Honor of Stanley Fisher, International Monetary Fund, 8 November. Transcript available at www.facebook.com/notes/randy-fellmy/transcript-of-larry-summers-speech-at-the-imf-economic-forum-nov-8-2013/585630634864563 [accessed 21 September 2017].

Summers, L. H. (2014). Reflections on the 'New Secular Stagnation Hypothesis' in C. Teulings and R. Baldwin, *Secular Stagnation: Facts, Causes and Cures*, 15 August. http://voxeu.org/content/secular-stagnation-facts-causes-and-cures [accessed 21 September 2017].

Teulings, C. and Baldwin, R. (2014). *Secular Stagnation: Facts, Causes and Cures*, 15 August. http://voxeu.org/content/secular-stagnation-facts-causes-and-cures [accessed 21 September 2017].

Wicksell, K. (1898a). *Interest and Prices*, translated by R. F. Kahn (1936), reprinted (1965), New York: Augustus M. Kelley.

Wicksell, K. [1898b] (1958). *The Influence of the Rate of Interest on Commodity Prices*. Translated by Reginald S. Stedman, Sylva Gethin and Alan Williams. *Selected Papers on Economic Theory*.

8 The interruption of industrialization in Southern Europe

A centre-periphery perspective

1 Introduction

In the previous chapters we have reviewed the by now rather widespread consensus on the euro's structural design flaws. Rather less investigation has been devoted to identify the distant origins of these flaws in the growth patterns, policy actions and narratives of Southern European countries *before* implementation of the Monetary Union. With no claim to completeness, in what follows we shall try to provide an inevitably broad and rough picture of these developments.

2 The embeddedness of centre-periphery relations

We argued in Chapter 4 that one of the side-effects of the economic crisis that began in 2008 was the rediscovery of the term 'centre-periphery' to analyse the economic situations of the European countries. This perspective, defined as the study of the evolution of the centre-periphery relations, may be helpful to analyse the dynamics of the European integration processes of the second half of the twentieth century, adopting the 'two eyes of history', chronology and geography (Vico, [1725–1728] 2011: 61). Concerning chronology, in reconstructing the relations between centre and periphery after the Second World War, it should be recalled that all the countries of the Southern European periphery can be defined as latecomers, although Italy embarked on a path of industrialization and integration into European trade earlier than all the other peripheral countries. As regards geography, 'changing geographies of production', wrote Hudson (2002: 262),

> are a product of the interplay of (*inter alia*) corporate, state and trade unions strategies, as companies pursue profitability, trade unions and workers seek new employment and/or protect existing jobs, and states attempt to balance the pursuit of accumulation in their territory with the claims of equity and socio-spatial justice.

While it is questionable whether this formulation adequately describes the strategies pursued by the European states, it remains true that, again quoting Hudson (ibid.), these geographies are contingent outcomes of the co-evolution of the asymmetric power relationships between these individual and collective actors and institutions. Conceptually, this represents an attempt to recognize the variety of ways in which agency and action and the structural determinants of capitalist economies co-evolve in particular ways.

It is important to remember the context in which this co-evolution occurs, namely the European integration of peripheral countries and globalization,[1] 'for these are both a partial product of the strategies of companies, states and trade unions and in turn help set the parameters that shape these processes' (Hudson, ibid.).

When one speaks of 'structural determinants', it is customary to refer to price competitiveness, and thus to labour costs and productivity. Developments in relative unit labour costs are then used to explain differential GDP trends. But, as we argued in Chapter 2, the experience of the past 15 years has clearly shown the limitations of focusing only on this unit costs indicator and on this definition of competitiveness. Moreover, in the presence of bubbles or unsustainable increases in net public (or private) spending, the short-period GDP performance can hide the structural fragility of the underlying economic conditions. Furthermore, a policy implication of focusing only on price competitiveness is that the only necessary and sufficient measure to heal a distressed economy and restore growth is the reduction of relative costs, obtained mainly through an increase in 'labour flexibility'. This measure would be unnecessary and probably counter-productive if the underlying problem stemmed not from price competitiveness but from 'product competitiveness, rooted in limited production capabilities' (Best, 2013: 1; see also Ginzburg, 2012). In a regime where product-led competition and innovation prevails, the problem is the *rigidity* of the productive structure (associated with what may be called, to be brief, its insufficient 'quality'), not labour flexibility. We share with Michael Best the idea that 'the evidence is abundant that peripheral economies suffer from a dearth of business enterprises that meet the performance standards required to compete and grow in the Single European Market' (2013: 2).

In order to understand the divergent trajectories of the core and the peripheral European countries in terms of interdependent economies with different productive capabilities (see Figure 8.1 for the trend of GDP per capita in the years 1960–2016), it is therefore necessary to start from two concepts. The first is the crucial distinction of countries between first-comer industrializers (the 'centre') and latecomers (Italy) and late-latecomers (Spain, Portugal and Greece) in the periphery. The second concerns the concept of level of productive structure:[2] although differences in the production structure between centre and periphery were very large at first, they were reduced until the beginning of the 1970s, especially during the 'glorious thirties', but reopened again in the subsequent years, and especially after the crisis of 2008.

What is meant by 'productive structure'? As noted by Best (2013: 2), 'the absence of the concepts of productive structure and product-led competitiveness from public discourse and academic economic analysis deflects "growth" policy away from its proper focus'. This absence, we might add, also hinders

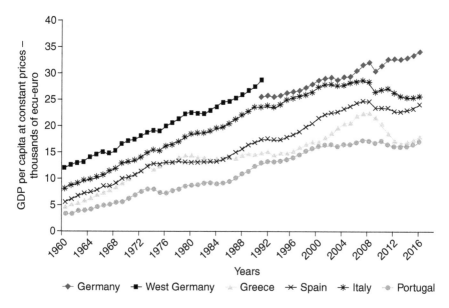

Figure 8.1 GDP per capita at constant prices (values in ecu-euro, '000) – selected countries (1960–2016).

Source: authors' elaborations on AMECO data.

understanding of the determinants of the divergent development paths taken in Europe by the centre and the periphery. We adopt a theoretical perspective that ideally combines the contributions of Albert Hirschman, Edith Penrose and Sebastiano Brusco. Here, the central role generally attributed to labour productivity in the development process is replaced by three circumstances, which, by mutually interacting, turn *ex post* into productivity performance: (i) presence of innovative businesses whose organization is aimed 'to compete on the basis of new products or processes and/or more effective use of new technologies and not primarily on the basis of price' (Best, 2013: 3–4); (ii) the activity of the firm is never isolated: its performance crucially depends on both the structured interrelationships (the linkages) that it can establish upstream and downstream, and the support received from the material and immaterial infrastructures, development agencies and financial institutions that sustain the process of innovation in the long term; (iii) in product-led competition, a central role is played by industrial policy. It is the result of 'triangular relations intersecting the three spheres of government, education and industry' (ibid.). From this it follows that a strategic policy of industrial development is incompatible with cuts in public budgets, and more generally in aggregate demand, which weaken or extinguish this triangular relationship. Industrial policy can encounter insurmountable obstacles if it is inconsistent with the main directions of macroeconomic policy. Finally, it should be emphasized that the notion of product-led competition is a relative concept. Indeed, it relates to the creation of new products and new markets *in a given productive system*. Thus, it does not concern only countries and markets at the frontier of knowledge, both technological and organizational; on the contrary, it takes on special importance in peripheral countries. Obviously, apart from the advantages deriving from experience, the transfer/adaptation of technologies, organizations, business strategies originally designed in other socio-economic systems poses difficult, specific problems in both the supply and demand domains.

The three circumstances described above were asymmetrically distributed between the countries of the centre and the Southern periphery of Europe at the beginning of the new stage of the Europeanization process of the early 1980s, associated with the enlargement of the EEC to Greece (1981) and Spain and Portugal (1986). In 1980, in a report on *Problems of Lagged Development in OECD Europe: A Study of Six Countries*,[3] Fuà observed – implicitly recalling Gerschenkron's theses – that the structure and tendencies of latecomer European countries were different from those observed during the initial development phases of the older industrialized countries. The major differences concerned the technological gap, the demonstration effect on consumption and the challenge of competition from more developed countries. These differences translated into strong internal productivity differentials across industries and regions ('dualism'), serious difficulties in providing regular employment to the potential labour supply, higher propensity to price instability and public deficits, and 'a peculiar fragility of the balance of payments'. Fuà concluded that the weaker competitive position originated from persistent trade deficits: at the end of the 1970s in all five countries, with the exception of Italy, that had succeeded to reach a more balanced position, persistent trade deficits had to be permanently compensated by remittances and tourism. Subsequent developments led to believe that this type of analysis had been overtaken by events: the per capita income grew also in the countries of the periphery, kindling hopes of a reduction also in relative income differentials. However, as shown by Figure 8.1, the undeniable, important *absolute* growth of per capita income in all the peripheral countries was accompanied by an increase in *relative* per capita income *gaps*, with respect to core countries (but also internal), heightened during the crisis that began in 2008. This suggests that an excessive focus on short-term, sometimes unsustainable, GDP increases may lead to ignore too hastily long period considerations. Also for this reason, it is important to complement aggregate national account data with indicators of productive structure.

Over the 30 years of European integration since the early 1980s, the Southern peripheral countries were exposed to macroeconomic and industrial policy measures that, though apparently neutral, generated increasing regional disparities, both between centre and periphery and within countries. In what follows, we retrace the main phases of the process of the relative hollowing-out of the productive structures of the peripheral countries.

In conformity with our main thesis, we make two assumptions. The first is that the crises of the centre (which here, for simplicity, is Germany, West

Germany until 1989), reflecting domestic and international circumstances, lead to internal reorganizations of its production structure that deeply affect the countries of the periphery. The centre is enabled to strengthen its ability to stay in the market in the product-led competition by processes of 'creative destruction' and reconstruction undertaken with the support of industrial policies.[4] Conversely, the countries of the periphery fall behind and, also as a consequence of their policies, implement what might be called a 'plain destruction' of their capabilities to create new products, market niches and markets.

The second, related, hypothesis is that the crisis of the 1970s, traditionally associated with oil price hikes, marked a profound break in the history of the relations between the centre and the periphery of Europe: until then, even if at unequal speeds, the countries of the European periphery had taken significant steps along the path of industrialization. After the 1970s, these processes were, again unevenly, disrupted. With reference to this pattern, Sapelli speaks of 'weak industrialization', or 'incomplete modernization' (see Table 8.1 for data on employment by sector as a percentage of total employment). According to this author (Sapelli, 1995: 63–64), the Southern European countries belong to

> socio-economic formations which cannot be defined simply as capitalist. They were of a new type. They had been determined by the character of the mixed economy and by the stratification of classes typical of societies where services had become predominant either after a very brief period of industrialization or by skipping industrialization completely.

In these societies, 'market forces were more evident than before, but in a social context dominated by reciprocity and patronage which did not allow the development of a complete contractual system'. Obstacles to the completion of industrialization in the countries of Southern Europe therefore derived from the prevalence of cultural values and power systems based on status and clientelism, with respect to those based on contracts 'typical of societies where the market economy has prevailed. The Weberian capitalistic society is the ideal example. However, this model has had little success in Southern Europe' (ibid.: 16). A

Table 8.1 Employment by sector as percentage of total employment (average values)

	1960–1968			1968–1973		
	Agriculture	*Industry*	*Services*	*Agriculture*	*Industry*	*Services*
Germany	11.9	47.7	40.4	8.5	47.9	43.6
Italy	27.7	36.4	39.5	20.4	39.1	40.4
Spain	33.4	32.7	33.9	26.7	35.6	37.7
Portugal	39.4	32.2	28.3	29.9	33.4	36.6
Greece	51.9	19.9	28.2	40.3	25.4	34.3

Source: Sapelli (1995) and elaborations on OECD data.

late and crony capitalism, brought in from outside, with a strong presence of the state in society, gave rise to what Sapelli, citing Huntington (1968), calls 'a weak degree of institutionalization of the political-democratic system': that is, a poor ability to create 'norms and democratic procedures of negotiation, compensation and regulation of interests' (Sapelli, ibid.: 17). This interpretation of the industrialization processes (i.e. of the transitions to tertiarization) of the Southern European countries seems unconvincing. It is an 'essentialist' interpretation unable to explain either the first phase of industrialization or why the process halted precisely in the 1970s. Moreover, the relations between centre and periphery play no role in the 'early tertiarization' hypothesis. Despite attempts to complicate the picture with many descriptive details, sometimes inconsistent with the basic thesis, the interpretative scheme appears to be a variant of the modernization theory, which reflects an idealized, atomistic development model of nineteenth-century England (or of the twentieth-century United States). This scheme refers to deviations from a unique optimal development model based on the choices of rational economic agents operating under perfect competition and favoured by an institutional framework consistent with it. Like all 'essentialist' models, also the optimal scheme tacitly assumes the end of history, as well as that of geography.

3 The global crisis of the mid-1970s in Southern Europe: peripheral tertiarization and impoverishment of the productive structures

The global economic crisis of the mid-1970s, related to the synchronization of the recessive cycles of the major countries, was at the time the deepest since the end of the Second World War. Those events are well known: the 1971 devaluation of the dollar; the huge increase in the price of oil[5] and other commodities in 1973; the 1974 drastic monetary and fiscal restriction aimed at addressing cost-push inflation (also associated with the strong wage increases in the previous years); and the deep balance of payments deficits of the commodity-importing countries. The economic and social effects of the crisis, in terms of employment reduction and productive capacity destruction, are also well known.

In a longer-term perspective, other aspects of a more enduring character emerge. The crisis can be analysed from the perspective of the alternation of phases of homogeneization and heterogeneization of the major countries' productive structures, separated by moments of crisis and restructuring. According to the Japanese economist Akamatsu,[6] this alternation of phases characterizes the evolution of international economic relations. Between the late 1960s and early 1970s the competitive gap among the US, the major European countries and Japan was narrowing (as evidenced by the forces that led to abandonment of the Bretton Woods regime). Meanwhile, in the major central countries, given the prevailing income distribution, the long-term post-war development was leading to the saturation of the domestic demand for consumer goods – especially durable consumer goods, including cars, the greatest drivers of post-war growth.[7]

The fact that the demand for consumer goods had become largely a question of replacement (rather than expansion in sales volumes) led to a strong differentiation of brands, to the multiplication of models (vertical differentiation) and to a dramatic shortening of products' lives.[8] In an environment of fierce oligopolistic competition, important consequences ensued: on the demand side, a boost to the search for still unexplored foreign market spaces; in terms of costs, a pressure to relocate production stages in lower-wage areas, which, favoured by ITC technologies, eventually led to international fragmentation. In some areas there was a prevalence of manufacturing over distribution (producer-driven global value chains), in others a prevalence of distribution over manufacturing (buyer-driven global value chains). In the countries of the centre, the shift in the forms of competition from quantitative expansion to qualitative product differentiation promoted a plurality of 'services based' sales strategies. None of this could have happened without a strong expansion of financial services, first to finance direct investments in the peripheral countries, then to cover the time gap between sales and disposable income, and finally to finance mergers, acquisitions and alliances prompted by excess capacity and (organizational more than technological) economies of scale. For their part, financial institutions were only eager to find outlets for the petrodollars recycled by the oil producers. Hence one witnesses a general drive towards the hasty deregulation of capital movements, from which the receiving countries expected to finance imports of goods and technologies necessary for their growth. Logistics, transport and communications – not coincidentally areas where, as in finance, the impact of new technologies had been more disruptive of current practices – assumed strategic importance in accommodating the international reorganization of production.

We have described in the previous chapter the empowerment of finance in the areas of speculation in the flex-price segments (securities, bonds, commodities, real estate, etc.). Uncontrolled deregulation led to a series of financial crises that were particularly severe and long-lasting in the periphery (from Mexico in 1981 to Greece in 2010 and following years). In response to inflationary pressures and/or balance of payments crises due to monetary expansion and/or asset price bubbles of centre-countries, recourse to drastically restrictive monetary policies had asymmetric effects: the fall in the prices of 'flex price' items hit countries in the periphery relatively harder, because of both their mono-specialization in commodities and the hasty return of capital to the safe-haven centre countries (the 'sudden stop' rediscovered during the occasion of the Eurozone sovereign crisis).

To conclude, by raising the bar in the standards of quality required to compete, the 1970s global crisis – as in different ways the next 2008–2015 global crisis – marked a turning point[9] in the diverging fortunes of centre and periphery. In particular, when tracing the evolution of the economies of the European periphery, it is necessary to bear in mind that, from the early 1970s onwards, they were operating in an international market regime increasingly dominated by the competition of differentiated products which led to the reorganization of a wide range of manufacturing and services operations. This new environment created highly selective opportunities for different countries and regions. Within the periphery, greater opportunities were opened for those firms provided with capabilities and inserted in productive structures better suited to filling the vacuum left by the core countries' shift in specialization and diversification, or better able to fit in the subcontracting chain of relatively sophisticated industrial components. Conversely, firms specialized in traditional products and unable to adapt, in a deflationary environment, to the new forms of competition encountered severe difficulties. The crisis also opened a gap in aggregate demand that political coalitions wanting to consolidate democratic institutions and/or reduce opposition eventually filled with welfare and construction expenditures. While, crisis after crisis, 'free-trade imperialism' (to recall Gallagher and Robinson's famous expression) accentuated the impoverishment of the productive structure of Southern countries, the 'peripheral tertiarization' based on construction and welfare found it increasingly difficult to reverse the hardships and inequities brought about by a limited and dependent capital accumulation.

The different transitions to tertiarization may be better understood by analysing the specific circumstances leading, in each country, to a halt in the industrialization process. We also raise doubts about the thesis of 'premature tertiarization' attributable to some 'original' ('pre-modern') features of those countries' institutions. In our opinion, the focus should instead be on the 'premature liberalization' of these economies and on the political confrontation that eventually led to the choice of this development path. The following section will be devoted to analysis of the first halt, in 1963, in the Italian industrialization process. Like the other Southern countries' analogous successive interruptions of industrialization, the Italian crisis was associated with a difficult phase of the European integration process. We shall argue that in all peripheral countries the 'solution' given to the specific crisis weakened, along with the productive structure, also the country's resilience to the following, systemic crisis. In all peripheral countries, and with greater intensity in Greece and Portugal, even before the 2008 crisis, a reduced growth rate was associated with a higher current account deficit as a percentage of GDP (see Table 8.2), a tendency that we interpret as evidence of an increasing mismatch between aggregate demand and output composition (negative substitution of net imports).

4 The European integration of a latecomer country: Italy

In 1948, per capita income in Italy was about three-quarters of that in Germany, two-thirds of that in France and half of that in the US (Barca, 1997: 6); however, Italy's industrial base was more diversified than those of the other Southern European countries (Sapelli, 1995: 76–77). Following the policy of import-substitution of investment goods implemented in the years before and after the Second World War, and during the 20 years of fascist dictatorship, Italy continued to develop a 'military-industrial' apparatus (mechanical engineering and steel industry, shipyards, automobiles, electricity and minerals). Industry, heavily protected by import barriers, was mainly concentrated in the North-West

Table 8.2 Rate of growth of real GDP and current accounts as a percentage of GDP (average values)

	Germany		Italy		Spain		Portugal		Greece	
	GDP	C/C	GDP	C/C	GDP	C/C	GDP	C/C	GDP	C/C
1960–1967	3.8	0.5	5.6	1.4	7.7	–0.9	6.0	–3.6	8.3	–1.8
1968–1973	5.0	1.2	5.1	1.3	6.7	0.4	7.0	–1.4	9.0	–1.5
1974–1979	2.6	0.5	3.7	–0.2	2.3	–0.6	3.2	–7.4	3.4	0.9
1980–1991	2.5	2.1	2.4	–1.1	2.8	–1.5	3.7	–7.9	0.9	–0.9
1992–1998	1.4	–0.9	1.4	1.2	2.2	–1.5	2.7	–6.0	2.1	–2.1
1999–2007	1.6	2.5	1.5	–0.6	3.9	–5.6	1.8	–9.5	4.0	–10.4
2008–2014	0.7	6.4	–1.3	–1.3	–0.7	–2.7	–0.9	–6.0	–4.1	–8.8

Source: authors' elaborations on AMECO data.

Note
1960–1991 West Germany.

'triangle' (Lombardy, Piedmont, Liguria). After the 1929 crisis, in 1933 the state created IRI, a public body[10] that brought together a group of bailed-out banks and firms in various sectors.[11]

Between 1948 and 1962, and in particular after 1953, the Italian economy underwent an intense phase of industrialization that in the space of a few years transformed the main features (and the landscape) of the Italian economy and society. Since 1951, gradual measures of foreign trade liberalization had favoured intra-European trade, resulting in 1957 in the Treaty of Rome. However, until 1956–1957 Italian growth was driven mainly by domestic demand, and in particular by private investment (public investment would rise only in 1961–1962): 'At this stage, steel and energy investments of public bodies owe their importance to their strategic role in directing and enabling private investment, not to their size' (Barca, 1997: 68). Moreover, these investments, 'aimed at substituting imports [sought] to mitigate the old constraint of the limited availability of raw materials and energy' (Ciocca *et al.*, 1973: 92).[12] Investment growth was stimulated by high profitability and strong consumption growth. Profit margins were high because of stagnant nominal industrial wages and stable prices, associated with high labour productivity growth. Total consumption growth was driven by the increase in average per capita income, brought about by huge, inter-sectoral, geographical and demographic shifts: between 1951 and 1963 more than three million people moved from agriculture to the industrial and the services sectors, and about 6–7 million from the countryside to the city (Barca, 1997: 69). From the second half of the 1950s onwards, also exports started to grow vigorously. In 1962, the current account was still in surplus: this was the culmination of the so-called 'economic miracle'.

Growth resulted in a rapid reduction in unemployment, which throughout the 1950s had contributed, together with trade union repression, to dampening demands for wage rises. The resumption of trade union militancy was accompanied by a strong increase in wages, and thus of consumption, and, given important supply bottlenecks, huge consumer goods imports. The result was a strong price hike, a high current account deficit and massive capital flights, caused also by fears of radical reforms by the new centre-left government (for the first time since 1947, in 1962 the Socialist Party decided to support by an abstention vote the Government led by Christian Democrats, taking an active part in the following year). On the eve of the April 1963 political elections, the new Governor of the Bank of Italy, Guido Carli, implemented a too expansionary monetary policy; and also for this reason – he said later – he had to apply the monetary brakes 'very vigorously'.[13] The monetary squeeze produced a steep fall in private investments, which would recover only very slowly in the following years, despite a quick recovery in profit margins, amid high and persistent unemployment. A rapid increase in exports, with stagnant imports, led to almost a decade of highly positive current accounts, which were considered evidence of the success of the economic policies adopted. The other side of these policies was the quantitative, and above all qualitative, destruction of productive capacity epitomized by the irreversible crisis of the Olivetti Electronic Division, which had just put an innovative portable computer model on the market (the Division would be sold to General Electric, which did not seize the opportunity to develop this new product line).

There was an obvious contradiction between the deflationary measures adopted by the coalition government to stabilize the economy and the longer-term policies needed to cope with the old and new imbalances in the Italian productive structure. In a longer-term perspective, inflation and external imbalances could be read as symptoms of the incompleteness of a 'viable' productive structure compatible with a more equitable income distribution. The experience of the Italian 'economic miracle' (before it abruptly came to a halt) – and the more lasting and administratively guided development model of the East Asian countries in the 1960s and 1970s – suggest that a broader internal market could have been obtained through import substitution *and* the creation of a sufficiently large (and territorially extensive) export base able to finance continuation of the industrialization process.

Could the 1963 crisis – with its important long-run repercussions – have had a different outcome? It is customary to answer this question in terms of choice between abstract principles, in this case between automatism (the market, possibly integrated by a legal framework[14] to achieve the competitive equilibrium described by the textbooks) or discretion (often assimilated to central planning). But an ill-formulated question leads to misleading simple answers. There is a different way – between automatism and discretion – that requires reducing the level of abstraction from abstract principles down to deeper analysis of the insertion of the Italian productive structure in the international trade network, and careful assessment of the difficulties that the spontaneous forces of *this* market economy are able to solve.

In an important document – the *Nota Aggiuntiva* (1962), presented to the Parliament in 1962 – the Minister of the Budget, Ugo La Malfa, argued that Italy's rapid post-war growth had been accompanied by sectoral, regional and social imbalances, and by distortions in the level and the composition of consumption and investment. This analysis prompted the proposal for a plan of coordinated actions targeted, not on the market, but on its extension and transformation, through state support for the creation of new activities. The two most dynamic components of effective demand – private consumption and exports – could slow down, the former because of saturation and the latter because of unpredictable external events, with serious consequences for the whole of industry, and especially for the more backward sectors and areas. As regards investments, a programme for development could reduce the persistent underestimation by private investors of the convenience of investing due to uncertainty, a limited horizon, private risk versus collective benefits. These policies today appear far-sighted and very distinct from a proposal of centralized planning. Compared with the views and actions of the protagonists of the economic policy of the time,[15] they reveal a wider breadth of vision, coupled with a more realistic consciousness of the latecomers' difficulties to expand the productive basis through spontaneous market forces. Guido Carli, for instance, was less inclined than his predecessor to recognize the backwardness of the country and the need to broaden its industrial base. In 1959, while advocating an expansion of the tertiary employment, Carli remarked that a sustained effort to extend the industrial base was needed by economies 'more backward' than Italy (Carli, 1993: 162). After a political clash in which at a certain moment even the threat of a military coup was envisaged,[16] the automatism of stabilization policies, which were presented as merely short-term measures, eventually prevailed.

By directing the economy away from indicative planning, the 1963 interruption of the Italian industrialization process had long-term effects that became evident at the time of the Treaty of Maastricht and the Stability Pact. It also affected the path of development in the Southern Italian regions – the so-called Mezzogiorno, which was severely hit by the stagnation of domestic demand in the 1960s. This strengthened the pressure to use direct state intervention to promote the creation of basic industries (steel, chemicals, oil refineries). The declared intention was to provide cheaper inputs to the existing firms located in the North and to create new industrial initiatives in the South through forward linkages.[17] The vehicle of the public intervention was IRI, which in fact enormously expanded its activities in a variety of sectors. The per capita income gap between central-northern and southern Italy, which had increased in the early 1950s, narrowed rapidly in the 1960s largely as a result of state intervention. But it again widened drastically in the 1970s in parallel with its crisis, and remained stable for almost 40 years (to worsen again during the last crisis).

The failure of state intervention in the South was the result of a constellation of different circumstances that in the end proved to be cumulative: among them was the political conflict on whether government spending should be used for self-sustained industrial development or for the creation of an electoral consensus. The 1973–1974 crisis shifted the balance between these two objectives in favour of the latter. The steep fall in demand, the ensuing collapse of basic commodities prices, due also to the entrance of new Asian competitors, led to huge

IRI debts (Ravazzi, 2013: 173). The crisis of the steel and shipbuilding industries accounted for more than 100 per cent of the group's losses. The firms in the IRI group, having lost their financial and decision-making autonomy, had to ask the state to refinance even their current activities and to allow price adjustments.

The Mezzogiorno industrialization process was interrupted when a selective investment effort was needed to upgrade products and processes. In a situation of widespread distress, state intervention shifted towards creating dependent and assisted subjects through the nomination of incompetent but loyal managers, and increasing disability pensions and other transfers. Amid growing social unrest, new forms of rampant corruption and organized crime – both instrumental to social control and electoral support – also succeeded in seizing new opportunities for expansion. The increase in interest rates during the 1980s led to an explosion of interest expenditures in the presence of a weaker productive structure. Also fiscal adjustment, long delayed but finally accelerated in the mid-1990s to meet the Maastricht criteria, penalized southern Italy, since it was implemented through tax increases and spending cuts (and not through the reduction of tax evasion): fixed investment and transfer expenditures have a proportional higher weight in the southern regions. After 1999, with the entry into force of the Treaty of Maastricht, the narrow export base of southern Italy (9 per cent of GDP) contributed to the reduction of the overall growth rate, thereby raising, together with southern poverty, the debt parameters, given that exports are the only dynamic item in aggregate demand.

As regards private large firms, when in the 1980s and 1990s exchange rate devaluations became less frequent, rather than adopting the strategy of product innovation they preferred to de-localize their plants abroad. It was unexpectedly left to the industrial districts of the North-East and the Adriatic coast to take up the challenge of the new, post-Fordist competition based on small batches and differentiated products. In 1979, Wade (1979: 216), assessing the situation of the Italian Mezzogiorno, wrote words that today sound prophetic and not only restricted to North–South relations within Italy:

> Before 1950 the South was poor and in the large part self-sufficient. Now the development mechanism has transformed it into a place which is much less poor and much more dependent on the North. Whether one says that southerners are on the whole better or worse off depends on how much normative weight one gives to consumption on the one hand and 'autonomy' on the other. Some critics go so far as to say that the development programme has failed because the South is now more dependent. I would wish to give more weight to the improvement in consumption, as a goal in itself, whether 'dependent' or 'independent'. However, the point is not only one of the values, but also whether the North will be able to continue underwriting the Southern living standards if the European economy expands more slowly or not at all over the next few decades. If not, the consequences for consumption standards of having become so dependent on northern transfers will be severe.

5 The late-latecomers' European integration

After a brief spell of autarchy and import substitution, by the end of the 1950s also the late-latecomer economies of Southern Europe moved, at different speeds and with diverse results, towards increasing commercial and economic integration with the core of the European Union.

The three countries started from different levels of industrial development: in the 1960s employment in agriculture was 33.4 per cent in Spain, 39.4 per cent in Portugal and 51.9 per cent in Greece (Sapelli, 1995 and Figure 8.2) – but they all recorded high income growth (see Table 8.2) led first by investment and consumption, and then by exports. With the partial exception of Greece, where investment went mostly to construction, all countries placed especial emphasis on basic industry, which was deemed essential for the expansion of the industrial sectors of comparative advantage. The state supported accumulation either directly, through publicly owned companies, or indirectly through subsidies and other incentives to domestic and foreign capital. In Spain the state attempted to counter the excessive power of the private oligopolies – steel, electricity and coal – by direct public investment in heavy industry through the Instituto Nacional de Industria (INI, funded in 1941 along the lines of the Italian IRI) (Balbín, 1999). In Portugal, national groups, with state support, invested in the machinery and chemicals industries (Mamede *et al.*, 2014), while in Greece it was foreign companies that came to control the basic industry (steel and metallurgic industries, chemicals, plastics, electricity) producing inputs for the domestic market and for exports to their parent companies (Sapelli, 1995). In the heyday of the Fordist regime of mass production, cost reduction was a strategic competitive factor in the core countries. Increasingly, the lower wages of peripheral countries attracted FDI[18] from the centre to produce for export: cheap intermediate inputs for the capital and durable consumption goods sectors, and cheap final consumption goods. With the openness of their economies progressing, the commercial integration with the core deepened, and their economies grew increasingly attuned to the European cycle.

The process of growth changed the structure of the economy: the share of industry (measured at constant prices) increased in all countries; and it did so especially in Spain, the most advanced of the group. In that country, capital accumulation and consumption drove the expansion of the consumer goods industries and the transformation of the economic structure. The capital goods sectors were among the most dynamic: chemicals and petrochemicals, metallurgy and steel, transport equipment (Banyuls and Recio, 2014). In spite of the suppression of free trade unions and the restriction of wage bargaining, under the Franco regime wages grew by and large in line with productivity (Toharia, 1988, refers to it as 'pseudo-Fordism'). By ensuring the enlargement of the domestic market, the pattern of wages was an important factor supporting the economy's high rate of growth: between 1961 and 1972 private consumption increased by an average 7 per cent per annum. In the same period the share of industry increased by 10 points at constant prices, while remaining practically

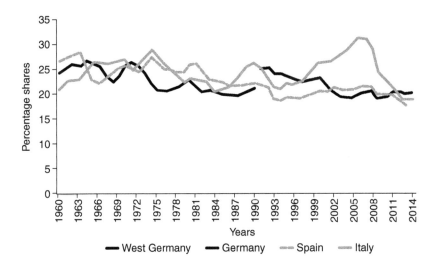

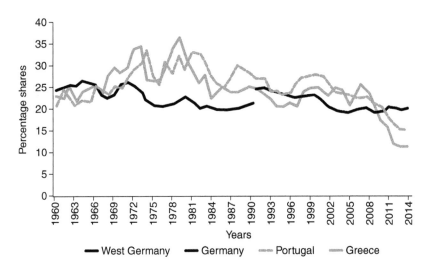

Figure 8.2 Gross fixed investment as a percentage of GDP (1960–2014).

Source: authors' elaborations on AMECO data.

constant at current prices. Productivity increases in industry, while allowing for comparable rate of growth of wages, translated into worsening terms of trade vis-à-vis services.

However, behind the apparent success in growth rates, the pattern of industrialization of the late-latecomers exhibited several weaknesses, similar to those evidenced for Italy, and, as anticipated by Fuà (1980), all linked to the narrow base of productive structure: unequal internal development, external disequilibria and an unsustainable demand pattern.

The rapidly increased liberalization and openness to the world economy was not preceded or accompanied by the creation of a competitive productive base. Indicative planning remained largely on paper, while the process of industrialization responded to market incentives: it was left to the market to decide what to produce and where. Subsidies and incentives were poured into all sectors, but investment and industrial production remained strongly geographically concentrated (in the Basque countries, Catalonia and Madrid in Spain; in the Lisbon and Oporto area in Portugal; in Thessaloniki and Athens in Greece), leaving the largest part of the country behind. The industrial structure became even more polarized between big, domestic and foreign firms in key sectors (finance, basic industries, utilities, durable consumption in Spain; aluminium, oil refineries and chemicals in Greece) and a large number of small, non-competitive firms. This resulted in a dualistic pattern of industrialization divided between the 'modern' sectors – characterized by higher capital/labour ratio and productivity – and the traditional ones. Overall, the technical content of production remained low and FDI had the effect of increasing the specialization of these countries' manufacturing industry in activities with low value added and low technological intensity (Mamede *et al.*, 2014).

The process of accumulation and the build-up of a domestic industry of consumption goods were heavily dependent on a large and increasing flow of imports – of capital, intermediate and 'sophisticated' consumption goods – only partly matched by an increasing volume of exports based on competitively low labour costs (see Figure 8.3). The negative balance of trade was financed by remittances, tourism, FDI and financial flows (aid, subsidies and credits). The export of the growing surplus of labour, which the expansion of industry and services was insufficient to absorb, was made possible by the process of growth in the core European economies, and responded to the double goal of defusing the time-bomb represented by a potential massive unemployment and financing the external deficit and the continuous expansion of domestic living standards (Fotopoulos, 1992).[19]

The rapid expansion of incomes (Figure 8.1) and a high degree of inequality in their distribution, a huge black economy, significant capital inflows (remittances, aid, loans) and 'demonstration effects' skewed consumption away from basic goods and services towards a pattern of consumption in stark contrast with the level of development of these economies and with the quality of their production structures. In the poorest of the latecomer countries, Greece and Portugal, the volume and pattern of demand gave rise to the paradox of the emergence of a 'consumer society without a production base' (Fotopoulos, 1992).[20]

6 Democratic transition and restructuring without re-industrialization, 1975–1985

The transition of Spain, Portugal and Greece to democracy in 1975 coincided with international developments – change in the structure of demand and in the

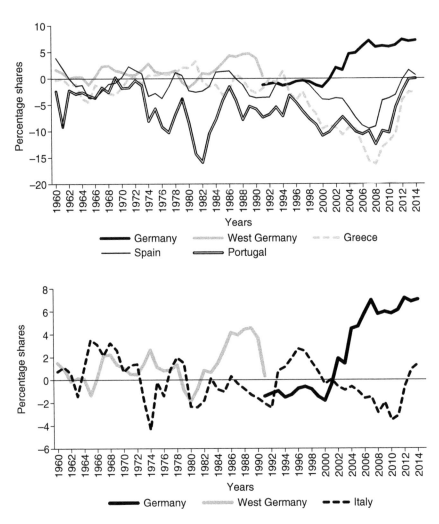

Figure 8.3 Current accounts as a percentage of GDP (1960–2014).

Source: authors' elaborations on AMECO data.

organization of production – that changed the context, the geography and the composition of industrial activity, transformed the factors of competitiveness, made a large part of the productive capacity obsolete or redundant, and ushered in a wave of restructuring and adjustment in core industries.[21]

The new governments had to face the consequences of this 'revolution': a difficult macroeconomic situation – high inflation rates and huge external deficits, swollen by the rise in the prices of oil and other raw materials, fall in domestic and foreign demand – and a hard process of adjusting the inherited industrial structure, at a time when the process of democratization had raised expectations of more widespread economic and social rights. The weight of basic industries in total production called for drastic cuts in productive capacity (steel, coal, shipyards), which meant a massive destruction of employment. Entry into the global trade network of new low-cost producers significantly increased the exposure of the Southern European industries to foreign competition due to the substantial overlap in industry structures, while the increase in wages and labour rights, entailed by the transition to democracy, eroded the price competitiveness of their exports, pushing the importing core countries to look for alternative cheaper sources.[22] The change in the patterns of consumption and the shift to product-led competition required an overhauling of their consumer goods industries that, left to market forces, they proved unable to perform. The domestic industry grew increasingly incapable of catering to domestic needs, let alone foreign ones. As the restructuring process gained momentum throughout Europe, unemployment soared,[23] drastically reducing emigration opportunities.

The socialist parties that came to government at the turn of the decade were committed to substantially transforming the structure of wealth, property and power, the purpose being to extend democracy from the political to the social and economic spheres (Tsakalotos, 1998). In the original PASOK programme, for instance,

> an all-round modernisation of the productive system was envisaged to take place through a significant expansion of the economic role of the state in the development process, with the aim to transform Greece from a dependent service economy, based on semi-skilled labour, to an independent industrial economy, based on skilled labour.
>
> (Fotopoulos, 1992: 55)

Similarly, the electoral programme of the Spanish Socialist Party

> referred to a 'policy of expansion' within a strategy which focused on employment as the number one priority, to government investment as the 'motor' of the economy, and even to the idea of concerted planning, although it also contained orthodox references, such as to the prevalent role of the market and to anti-inflation policy.
>
> (Recio and Roca, 1988: 140)

However, none of these governments were prepared (or able, or willing) to risk a conflict with local interests and foreign capital in order to fulfil their election development promises. Faced with the challenge of 'expanding the development role of the state, by adopting a radical restructuring program' (Fotopoulos, 1992: 40), they withdrew, attempting instead, at first, to expand the consumption function of the state, with the double objective of avoiding a massive rise in unemployment and reproducing the consumer society.

The public sector found itself under increasing pressure to absorb the rapidly rising surplus of labour and sustain demand in the face of a severe investment slump and the consequent fall in private consumption. The number of employees in the public sector increased, only partly in response to an increasing supply of social services (education, health and social security), which remained highly segmented and unequally accessed (Karamessini, 2008). With the public share in the economy increasing, internal and external deficits soared. Under pressure from the EEC creditor partners,[24] the socialist governments turned to the new liberal agenda (Tsakalotos, 1998: 118).

Thus, the crisis of the 1970s marks a turning point in the economic development of the late-latecomer economies, which started to diverge again from the core. As argued by Mamede *et al.* (2014: 259) with reference to the Portuguese economy, these countries were 'stuck in the middle': 'while insufficiently developed to compete in the most sophisticated markets, the price of [their] products in the international markets proved to be too high to compete with those of less advanced, emerging economies'. This applies also to Spain, which has seen the development of a few big holdings with important internationalized activities (especially in Latin America) and advanced technology (transport infrastructure, telecommunications, renewable energies, finance): however,

> they are far from being enough to drive the country behind them. The country does not have enough solidly grounded productive undertakings and general structure. The continuous surge of the real estate industry has hidden the weaknesses of the Spanish productive system but the crisis has exposed the poor base of Spanish economic dynamics.
>
> (Etxezarreta *et al.*, 2011: 15)

The implementation of orthodox macroeconomic policies pre-empted the space for adoption of those industrial policies required to upgrade the industrial structure. At the same time, EU membership provided policy-making elites with a legitimation for shifting policies towards disinflation and the market approach to restructuring.

7 The financialization of the European periphery

We know that the process of financialization in the Southern periphery played a crucial role in the emergence of imbalances between the centre and the periphery and in the outbreak of the recent crisis.

However, it had also long-term effects, hampering, retarding or diverting the process of development. Indeed, in the SP, the liberalization of capital flows in the late 1980s coincided with the retreat of industrial and development policies, with various effects on the SP economies. The opening of their financial markets attracted increasing financial flows from the centre, lured by higher interest rates. The opening of their product markets exposed their manufacturing sector, characterized by structural fragilities and relative backwardness, to the international competition. The reduction in profit margins diverted the funding required for modernization towards sectors that promised higher profits in the short term. Finally, as elsewhere, financialization mandated a reduction in state intervention, justified with the market efficiency ideology.

'Financial repression' – capital controls, selective credit ceilings and banks' portfolio allocation – had supplemented the development strategy pursued by the state. The process of European integration speeded up the process of liberalization, demanding liberalization of capital flows, privatizations and the withdrawal of the state from direct intervention. In the Eurozone, financial liberalization has been accelerated by institutional changes (Gambarotto and Solari, 2015; Rodrigues *et al.*, 2016), that added up in determining greater fragility and less resilience in case of a shock. Thus, we witness a common trend featuring the gradual retreat of the state from controlling and guiding the allocation of financial resources; the diversion of finance from industry to construction, retail and private consumption; privatization, market concentration and increasing relevance of foreign operators in the banking sector. However, we also observe different trends in private sector indebtedness and in the exposure to the formation of bubbles, in particular, in the construction sector.

We briefly review the specific trajectories of the process of financialization of each Southern European economy, to highlight commonalities and specificities, and their possible link with the evolution of the economy.

Greece

Still in the late 1980s, the Hellenic financial sector was a typical credit-based Mediterranean system (Pagoulatos and Quaglia, 2013), sharing the main characteristics of the other southern countries: extensive state control over the banking system, underdeveloped capital markets and pervasive financial interventionism. Following a policy approach common during the post-Second World War era, economic development was pursued through large direct state intervention in the economy combining government consumption and the activities of state-owned enterprises. Financial interventionism – capital controls, and subsidized credit to industry – ensured cheap finance to the targeted sectors (Perez, 1997; Woo-Cumings, 1999).

The deregulation of the Greek financial system was related to impending integration within the Common market. Following the state's retreat from direct ownership of banks, the financial sector came to be dominated by big private companies. During the 1990s, the Greek financial system experienced a radical transformation. Bank credit to the private sector surged and, after 1998, the Greek stock market boomed: the capital raised by private companies on the stock market went from 1.6 per cent of bank credits in 1996 to 5.6 per cent in 1997, to 27.7 per cent in 1999. A substantial penetration of foreign financial institutions took place, with the market share of foreign branches and subsidiaries over the total assets of the Greek banking system reaching 37 per cent in 2006 (down to 22 per cent in 2008) (European Central Bank, 2010). Greek banks embarked on a process of regionalization in the south-eastern part of Europe, through ownership of subsidiaries and participation in banking groups: Turkey, Bulgaria and Romania were Greek capitals' privileged foreign destination. They also increased purchases of foreign assets in emerging markets, namely Poland, Serbia, Albania, Ukraine and the FYR of Macedonia. In 2008, the total assets of foreign subsidiaries and branches of Greek banking groups amounted to 28 per cent of their total assets (€118 billion) and 49 per cent of Greek GDP (about half of them in emerging Eastern European economies) (Pagoulatos and Quaglia, 2013).

Although the liberalization of the financial market obviously exposed the Greek banking system and the Greek economy to new risks, according to Varoufakis and Tserkezis (2014: 52), 'internal' financialization was not the main cause of Greece's problems.

> The effects of financialization outside of Greece's borders on the evolution of the Greek real economy have been considerably stronger and more influential, as compared with the effects of the much slower financialization happening within Greece. The significant and growing imbalances in the current account (and the crises thereby engendered), which had such detrimental effect on Greece, would have been impossible without financialization's global onslaught.

If it is true that the economic growth in Greece in the past two decades relied heavily on private consumption (and public deficit, one should add), and that the Greek economy did see a dramatic proliferation of new financial instruments over the past 10–15 years, the levels of private debt are still quite low in comparison to other developed nations. 'Financialization arrived rather late in Greece and did not have the time fully to unfold due to the financial crisis of 2008' (ibid.: 39).

Thus, according to the two authors, the true effects of financialization operated through the current account.

> Financial sector deregulation, in conjunction with technological developments that make it possible for huge sums of money to be transferred through different jurisdictions at the touch of a button, imply that persistent, and even growing, deficits in the current account can be maintained, hence facilitating the emergence of severe instabilities.
>
> (Ibid.: 40)

Their conclusion is that

> Greece did not experience financialization like other developed countries did. Greece experienced financialization via the European Monetary Union

that it chose to enter into back in 2000. Thus a chronically deficit nation, with a weak and fragile state apparatus, entered into a monetary union that removed Greece's internal shock absorbers while guaranteeing that the impending shock, when it hit, would be impossible for the meek Greek economy to sustain.

(Ibid.: 63)

Moreover, the state's retreat from financial interventionism, that reduced the opportunity to channel capital towards sectors capable of reinforcing the industrial structure, paralleled its retreat from industrial policy, leaving to the market to decide which sector to develop, and to the financial market to decide which one to fund.

Spain

While Spain's pre-financialization story is similar to the one of its southern companions, it departs from them for the very special role played by the finance-construction linkage.[25] A set of institutional changes characterized the Spanish way to financialization. In 1992, securitization ('titulización') was legalized. The length of the loans was extended from 10–20 years to 30, 40 and even 50 years and the collateral required to obtain the mortgage was significantly reduced. In 1999, changes in the tax code made renting less convenient, by eliminating the deduction for rentals which had been in force between 1992 and 1998 to favour the market for house rentals (Santos, 2014). Several plans (*Planes de Vivienda*) offering direct subsidies to families seeking homeownership were implemented. Because of these measures, mortgages, that were previously mainly reserved for upper middle class families, became a product of mass consumption, affordable by any family, regardless of its income, social and professional status. As a result, mortgages soared, fuelled also by the fall in interest rates that followed the introduction of the euro and by inflows of foreign capital, when many foreign banks started to buy mortgage credits in Spain. In a decade, between 1997 and 2008, house prices increased by more than 200 per cent.

The pace of financialization of the Spanish economy engulfed the whole private sector. The private debt (total liabilities) incurred by financial institutions, households and non-financial corporations, which represented 314.9 per cent of the GDP at the beginning of the economic growth cycle in 1996, had risen to 587.4 per cent by 2006 (down to 569.3 per cent by the end of 2013), and household debt rose from 61 per cent of gross disposable income in 1997 to 139 per cent in 2007, significantly higher than that of major European economies – in 2007 French, Italian and German household debt was, on average, 85 per cent (Alvarez, 2012).

The financialization of the public debt – high density of trades; predominance of repo transactions; high volume of sovereign Credit Default Swaps (CDS) trading; and high share of foreign debt holders and market makers – represents the other peculiarity of the Spanish financialization (Massò, 2016). Designed to favour market liquidity and credit expansion, these features can dramatically worsen borrowing conditions in an economic context of uncertainty, when increased volatility, or outright selling determined by investors' fear of non-sustainability, can make non-sustainability possible.

Portugal

Before Rodrigues *et al.* (2016: 487) observe that, rates were set administratively, and credit was mostly directed towards the needs of the state and of the associated public enterprises in strategic sectors; there were also strict controls on capital flows and on the exchange rate.

This configuration, locked-in by a socialist leaning Constitution declaring nationalizations as 'irreversible conquests of the working-class', was antithetical to the wider neoliberal international trends of the early eighties with which Portugal eventually aligned, albeit, as typical in a semi-periphery, with a time lag, (Rodrigues *et al.*, 2016: 488–489).

The process of European integration spurred the financialization of the Portuguese economy: within the time-span of a mere decade, between the mid-1980s and the mid-1990s, the Portuguese financial system evolved from a state-controlled and 'repressed' financial regime to become a fully integrated and liberalized one. In 1989, a revision of the Constitution allowed reversing the nationalization of banks. Following the large number of privatizations, between 1990 and 1996 the market share of state banks fell from 74 per cent to 24 per cent. During the same period, the presence of foreign banks increased, their market share tripling from a mere 3 per cent in 1991 to 9 per cent in 2000. Because of mergers and acquisitions, the Portuguese banking sector came to be concentrated around five major banks (Rodrigues *et al.*, 2016).

The 1989 European Directive, transposed into a Portuguese Law, introduced the deregulation of the financial sector and opened it to the market. With credit ceilings and administrative interest rates removed, for the first time, Portugal had unlimited access to hard currency and loanable capital at low interest rates. Abundance of financial resources, confronted with the structural weaknesses of the Portuguese economy, fed a persistent and growing current account deficit. The fall in real interest rates and expectations of an economic boom following the euro introduction pushed Portugal's private sector indebtedness – that, until the mid-1990s, was below the European average – to levels similar only to the UK and Ireland. Banks channelled credit towards sectors such as construction, retail or privatized utilities, contributing to the acceleration of the process of structural weakening.

From 1990, Central Bank-treasury relationships changed. The Bank of Portugal restricted its funding to the Treasury, which became completely dependent on the financial markets to fund its deficits. The public debt was gradually securitized, traded on secondary markets and opened up to foreign investors.

Italy

Until the 1970s, Italy shared with the other Southern periphery's economies a significant state-driven financial interventionism. Banking activity was subject to strict administrative controls, foreign exchange restrictions kept the cost of public sector borrowing under control, and financial interventionism complemented demand management and industrial policy. During the 1970s, credit ceilings and banks' portfolio allocation – requiring banks to devote a fraction of their deposits to the purchase of long-term fixed rate bonds – aimed to guarantee appropriate funding to small and medium enterprises and long-term financing of firms and government (Gaiotti and Secchi, 2012).

From the mid-1970s, the Bank of Italy started to assign increasing importance to price stability (as described in Chapter 1). In 1981, following the 'divorce' between the Bank of Italy and the Treasury (Ciocca, 2005), the Bank of Italy ceased being the residual buyer of government securities at primary market auctions, and price stability became the fundamental objective of the monetary action. However, until the 1990s, Italy's bank-based system operated within a context of pervasive administrative controls and financial interventionism.

In the early 1990s, in coincidence with the early stages of the Common Market, a set of key reforms imprinted a market orientation. The banking sector was privatized and banks' trading in securities increased. In 1992, with the transposition of the 1988 Second Banking Directive, the 'all-purpose universal' bank was introduced in the Italian jurisdiction, putting an end to functional segmentation of the banking sector. The process of consolidation, favoured by these institutional changes,[26] accelerated after the establishment of the EMU in 1999. In 2008, the five biggest Italian banks held over 50 per cent of total assets, and the first two – Unicredit and Intesa San Paolo – accounted for more than 35 per cent, ranking them among the top European banks (Pagoulatos and Quaglia, 2013). While the top five banking groups' foreign operations increased rapidly to reach about a third of total assets, mostly towards the Central and Eastern European countries (CEEC), up to the 2000s, the penetration of foreign operators remained limited. Increasing pressure on the part of the EC for greater openness of the financial sector[27] eventually led to a presence of foreign operators in Italy comparable to the level experienced in the other EU member states, also through acquisitions.

As in the other Southern European countries, the main effects of the process of financialization on the Italian economy concern the allocation of funds to the economy. The elimination of restrictions on capital flows and the privatization of the banking system deprived the government of its power to 'guide' the allocation of funds to firms and sectors. Meanwhile, the difficulties of the real economy, exposed to the competition of the rest of the Eurozone with no longer the defence of the exchange rate, reduced its prospective profitability. Sustained by the fall in interest rates, a construction bubble contributed in diverting funds from the productive to the services sector. Between the late 1990s and 2006, the construction sector recorded a momentous increase: the share of bank credit associated with construction activities increased from about 25 per cent in 2000 to 48 per cent in 2012 (Gobbi and Zollino, 2013), and house prices recorded their highest increase. Although private credit did not reach the excesses observed in Spain and Portugal, financialization and the resulting mechanism of funds allocation may have contributed to the weakening of the industrial structure, exposing the Italian banks to a different solvency risk.

To conclude, since the 1980s all the Southern European economies moved from financial repression to financial liberalization. European integration was central in guiding and accelerating the process. Financial liberalization and economic integration had several consequences on the structure and resilience of these economies. First, the opening of the financial markets and the dismantling of internal controls, not replaced by a suitable alternative supervisory structure, exposed these economies to the risk of bubbles. Second, by eliminating the balance of payments constraints, the monetary union waved the early backstop to the accumulation of unsustainable external imbalances, but its incomplete construction exposed the economies to the risk of sudden stops. Third, the process of financialization went hand in hand with the dismantling of the institutions of industrial policy and state's guidance, replaced by the European flagship of competition as industrial policy. Opened to Europe-wide competition, the southern industry proved unable to restructure and modernize; its profitability could not compete with the perspectives that the processes of privatization and deregulation were opening in the services. Following the privatization of the banking sector and the process of concentration of the industry, the financial flows were redirected towards short-term profitability, favouring the formation of bubbles, while weakening the links with industry and depriving it of financial resources. Reliance on bank credit made the distortion of the financial flows all the more harmful. Finally, when the sovereign debt crisis backfired on the national banks, the austerity policies froze the domestic market and the product demand for firms evaporated, the problems of liquidity and solvency of the banking system, overloaded with bad credits and doubtful government bonds, led the economic, financial and productive system to a complete halt.

8 The German internationalization strategy: 'widen the market and narrow the competition'[28]

According to conventional wisdom, the major force behind Germany's growth are its exports. The traditional 'neo-mercantilist'[29] model adopted by Germany in the 1960s and 1970s was (and still is) based on the accumulation of current account surpluses, which enable the financing of a huge flow of trade credits, direct investment, and aid in support of Germany's exports of investment goods. Until the establishment of the Monetary Union,

> appreciation in the exchange rate allowed for reductions in the prices of imported raw materials, consumer goods and intermediate goods, thus

helping curb the increase in domestic prices and safeguard the social pact upon which the system of industrial relations rested.

(Simonazzi and Vianello, 1999: 264)

While the investment goods sector acquired increasing weight in the German industrial structure, the interests of the other sectors, more exposed to foreign competition, were taken care of by promoting an area of integrated trade within Europe to which they could delocalize the production of their inputs and export their final products. When the sharp appreciation of the D-Mark in the 1970s risked putting also the powerful German industry (or at least its weakest, more price-elastic, products) in jeopardy, the German Government fostered the institution first of the European Monetary System (EMS), and then of the Monetary Union, accepting – albeit reluctantly – a more flexible interpretation of the criteria for admission (ibid.: 265). The creation of the EMS responded to German industry's need to restrain the pressure of foreign competition, and to create an area of relative stability within which to establish and consolidate stable networks of reliable suppliers in selected countries/regions (northern Italy, Spain, centre-northern Portugal). By securing an outlet for its mature sectors, the closer integration within the Single Market in the difficult times of the post mid-1970s downsizing and restructuring gained precious time for their reorganizing.[30] Later, de-localization of stages of production beyond the European tariff wall via outward processing trade (OPT) represented the first step of a process of Eastern integration[31] with German industry; a process which reached full speed after the fall of the Berlin Wall and enlargement of the European Union. After establishment of the euro, the rapid increase of intermediate imports, especially from Eastern Europe, evidenced the transformation of the German economy into a 'Bazaar Economy'. On the cost side, it exploited, for instance in the case of Poland, the double advantage of lower labour costs and a stronger exchange rate. On the demand side, foreign loans and structural funds to the European periphery[32] financed its increasing gulf between imports and exports, allowing maintenance of a model that was no longer viable in the changed national and international context, but that continued to perform the task of providing a vent for the core country's increasing surpluses.

Given the much more fragile industrial structure of the peripheral economies, the successful restructuring of their industry would have required an overhauling of their policies of state intervention so that their enterprises would be able to compete on the basis of new products/technologies and not only on price. It was necessary to tackle the lack of business enterprise, create new competences, favour the establishment of backward and forward linkages to thicken the industrial fabric, and strengthen the formation of networks. That is, to implement the same policies that Germany, Japan and free-market economies such as the UK and the US had never relinquished.[33] It is true that the progressive tightening of macroeconomic conditions imposed by the Maastricht Treaty and the subsequent Stability Pacts reduced the room for implementation of selective industrial policies: the industrial retooling of the Southern European countries occurred in a context of economic stagnation and within a market philosophy of non-intervention. But tough external conditions do not reduce the responsibility of the peripheral countries' governments, which placed uncritical faith in the drive to efficiency that the tougher competition resulting from the creation of the single market would mean for European firms.

> That the contemporaneous reduction of the possibility to intervene in support of national industries ... would inevitably add to the pressure on the more exposed sectors was judged a price to be paid for progress along the road to efficiency.
>
> (Simonazzi and Vianello, 1999: 271)

9 Conclusions

We have argued that, by confusing the trigger for its underlying causes, the 1970s crisis was mistaken as the 'oil crisis'. Only later was the major role played by other, more irreversible factors fully recognized: the collapse of the Fordist system and the overhauling and fragmentation of the international division of labour, with the disrupting entry of the NICs in heavy industry[34] and in the labour-intensive stages of production, to rapidly climb the technological ladder. Likewise, the current European crisis has been interpreted as the 'financial and sovereign debts crisis', which is once again to miss its deeper-lying causes. The financial crisis has exposed the unsustainability of the old core-periphery model, which was required to tackle the broader context of change in technology and demand within a faulty institutional and macroeconomic framework.

The outbreak of the crisis coincided with the deployment of a new phase in the paradigm of international production and technology, with new emerging countries entering the scene. As in the 1970s and 1980s, this new phase calls for an overhaul of the production systems in the advanced countries: obsolete capacity will need to be scrapped, declining sectors will have to be abandoned. But the birth and growth of new sectors presupposes recognition of 'the "collective" character of innovation. 'Different types of firms (large and small), different types of finance and different types of State policies, institutions and departments interact sometimes in unpredictable ways' (Mazzucato, 2013: 194). When the innovation process is visualized as occurring through 'separate and isolated activities of the State and the firms' (ibid.), the innovation process fades and dies out. The lack of alternatives will mean greater demand for protection or soaring unemployment. No amount of labour flexibility can turn the industry-specific skills of laid-off workers into the new skills now in demand; and no amount of domestic deflation can stimulate the growth of innovative industries.

Once again the core country has found itself in a favourable position to tackle the crisis: it is true that the debt crisis in the countries of the periphery and the austerity imposed upon them has drained their demand for German products, but it has also crippled their economies, reduced their prices; while the low – even negative – interest rates accruing to Germany by virtue of its safe haven status have allowed its industry – and its government, directly or through its national investment banks[35] – to play the old game again. Restructuring at no cost, picking and choosing suppliers in the South, the East and the Far East, and selling its quality products on credit to the world. However, if debts must be repaid, debtor countries must be enabled to produce income gainfully, or the core-periphery relation will be condemned to cyclical waves of financial crises.

As noted by Schulmeister (2012), systemic crises require systemic solutions. But they need also suitable spectacles to focus on those systemic links that, ignored by the prevailing theories, tend to emerge with dramatic emphasis in the course of the crises. At a higher level of generality, these links include the co-evolution, in the long term, of aggregate demand and supply (which in the crisis manifests itself as hysteresis, that is, permanent destruction of productive capacity), the relationship between the quantity of money and the level of activity of the real sector (which refutes the supposed neutrality of money on which the European Monetary Union was built), the interweaving of monetary and fiscal policy (with the associated link, under certain conditions, between bank risk and sovereign risk). At a lower level of generality, we find systemic links in the relations between the centre and Southern European peripheries, that we have analysed in the previous pages. These links concern also the relationships between productive sectors, for example between industry and the services. We found unconvincing the argument proposed by Sapelli, who attributes the slower growth of the peripheral economies to the prevalence of cultural values based on status and clientelism, instead of 'modern', contract-based 'weberian' relations. An incomplete liberalization would have given rise to a weak industrialization, and therefore (tautologically) to an 'early' tertiarization. We have argued instead that the arrest of industrialization processes, which began in the mid-1960s in Italy and in the mid-1970s in all the countries of Southern Europe, must be attributed to the raising of the bar in the quality of performance standards required to compete, associated with the market saturation for the main durable consumption goods. Just when the state should have taken up new tasks to strengthen the quality of the productive structure, 'early liberalization' policies prevented public investment guidance in the peripheries: industrial policies were redefined as policies for the guarantee of competition, thus hindering policies addressed to sustain diversification and upgrading. These policy decisions did not occur smoothly, but were associated with political and social conflicts (where also the cultural values highlighted by Sapelli played a role).

For the sake of brevity, we shared with Sapelli the restrictive assumption of an aggregate tertiary sector, without distinguishing between advanced and 'routine' services sectors and disregarding their linkages with the other sectors of the economy, that we showed, however, in the previous chapters to be extremely important. The alleged economic miracles of Ireland (the 'Celtic Tiger') and Spain (flagship of the liberalization policy of the labour market), in the first half of the 2000s, have been interpreted as an exemplary model of 'highly skilled' tertiarization, as proved by the high percentage increase of employment in the Financial Intermediation and Business Services sectors. Only after the crisis was it realized that the other side of the miracle was the piling up of a high private debt, quickly turned during the crisis into a huge debt. Moreover, much of the employment in these sectors was less skilled than anticipated. In Ireland, for example, the expansion of the economy was based largely on the relocation of lower-end stages of the electronics value chain, attracted from very high tax benefits: a model that can hardly be generalized and, as it turned out, not sustainable.[36]

Notes

1 We provided a broad picture of the financialization in the previous chapter. A more precise description of the context in which the transition from the Fordist to the post-Fordist regime (to use a synthetic current terminology) assumes prominent importance is presented below.
2 In some recent studies (Hidalgo et al., 2007; Hidalgo and Hausmann, 2009), the productive structure of an economy is seen as a network that links specific products to specific capabilities. Economies that are more diversified and able to produce and export more exclusive products are defined as 'more complex'. For a study of the evolution of the production structures of the EU and its members based on the relationship between indicators of the complexity of the products exported and international trade patterns, see Reinstaller et al. (2012).
3 Cf. Fuà (1980: 18–19). The six countries included Greece, Ireland, Italy, Portugal, Spain, Turkey.
4 For the events associated with the mid-1970s crisis, see below, while for a reconstruction of the changes of the German development model in the early 2000s, see Simonazzi et al. (2013).
5 On the endogenous determination of the oil prices trend, namely its link with the dollar exchange rate and the domestic policy targets of the United States, see Schulmeister (2000).
6 See Akamatsu (1962) and Ginzburg and Simonazzi (2005).
7 Piore and Sabel (1984: 184), among the first authors to call attention to this crucial aspect, observe that 'the saturation was especially true in the United States, where in 1979 there was one car for every two residents, compared with one for every four in the early 1950s.' Similarly, 99 per cent of American households had refrigerators and television sets and more than 90 per cent had washing machines. Evidence of the saturation of product markets has also been drawn from the constancy, in the 1970s, of the ratio between goods and services growth at constant prices in the major industrial countries, despite the reduction in the relative prices of goods. Markets in which the elasticity of demand is price inelastic are generally termed 'saturated markets'. See on this Appelbaum and Schettkat (1999: 395–396).
8 According to Volpato and Stocchetti (2008: 30), during the period 1984–2006 in Italy, in the car sector 'the number of brands … remained almost constant while the number of models increased from 170 to 281 and the number of versions from 696 to 3440'. For data on market saturation of 'white goods' in Italy, see Paris (2013).
9 For an overview of the global implications of the mid-1970s crisis, although without reference to the centre-periphery relation, see Cipolletta (2013).
10 With respect to classical nationalizations, in the 'IRI formula' listed companies were funded by both public and private capital, and public and private firms often coexisted in the same sector.
11 After having played a decisive role in the 1950s and 1960s Italian industrialization process, IRI, overburdened with debts, was liquidated in 2002 under the pressure of the European Economic Commission.

12 For data on import substitution of investment goods, possibly carried out to face the challenge of international competition, see Ciocca *et al.* (1973: 98).
13 In his memoirs (1993: 268–269), Carli writes that the expansionary monetary policy responded not only to the desire not to interrupt the investment cycle under way, but also to the goal of 'saving private property from the nationalizing fury of the socialists … I was on the side of capitalists. What I was never able to make people understand is that also unions should have been on the capitalists' side.'
14 According to Barca (1997), the 'original sin' of Italian capitalism was the absence of rules governing competition and procedures to monitor public actions. In this framework, rules and procedures are set exogenously by the state, since institutions and markets are considered separate entities whose interplay determines governance of the markets. Adopting the same dichotomic perspective, Bank of Italy officials placed high expectations in the 'modernizing' discipline enforced by external pressures (Monetary Union and the Single Market). However, in Italy the Authority for Guaranteeing Competition and Markets (CONSOB) was established in 1991 with no appreciable impact on the collusive and opaque functioning of the markets. From a different perspective that does not separate economics and politics, governance and rules are endogenous to the market system and depend on the specific configuration of economic activity: 'the institutions of governance are influenced and often "peopled" by the same producer constituencies with limited interest in market efficient outcomes' (Underhill, 2007: 100). For a realistic account of the European process of establishing competition rules in the finance area, see Mügge (2010).
15 In 1993, Carli argued that the *Nota Aggiuntiva*, interpreted as a document advocating Stalinist-like coercive planning, was presented by the Minister of the Budget only to gain the benevolence of the socialists. In a recent testimony, the Treasury Ministry, Emilio Colombo, said:

> Tactically I supported programming, highlighting its progressive aspects; the socialists were passionate about programming … [Their] approach … to programming proved to be overambitious and unrealistic and diverted their attention from less ambitious but more concrete and therefore potentially more dangerous measures for the stabilization of the economy.
>
> (Carli, 2014: 114)

16 See the *Piano Solo* prepared in 1964 by General De Lorenzo.
17 According to Hirschman (1958), the impact of forward linkages is in general weaker and more uncertain than that of backward linkages.
18 When comparing the evolution across countries of fixed investment as a percentage of GDP (Figure 8.2), an asymmetry between centre and peripheral countries should be borne in mind. From the point of view of firms – as distinct from that of countries of belonging – FDI is much more important for the centre countries, and should be ideally added to their fixed investment.
19 In Portugal in the 1980s remittances reached more than 10 per cent of GDP (Confraria, 1999: 271).
20 Malthus ([1834] 1974: 406) wrote:

> if the master-producers, from the laudable desire they feel of bettering their condition, and providing for a family, do not consume their revenue sufficiently to give an adequate stimulus to the increase of wealth; if the working producers, by increasing their consumption, supposing them to have the means of so doing, would impede the growth of wealth by diminishing the power of production, than they could encourage it by increasing the demand for produce; and if the expenditure of the landlords, in addition to the expenditure of the two preceding classes, be found insufficient to keep up and increasing the value of that which is produced, where are

we to look for the consumption required but among the unproductive labourers of Adam Smith?

21 See Fotopoulos (1992); Balbín (1999); Banyuls and Recio (2014); Mamede *et al.* (2014).

22 In 1987, gross hourly earnings of manual workers in Greece (expressed in purchasing power parities) were still about 56 per cent of the EEC average (from 47 per cent in 1977), but they were rapidly becoming uncompetitive with respect to wages in Eastern Europe, North Africa and the developing world.

23 In Germany unemployment increased from less than 1 per cent in the early 1970s to a peak of 7.2 per cent in 1985. In the same period, in Greece unemployment quadrupled (from about 2 to 7 per cent); in Spain it soared from an average 3 to 18 per cent; in Portugal from 2–3 to 10 per cent; from about 5 to over 8 per cent in Italy. It should be remembered that unemployment figures are very imperfect estimates of employment conditions, especially in peripheral countries.

24 The Greek government had to agree to macroeconomic stabilization packages with the IMF in the late 1970s and had to resort to emergency borrowing from its EEC partners in 1985 and in 1990. The two loans (1.3 billion dollars and three billion dollars respectively) were made conditional on the implementation of increasingly stricter Stabilization Programmes. Portugal first received EC aid in 1974 and in the early 1980s (Confraria, 1999: 281).

25 During the period 1996–2007, the Spanish economic model was largely considered a 'success' case: economic growth remained above the European average, job creation rates were significant, inflation was under control and public budgets were in surplus. As we now know, behind this success loomed the increasing over-indebtedness of the economy (Massò, 2016).

26 A turning point was the Financial Services Action Plan (FSAP), promoted by the EC to create a single market for financial services.

27 The substitution of the former Bank of Italy's governor, Antonio Fazio, considered 'hostile' to the opening of the banking system, with Mario Draghi, explicitly in favour of internationalization, speeded up the process.

28 Adam Smith ([1776] 1996: 278), wrote:

> The intent of the dealers ... in any particular brand of trade and manufacture is always in some respect different from, and even opposed to that of the public. To widen the market and to narrow the competition is always the interest of the dealers.

We borrow the quotation from Mügge (2010).

29 The German neo-mercantilist policy has old roots. As Hirschman ([1945] 1980: 146) recalls, since the beginning of the nineteenth century, 'in the minds of the public and of many economists, the increasing importance of German foreign trade was coupled with an increasing precariousness of its economic basis'. In 1903, Sombart had stated the so-called 'law of the declining importance of export trade'. His forecast was that the gradual industrialization of the agricultural countries, coupled with the increasing capacity to consume on the part of the home market, would lead to a reduction of the growth of foreign trade with respect to internal demand. This forecast raised in Germany the apprehension of being shut off from food and raw material supply, especially in wartime, and of depriving exports of their markets abroad. The collapse of foreign trade could be prevented either by obtaining 'sufficient colonies, or, directly, by *preventing the industrialization of foreign nations*' (ibid.: 148, italics added). An echo of this position may perhaps be detected, for instance, in the German fierce opposition to the exemption of investment expenditures from Maastricht parameters on public deficit. Or in an October 1974 statement by Helmut Schmidt (De Cecco, 1976):

We must not save Italy, but give only as much help which enables it to be with his head out of the water, not on the beach. The Italian industry must be strengthened without chasing the mirage of product diversification, because in Europe we have to accomplish a precise division of labour.

30 In the early 1980s, 50 per cent of West German foreign trade was directed to the EC (including Austria and Switzerland), the figure rising to 60 per cent when Great Britain and Spain joined the EC.
31 The OPT of German 'mature' industries was not confined to Eastern European countries; nor was Germany the only European country to resort to it. Italy, France and the Netherlands all resorted to the de-localization of stages of production – to Turkey, the North African countries and the Balkans – taking advantage of their lower labour costs to meet the increasing competition of the NICs (newly industrializing countries) in mature sectors (textiles and clothing, footwear, etc.). In the UK, where the market was dominated not by producers but by large retailers, the phenomenon took the form of de-localization of the entire production process, retaining only the two extreme stages – design and commercialization – within the country (Ginzburg and Simonazzi, 1995).
32 To which one should add the role played by KfW (*Kreditanstalt für Wiederaufbau*) in providing long-term subsidized financing to the importers of German capital goods.
33 See for instance Block (2008), FINNOV (2012) and Mazzucato (2013).
34 On changes in the geographical distribution of world steel production, see Hudson and Sadler (1989: 18).
35 The German Government has been very active in supporting change in the industrial composition and organization of production. Its actions have ranged from sustaining the network of local banks committed to financing the German Mittelstand to heavily subsidizing the growth of new sectors, as in the case of energy policy.
36 Wren (2013: 23, graphs 1 and 2) has highlighted the existence of a positive relationship between 'the expansion of employment in low-end service sectors and the expansion of credit [indebtedness] to the private sector'. She adds, 'In contrast there is no such link with manufacturing.' The author does not connect this relationship with the lower wages paid in the tertiary sector, but with 'the illusion of wealth' associated with the expansion of cheap credit. However, the author wonders whether in the economies that have adopted a service transition strategy 'it is feasible to maintain the same levels of employment in the non-traded services sectors under more restrictive credit conditions'.

References

Akamatsu, K. (1962). A historical pattern of economic growth in developing countries. *The Developing Economies*, 1(s1), 3–25.
Alvarez, N. (2012). The financialization of the Spanish economy: Debt, crisis and social cuts. *Workshop on Debt*, organized by Rosa Luxemburg Stiftung, Berlin.
Appelbaum, E. and Schettkat, R. (1999). Are prices unimportant? The changing structure of the industrialized economies. *Journal of Post Keynesian Economics*, 21(3), 387–398.
Balbín, P. F. (1999). Spain: Industrial policy under authoritarian politics. In J. Foreman-Peck and G. Federico (eds), *European Industrial Policy*. Oxford: Oxford University Press, 233–267.
Banyuls, J. and Recio, A. (2014). *Industrial Policy in Spain* (mimeo).
Barca, F. (1997). Compromesso senza riforme. In F. Barca (ed.), *Storia del capitalismo italiano dal dopoguerra a oggi*. Roma: Donzelli, 3–115.

Best, M. H. (2013). Productive structures and industrial policy in the EU. www2. euromemorandum.eu/uploads/best_productive_structures_and_industrial_policy_in_ the_eu.pdf [accessed 9 March 2013].

Block, F. (2008). Swimming against the current: The rise of a hidden developmental state in the United States. *Politics and Society*, 36(2), 169–206.

Carli, F. (ed.) (2014). *La figura e l'opera di Guido Carli. 2. Testimonianze*. Torino: Bollati Boringhieri.

Carli, G. (1993). *Cinquant'anni di vita italiana*. Bari: Laterza.

Ciocca, P. (2005). *The Italian Financial System Remodelled*. London: Palgrave Macmillan.

Ciocca, P., Filosa, R. and Rey, G. M. (1973). Integrazione e sviluppo dell'economia italiana nell'ultimo ventennio: un riesame critico. *Contributi alla Ricerca Economica*, Servizio Studi della Banca d'Italia, 3, 57–135.

Cipolletta, I. (2013). Gli anni Settanta: una frattura nel processo di crescita. In F. Silva (ed.), *Storia dell'IRI. I difficili anni '70 e i tentativi di rilancio*. Bari: Laterza, 70–112.

Confraria, J. (1999). Portugal: Industrialization and backwardness. In J. Foreman-Peck and G. Federico (eds), *European Industrial Policy: The Twentieth-Century Experience*. Oxford: Oxford University Press, 268–294.

De Cecco, M. (1976). L'economia tedesca e il bastone Americano. *La Repubblica*, 22 July.

Etxezarreta, M., Navarro, F., Ribera, R. and Soldevila, V. (2011). Boom and (deep) crisis in the Spanish economy: The role of the EU in its evolution. *17th Workshop on Alternative Economic Policy in Europe*, Vienna, September.

European Central Bank (2010). *Structural Indicators for the EU Banking Sector*. Frankfurt: ECB Publishing.

FINNOV (2012). *Finance, Innovation and Growth: State of the Art*. Report for European Commission. www.finnov-fp7.eu/publications/finnov-policy-papers/finnov-final-policy-brief-reforming-a-dysfunctional-system [accessed 21 September 2017].

Fotopoulos, T. (1992). Economic restructuring and the debt problem: The Greek case. *International Review of Applied Economics*, 6(1), 38–64.

Fuà, G. (1980). *Problems of Lagged Development in OECD Europe: A Study of Six Countries*. Paris: OECD (Italian translation 1985, Bologna: Il Mulino).

Gaiotti, E. and Secchi, A. (2012). Monetary policy and fiscal dominance in Italy from the early 1970s to the adoption of the euro: A review. *Questioni di Economia e Finanza, Bank of Italy Occasional Papers No. 141*.

Gambarotto, F. and Solari, S. (2015). The peripheralization of Southern European capitalism within the EMU. *Review of International Political Economy*, 22(4), 788–812.

Ginzburg, A. (2012). Sviluppo trainato dalla produttività o dalle connessioni: due diverse prospettive di analisi e di intervento pubblico nella realtà economica italiana. *Economia & Lavoro*, 46(2), 67–93.

Ginzburg, A. and Simonazzi, A. (1995). Patterns of production and distribution in Europe: The case of the textile and clothing sector. In Roberto Schiattarella (ed.), *New Challenges for European and International Business*. Roma: Litografia Ranieri, 259–283.

Ginzburg, A. and Simonazzi, A. (2005). Patterns of industrialization and the flying geese model. *Journal of Asian Economics*, 15(6), 1051–1078.

Gobbi, G. and Zollino, F. (2013). Tendenze recenti del mercato immobiliare e del credito. *Banca d'Italia, Le tendenze del mercato immobiliare: l'Italia e il confronto internazionale, Seminari e convegni No. 15*.

Hidalgo, C. and Hausmann, R. (2009). The building blocks of economic complexity. *Proceedings of the National Academy of Sciences*, 106(26), 10570–10575.

Hidalgo, C., Klinger, B., Barabási, A. and Hausmann, R. (2007). The product space conditions the development of nations. *Science*, 317(5837), 482–487.

Hirschman, A. O. (1958). *The Strategy of Economic Development*. New Haven, CT: Yale University Press.

Hirschman, A. O. [1945] (1980). *National Power and the Structure of Foreign Trade*. Berkeley: University of California Press.

Hudson, R. (2002). Changing industrial production systems and regional development in the New Europe. *Transactions of the Institute of British Geographers*, 27(3), 262–281.

Hudson, R. and Sadler, D. (1989). *The International Steel Industry: Restructuring, State Policies and Localities*. London: Routledge.

Huntington, S. (1968). *Political Order in a Changing Society*. New Haven, CT: Yale University Press.

Karamessini, M. (2008). Continuity and change in the southern European social model. *International Labor Review*, 147(1), 43–70.

Malthus, T. R. [1834] (1974). *Principles of Political Economy: Considered with a View of their Practical Applications*. Clifton: Kelly.

Mamede, R., Simões, V. and Godinho, M. (2014). Assessment and challenges of industrial policies in Portugal: Is there a way out of the 'stuck in the middle' trap? In A. Teixeira, E. Silva and R. Mamede (eds), *Structural Change, Competitiveness and Industrial Policy: Painful Lessons from the European Periphery*. London: Routledge, 258–277.

Massó, M. (2016). The effects of government debt market financialization: The case of Spain. *Competition & Change*, 20(3), 166–186.

Mazzucato, M. (2013). *The Entrepreneurial State: Debunking Public vs. Private Sector Myths*. London: Anthem Press.

Mügge, D. (2010). *Widen the Market, Narrow the Competition: The Emergence of Supranational Governance in EU Capital Markets*. Colchester: ECPR Press.

Nota Aggiuntiva alla Relazione generale sulla situazione economica del paese 1961 (1962). Camera dei Deputati, May. www.fulm.org/doc/2974/nota-aggiuntiva-20140326125800. pdf [accessed 21 September 2017].

Pagoulatos, G. and Quaglia, L. (2013). Turning the crisis on its head: Sovereign debt crisis as banking crisis in Italy and Greece. In I. Hardie and D. Howarth (eds), *Market-Based Banking and the International Financial Crisis*. Oxford: Oxford Scholarship Online, 179–200.

Paris, I. (2013). White goods in Italy during a Golden Age (1948–1973). *Journal of Interdisciplinary History*, 44(1), 83–110.

Perez, C. (1997). *New Technologies and Socio-institutional Change*. Cologne: Lindenthal Institute.

Piore, M. and Sabel, C. (1984). *The Second Industrial Divide: Possibilities for Prosperity*. New York: Basic Books.

Ravazzi, P. (2013). L'IRI negli anni Settanta: accelerata espansione, 'ipertrofia' e crisi. In F. Silva (ed.), *Storia dell'IRI. I difficili anni '70 e i tentativi di rilancio*. Bari: Laterza, 165–266.

Recio, A. and Roca, J. (1998). The Spanish socialists in power: Thirteen years of economic policy. *Oxford Review of Economic Policy*, 14(1), 139–158.

Reinstaller, A., Hölzl, W., Kutsam, J. and Schimd, C. (2012). The development of productive structures of EU member states and their international competitiveness. *Final Report for the European Commission*. Vienna: WIFO.

Rodrigues, J., Santos, A. C. and Teles, N. (2016). Semi-peripheral financialization: The case of Portugal. *Review of International Political Economy*, 23(3), 480–510.

Santos, J. (2014). Evidence from the bond market on banks' 'too-big-to-fail' subsidy. *Economic Policy Review*, 20(2), 29–39.

Sapelli, G. (1995). *Southern Europe since 1945: Tradition and Modernity in Portugal, Spain, Italy, Greece and Turkey.* London: Longman.

Schulmeister, S. (2000). Globalization without global money: The double role of the dollar as national currency and world currency. *Journal of Post Keynesian Economics*, 22(3), 365–395.

Schulmeister, S. (2012). The European Monetary Fund: A systemic problem needs a systemic solution. *WIFO Working Papers No. 414.* http://stephan.schulmeister.wifo.ac.at/fileadmin/homepage_schulmeister/files/EMF_Concept_07_11.pdf [accessed 21 September 2017].

Simonazzi, A. and Vianello, F. (1999). Financial liberalization, the European single currency and the problem of unemployment. In M. Franzini and F. R. Pizzuti (eds), *Globalization, Institutions and Social Cohesion.* Berlin: Springer, 257–282.

Simonazzi, A., Ginzburg, A. and Nocella, G. (2013). Economic relations between Germany and Southern Europe. *Cambridge Journal of Economics*, 37(3), 653–675.

Smith, A. [1776] (1996). *An Inquiry into the Nature and Causes of the Wealth of Nations.* Chicago: University of Chicago Press.

Toharia, L. (1988). Partial Fordism: Spain between political transition and economic crisis. In R. Boyer (ed.), *The Search for Labour Market Flexibility: The European Economics in Transition.* Oxford: Clarendon Press.

Tsakalotos, E. (1998). The political economy of social democratic economic policies: The PASOK Experiment in Greece. *Oxford Review of Economic Policy*, 14(1), 114–138.

Underhill, G. (2007). When will politics end and the market begin? Whither 'free' trade after Doha. *Journal of International Trade and Diplomacy*, 1(1), 91–126.

Varoufakis, Y. and Tserkezis, L. (2014). Financialization and the financial and economic crises: The case of Greece. *FESSUD Studies in Financial Systems No. 25.*

Vico, G. [1725–1728] (2011). *Princìpi di scienza nuova.* Milano: Mondadori.

Volpato, G. and Stocchetti, A. (2008). Managing product life-cycle in the auto industry: Evaluating carmakers' effectiveness. *International Journal of Automotive Technology and Management*, 8(1), 22–41.

Wade, R. (1979). Fast growth and slow development in Southern Italy. In D. Seers, B. Schaffer and M.-L. Kiljunen (eds), *Underdeveloped Europe: Studies in Core-Periphery Relations.* Hassocks: Harvester Press.

Woo-Cumings, M. (ed.) (1999). *The Developmental State.* Ithaca, NY: Cornell University Press.

Wren, A. (2013). Introduction. In A. Wren (ed.), *The Political Economy of the Service Transition.* Oxford: Oxford University Press.

9 A policy divide

Industrial policies in 'core' and 'peripheral' countries

1 Introduction

Since 2008, tight fiscal policies, belated monetary stimulus and perverse adjustment policies have led to profound crisis in the European periphery. Many areas have suffered destruction of productive capacity and permanent loss of output (see Chapters 2 and 4). The severity and extent of the crisis and its unequal effects have increased the risk of fragmentation of the EU and threatened the very survival of the Monetary Union.

As argued in the previous chapters, the effects of crises differ for first and latecomer countries. Crisis after crisis, their different capacities to cope with change aggravated the impoverishment of the productive structures of the Southern countries. The first crisis (in the 1970s) opened a gap in aggregate demand that political coalitions, anxious to consolidate democratic institutions and/or reduce opposition, eventually filled through welfare and construction expenditures. The 'peripheral tertiarization' based on construction and welfare came up against increasing difficulty in tackling the hardships and inequities brought about by limited and dependent capital accumulation. The current economic crisis together with the institutional structure of the EMU have increased the divergence. With Europe's internal demand curbed by the recession, it remains with exports to sustain growth. Two different industrial models now co-exist: a strong industrial basis in the core countries, which is export-oriented and has a solid position on the global markets, and a less diversified industrial sector in the periphery (with appreciable differences across and within countries). The crisis has increased the divergence not only between core and periphery, but also within the two macro-areas, with Southern Europe and France falling behind the eastern periphery and Germany respectively. We have argued that reducing the gap in industrial capabilities would have called for a multilevel policy, combining support for demand with diversified industrial policies across the EU. This has proved impossible for two reasons: the predominance of national interests and the prevalence of the idea that the market would bring about the required convergence.

This chapter builds on the arguments developed in the previous chapters to substantiate our claim that, in order to restore sustainable growth, EU policy must pursue a rebalance between the core and the peripheries of the EU. The current Eurozone crisis has two components: a structural core-periphery divide and a chronic lack of demand, due to the initial crisis and the austerity policies subsequently implemented.[1] EU policies must address both problems: sustaining the EZ overall demand while addressing the fragility of the periphery's industrial basis. To this end, reconstruction of the EU must start from three interrelated objectives:

1   Rebuilding the economic and productive fabric of the areas which have been devastated by the crisis (not only Greece, but the South of Italy, several regions in Spain, Portugal, and elsewhere in Europe).[2]
2   Expanding the range of efficient or viable firms. To this end, the need is not only to focus on the export market or 'the most innovative sectors', but also to promote an investment programme targeting the domestic market, as well as the physical and social infrastructures.
3   Upgrading the production structure.

These objectives can only be achieved with a combination of a macroeconomic policy favouring recovery of demand coupled with an industrial policy focused on creating conditions for the areas left behind to catch up.

The level and composition of demand

There is, by now, increasing consensus on the need for expansionary fiscal policies. Even the IMF supported the view that the need is to relax the fiscal rules and expand government spending to end the recession. In a period of deleveraging, when households and firms refrain from spending, the state must step in to support the level of demand (Koo, 2016). The need for fiscal policy is all the more evident if we consider the ineffectiveness of quantitative easing to create demand. With an extremely expansionary monetary policy, public investment in infrastructure would entail almost no cost for the public budget. Hence the call for countries with fiscal space to expand public investment in infrastructure. In the previous chapters, we argued that recovery and growth in Europe cannot rely solely on the core countries' expansion. Since the composition of demand is of equal importance for short- and long-term growth, convergence of the periphery would not be achieved simply by relying on exports. The Southern European countries need to invest more, since investment affects capital accumulation and innovation, income distribution, living standards and sustainable development: interdependences between supply and demand prove crucial for the rate and the quality of growth.

The new industrial policy

The urgency to rethink EU policy lies behind the resurgence of industrial policy. Industrial policy should steer investment towards those activities that are desirable in both economic and social terms, fostering structural change, reallocation of resources, diversification and upgrading. We argued that this process of development is not automatic, and it is especially hard for the latecomer countries, which operate far from the frontier. It calls for the active intervention of the state, which must be tailored to the various areas' levels of capabilities, while aiming at the same time to promote their extension and upgrading. The need for a 'new' industrial policy has at last been accepted also at the EU level.

The first part of this chapter briefly reviews the historical evolution of the theory of development and the very concept of industrial policy (Section 2). It outlines the background for analysis of the evolution of this concept within the EC as well as the recent debate on the industrial policies required to sustain and rebalance growth within the EU (Section 3). The chapter concludes with an assessment of two examples of implementation of industrial policy. With the first, at the EU level, we look at the Investment Plan for Europe, known as the Juncker Plan, while with the second, at the national level, we briefly consider the recent debate on Industry 4.0. These two cases substantiate our point that any policy aiming at reversing the disintegration of the Eurozone must take into account the diversity in the levels of development of the various regions.

2 The vicissitudes of a concept

The rise and decline of development economics

'The development ideas that were put forward in the forties and fifties', argues Hirschman (1981: 3), 'shared two basic ingredients in the area of economics'. The first was rejection of the *monoeconomics* claim: claiming universality, traditional economics extended analysis appropriate for the 'special case' of a minority of developed economies to the underdeveloped countries. This new body of research was far from unified. It was still the monoeconomics view that inspired Rostow's five 'stages' of development, 'with identical content for all countries, no matter when they started out on the road to industrialization'. Gerschenkron's analysis of the process of industrialization of latecomers, such as Germany and Russia, with respect to the English industrial revolution, by contrast, showed that latecomers may have to overcome greater difficulties in their efforts to catch up, and that there can be more than one path to development (Hirschman, 1981). For latecomer countries, industrialization represented a formidable undertaking that could not be left to market forces. Development economics therefore endorsed a stronger steering role for the state of the developing country than did the mainstream, and new rationales were developed for protection, planning, and industrialization itself. 'Industrial policy' came to identify the set of policies aiming to change the structure of the economy with a deliberate, intensive and guided effort.

The second ingredient was the mutual benefit claim, namely the assertion that economic relations between the two groups of countries 'could be shaped in such a way as to yield gains for both' (Hirschman, 1981: 3). In contrast with this view, the doctrine of unequal exchange proposed by Prebisch and Singer gave support to the argument for protection and industrialization, while Myrdal and Hirschman's principle of cumulative causation advocated the need for public policy to counteract polarization.

The difficulties encountered on the path of development, the many failures and dramatic reversals in many countries, exposed the naiveté of the idea that progress 'would be smoothly linear if only [the developing countries] adopted the right kind of integrated development program' (Hirschman, 1981: 24). Criticism came from two opposite fronts: from the neo-Marxist camp (the dependency theory), and from the neoclassical camp, which stressed the risk of misallocation of resources. From the early 1980s, development economics – as articulated by what in 1989 John Williamson called the Washington Consensus, namely the World Bank, the IMF, the US Treasury and economics departments in western universities – changed direction and more or less merged its priors with those of the mainstream, dragging in industrial policy and public intervention in the economy with them. According to the new conventional wisdom, public intervention is only justified

> when (1) markets fail to produce social optima (due to some form of 'externalities'), and (2) the intervention can be presumed to move the outcome closer to the social optima at a cost less than the gain. It then asserts that in the real world, both conditions are rarely satisfied. With several more steps in between, the conclusion is drawn that 'Governments cannot pick winners, but losers can pick governments'.
>
> (Wade, 2012: 225)

It should be noted, however, that, even if shunned by the academia, industrial policy continued to enjoy a very concrete and lively existence within the industrial countries, although often 'under the radar', as documented by an increasing number of studies.[3] Eventually, 'after three decades of ideologically-motivated wilful neglect ... Unexpectedly ... industrial policy is now back in fashion, both in the academia and in the real world' (Chang and Andreoni, 2016: 3).

The rise of the 'new' industrial policy

The arguments in favour of a national industrial policy rest on the observation that the process of development is far from linear. In the mainstream approach, the problem of development is mainly a matter of achieving static efficiency, allocating resources better by countering the market failures caused by monopolies, asymmetric information and externalities. The assumption of a continuum in the product space ensures that, by shifting resources to the more efficient production, it is possible to move up in the product space, thus achieving dynamic efficiency. Conversely, the existence of discontinuities in the product space and the need to develop and coordinate those capabilities that growth industries demand prove a formidable obstacle to the process of development. In this view, development consists in broadening the range of activities and capabilities and moving up towards more complex, less ubiquitous, products rather than, as the theory of comparative advantage would have it, specializing in what one does better (Hausmann and Hidalgo, 2011).[4] Countries with a low diversity of capabilities can become stuck in 'quiescence traps' that make catching up more difficult. This is why government policy is called upon to coordinate the dispersed actions of firms, to help them identify new opportunities for differentiation and upgrading, and to contribute to developing the capabilities required for the production of more complex products.

The rediscovery of industrial policy is still mainly conducted in terms of 'market failures'. For instance, Hausman and Rodrik (2003) justify the need for direct state support for innovation in terms of information externalities. 'Pioneers' – those firms that enter a new sector or invest in a new production/technology – diffuse information on the feasibility of technologies and industries to the benefit of other potential entrants, providing value for the whole economy. State intervention is justified since the higher risk faced by 'pioneers' may result in sub-optimal entry into new industries. This approach has been criticized for overestimating intra-sectoral and underestimating inter-sectoral externalities (Chang and Andreoni, 2016). As for the former, by assuming that, once acquired by the 'pioneer', knowledge is then perfectly transferable within the industry, it neglects the firm-specific and tacit nature of knowledge, which implies that it is hard for imitators to free-ride on the pioneer; thus the information problem is not automatically solved with the establishment of a pioneer. At the same time, the latter implies a lack of systemic perspective. The focus on the representative 'pioneer' neglects the role played by inter-sectoral externalities – such as knowledge spillover through inter-sectoral labour mobility – and the development of supra-sectoral 'industrial commons' which can be used by many industries – such as quality and competence of the workforce, innovative management techniques, quality of the institutions – in sustaining development (Chang and Andreoni, 2016: 11). When these factors are properly accounted for, all industrial firms (and not just 'pioneers') may generate 'inter-sectoral' externalities for the rest of the economy.

Chang and Andreoni (2016: 13) also take issue with 'the Product Space approach' (Hidalgo and Hausmann, 2009) on two grounds. First, 'the approach defines the proximity between products in terms of their classifications in international trade, which is according to the character of the final product, rather than in terms of the technologies used in their productions'. However, apparently distant products can be produced with relatively similar technologies. Second, citing the experience of East Asian countries, they argue that 'it is not clear whether related diversification, which is advocated by the Product Space approach, is necessarily better or easier than unrelated diversification' (Chang and Andreoni, 2016: 14). By mapping the 'distance' between all exported products, the Product Space approach charts the 'natural' path of industrial diversification. In so doing, it does not recognize that the existing product space is not 'natural' but is to a great extent the outcome of the past industrial policies of the developed countries (ibid.).[5] They suggest a transition from a product-based taxonomy to a production technology-based taxonomy.... Technological linkages among different manufacturing processes may be used to define 'capability domains', that is, domains of techniques, productive knowledge, and production technologies/equipment that show high degrees of similarity and complementarity.

Abandoning the standard sectoral classification, 'a manufacturing process could be re-conceptualised according to the underpinning capability domain. Different manufacturing processes could be then clustered based on their reliance on particular capability domains.' It seems to us that the two approaches are complementary rather than alternative and the focus on the capabilities required in products or production technologies can help to broaden the scope of possibilities. Governments can target the development of capability domains in terms of technology (e.g. food processing, advanced materials, mechanics and control systems, ICT), and the development of particular industries defined in terms of the final product. An important point to note is that the

> capability domain constitutes a platform of competencies, technologies, productive knowledge, and experiences that can be deployed in a plurality of sectors.... By nurturing the development of complementary sets of capabilities, the scope for technological innovation within and across sectors can be increased and new development trajectories built.
>
> (Ibid.: 36)

When the Product Space approach is redefined in terms of capabilities, with reference to both products and production technologies, changes in a country's productive structure can thus be understood as a combination of two processes: (i) the process by which countries find new products through as yet unexplored combinations of the capabilities they already have, and (ii) the process by which countries accumulate new capabilities and combine them with other previously available capabilities to develop yet more products. Development occurs through diversification into products that are 'near' to those that are already being successfully produced and exported or that require the capabilities acquired in the production of more distant products. A country's ability to add new products to its production depends on having many near products and many capabilities that are being utilized in other, potentially more distant, products (Ginzburg and Simonazzi, 2017).

The distinction Rodrik makes between innovation (or R&D) and *cost discovery*, with its emphasis on 'self-discovery', is also relevant. It suggests, for instance, extending the range of policy actions to import substitution as a way of broadening the range of products and capabilities. 'What is involved is not [only] coming up with new products or processes, but "discovering" that a certain good, already well established in world markets, can be produced at home at low cost' (Rodrik, 2004: 7–8). Imports can signal the existence of unexploited opportunities – final demand for products or bottlenecks to development – that a well-integrated policy action can help to seize.[6] The focus on potential markets can reveal opportunities also in less obvious venues than exports or manufacturing. Mazzucato *et al.* (2016: 170) suggest focusing on societal challenges, in which many different sectors can interact, to create the potential for greater spillovers than a sectoral approach. They do not have to be restricted to frontier knowledge (the so-called mission-oriented policies). Public services, for instance, exhibit rapid growth in demand in cities and metropolitan areas. The provision of public goods for the productive sector can offer new opportunities for innovative firms, while exerting a strong activating capacity. The focus on welfare as an engine for growth calls for systemic action at different levels of governance (central, regional, municipal) and various institutions, in order to coordinate the supply and demand of innovative services (Cappellin *et al.*, 2015: 40–41).

Since market prices cannot reveal the profitability of products that have yet to come into existence, and dynamic externalities or uncertainty can limit firms' readiness to take up risky projects, without public incentive and support firms may be loath to adopt promising innovations. Production requires irreversible commitments under uncertainty: investment in physical capital embodying a specific technology, organizational innovations, new products, markets or a network of suppliers. Likewise, the transfer and adaptation of technologies, organizations, business strategies, products originally designed in other socio-economic systems pose difficult, specific problems in both the supply and demand domains. Thus, state intervention is needed not because 'the government officials [are] omniscient or cleverer than businessmen but because they [can] look at things from a national and long-term point of view, rather than a sectional, short-term point of view' (Chang, 2011: 92). It can support firms in their innovation processes and provide guidance for development strategies that promote products and capabilities as a way to create incentives to accumulate capabilities and develop new products in a cumulative, virtuous circle.

> By developing a joint vision as well as credible expectations among private companies around future public investments, not only does the government reduce the uncertainty faced by companies but it also sets the conditions for the creation of new markets … the government can play a major role in creating the future markets, more than simply fixing the failures of the existing ones.
>
> (Chang and Andreoni, 2016: 18)

Modern economies compete also, or chiefly, through their public policies, and those capable of orienting, accompanying and controlling complex systems will prevail. Drawing on a unique data set of prize-winning innovations between 1971 and 2006, Block and Keller (2011: 96) find that the expanded role of public institutions and public funding in the US has been a crucial factor in the innovation process. 'This leads us to the surprising conclusion that the U.S. increasingly resembles a Developmental Network State in which government initiatives are critical in overcoming network failures and in providing critical funding for the innovation process.' As argued by Chang and Andreoni (2016: 9), the way in which public, private and institutional actors are organized and the quality of their interactions are crucial for the working of an effective industrial policy. They mention: the degree of coordination between different ministries; the existence of effective 'intermediate institutions' in the public sector that provide critical inputs, like R&D, to the private sector; well-functioning associations at the national, regional and sectoral levels; and the existence of mechanisms for regular exchange of information between key policymakers and business leaders on technological and market realities.

Lack of the capabilities required to implement these policies – the most binding bottleneck in a plurality of situations – can be overcome through a sort of 'learning by doing' – for instance, by investing in the state's capacity to coordinate a selected set of economic agents, fostering their confidence in the state's behaviour, establishing national development as an urgent overarching project (Simonazzi *et al.*, 2013: 672). After so many years of stagnation, business is lacking a sense of where the future opportunities will lie (Mazzucato *et al.*, 2016). Governments must have a process in place which helps reveal areas of desirable intervention, facilitating structural change and collaboration with the private sector. Thus, although concern about government inefficiencies should be taken seriously, it should not justify inaction. Measures ensuring competition can reduce the risk of rent-seeking behaviours; monitoring can assess results. And, what is much more important, transformational change requires active investment on both the supply and demand sides.

To conclude, firms' performance crucially depends on both the structured interrelationships (the linkages) that they can establish upstream and downstream, and the support received from the material and immaterial infrastructures, development agencies and financial institutions that sustain the process of innovation in the long term (Ginzburg, 2012). Innovative countries rely on the presence of innovative businesses that compete on the basis of new products or processes and/or more effective use of new technologies, and not primarily on the basis of price. As argued in the previous chapters, these features were (and still are) asymmetrically distributed between the countries of the centre and the Southern periphery of Europe. If, as argued by Rodrik (2015), technical change and globalization are causing a process of 'premature de-industrialization', the EU latecomers are likely to get caught in the 'middle-income trap', no longer (price) competitive because of the developing countries catching up, and not yet capable of withstanding the worldwide (quality) competition. The growing commodification and private appropriation of knowledge makes it even more difficult to enter new product markets. One of the side-effects of the current economic crisis has been the rediscovery of the terms 'centre' and 'periphery' to analyse the dynamics of the European integration processes of the second half of the twentieth century (Simonazzi and Ginzburg, 2015). The divergent trajectories of the core and the peripheral European countries, interpreted in terms of interdependent economies with different productive capabilities, has led to revision of the concept of industrial policy also within the EU.

3 European industrial policy

We can distinguish three phases in European industrial policy: from product market intervention (1950s–1970s), to laissez-faire policies (1980s–1990s), to interventions increasingly focused on supporting 'innovative', science-based sectors. In the first phase, the challenges of reconstruction (1950s), catching up with the US (1960s) and response to the oil crisis (1970s) defined a national policy of intervention in the product market within a permissive European context.

In the second phase (1980s–1990s), following the developments in economic thinking, European industrial policy came to be conceived mostly in terms of market selection mechanisms. The idea of competition as industrial policy led to the dismantling of national policies. Intervention in traditional heavy capital- and scale-intensive manufacturing sectors, at a time when they were increasingly exposed to global competition, was phased down on the grounds that it protected declining industries, delaying adjustment. As argued in Chapter 8, early liberalization policies in the periphery shunned public investment guidance. Instead of devising new intervention policies to cope with the new international environment, the whole philosophy changed in favour of policies aimed at bolstering competition and enforcing antitrust measures. Ignoring the peculiar problems faced by countries at different stages of development, EU competition policy, epitomized by the Single European Act of 1986, de facto reinstated the monoeconomics paradigm. With the common market, new sectors were opened up to competition, public-owned companies were privatized[7] and new EU legislation was introduced to tighten control over public subsidies (Dhéret, 2014). Priority was given to horizontal measures, while upgrading was left to the market forces. Thus, partly as a consequence of these policies, in the 1980s growth in the periphery fell behind and the crisis associated with deregulation opened a gap in aggregate demand that was eventually filled by welfare and construction expenditure. This 'premature de-industrialization' – restructuring without industrialization – exposed the peripheral countries to stunted growth and persistent fragility with respect to external changes even before the formation of the Monetary Union.

As from 2000 European industrial policy gradually evolved from competition toward a 'soft' kind of industrial policy, focused on correcting 'systemic failures' and facilitating innovation. This new approach – a blend of horizontal and vertical policies, termed by Aiginger and Sieber (2005) 'matrix organization' of industrial policy – recognizes the role of governments in providing supportive institutions and of a broad set of horizontal policies conducive to competition, innovation and industrial change, though still initially eschewing the targeting of specific industries.

The shift towards selective intervention, embarked upon very cautiously in the Lisbon Strategy (2000), was reformed in the Europe 2020 strategy (2010) and accelerated with the crisis. In 2012, the Commission decided to complement its horizontal approach with a more vertical one, placing emphasis on specific technologies. Six lines of action were prioritized: advanced manufacturing technologies; key enabling technologies; bio-based products; sustainable industrial and construction policy and raw materials; clean vehicles; and smart grids. The strategy is still one of 'universal' policies across sectors and countries,[8] but the focus is increasingly on specific areas: primarily science, innovation and technology, but also textiles, tourism and steel. In January 2014, a new policy initiative, called the Industrial Compact, established the target of returning industrial activities from 16 to 20 per cent of GDP by 2020, and, in November, launched the Investment Plan for Europe (Juncker Plan) (see Section 4). The language now evokes many of the ideas promoted by the 'new industrial policy', from the 'smart specialization' strategy to calls for a process of 'self-discovery' by which firms, entrepreneurs and universities identify the domain of R&D and innovation in which their region can excel. Public action should aim at 'structuring policy initiatives on the basis of regional clusters' ... 'bringing together resources and expertise, fostering cooperation among business, public authorities and universities' (Aiginger and Sieber, 2005: 354), and envisaging public involvement through public-private partnership agreements.

Assessing the new European industrial policy

The success of the new European industrial policy in reducing the gap between the various regions of the Eurozone depends on three factors: sufficient funding; ensuring that latecomer countries can participate on an equal footing; and coordination across all levels. In all these respects, it still falls far short of what is needed to kick-start rebalanced growth in the Eurozone.

1   The attention commanded by the European industrial policy is disproportionate to its real relevance. The EU budget is trifling: only 1 per cent of total EU GDP. In the US the percentage of GDP accruing to the federal budget averages around 20 per cent. Only 16.5 per cent of the EU budget was dedicated to innovation policy over the period 2007–2013. The Structural Funds, representing the most important cohesion policy, had an endowment amounting to 0.38 per cent of the EU GDP (€347 billion). The European Investment Bank (EIB) (endowed with €72 billion in 2013), responds to a market principle, since it finances only public and private investments that promise to be profitable. The diminutive proportions of the EU budget reflect the very limited capacity and reach of its central institutions. The paucity of the EU budget devoted to innovation and cohesion is not offset by efforts at the national level: in 2011, the share of public spending on R&D in GDP was 2.7 per cent in the United States, 4 per cent in South Korea, 3.4 per cent in Japan and only 2 per cent in the EU. Moreover, the EU average hides the drastic fall of R&D expenditure in the crisis countries, which were already investing only half the amount of the northern and continental countries prior to the crisis. Thus, the crisis and the fiscal constraints work in the direction of increasing the divergence. On top of the

limitation of resources, the Union has no clear mandate to act in the industrial policy area. Measures aiming to drive industrial change are relying either on instruments from other policies, mainly internal market provisions, competition policy and trade policy, or on soft tools promoting consultation and coordination between member states (Pianta and Lucchese, 2014).

2   The second question concerns the principle of non-discrimination. No matter how general it may seem, any policy, or indeed the choice to have no policy, has discriminatory effects that amount to implicit targeting (Chang *et al.*, 2013). Supposedly horizontal policies, such as those regarding physical infrastructure, transport and R&D, are location/sector specific; tax credits to R&D will have greater effect on research-intensive sectors and will benefit countries with advanced productive structures more than regions with lower densities of research-intensive sectors. Thus, far from being non-discriminatory, horizontal measures may increase divergences when the participants are not on the same level playing field. For instance, the core countries seem to have been better able to adopt a long-term view in the selection of strategic sectors to invest in (Farla *et al.*, 2016: 367). Breschi and Cusmano (2004) speak of the unintended creation of an 'oligarchic core' made up of industry, academics, technology leaders and public actors.[9] 'The lobbying can mean that funding does not flow to regions and sectors most in need, but rather to those with a strong voice' (Farla *et al.*, 2016: 373). Conversely, the distribution of the European Structural and Investment Funds (ESI)[10] had 'been restricted to activities – such as infrastructure and education – less capable of leading to the emergence of new economic activities' (Pianta *et al.*, 2016: 6). In the 2014–2020 budget, allocation has been slightly revised to include 'over EUR 120 billion which will be strategically invested in research and innovation and provide support for small businesses and digital technologies' (EC, 2017).

3   The coexistence of very different industrial models in Europe, embedded within a free market approach at the EU level, makes multilevel coordination of industrial policies very difficult. Coordination between EU and national policies must find ways to reduce tensions between European and national competences, prevent the wasteful duplication of big projects and the build-up of excess capacity, curb conflicts between member states, and ensure catching up for latecomers (Dhéret, 2014). Partly because of their more advanced economies, and partly as a result of their greater capacity to direct EU priorities, the core countries seem to have been more capable of coordinating the EU strategy and policies with their own policies at the national and regional level.[11] They have also shown greater promptness in developing their own innovation clusters. The Top Cluster Competition in Germany, for instance, combines a network of applied research centres,[12] operating within a long-term strategy: Germany's Industrie 4.0 project (Section 5) aims at consolidating Germany's manufacturing leadership, mobilizing an impressive quantity of resources and public and private actors. In the periphery, the economic and fiscal crisis, in combination with

a still enduring pro-market bias, have contributed to extending the delay in adopting active strategic policies capable of providing firms with a long-term horizon.

To sum up, Europe needs to compete on a global market with nations that are engaged in active policies to support their own industrial champions. While the horizontal approach is still prevailing, the EU now proposes to support cooperation in industrial policy among the EU countries, focusing primarily on advanced technologies. If they are to avoid being shut out of the EU's fresh approach to industrial policy, the latecomer countries of the periphery wishing to follow this 'high path' to industrial renaissance will have to engage with this new agenda. To this end, they must make a significant contribution to the new industrial sectors at the European level, join in cooperative ventures to develop innovations in new, advanced fields, link up with the European value chains in the targeted sectors, and participate in the European cluster initiatives (Bartlett, 2014). This is an extremely difficult challenge: it calls for mobilization of the capabilities of their producers and policymakers alike, and it entails extensive industrial restructuring that will be difficult to achieve in a depressed economy. Actually, it is highly likely to fail if the instruments and policies at the EU level disregard the diverse conditions of the member states. With the peripheral countries' policies constrained by the fiscal compact, and their economies and indeed the entire EU stagnating, a common sectoral strategy across Europe will have unintended discriminatory effects. It will imply different incentives, and will result in different outcomes, if, as is now the case, firms operating in the same sector, but in different countries, are not on an equal playing field. Since firms' investments are linked in a circular and cumulative relationship with demand, a virtuous cycle of growth and innovation is possible only within buoyant macroeconomic conditions (Andreoni and Chang, 2016). Again, this plays against the countries in the periphery.

4 The Investment Plan for Europe (Juncker Plan)

The Investment Plan for Europe (IPE) well exemplifies the problems of the European industrial strategy. As argued in the previous section, the plan represents a significant reversal in EC philosophy, acknowledging the need for public support for investment, industrial recovery and structural convergence. In fact, the Plan was proposed by the European Commission in November 2014 in response to the drop of investment within the EU (–15 per cent since its peak in 2007), which left an investment gap estimated at €430 billion in 2013. It was expected that, by catalysing investment, in particular private investment, and by increasing companies' access to financing, this investment gap could be reduced, boosting growth, competitiveness and job creation in the European Union.

The IPE consists of three pillars: the first is the Investment Plan itself, run by the European Fund for Strategic Investments (EFSI). The second, comprising the European Investment Advisory Hub and the European Investment Project Portal, provides technical assistance and greater visibility of investment opportunities, as well as helping to create a stable pipeline of bankable projects and attract potential investors worldwide. Finally, the third pillar focuses on removing regulatory barriers at both the national and the EU level (EC, 2017).

Implementation of the EFSI, which is the financial pillar of the IPE, has been entrusted to the EIB Group. The Fund provides an EU guarantee amounting to €21 billion[13] and aims to mobilize additional investments in the order of €315 billion over three years (with a multiplier, or leverage effect, of 15 times).

The EFSI Regulation entered into force in July 2015. By June 2016, close to 270 transactions in 26 of the 28 EU member states had been accepted. By December 2016, the EIB Group had approved €30.2 billion under EFSI, mobilizing a total investment of 163.9 billion, or 52 per cent of the target of €315 billion over three years. In his 2016 State of the Union address, President Juncker announced the Commission's proposal to extend the EFSI, increasing its firepower and duration as well as reinforcing its strengths.[14] To improve the working of EFSI, the Commission plans to address the issue of geographical coverage by placing stronger emphasis on providing local technical assistance to those who wish to bid for funding and to further simplify the combination of EFSI funding with other sources in the EU, such as the European Structural and Investment (ESI) funds.[15]

Assessment of how the EPI project responds to the requirements discussed in the previous sections is mixed.

1   It does not respond to the immediate need to support recovery. According to Le Moigne *et al.* (2016), the plan came too late to prevent the liquidity trap and it is 'probably too little' to escape from it. In fact, the plan is under-financed, and the total amount of funds that can be activated (even taking the multiplier at its maximum face value) is largely insufficient for the task of supporting innovation and infrastructure and stimulating growth, as demonstrated by comparison with the fiscal stimulus launched by US President Obama. The reliance on a huge leverage effect – i.e. the lack of fresh money to fund the projects – and the time-to-build required from the inception of the procedure to the signing and implementation of an EFSI project, condemn it to irrelevance regarding its stated aim of providing an anti-cyclical stimulus.

2   It does not respond to a clear development strategy. The allocation of funds is demand-driven (from firms), within a very broad range of targets. The requirement that the projects be profitable constrains the scope of its policy to immediately commercially successful projects, leaving out projects that could generate new, interesting and potentially enabling capabilities (Ciuriak, 2016). For instance, the Social Investment Package, launched in 2013 by the EC with high hopes for a paradigm shift concerning social investment, did not find adequate room in the project (it accounted for 4 per cent of the total funded in 2016). Moreover, it is biased towards projects with a low, and/or deferred employment impact.

3   The requirement of 'additionality' of investment projects, finalized to create and finance new investment opportunities, is difficult to assess. Clayes and Leandro (2016) have attempted to assess the degree of additionality. According to their criteria of additionality, based on comparison of similar projects financed by the EIB, only one project among those financed would be considered additional.

4   Finally, in obeisance to the principle of non-discrimination, there is no sectorial or geographical pre-allocation. The equal treatment of unequal partners could leave weaker firms in weaker countries at a disadvantage, since investment opportunities or capability barriers could penalize these firms more. In contrast with this concern, the data published by EFSI seem to suggest that EFSI has gone more towards the periphery of the EU. This might be due to a more active role played by the National Promotional Banks and Institutions (NPBIs) (for instance, in the case of Italy, the Cassa Depositi e Prestiti, jointly with COSME – 'Competitiveness of Enterprises and small and medium-sized enterprises' – provided guarantees to finance investment to SMEs).[16] Their involvement follows recognition of the 'complementarity to the market' of National Promotional Banks and of their institutional role as pillars of the EFSI alongside the EIB. It may also reflect the fact that the financial guarantee is more valuable to firms in countries subject to a credit crunch. It is not clear, however, if these funds have been provided following a well-conceived national programme. Overall, and especially in consideration of its limited amount, it is doubtful that EPI can perform the twofold roles of sustaining recovery and reducing divergences between countries.

5 Industry 4.0: a Europe-wide opportunity or a new factor of divergence?

In Chapters 2 and 6, we showed that the creation of a German-based Eastward-oriented manufacturing network has proved a key driver of the core-periphery divergence, reinforcing the hierarchical reorganization of the European industry that the process of European integration had favoured. From a geographical perspective, this reorganization was characterized by the strengthening of the core and the weakening of the Southern periphery. From a structural perspective, it saw the increasing concentration of power, along the value chains (VCs), in the core-based multinational firms (MNFs). Particularly in key manufacturing sectors such as automotive and machineries, the latter have been increasingly capable of deciding what, how, where and when to produce (see Chapter 6). Stehrer and Stöllinger (2015) report that, between 1995 and 2011, the share of the '*German manufacturing core*' in total EU manufacturing exports increased from 34.5 per cent to 42.6 per cent, while the share of the other two largest manufacturing economies – France and Italy – fell from 23.8 per cent to 20 per cent.[17] The ability to govern a network of geographically close suppliers, providing low- and medium-tech intermediate inputs at a relatively low cost, gives

German firms a significant competitive advantage over the other European producers. Partially crowding out Southern-based suppliers from the German network (Simonazzi *et al.*, 2013 and Chapter 2), it has contributed to widening the core-periphery divergence since the 2000s.

As Garibaldo (2012: 15–16) emphasizes, the German-based manufacturing network is 'very different from the VCs of the past, which had the only objective of making the firm more flexible ... it represents a new structural division of labour between firms'. This production hub emerges as a network of suppliers structured in different levels and poles, within a hierarchical system.

> The companies engaged in the upstream activities are no more merely on the buy side of the option Make-Or-Buy; they are in some way under the authority of the firms controlling the specific supply chain as a whole – the so-called Original Equipment Manufacturers (OEMs) – or of the other key players in each tier. To be 'under the authority' means that key players decide for the other companies on how to plan the output's quantities in a given period, pace and speed to deliver the output's batches, how to arrange in sequences a mix of different items, etc. By and large, [these players] have the classical prerogatives of the managers. Sometimes, namely for the highly specialized companies, such as the modules suppliers, the degree and the nature of the integration in the network is such that the border lines between companies blur and new ways of co-operation start within original corporate governance schemes.

The core-periphery polarization may potentially be deepened by a new radical change affecting, in a *non-neutral* way, the European industrial structure. The source of this change is a set of new technologies – popularized with the name 'Industry 4.0' – designed to renew and reshape manufacturing processes and VCs. With particular reference to manufacturing, Industry 4.0 refers to the technological evolution from *embedded systems (ES)* to *cyber-physical systems (CPS)*.[18] By means of technologies such as *Internet of Things, Advanced Manufacturing* and *Decentralized Artificial Intelligence* efficiency and flexibility in governing production lines and VCs is expected to rise substantially. While the increase in efficiency and flexibility is, on the one hand, likely to spur the productivity and competitiveness of those firms, sectors and countries that are quicker in *absorbing* these technologies, it is, on the other hand, likely to endow the VC leaders with new instruments to govern production chains.

Pfohl *et al.* (2017) illustrate the effects that Industry 4.0 may exert on manufacturing processes and, more specifically, on VC organization and management. Introduction of CPS in production enables high levels of automation both within – i.e. the 'smart factory' – and between plants. In this respect, VCs become flexible networks of CPS-based production systems, endowed with infrastructures allowing for automatic overseeing of production processes. The adoption of CPS enables production processes to respond to varying conditions almost in real-time, radically enhancing optimization. As a result, the VC leaders' ability to coordinate activities and enforce decisions along the layers of the chain is considerably enhanced. The basic elements characterizing the effects of Industry 4.0 on the organization and management of VCs can be listed as follows (Pfohl *et al.*, 2016).

- *Control*. The availability of large amounts of constantly updated data enhances the ability to control the stages of production within the firm and the interactions between the VC layers.
- *Communication*. The dissemination of mobile devices combined with the use of data sharing and remote control boosts the effectiveness of communication between VC layers enabling customization.
- *Customization*. Continuous adaptation of product quantity and quality according to real-time changes in demand flows and customers' needs would positively affect the VCs' overall productivity. However, it will expose the weakest layers of the chain – i.e. the suppliers of the more labour-intensive components – to the risk of bearing the entire cost of adjustment to real-time changes in production plans.
- *Network-collaboration*. Interactions among the firms populating a VC are coordinated through the interaction of machines and human beings within specific networks within and outside the companies' organizational borders.

This coordinated collection of new technologies can affect production systems in different ways, and there are reasons to fear that they can deepen the core-periphery divergence. To set the Industry 4.0 project in its current European context, let us take a brief look at the origins of this 'technological revolution'.

Industry 4.0 originated as a German project explicitly aimed at consolidating the leadership of Germany in global manufacturing industry.[19] The prelude was in 2009, just one year after the outbreak of the crisis. A group of more than 40 German decision-makers, from large companies, research institutes and industry associations, met and gave birth to the '*National Roadmap Embedded Systems, for the further development of embedded systems technology*' (GTAI, 2014). Key German industry associations – specifically, automotive, machineries and automation technology – committed to spending more than €2.5 billion on a ten-year project to finance all the research areas linked to ES (the technological forerunner of Industry 4.0). In January 2011, Industrie 4.0 was launched as a 'Future Project' of the German Federal Government. The project, with a 10–15-year horizon, involves a large number of private and public partners: the Federal Government, the National Academy of Science and Engineering (ACATECH), the Fraunhofer-Gesellschaft, the Platform Industrie 4.0 consortium[20] and private corporations, such as Bosch and Festo. The Industrie 4.0 project, the cornerstone of the German Government's High-Tech Strategy 2020, has been allocated funding of up to €200 million within the Strategy Action Plan. Finally, in December 2013, the CDU-CSU-SPD coalition government singled out Industrie 4.0 as a key measure in consolidating Germany's technological leadership in the manufacturing sector. This short *excursus* on the *Industrie 4.0 plan for Germany*, offers effectual representation of the asymmetry characterizing the European political and economic environment.

Given the features that the German industrial VCs have taken on over the last few decades, the Industry 4.0 design responds to, and is strongly intertwined with, the technological needs and characteristics of the German manufacturing sector, which accounts for the coordinated efforts made by all the relevant public and private German actors. Conversely, for a number of reasons the periphery risks not only lagging behind, but also falling back in the industrial race. First, Industry 4.0-related opportunities are maximized when they interact with a closely connected, technologically advanced network. It represents a formidable advance along the lines of coordinated and just-in-time manufacturing production. As argued above, the diffusion of CPS is likely to strengthen the position of the firms and countries that are leaders in their manufacturing VCs (Garibaldo, 2012). Industry 4.0 may thus consolidate Germany's position as VC leader, providing instruments to coordinate the Eastward-oriented network more effectively. This is hardly the case of the industries of the Southern periphery. Differences in productive structures determine marked core and periphery heterogeneity in terms of absorptive capacity, or in other words their ability to recognize the value of new knowledge and technologies, and to assimilate and apply them to productive and commercial ends (Cohen and Levinthal, 1990). Their inability is even greater in terms of the magnitude, scope and pace of diffusion of Industry 4.0 technologies. Preventing Industry 4.0 from becoming an additional factor of polarization would call for a plan, coordinated at the national and EC levels, aimed at narrowing the core-periphery technological and competitive gap and creating the favourable environment that market actors cannot create alone. This requires massive investments aiming at strengthening infrastructure facilities, industrial capabilities and technology transfer mechanisms in the weakest areas: investment in digital infrastructures and higher education; European patents allowing generalized (across member states) access to relevant Industry 4.0 technologies; and strategic decisions on where to locate production of Industry 4.0-related goods. This is the field where the dimensional adequacy and the strategic vision of EC industrial policy is more lacking.[21] The largest Europe-wide action plan – the Juncker Plan – is far from ensuring a balanced diffusion of Industry 4.0 technologies.

The European authorities and national governments have recently adopted Industry 4.0 as a common goal (European Parliament, 2015). However, as a non-neutral change rapidly affecting the European industrial fabric, Industry 4.0 implies both threats and opportunities. The European and member states' authorities must take account of the factors described above: the structural heterogeneities characterizing different countries and regions, the Southern periphery's debilitated manufacturing sectors, the deep-reaching macroeconomic crisis that has reduced per capita income and spread poverty, and fiscal constraints reducing the Southern governments' capacity to promote a balanced diffusion of Industry 4.0 opportunities. Given these conditions, it is likely that, in the absence of an industrial policy to guide the sectoral and geographical allocation of investment, Industry 4.0-related technologies will reach only the more developed areas, populated by clusters of large internationalized firms, thus also widening the internal divide. A targeted industrial policy is urgently needed to rebalance the regions within each country, and so to reverse the trend that has seen the backward non-exporting regions falling behind, with hysteresis resulting in reductions in productive capacity, the development of bottlenecks and lower long-term actual and potential growth rates.

6 Conclusions

The Eurozone crisis has been interpreted as a balance of payments crisis. Given the impossibility to depreciate, the deficit countries' lack of competitiveness called for domestic devaluation. Fiscal austerity was deemed able to solve the sovereign debt crisis and restore price competitiveness. While contesting this interpretation (in Chapters 2 and 7), we have argued that the Southern European countries' crisis can be interpreted within a core-periphery model. Adopting a long-term view, we claimed that the problems of the periphery are of a structural nature, and have been exacerbated by the policies implemented before and during the current crisis. Keynesian policies stimulating demand are indispensable to enable broadening of the production structure and the increase in production and income that are required to ensure full employment. However, structural problems demand structural policies. We have surveyed the recent theoretical re-evaluation of the reasons in favour of an industrial policy and concluded that the convergence of the periphery can only be achieved with reorientation of industrial policies at the national and European level. These policies have to target the disadvantages that handicap latecomers in a world where, as observed by Smith ([1776] 1996: 278), 'to widen the market and to narrow the competition is always the interest of the dealers'. The market power accruing to incumbents with the new technologies – dynamic economies of scale, private appropriation of knowledge, patents, hierarchical organization of VCs – makes it impossible to catch up if unassisted by the state. While all the advanced countries (like the rapidly developing countries in Asia) have always implemented industrial policies to sustain innovation in their industries, only recently has the 'new' industrial policy started to permeate the EC institutions. However, despite recent weak signs of resipiscence,[22] its approach is still based on the assumption that all member states are on the same level playing field. In a context of unequal participants, policies inspired by the principles of universality and equality of treatment risk (in practice) sustaining inequality. The strengthening of the EC industrial policy actions should work in the direction of restoring convergence: they should be coordinated with national (and regional) policies targeting the specific regional and sectoral weaknesses. A more effective national and supranational industrial policy cannot disregard the financing problem. Suggestions are not lacking, from enlargement of the community budget to a golden rule that allows exclusion of public investment from the fiscal compact, as well as state investment banks or public venture capital funds and 'blue bonds' to finance

EU-wide investment projects. The survival of the Eurozone must be pursued contemplating some of these proposals to promote the convergence of the areas that are left behind.

Notes

1 The crucial problem lying in the flawed institutional basis of the euro construction, analysed in Chapter 1, plays an important role in as much as it constrains the range of the possible solutions; it will be addressed in the final part of this chapter.
2 See Annoni *et al.* (2017).
3 See Mazzucato (2014). The rediscovery of industrial policy, and of industrial and technological clusters, has also drawn attention to the literature on industrial districts (Brusco, 1982; Becattini, 1990; Best, 1990).
4 'Countries do not become rich by making more of the same thing. They do so by changing what they produce and how they produce it. They grow by doing things that are new to them; in short, they innovate' (Hausmann, 2013).
5 Somewhat contradictorily, they continue: 'Even if there are "natural" paths of progression between different products, industrial policy will still benefit countries if it allows them to travel along those paths more quickly than otherwise or to skip steps within the given path.'
6 As Hirschman put it, economic development 'depends not so much on finding optimal combinations for given resources and factors of production as on calling forth and enlisting for development purposes resources and abilities that are hidden, scattered, or badly utilized' (Hirschman, 1958: 5, quoted in Rodrik, 2004: 13).
7 With privatization, public companies were often transformed into private monopolies (see Costi and Messori, 2005 for the Italian record).
8 The two flagship initiatives devoted to innovation and industrial policy by Europe 2020 – the 'Innovation Union' and 'An integrated industrial policy for the globalization era' – are still based on a horizontal approach. Their main policy tools are provision of infrastructure, reduction of transaction costs across the EU, a more appropriate regulatory framework favouring competition and access to finance (Pianta and Lucchese, 2014).
9 Farla *et al.* (2016: 372) note that 'the inclusion of some sectors, the recurrence of others, the practice of establishing priorities after consultations with industry stakeholders suggest a lobbying process in the workings of industrial policy that is more evident in some contexts than others'.
10 The European Regional Development Fund (ERDF), the Cohesion Fund (CF) and the European Social Fund (ESF).
11 For instance, the UK Technology Strategy Board was set up by the government in 2007 to finance private investments in innovation and to promote access to UK and EU funding schemes and network opportunities for them (Farla *et al.*, 2016: 365).
12 The Fraunhofer Gesellschaft – 69 institutes and research units in Germany, the largest organization for applied research in Europe – undertakes applied research that drives economic development and serves the wider benefit of society. The majority of the more than 22,000 staff are qualified scientists and engineers, who work with an annual research budget of €1.9 billion. Similarly, in the UK the Catapult programme brings together a network of world-leading centres designed to transform the UK's capability for innovation in specific areas and help drive future economic growth. France has developed its Poles of Competitiveness.
13 It consists of €8 billion detracted from the EU budget, mostly Horizon 2020 (H2020) and the Connecting Europe Facility (CEF), plus €8 billion as an EU Guarantee. The €16 billion are complemented by an EIB contribution (€5 billion), provided from its own resources.

14 It also proposed to set up a new European External Investment Plan (EIP) to encourage investment in Africa and the EU Neighbourhood to strengthen partnerships and contribute to achieving the Sustainable Development Goals.

15 http://europa.eu/rapid/press-release_IP-16-3002_en.htm.

16 The NPBIs, which have a comprehensive knowledge of local stakeholders and their respective domestic markets, positioned themselves from the outset as 'facilitators' in the national roll-out of the IPE. They have grouped together under the banner of the European Long-Term Investors association (ELTI).

17 Stehrer and Stöllinger (2015) use the value added of exports, i.e. the value added generated in a country that is finally absorbed abroad. In Chapter 4 and 6, we use this indicator to highlight the core-periphery divergence in key manufacturing sectors and its deepening after the 2008 crisis.

18 In the industry domain, the CPS endows factories with a digital twin of the real productive process by means of cloud platforms and Big Data. The 'coupled model' can be interpreted as a digital image that materializes from the early design stage. This model, thus, is a mirrored image of the real process enabling continuous recording and tracking of machines and product conditions during the various production stages. Thanks to the ubiquitous connectivity offered by cloud computing technology, managers are substantially empowered as regards control and ongoing adaptation of the production process. This very strong control as well as the possibility of real-time changes in production conditions improve efficiency and governance effectiveness both within the plant and along the VCs.

19 The foreword to the Industrie 4.0 project official report is indicative:

> Germany has the ideal conditions to become a global leader in innovative, internet-based production technology and service provision. Technological leadership and vision in the fields of manufacturing, automation and software-based embedded systems, as well as historically strong industrial networks, lay the cornerstone for the long-term success of the Industrie 4.0 project.

20 See fn. 12 for a description of the Fraunhofer Gesellschaft. The Plattform Industrie 4.0 is a joint initiative of the industry organizations BITKOM (Federal Association for Information Technology, Telecommunications and New Media), VDMA (German Engineering Federation) and ZVEI (Electrical and Electronic Manufacturers' Association) and acts as a central point of contact for companies, employee representatives, politicians and scientists related to Industry 4.0.

21 Recognition of the threats entailed by uneven adoption of Industry 4.0 across Europe can be found in the EC documents (see, for example, the EC Industry 4.0 briefing of September 2015 and the analytical study commissioned by the European Parliament in 2016). However, as noted in the text, this awareness has not yet translated into a concrete industrial policy.

22 New principles have been introduced that can represent seeds of potential future transformations: the principle of fiscal flexibility – the 'investment clause', for the first time contains some timid hints at the 'Golden Rule'; the principle of additivity ('filling market failures or sub-optimal investment situations'); the principle of 'good aid' – defined as 'the decision on state aid on well-defined market failures and on objectives of general interest'; the 'complementarity to the market' of National Promotional Banks; and finally the Capital Market Union with its recently released 'Action Plan' (Reviglio, 2015).

References

Aiginger, K. and Sieber, S. (2005). *Towards a Renewed Industrial Policy in Europe.* Background Report of the Competitiveness of European Manufacturing. European Commission, DG Enterprise. Brussels: WIFO.

Andreoni, A. and Chang, H.-J. (2016). Industrial policy and the future of manufacturing. *Economia e Politica Industriale*, 43(4), 491–502.

Annoni, P., Dijkstra, L. and Gargano, N. (2017). *The EU Regional Competitiveness Index 2016*. European Commission, Directorate-General for Regional and Urban Policy, Working Paper 02/2017.

Bartlett, W. (2014). Shut out? South East Europe and the EU's new industrial policy. *LEQS Paper No. 84*.

Becattini, G. (1990). The Marshallian industrial district as a socioeconomic notion. In F. Pyke, G. Becattini and W. Sengenberger (eds), *Industrial Districts and Inter-firm Co-operation in Italy*. Geneva: ILO.

Best, M. (1990). *The New Competition: Institutions of Industrial Restructuring*. Cambridge, MA: Harvard University Press.

Block, F. and Keller, M. (2011). Where do innovations come from? Transformations in the US economy, 1970–2006. In L. Burlamaqui, A. C. Castro and R. Kattel (eds), *Knowledge Governance: Reasserting the Public Interest*. London: Anthem Press, 81–104.

Breschi, S. and Cusmano, L. (2004). Unveiling the texture of a European Research Area: Emergence of oligarchic networks under EU Framework Programmes. *International Journal of Technology Management*, 27(8), 747–772.

Brusco, S. (1982). The Emilian model: Productive decentralisation and social integration. *Cambridge Journal of Economics*, 6(2), 167–184.

Cappellin, R., Baravelli, M., Bellandi, M., Camagni, R., Ciciotti, E. and Marelli, E. (2015). *Investimenti, innovazione e città. Una nuova politica industriale per la crescita*. Milano: Egea.

Chang, H-J. (2011). Industrial policy: Can we go beyond an unproductive confrontation? In *Annual World Bank Conference on Development Economics*. Washington, DC: World Bank Group, 83–109.

Chang, H-J. and Andreoni, A. (2016). Industrial policy in a changing world: Basic principles, neglected issues and new challenges. *Cambridge Journal of Economics 40 Years Conference*, Cambridge, 12–13 July.

Chang, H.-J., Andreoni, A. and Kuan, M. L. (2013). International industrial policy experiences and the lessons for the UK. *Future of Manufacturing Project: Evidence Paper 4*, Foresight, Government Office for Science.

Ciurak, D. (2016). *Rebooting Europe*. The McKinsey Global Institute. An opportunity for Europe? 2016 Europe Essay Prize.

Clayes, G. and Leandro, A. (2016). The Juncker Plan needs to be turned on its head. *Bruegel*, 8 June. http://bruegel.org/2016/06/the-juncker-plan-needs-to-be-turned-on-its-head/ [accessed 8 June 2016].

Cohen, W. and Levinthal. D. (1990). Absorptive capacity: A new perspective on learning and innovation. *Administrative Science Quarterly*, 35(1), 128–152.

Costi, R. and Messori, M. (eds) (2005). *Per lo sviluppo. Un capitalismo senza rendite e senza capitale*. Bologna: Il Mulino.

Dhéret, C. (2014). Sharing the same vision: The cornerstone of a new industrial policy for Europe. *EPC Discussion Paper*, 20 March.

EC (2017). *Industry in Europe. Facts & Figures on Competitiveness & Innovation*. Brussels: European Commission.

European Parliament (2015). *Industry 4.0. Digitalisation for Productivity and Growth*. www.europarl.europa.eu/RegData/etudes/BRIE/2015/568337/EPRS_BRI(2015)568337_EN.pdf [accessed 22 September 2017].

Farla, K., Guadagno, F. and Verspagen, B. (2015) Industrial policy in the European Union. In J. Felipe (ed.), *Development and Modern Industrial Policy in Practice. Issues and Country Experiences*. Cheltenham: Edward Elgar.

Garibaldo, F. (2012). The social roots of the democratic crisis of the EU and the role of Trade Unions. In F. Garibaldo, M. Baglioni, C. Casey and V. Telljohann (eds), *Workers, Citizens, Governance. Socio-Cultural Innovation at Work*. Frankfurt: Peter Lang, 13–28.

Ginzburg, A. (2012). Sviluppo trainato dalla produttività o dalle connessioni: due diverse prospettive di analisi e di intervento pubblico nella realtà economica italiana. *Economia & Lavoro*, 46(2), 67–93.

Ginzburg, A. and Simonazzi, A. (2017). Out of the crisis: A radical change of strategy for the Eurozone. *The European Journal of Comparative Economics*, 14(1), 13–37.

GTAI (2014). *Embedded Systems and Networks*. http://industrie4.0.gtai.de/INDUS TRIE40/Navigation/EN/Topics/The-internet-of-things/embedded-systems-and-networks.html [accessed 22 September 2017].

Hausmann, R. (2013). The conglomerate way to growth. *Project Syndicate*. www.project-syndicate.org/commentary/bigcompanies-and-economic-growth-in-developing-countries-by-ricardo-hausmann [accessed 25 October 2013].

Hausmann, R. and Hidalgo, C. (2011). The network structure of economic output. *Journal of Economic Growth*, 16(4), 309–342.

Hausmann, R. and Rodrik, D. (2003). Economic development as self-discovery. *Journal of Development Economics*, 72(2), 603–633.

Hidalgo, C. and Hausmann, R. (2009). The building blocks of economic complexity. *Proceedings of the National Academy of Sciences*, 106(26), 10570–10575.

Hirschman, A. O. (1958). *The Strategy of Economic Development*. New Haven, CT: Yale University Press.

Hirschman, A. O. (1981). The rise and decline of development economics. In *Essays in Trespassing: Economics to Politics and Beyond*. Cambridge: Cambridge University Press.

Koo, B. H. (2016). Sociocultural factors in the industrialization of Korea. In B. H. Koo and D. H. Perkins (eds), *Social Capability and Long-term Economic Growth*. Berlin: Springer.

Le Moigne, M., Saraceno, F. and Villemot, S. (2015). Le plan Juncker peut-il nous sortir de l'ornière?. *Revue de l'OFCE*, (8), 357–386.

Mazzucato, M. (2014). Ripensare la concezione di Stato. *Il Mulino*, 63(3), 484–491.

Mazzucato, M., Onida, F. and Viesti, G. (2016). Industrial policies in advanced countries: A brief introduction. *Politica Economica*, 32(2), 167–178.

Pfohl, H. C., Yahsi, B. and Kurnaz, T. (2017). Concept and diffusion-factors of Industry 4.0 in the supply chain. In M. Freitag, H. Kotzab and J. Pannek (eds), *Dynamics in Logistics*. Lecture Notes in Logistics. Berlin: Springer.

Pianta, M. and Lucchese, M. (2014). Una politica industriale per l'europa. *Economia & Lavoro*, 48(3), 85–98.

Pianta, M., Lucchese, M. and Nascia, L. (2016). *What is to be Produced? The Making of a New Industrial Policy in Europe*. Brussels: Rosa Luxemburg Stiftung.

Reviglio, E. (2015). Moving the first steps towards an 'European Infrastructure Union'. *Confrontations Europe*. http://confrontations.org/la-revue-en/moving-the-first-steps-towards-an-european-infrastructure-union?lang=en [accessed 11 October 2015].

Rodrik, D. (2004). Industrial policy for the twenty-first century. *CEPR Discussion Paper No. 4767*.

Rodrik, D. (2015). Premature deindustrialization. *NBER Working Paper No. 20935*.

Simonazzi, A. and Ginzburg, A. (2015). The interruption of industrialization in Southern Europe: A center-periphery perspective. In M. Baumeister and R. Sala (eds), *Southern Europe? Italy, Spain, Portugal, and Greece from the 1950s until the Present Day*. Frankfurt: Campus, 103–137.

Simonazzi, A., Ginzburg, A. and Nocella, G. (2013). Economic relations between Germany and southern Europe. *Cambridge Journal of Economics*, 37(3), 653–675.

Smith, A. [1776] (1996). *An Inquiry into the Nature and Causes of the Wealth of Nations*. Chicago: University of Chicago Press.

Stehrer, R. and Stöllinger, R. (2015). The Central European Manufacturing Core: What is driving regional production sharing? *FIW Research Reports No. 2014/15–02*.

Wade, R. H. (2012). Return of industrial policy? *International Review of Applied Economics*, 26(2), 223–239.

10 Conclusions

1 Institutional flaws and policy mistakes

The current crisis has distant origins. Erroneously interpreted as a standard fiscal/balance of payments problem, it was in fact the result of the incomplete nature of the European institutions and a disregard for the consequences of differences in the stages of development of the member countries. We argued in Chapter 1 that a viable currency union needs to be fully embedded in the existing social and political institutions. 'The main euro problem', Matthijs and Blyth (2015: 252–253) write, quoting McNamara (2015), 'is, and remains, one of missing "systemic" institutional embeddedness, rather than a lack of "national" competitiveness, labour mobility, or fiscal restraint'. The crisis revealed serious institutional and political flaws in Eurozone governance. Subsequent policy errors deriving from theoretical prejudices, economic interests and political myopia, combined to implement short-sighted, economically damaging and politically divisive policies. The dominant dogma that markets are self-equilibrating prevented the EZ authorities (and those in the United States) from taking action to limit financial excesses in the pre-crisis years. The European banks, actively engaged in global financialization, recycled international liquidity to the European periphery. When the banks went bust, the national governments had to step in to bail them out, creating a 'doom loop', 'with weak banks dragging down weak governments, which in turn dragged banks down further' (Legrain, 2014: 12). While the banking crisis exposed the 'absence of a common mechanism for dealing with bank failures and a fear of imposing losses on banks' creditors', the Greek crisis 'highlighted the absence of a formal mechanism for restructuring sovereign debt within the Eurozone and great resistance to doing so' (ibid.). The crisis also revealed the risks of having a central bank that, formally independent, interferes in political questions, with significant distributional consequences for creditor and debtor countries, and for different social groups within countries. Finally, price competition has been used to justify disastrous internal devaluation policies in the belief that an austerity regime associated with institutions close to those assumed to prevail in 'core' countries would create the 'right' environment for resuming growth in the periphery.

What began as a community of equals is now a deeply divided Europe, with debtor countries resenting the conditionality and costs imposed by the creditor countries, and the latter feeling constantly threatened by the debtors' free-riding behaviour.

2 Structural differences

Our analysis of the main phases of the development of European countries since the aftermath of the Second World War reveals great differences in the productive structures of the countries of the centre and the Southern periphery of Europe at the start of the Europeanization process. These differences entailed an asymmetric capacity of countries at various levels of development to adjust to external shocks. Moreover, the slow growth of the euro area failed to sustain the Southern European countries in pursuit of a sufficient level of diversification and specialization in their productive structures; indeed, it may even have contributed to worsening it (as seems to be the case with Southern Italy). Given the differences in the levels of development of the various EU countries and their varying capacities to cope with change, public policy should have played the role of actively promoting – through investment – the removal of development bottlenecks and renewal of the productive base. Instead, the integration of these economies into the EU, and the process of Europeanization meant opting for (premature) liberalization. In the absence of guidance, the forces protecting and freezing the status quo of institutions and productive specialization thus prevailed. The way was open for a kind of bank-led 'privatized Keynesianism' that concealed – until the outbreak of the global crisis – the existence of a demand-and-supply constraint on development in the European peripheral countries.

Conversely, the increasing integration of the Central and Eastern European economies into the supply chain of the German industry speeded up their diversification and specialization processes. The eastward integration of German industry sustained the EP's growth by reactivating the two engines of growth, investment and exports, which had supported the capitalist countries' growth in the 'trente glorieuses'. However, unlike that scenario, their growth was now combined with persistent containment of internal demand in the major economies of the euro area. Hence, it did not spread its effects across the region, but went hand in hand with an impoverishment of the productive matrix of the southern regions less connected with Germany and, more generally, with a broad rerouting of trade flows. The different experiences of the two peripheries highlight the importance of understanding the divergent trajectories of the core and peripheral countries in terms of *interdependent* economies with different productive capabilities. The story of the Southern periphery cannot be told 'in isolation' – without, that is, taking into account the repercussions of the choices of the core, which does not imply exonerating national actors from their responsibilities (Simonazzi and Ginzburg, 2015: 104–106).

3 Partial, cautious reforms

The severity of the crisis and the risks of EMU disintegration called for the adoption of partial and belated reforms of the community's institutions. As a result, Eurozone governance has changed a great deal during the crisis, often in the wrong direction, but falling short of tackling the fundamental problem of the 'missing unions' (McNamara, 2015). A limited banking union and a common resolution mechanism have at last been agreed upon (but with no consensus on a common deposit insurance scheme). Its rules, rigidly interpreted, have opened new divisions and stirred greater acrimony among the weaker countries, whose struggling banks would have to fend for themselves, rationing credit to the economy and crimping growth (Bastasin and Messori, 2017). The no-bail-out rule, first breached in 2010 in the case of Greece, to the benefit of its centre creditor banks, was subsequently formalized with the creation of the European Stabilization Mechanism (ESM), which operates under strict conditionality. The fiscal discretion of individual nations has been further constrained with approval of various rounds of new rules (six-packs, two-packs, European semester, fiscal compact), but any proposal to broaden EU fiscal responsibility met with firm opposition. The evolution of the fiscal rules highlights the looming flaw in Eurozone fiscal governance: 'the fact that EU rules and Eurozone policy-makers' decisions ignore the collective impact of individual countries' fiscal decisions' (Legrain, 2014: 20). The ECB has intervened, performing the function of lender of last resort for banks and for sovereigns, but in an ad hoc, conditional way, often stepping outside the boundaries of the monetary area.

Overall, the EU's macroeconomic stance is unbalanced (for instance, more lenient towards countries with current account surpluses than to those with deficits) and distorted by an increasingly uneven distribution of power. Interventions proving too little and too late have inflicted enormous costs on the European community and single member countries, often simply preparing the ground for the next crisis. Above all, there has been no complementary pooling of sovereignty, nor convergence towards shared decision-making.

4 Institutional reforms

For long-term sustainability the European project needs a multilevel policy. The first step, and an urgent one, calls for a shared solution offering respite to the heavily battered economies of Southern Europe. As stressed by Koo (2011), the EZ is in a debt deflation trap. The productive system of the Southern periphery is in tatters, and it is dragging the banking system down with it in a new round of industry-bank debt loop. There is no way to resume growth without solving the problem of debt and the connected process of de-leveraging, which is killing demand. As the history of past debt deflations shows, when things get sour, the creditor will sink with the debtor, a lesson well understood by the US administration on the occasion of the less developed countries' debt crisis, which broke out in 1982 and simmered for the next seven years.

From 1982 through 1988, debtor nations and their commercial bank creditors engaged in repeated rounds of rescheduling and restructuring sovereign
and private sector debt, in the belief that the difficulty these nations experienced in meeting their debt obligations was a temporary liquidity problem
that would end as the debtor nations' economies rebounded. However, by
the time the Brady Plan was announced, it was widely believed that most
debtor nations were no closer to financial health than they had been in 1982,
that many loans would never be entirely repaid, and that some form of substantial debt relief was necessary for these nations and their fragile economies to resume growth and to regain access to the global capital markets.

(EMTA, 2009)

In 1989, Treasury Secretary Nicholas Brady formulated a new strategy to tackle
the developing country debt. The Brady Plan focused on debt and debt service
reduction by commercial bank creditors for those debtors who agreed to implement substantial economic reform programmes. The Plan offered banks credit
enhancements in exchange for agreement to reduce claims.[1] By coupling economic
reform with debt reduction, the Brady Plan represented a market-oriented solution
that served as a catalyst to restart growth in the emerging markets. It was not meant
as an act of solidarity: drawing on his experience on Wall Street, Brady recognized
that reversing the exodus of capital from debtor nations was critical for creditor
banks' survival: it was an (enlightened) policy of self-defence, which was deemed
necessary to free the US bank's frozen resources and restart lending. The EZ needs
a similar capacity to see beyond the immediate, narrow interest, and to avoid the
fallacy of composition represented by the systemic risk. A variety of solutions has
been offered to defuse the bomb made up of private and public indebtedness, battered banks and generalized impoverishment in the periphery. However, any proposal for debt mutualization[2] must overcome the German obsession with moral
hazard. And yet, as has been remarked, the problem of moral hazard should be
tackled ahead of the creation of a bubble. When the bubble has burst, the only
thing to do is try to limit the damage.

The second step concerns the institutional architecture. Here, too, the suggestions cover a wide range, from mild to bold proposals[3] to address the problems
in the functioning of the EMU, exposed by the crisis and mostly left unanswered.
Essential as they are to exit the crisis, and indeed economically sensible and
plausible, they are hardly realistic in the present circumstances. The problem is
obviously a political one. In fact, 'There are no sustainable technocratic solutions to the euro problem, which is an inherently political one, and will need
political solutions' (Matthijs and Blyth, 2015: 268). And here the problem is
obviously Germany.

5 A German Europe[4]

At present, the European Union is heading towards a predominantly Germanic
Eurozone – one, that is, whose rules, institutions and policies are shaped by

Germany's ideas and interests, rather than a coherent vision of the interests of the area as a whole. Thus, while desperately needed, reforms to repair the institutional flaws in the EMU do not seem likely in the immediate future. Risk and cost sharing are not very popular in Berlin. As Kundnani (2015) argued, the 'German question', which emerged in 1871 when, after unification, Germany became too powerful for any of the other great powers of the time to challenge, has re-emerged in geo-economic form. 'The size of Germany's economy, and the interdependence between it and those around it, is now creating instability within Europe as its military power once did.' However, now as then, Germany's position can be described as one of 'semi-hegemony'. 'Although Germany's increasing power and France's relative weakness have allowed Germany to impose its preferences on others in the Eurozone, it is too small to be a European hegemon.' This seems to be leading to a geo-economic version of the old German fear of encirclement. In any domain – financial, fiscal, economic or social – everything which is 'joint' smacks of 'a common front' of weak countries, eager to go free-riding on (or raiding) the German taxpayer. Fiscal transfers, deposit-insurance schemes, unemployment insurance schemes, safe sovereign assets or Eurozone-wide risk-free securities, are seen as a 'blank check' for the crisis countries.[5] Germany has been active on all fronts in the Eurozone crisis, but has played the role of reluctant leader 'cautious and circumscribed' (Newman, 2015), always 'stressing the "moral hazard frame of policy" over alternative frames that would legitimate a more aggressive response … [thus managing] to both help resolve and help exacerbate the crisis' (Matthijs and Blyth, 2015: 12). Germany's cautious response to crisis reflects the German leaders' concern over the 'politics of timing' – the need, that is, to launch new interventions only when they have properly prepared their voters (Jacoby, 2015). The future of the euro depends on how Germany resolves this dilemma between the urgency to act and voters' preparedness.

It is hard to see how the leaders of France, Italy and Greece can create growth and jobs without a big shift in Eurozone economic policy. However, it is also increasingly hard to see how they can force such a shift unless they join forces and take a more confrontational approach to Germany – as many are now urging them to.

6 A European Germany

In 2011 George Soros expressed the view that 'with Germany's reunification, the main impetus behind the integration process was removed' (Soros, 2011, quoted in Simonazzi, 2015: 89–90). The impetus might have been weakened further by the crisis, which has debilitated the Southern periphery and France, and by the formation of the Central European Manufacturing Core, which changed the barycentre of Europe. Yet, can Germany (and its northern peers) stand alone?

Since the inception of the Monetary Union, Germany has been able to profit from a nominal exchange rate lower than would have prevailed had it not belonged to the Euro system, and from an undervalued real effective exchange rate due to internal and 'external' wage moderation (that is, the cost effect embodied in its imports of intermediate and consumption goods from lower-wage countries). Since the crisis German borrowers have been enjoying a subsidy from Southern European countries through the lower rates of interest due to the 'flight to quality' effect (the upside of the increasing spreads in government bonds in the crisis countries). Thanks to this subsidy, during the years of the crisis Germany was able to finance an increase in construction (the only investment to some extent responsive to low interest rates), which somewhat mitigated the slowdown in external demand.

It is doubtful whether the conditions that favoured the success of German exports (and by implication of export-led models in general) will continue into the next decade. Contrary to the expectations built on supply-side models, recent experience shows that the tendency towards convergence in unit labour costs and current accounts, prompted by simultaneous austerity measures across European countries, is associated with a pronounced slowdown of the economies in the Eurozone, with negative effects on their debt/income ratios as well. Since 2008, the deflationary forces originating from within the Eurozone have been added to the forces from outside, particularly from China. Since Europe's biggest country is reliant on exports and Germany has been a particular beneficiary of China's sustained investment-led boom, the 'rebalancing strategy' carried out by China since 2007 creates growing uncertainty and concern that goes beyond Germany's borders. Since the 2007 subprime crisis, the Chinese government has been implementing measures targeted at reducing various imbalances (and gaining greater strategic autonomy from external influences): the imbalance in domestic expenditure (an excessive share of investment relative to consumption); the urban-rural income divide; the coast-hinterland divide; asymmetries in access to credit, social security, housing and education. This inward reorientation (which is not free from the risk of derailment, given the high private debt/income ratio; see Pettis, 2013) has already produced a reduction in the aggregate import/GDP ratio, as well as major changes in the composition of imports: a lower share of intermediate imports to be processed by foreign firms, and a higher share of luxury consumption goods, such as high-quality cars. This last feature, which helps explain the performance of German exports to China even after the subprime crisis, entails vulnerability to developments in the political campaign aiming at reducing ostentatious consumption, and more generally to the policy seeking to reduce the greatest inequalities in income distribution, eliminating corruption and speculation (see Lemoine *et al.*, 2015: 42).

The spectacular German surplus is also stirring protectionist feelings in the very homeland of liberalism and free trade. President Trump has made no mystery of his displeasure at German surpluses. The economic weight of the Chinese and the US markets in German exports suggests the urgency of countering the exogenous deflationary/protectionist forces by envisaging an international – and in particular European – strategy targeted at reducing the major imbalances within and across European countries. Since the inception of the

Monetary Union, internal and external income inequalities have increased due to the combined effect of each European country's policy of promoting exports at the expense of domestic demand and synchronized austerity policies. While a few exporting firms in certain regions are able to reap the benefits of these policies, their effects, far from trickling down to the economy as a whole, increase the existing divergences and create new ones. As the case of Asia has shown, any successful development strategy has always been a combination of an import substitution policy geared to enlarging the internal market and an export promotion policy (Ginzburg and Simonazzi, 2005: 1057–1058). Export promotion has been used to support import substitution, which, sustained by a set of governmental and financial institutions, has been the key focus of the development strategy (see Zhu, 2006). The EU domestic market can offer fundamental support to demand and growth.

7 A longer-term perspective

The creation of a Monetary Union without fiscal and political union has meant that both the problems of the transition to full integration and the crucial issue of who should eventually pay the costs of this incompleteness were ignored. The assumption of an equal level playing field has led to disregarding the need for industrial policies geared towards coping with the peculiar problems faced by countries at different stages of development.

A longer-term perspective helps us better to assess the limitations of the solutions proposed to steer the EZ economy out of its present quagmire. Austerity measures, structural reforms and internal devaluation (wage flexibility) in the deficit (Southern European) countries, or expansion of internal demand in the 'core' countries (Germany) do not get to the root of the development and debt sustainability problems of Southern European countries, which have seen their productive structures devastated by the long crisis, and indeed by the policies that have been implemented. There can be no escape from the crisis unless the deflationary measures strangling the Eurozone are rescinded. However, long-term sustainability entails a new strategy that assigns a key role to investment guidance by the state through industrial policies geared to diversifying, innovating and strengthening the economic structures of the peripheral countries.

This change of strategy is even more urgent today, since the crisis marks another major structural break in world trade, similar to those of the 1970s and the first decade of the new millennium. In the mid-1970s, saturation of the main mass consumer goods markets led to stiff product-led competition based on quality and product differentiation. The countries of the periphery, which failed to restructure their economic systems to meet this challenge, suffered a halt in their industrialization process and lost ground to those 'core' countries that were able to implement the required macroeconomic and structural policies. In the first decade of the millennium, Germany once again succeeded in reorganizing its economy to meet the demand for investment goods sustained by the industrialization of the emerging countries. On the cost side, it exploited the benefits of wage restraint, industrial outsourcing to Eastern European countries, and the 'exorbitant privilege' of belonging to the Monetary Union and having a dominant position within it. The crisis has shown not only an inability to replicate the German export-led model across Europe, but also the limitations of this model for Germany itself. In fact, the conditions that ensured the success of German exports in the years between 2005 and 2007 no longer hold. China's new policy will have major repercussions on Europe's 'core' and 'periphery' alike because of its quantitative (slowdown in growth) and qualitative (changes in the composition of imports due to import substitution) effects. Unfortunately, Europe's leaders still tend to tackle the problems they face exactly as they did in the past, and expect to achieve the same outcome, even where the circumstances have changed.

8 Income distribution and the European social model for long-term sustainability

The peripheral countries need public investment targeted to their specific needs, public guidance able to envision and encourage the direction of change and innovation that best ensures the attainment of autonomous development. Only in this way, by reinstating the two engines of growth represented by investment and exports, can the Southern European countries tackle the supply and demand bottlenecks that prevented the continuation of convergence in per capita income and sustainable growth. Simply investing in infrastructure is not the goal: it is necessary to align production and consumption infrastructures in ways that foster socially rational long-term growth (Best, 2013). Positive complementarities between equity and efficiency suggest that 'investing in people' and targeting inequality more closely may respond to the urgent need to create employment while also favouring innovation and long-term sustainability. Higher employment is an indispensable prerequisite for the long-term sustainability of an inclusive system, while an increase in the supply of skilled capabilities needs to be matched by an increase in the creation of quality jobs. Capacitating public services can yield better long-term results than the neoliberal deregulation of labour markets, which works by lowering labour costs and providing incentives for the unemployed to take on poorly paid jobs. Accommodating critical life-course transitions reduces the likelihood of people getting trapped in inactivity and welfare dependency.

An independent strategic policy of industrial development calls into question the institutional construction of the Eurozone, the fiscal compact, the monetary policy rules and the whole adjustment agenda of the ECB and the EC. Austerity policies, constraining the spending capacity of governments, force reductions in social investment, while structural reforms interpreted solely as favouring more 'flexible' labour markets undermine long-term growth. As argued in Chapter 9, strengthening EC industrial policy actions should work in the direction of restoring convergence: they should be coordinated with national (and regional) policies targeting the specific regional and sectoral weaknesses.

The difficulty in implementing such a policy is not to be underrated. As Levy (2016) demonstrated in the case of France, the dismantling of most of the tools of statist industrial policy in the 1980s and 1990s stripped the state of critical institutional and fiscal capacities. After decades of neoliberalism, the French state of 2008 was unable to respond in the same way it had in the 1960s or 1970s. The French authorities lacked the vision, policy instruments and financial means to forge an effective, statist response to the 2008 crisis. Levy concludes (2016: 20) that

> The dirigiste spirit may have been willing, but the statist flesh was weak. Thus, breaking with the neo-liberal paradigm requires more than political will; it also requires state capacity, and such capacity cannot be presumed, even in a country like France with a long tradition of state intervention in the economy and a relatively positive view of the state.

For some decades the infrastructure of knowledge, experience, ideas and culture required to implement a new industrial policy has not been maintained in the universities, ministries, think-tanks or society at large, overwhelmed by the market paradigm; by now it needs rebuilding almost from scratch.

9 Towards a shared alternative programme

As Kevin O'Rourke (2014: 16) has rightly remarked, 'Europe is now defined by the constraints it imposes on governments, not by the possibilities it affords them to improve the lives of their people. This is politically unsustainable.' We have argued throughout this book that the Southern countries' elites were not blameless for this turn of economic theory and policy. What prompted the Southern political elites to accept convergence on what has been defined a 'neoliberal consensus' – which served as a basis for the creation of the Monetary Union, placing it before political and fiscal union – was a mix of pragmatism and myopia. German economic policy provided a model to follow in order to emerge from the quagmires of the oil crises, stagflation and the first great industrial restructuring. Viewed through monetarist glasses, the 'facts' appeared to agree with the framework offered by academic monetarism. Once in the EMU, acceptance and implementation of austerity became difficult to resist for economically enfeebled countries and politically weak coalitions. The Southern European leaders have proved incapable of joining forces to counter Germany's dogmatism. In many cases, centre-left politicians have eagerly embraced austerity to prove their bona fide to the markets (and to the creditor countries). In the process of building a European 'neoliberal consensus', the shift towards austerity in France was decisive. With the new presidency of Emmanuel Macron, an enfeebled France is trying to relaunch 'la ligne droite' of its special relations with Germany, once again embracing the German model as a way to solve its problem.

There is very little hope of a radical change of policies, which would mean changing the EZ rules. There is no real will to move in the direction of budgetary and political union in Europe today. As in the neo-functionalist approach, the expectation is that muddling through along the austerity route would eventually get the Southern periphery out of its mess and return to growth. Ironically, both in the US and in Europe the attempt to replace explicitly political decisions with technocracy and automatism eventually led, after drastic austerity measures, to the reappearance of politics in the guise of demagogy ('populism'). European leaders will have to acknowledge that technocratic fixes cannot paper over the failures of 'functionalism' indefinitely. The costs have been high not only for the debtor countries of the periphery, but also for the core: the waste represented by the German external surplus is appalling when considered in the light of its population's increased inequality and poverty. Europe is at a crossroads. On one way, there is the stiffening of core-periphery hierarchical relationships and a further narrowing of democratic space, with its worrisome populist corollary. On the other, the attempt to unify progressive forces across debtor and creditor countries to redirect voters' protest away from populism to the solution lying in the political identity of Europe.

Notes

1 These credit enhancements were created by first converting commercial bank loans into bonds, and then collateralizing principal and rolling interest payments on those bonds with US Treasury zeroes purchased with the proceeds of IMF and World Bank loans.
2 There have been proposals of debt mutualization also from the German side. See for instance the 'Debt Redemption Fund' (DRF) by the German Council of Economic Experts and the 'Blue Bond Proposal' (BBP) by von Weizsäcker and Delpla (2010). While 'the Bond Proposal entails a pooling of sovereign debt up to a level of 60% of GDP, the Debt Redemption envisages a pooling of debt exceeding the 60% threshold'. A specific problem of the Redemption Fund is the disproportionate share of member states in Southern Europe that would by far exceed their share in the EZ's GDP (Bofinger, 2016: 232).
3 Closer economic and institutional integration in the EMU; progressive centralization of national fiscal policies and partial mutualization of the public debts of member states; greater fiscal flexibility and EU-level support to eurozone countries that lack the budgetary space to spur growth on their own; fiscal harmonization and transfers; the creation of an EMU Minister of Finance endowed with a significant amount of own resources; an increased integration towards an economic, fiscal, banking and finally political union.
4 Speaking in 1953 to the students of the University of Hamburg, Thomas Mann: 'We do not want a German Europe, but a European Germany.'
5 This is how Holger Stelzner, one of the publishers of the Frankfurter Allgemeine Zeitung, saw the ruling by the European Court of Justice that cleared the way for OMT (quoted in Kundnani, 2015).

References

Bastasin, C. and Messori, M. (2017). A joint intervention for Italy: A non-punitive plan for investment and reform. *Luiss School for European Political Economy, Policy Brief*, February, 13.

Best, M. H. (2013). Productive structures and industrial policy in the EU. www2.euromemorandum.eu/uploads/best_productive_structures_and_industrial_policy_in_the_eu.pdf [accessed 9 March 2013].

Bofinger, P. (2016). The way forward: Coping with the insolvency risk of member states and giving teeth to the European Semester. In R. Baldwin and F. Giavazzi (eds), *How to Fix Europe's Monetary Union: Views of Leading Economists*. Voxeu.org, 228. http://voxeu.org/sites/default/files/file/epub/rebooting2_upload.pdf [accessed 22 September 2017].

EMTA [Emerging Markets Traders Association] (2009). The Brady Plan. www.emta.org/template.aspx?id=35&terms=brady+plan [accessed 22 September 2017].

Ginzburg, A. and Simonazzi, A. (2005). Patterns of industrialization and the flying geese model. *Journal of Asian Economics*, 15(6), 1051–1078.

Koo, R. (2011). The world in balance sheet recession: Causes, cure, and politics. *Real-world Economics Review*, 58. http://rwer.wordpress.com/2011/12/12/rwer-issue-58-richard-koo/ [accessed 22 September 2017].

Kundnani, H. (2015). The return of the German question. *Social Europe*, 27 January. www.socialeurope.eu/2015/01/return-german-question/ [accessed 27 January 2017].

Jacoby, W. (2015). Europe's new German problem: The timing of politics and the politics of timing. In M. Matthijs and M. Blyth (eds), *The Future of the Euro*. Oxford: Oxford University Press, 187–209.

Legrain, P. (2014). *How to Finish the Euro House*. CER (Centre for European Reform), June. www.cer.eu/sites/default/files/publications/attachments/pdf/2014/report_legrain_euro_house_june14-9111.pdf [accessed 22 September 2017].

Lemoine, F., Poncet, S. and Ünal, D. (2015). Spatial rebalancing and industrial convergence in China. *China Economic Review*, 34(C), 39–63.

Levy, J. D. (2016). The return of the state? France's response to the financial and economic crisis. *Comparative European Politics*, 1–24.

Matthijs, M. and Blyth, M. (2015). Conclusion. The future of the euro. Possible futures, risks, and uncertainties. In M. Matthijs and M. Blyth (eds), *The Future of the Euro*. Oxford: Oxford University Press, 249–269.

McNamara, K. (2015). The forgotten problem of embeddedness: History lessons for the euro. In M. Matthijs and M. Blyth (eds), *The Future of the Euro*. Oxford: Oxford University Press, 249–269.

Newman, A. (2015). The reluctant leader: Germany's euro experience and the long shadow of reunification. In M. Matthijs and M. Blyth (eds), *The Future of the Euro*. Oxford: Oxford University Press, 117–135.

O'Rourke, K. H. (2014). Whither the Euro. *Finance and Development*, 51(1), 14–16.

Pettis, M. (2013). *The Great Rebalancing: Trade, Conflict and the Perilous Road Ahead for the World Economy*. Princeton, NJ: Princeton University Press.

Simonazzi, A. (2015). Italy's long stagnation. In S. Lehndorff (ed.), *Divisive Integration: The Triumph of Failed Ideas in Europe – Revisited*. Brussels: ETUI, 69–93.

Simonazzi, A. and Ginzburg, A. (2015). The interruption of industrialization in Southern Europe: A center-periphery perspective. In M. Baumeister and R. Sala (eds), *Southern Europe? Italy, Spain, Portugal, and Greece from the 1950s until the Present Day*. Frankfurt: Campus, 103–137.

Soros, G. (2011). Europe needs a Plan B. *Project Syndicate*, 11 July. www.project-syndicate.org/commentary/europe-needs-a-plan-b [accessed 22 September 2017].

Von Weizsäcker, J. and Delpla, J. (2010). The Blue Bond Proposal. *Bruegel policy brief 2010/03*.

Zhu, T. (2006). Rethinking import-substituting industrialization. *UNU-WIDER Research Paper No. 2006/76*.

Index

Page numbers in *italics* denote tables, those in **bold** denote figures.

Taylor & Francis eBooks

Helping you to choose the right eBooks for your Library

Add Routledge titles to your library's digital collection today. Taylor and Francis ebooks contains over 50,000 titles in the Humanities, Social Sciences, Behavioural Sciences, Built Environment and Law.

Choose from a range of subject packages or create your own!

Benefits for you

» Free MARC records
» COUNTER-compliant usage statistics
» Flexible purchase and pricing options
» All titles DRM-free.

Benefits for your user

» Off-site, anytime access via Athens or referring URL
» Print or copy pages or chapters
» Full content search
» Bookmark, highlight and annotate text
» Access to thousands of pages of quality research at the click of a button.

REQUEST YOUR FREE INSTITUTIONAL TRIAL TODAY

Free Trials Available
We offer free trials to qualifying academic, corporate and government customers.

eCollections – Choose from over 30 subject eCollections, including:

Archaeology	Language Learning
Architecture	Law
Asian Studies	Literature
Business & Management	Media & Communication
Classical Studies	Middle East Studies
Construction	Music
Creative & Media Arts	Philosophy
Criminology & Criminal Justice	Planning
Economics	Politics
Education	Psychology & Mental Health
Energy	Religion
Engineering	Security
English Language & Linguistics	Social Work
Environment & Sustainability	Sociology
Geography	Sport
Health Studies	Theatre & Performance
History	Tourism, Hospitality & Events

For more information, pricing enquiries or to order a free trial, please contact your local sales team: www.tandfebooks.com/page/sales

Routledge
Taylor & Francis Group

The home of Routledge books

www.tandfebooks.com

For Product Safety Concerns and Information please contact our EU
representative GPSR@taylorandfrancis.com
Taylor & Francis Verlag GmbH, Kaufingerstraße 24, 80331 München, Germany